VIENNA LECTURES ON LEGAL PHILOSOPHY, VOLUME 2: NORMATIVISM AND ANTI-NORMATIVISM IN LAW

What is law? Is it a set of obligations imposed on courts and officials to guide their conduct and to assess the conduct of others; or is it the result of various, ever negotiable, settlements reached by contending forces that accept, for the time being, arrangements and understandings in order to sustain conditions of peaceful cooperation?

If law is the former, its import and meaning are independent of a shifting constellation of forces; if the latter, then what the law says depends on the relative power and prestige of the actors involved.

If scholars and practitioners believe that law imposes such obligations that demand allegiance, they are considered normativists. Alternatively, if they view legal constraints as transient arrangements between and among contending groups, they are not. Hardly any issue in contemporary legal philosophy is as controversial as the normativism/anti-normativism debate; while some believe law's (claim to) 'normativity' to be at the very core of the concept of law, others brush it aside as a pseudo-problem, frequently discussed (and oftentimes resolved) in the history of legal thought.

The second volume of the Vienna Lectures on Legal Philosophy presents the positions of some of the leading scholars working on the problem and allows them to take a stand on the issue. In providing a forum of discussion for proponents and opponents alike, it allows for a nuanced assessment of a debate that all too often is led by one side without paying attention to the arguments of the other.

Vienna Lectures on Legal Philosophy, Volume 2

Normativism and Anti-Normativism in Law

Edited by
Christoph Bezemek
Michael Potacs
and
Alexander Somek

•HART•

OXFORD • LONDON • NEW YORK • NEW DELHI • SYDNEY

HART PUBLISHING

Bloomsbury Publishing Plc

Kemp House, Chawley Park, Cumnor Hill, Oxford, OX2 9PH, UK

1385 Broadway, New York, NY 10018, USA

29 Earlsfort Terrace, Dublin 2, Ireland

HART PUBLISHING, the Hart/Stag logo, BLOOMSBURY and the Diana logo are trademarks of Bloomsbury Publishing Plc

First published in Great Britain 2020

First published in hardback, 2020
Paperback edition, 2022

A catalogue record for this book is available from the British Library.

Library of Congress Cataloging-in-Publication Data

Names: Bezemek, Christoph, editor. | Potacs, Michael, editor. | Somek, Alexander, 1961-, editor.

Title: Vienna lectures on legal philosophy / Edited by Christoph Bezemek, Michael Potacs and Alexander Somek.

Description: Portland, Oregon : Hart Publishing, 2018- | Includes bibliographical references and index.

Identifiers: LCCN 2018005368 (print) | LCCN 2018005869 (ebook) | ISBN 9781509921720 (Epub) | ISBN 9781509921713 (hardback : alk. paper) | ISBN 9781509921713 (hardcover ;vol. 1 ;alkalinepaper) | ISBN 9781509935901 (hardcover ;vol. 2 ;alkaline paper) | ISBN 1509921710(hardcover ;vol. 1 ;alkaline paper) | ISBN 9781509935918 (ePub ;vol. 2)

Subjects: LCSH: Law—Philosophy. | Law—Methodology.

Classification: LCC K212 (ebook) | LCC K212 .V54 2018 (print) | DDC 340/.1—dc23

LC record available at https://lccn.loc.gov/2018005368

ISBN: HB: 978-1-50993-590-1
PB: 978-1-50994-450-7
ePDF: 978-1-50993-592-5
ePub: 978-1-50993-591-8

Typeset by Compuscript Ltd, Shannon

To find out more about our authors and books visit www.hartpublishing.co.uk. Here you will find extracts, author information, details of forthcoming events and the option to sign up for our newsletters.

Preface

IF THERE IS any question that has significantly animated the project of legal theory it has been the question of what it takes to know what the law is. Answering this question, however, presupposes answering another, ostensibly more fundamental question, namely that of what the law is.

Ordinarily, the discipline is inclined to perceive a fork in the road at this point and to confront us with the choice between natural law, on the one hand, and positive law, on the other. And yet, at a deeper level another question needs to be answered first – a question that has been raised historically in the debate between legal realists and their opponents – namely, whether the law is manifest in standards guiding human conduct or, alternatively, borrowing Felix Cohen's felicitous expression, in 'patterns of behaviour'. Is the law something normative or is it something factual?

Arguably, this is, if anything is, the first question of legal theory. In the work of legal theorists it recurs at different levels. Hard-core 'normativists', ie those believing that the law is manifest in standards guiding human conduct, are disposed to tie legal interpretation to the meaning of language and to disregard any change in factual circumstances for the purpose of construction. In their view, changes of the factual circumstances cannot affect the significance of norms. At the same time, such a normativist creed can be easily challenged by taking into account that the interpretation of legal norms is a real-world process that always and invariably bears the imprint of social forces. The construction of the meaning of norms goes on in a context in which social actors pursue their 'self-interested' agendas. Hence, determinations of what 'the law requires' are arrived at on the basis of a more or less stable equilibrium between and among such forces. Insight into social background facts is decisive for understanding why certain normative claims appear to be de facto 'feasible', while others do not.

The divide between 'normativists' and their opponents – the 'anti-normativists' – concerns legal scholarship and theory at different levels. Ordinarily, anti-normativism has more traction in legal cultures in which a variety of legal realism, either Scandinavian or American, has left its mark. Not surprisingly, the anti-normativism of the realist movements resounds in approaches that regard social sciences as an integral part of legal studies proper. If social facts determine what is regarded as law in society, scholarship had better attend to these facts. Alternatively, normativism has its home in legal cultures in which the doctrinal study of law in the shape of 'legal dogmatics' and the belief in a 'science of law' have, for better or worse, withstood all attacks.

The chapters collected in this volume explore this contested field from a variety of perspectives, ranging form ancient constitutionalism and moral philosophy all the way up to contemporary behavioural law and economics, social systems theory and empirical legal studies. With the exception of the two contributions by co-editors the texts assembled in this volume were originally presented in Vienna. The two other texts were discussed at different places and outside of the lecture series. The editors decided, however, to add them to the set, not least because they demonstrate that the split between the two camps is part of the new Viennese milieu.

This second volume of the Vienna Lectures on Legal Philosophy presents the positions of some of the leading scholars working on the issue. The editors have encouraged the authors to take a stand. In providing a forum of discussion for proponents and opponents alike, the volume seeks to prepare the ground for a nuanced assessment of a debate that all too often is led by one side without paying attention to the arguments of the others.

Christoph Bezemek
Michael Potacs
Alexander Somek

Table of Contents

List of Contributors

Ino Augsberg, Professor of Legal Philosophy and Public Law, Kiel University.

Aditi Bagchi, Professor of Law, Fordham University School of Law.

Sylvie Delacroix, Professor in Law and Ethics, University of Birmingham.

Jakob v H Holterman, Associate Professor, Faculty of Law, University of Copenhagen.

Peter Koller, Professor Emeritus of Legal and Social Philosophy and Sociology of Law at the Karl-Franzens-University of Graz.

Stanley L Paulson, Sometime Mercator Professor, Faculty of Law, University of Kiel, Germany, and fellow of the Hermann Kantorowicz Institute, Faculty of Law, University of Kiel; formerly Professor of Philosophy and William Gardiner Hammond Professor Emeritus of Law, Washington University, St. Louis.

Jiří Přibáň, Professor of Law, School of Law and Politics, Cardiff University.

Michael Potacs, Professor of Law, University of Vienna.

Urška Šadl, Professor of Law, European University Institute.

Alexander Somek, Professor of Law, University of Vienna.

Torben Spaak, Professor of Jurisprudence, Department of Law, Stockholm University.

Anne van Aaken, Professor of Law and Economics, Legal Theory, International and European Law, University of Hamburg.

1

The Normality of Normativity

I. INTRODUCTION

IMAGINE THAT I had not begun this lecture by taking the floor and starting to say something. Imagine that instead I had begun by flipping several somersaults on stage and then had gone on to sing 'Jingle Bells', with all the verses, on and on, in spite of the flushed faces of those who kindly gave me the opportunity to speak to you and who were now hectically sliding back and forth on their chairs. How would you react to such a performance? To say the least, you would presumably think, and rightly so, that this kind of behaviour – and even more so: this person – is not entirely normal. Yet what does 'normal' mean in this context? What does 'presumably' refer to? And what does it mean to say that the presumed reaction of yours is 'right'?

On closer examination, the presumption refers to a double form of expectation, namely to my own expectation of a specific expectation from your side. This second expectation, for its part, is directed towards a certain notion of normality which my sketched imaginary behaviour obviously contradicts. More precisely, it is not only a question of the gradation of two structurally largely identical expectations, in the sense of distinguishing a first order expectation from a second order expectation. Rather, we are talking about two expectations that differ significantly from each other in another respect, too. This difference is expressed in German in the specific linguistic differentiation which distinguishes the mere non-fulfilment of an expectation from its frustration or disappointment. A frustrated expectation is something other than the mere amazement that a statistically probable event does not occur, but instead something different, rather unusual takes place. This kind of expectation can also be linked to subjective feelings marking the expected event as a positive, devoutly wished-for

* Professor of Legal Philosophy and Public Law at Kiel University. The paper was originally presented as one of the 'Vienna Lectures on Legal Philosophy'. For the invitation as well as for a highly stimulating and challenging debate I am indebted to Christoph Bezemek, Michael Potacs and Alexander Somek.

kind of thing; for example, if one dreams of a 'white Christmas' in Southern Italy or hopes for a 'straight flush' in a poker game. The frustrated expectation, however, goes beyond that. Its characteristic elements include something else: a certain resistance to accept what has happened, that is, a resistance to adapt one's own expectations to the unexpected event. So, if I stood here and sang, you probably would not just say to yourself or to your neighbour: 'Oh, how interesting, I didn't expect that, is this the new academic style now?' You would probably say, 'What's this idiot thinking?' And you would expect the singing to finally stop and the lecture to begin. Rightly so.

II. NORMATIVE AND COGNITIVE EXPECTATIONS

Niklas Luhmann describes expectations that ought to be preserved even if the actual events contradict them as expectations that 'resist learning'. This specific resistance of certain expectations is the fundamental element of Luhmann's sociological reconstruction of what in his view is to be called 'normativity'. He already developed this idea in the early work *Rechtssoziologie* (sociology of law) and maintained this perspective in the later works.[1] In this way, normativity is not primarily defined by the violation of norms and their sanction, as is the case from the perspective of theories justifying the quality of law in terms of the coercive character of norms, ie in terms of the peculiarity of the measures taken in order to react to infringements of legal obligations. Rather, normativity begins with a certain imaginative power with which a current observer of current conditions imagines the future development of things. This imaginative power becomes normative at the moment in which it maintains its own idea even though the actual events run in a different direction than originally thought. This stability of expectation, notwithstanding a contrary factual development, is what the term 'counterfactuality' of normative expectations indicates. In this way, it directly corresponds to the resistance to learning.

In contrast to this first kind of expectations, Luhmann calls expectations cognitive when they react to factual developments by adapting their own earlier drafts to these developments. Such cognitive expectations are not excluded in law. Rather, under the keyword of 'cognitive openness' a certain ability to react to irritations from the system's environment not only by ignorance, but also by correcting one's own previous assumptions, ie to learn, is also asserted for the law. However, for the operative level of law in the narrower sense, that is to say, for its own specific function, the normative qua learning-resistant expectation is indispensable. From Luhmann's point of view, a law capable of learning, as it

---

[1] See N Luhmann, *Rechtssoziologie 1* (Reinbek bei Hamburg, Rowohlt, 1972), 40 ff.; id., *Das Recht der Gesellschaft* (Frankfurt a.M., Suhrkamp, 1993), 77 ff.

has been conceived of in recent legal theory, especially in the context of considerations on the connection between risk and law, is an oxymoron.[2]

It is fairly easy to see in this differentiation between cognitive and normative expectations a remodeling of the classical dichotomy of 'Is' and 'Ought' (or, to put it more modernly: the difference between facts and norms), a remodeling that resumes the basic idea, but moves beyond the philosophical paradigm of subjectivity and individual consciousness shaped by Kant. In any case, Luhmann expressly places the functional specificity of modern law in this historical context. His sociological observation of law thus carries out a double movement: on the one hand, it takes up Kelsen's old criticism of Ehrlich's idea that the law has a sociological foundation, stating that this foundation would not distinguish exactly enough between what usually happens anyway and what is normatively supposed to happen.[3] On the other hand, Luhmann also undertakes to sociologically enlighten Kelsen's critique by explaining its function within the general framework of systems theory. In a remarkably platonic rhetoric confronting the supposedly actual situation with a point of view which offers merely perspectively shortened perceptions (thus coming close to the otherwise always incriminated 'ontological distinction between being and appearance'[4]), Luhmann remarks: The 'fact' that 'the social function of law [...] is exclusively perceived in the legal system and nowhere else' 'appears' in the 'theory of law [...] as the logical impossibility of deriving norms from facts.'[5] The difference between what usually happens anyway and what ought to happen is thus rewritten from a logical-categorical into a functional register. Yet at the same time, it is stabilised by the insertion into this new context as a further binding figure of thought. Normality and normativity remain strictly separate areas. There is no zone of gradual transition between genesis and validity. Obviously, in this basic assumption it is not only the theoretical constructions of Kelsen and Luhmann that converge.[6] What is more, our everyday intuitions seem to

[2] See for such a concept of 'learning law' KH Ladeur, *Postmoderne Rechtstheorie. Selbstreferenz – Selbstorganisation – Prozeduralisierung* (Berlin, Duncker & Humblot, sec. ed. 1995), 103 ff. For a critique from a systems theory point of view P Hiller, 'Probleme prozeduraler Risikoregulierung' in A Bora (ed), *Rechtliches Risikomanagement. Form, Funktion und Leistungsfähigkeit des Rechts in der Risikogesellschaft* (Berlin, Duncker & Humblot, 1999), 29 ff.

[3] See H Kelsen, 'Eine Grundlegung der Rechtssoziologie (1915)' in S Paulson (ed), *Hans Kelsen und die Rechtssoziologie. Auseinandersetzungen mit Hermann U. Kantorowicz, Eugen Ehrlich und Max Weber* (Aalen, Scientia, 1992). Kelsen maintains this perspective even in his late work. See, eg, H Kelsen, *Allgemeine Theorie der Normen* (Wien: Manz, 1979), 3. On Kelsen's general perspective in more detail, see, eg, N Bersier Ladavac, '*Sein* and *Sollen*, 'Is' and 'Ought' and the Problem of Normativity in Hans Kelsen' in N Bersier Ladavac/C Bezemek/F Schauer (eds), *The Normative Force of the Factual. Legal Philosophy Between Is and Ought* (Heidelberg/New York, Springer, 2019), 29.

[4] N Luhmann, *Die neuzeitlichen Wissenschaften und die Phänomenologie* (Wien, Picus, sec. ed. 1997), 32. (Unless noted otherwise, all translations are my own.)

[5] N Luhmann, *Die soziologische Beobachtung des Rechts* (Frankfurt a.M., Alfred Metzner, 1986), 21.

[6] See for a comparison of the two conceptions, eg, H Dreier, 'Hans Kelsen und Niklas Luhmann. Positivität des Rechts aus rechtswissenschaftlicher und systemtheoretischer Perspektive' (1983) 14 *Rechtstheorie*, 419.

follow the same distinction, since they for their part know different forms of expectation and different forms of merely unfulfilled and frustrated or disappointed expectations and explicitly distinguish between them.

III. BRIDGING THE DIVIDE

However, one may also doubt the necessity of this strict distinction which echoes clearly discernable older differentiations such as the difference between *physis* and *nomos* or between nature and culture. Indeed, instead of adhering to these time-honoured dichotomies, one might refer to a number of indications that point in the direction of a certain overlapping of the areas.[7]

A first, and as it may seem rather superficial indication can be found with regard to the use of language. In contrast to the allegedly clear difference, one can observe that the relevant words are always ambivalent. Norm, standard, yardstick, rule, even law must each first be traced back to their specific context of use in order to clearly mark the concrete use of language as exclusively descriptive or already prescriptive. Even right is not only opposed to the not right in the sense of the unlawful, but also to the wrong in the sense of the skew, that is to say, the clumsy tendency to leave the right way, moving waveringly to the side.[8] In this respect, even those who do not want to go so far as to assume with Jacob Grimm's romantic idea that there is a 'most profound relation of the words to the things'[9] can ask how this remarkable 'ambiguities in primitive words'[10] in the area of the normative relates to Kelsen's assertion that the difference between 'Is' and 'Ought' is 'directly given to our consciousness'.[11] By contrast, according to these ambiguities, language and consciousness obviously go different ways. Of course, one might stress that these ambiguities do not create particular difficulties. Typically, the intended meaning can be easily clarified with reference to the specific context in which the word in question is used. What is more, we can broaden the perspective, emphasising that, rather than being an exception

---

[7] See for a remarkably parallel attempt 'to pay some attention to the relation between facts and norms' and to analyse the general difficulty of how 'to transform *regularity* into *ruleness*', with an emphasis on Georg Jellinek's idea of the 'normative force of the factual' and its 'transformative potential', C Bezemek, 'The 'Normative Force of the Factual: A Positivist's Panegyric' in Bersier Ladavac/Bezemek/Schauer (eds), *The Normative Force of the Factual* (n 3), 65.

[8] See G Canguilhem, *The Normal and the Pathological*, trans CR Fawcett (New York, Zone Books, 1991), 239: 'The concept of right, depending on whether it is a matter of geometry, morality or technology, qualifies what offers resistance to its application of twisted, crooked or awkward.'

[9] J Grimm, 'Von der Poesie im Recht' (1815) 2 *Zeitschrift für geschichtliche Rechtswissenschaft* 25; quoted from: id., *Kleinere Schriften, Band 6: Recensionen und vermischte Aufsätze. Dritter Theil* (Berlin, Ferd. Dümlers Verlagsbuchhandlung, 1882 [reprint Hildesheim et al., Olms-Weidmann, 1991]), 152 ff. (157).

[10] See S Freud, 'Über den Gegensinn der Urworte' in id., *Gesammelte Werke, Bd. VIII: Werke aus den Jahren 1909–1913* (Frankfurt a.M., Fischer, 1969), 213 ff.

[11] H Kelsen, *Reine Rechtslehre* (sec. ed. Wien, Deuticke, 1960), 5.

from the rule, the necessity of context-related specifications corresponds to a general pragmatic understanding of the use of language. Yet with regard to the relevance of the 'Is' and 'Ought' dichotomy this is hardly a consolation. In any case, there seems to be no close connection between the structure of our consciousness and semantics. Given the supposed self-evidence of the dichotomy for our way of thinking and the linguistic ambivalences pointing in the opposite direction, it is all the more remarkable that this divergence arouses no particular interest in current legal-theoretical debates.[12] It hardly receives any special attention, comparable to the interest in ambiguities in other fields of research, namely within the Freudian theory. The typical (not to say: normal) manoeuvre is rather a kind of approach demonstrated by a much-noticed recent study on the phenomenon of normativity, which asks for the 'possibility of norms', but in the very first footnote expresses its explicit disinterest in conceptual-historical investigations.[13]

On the other hand, analyses by Edmund Husserl, which deal with the question of 'solipsistic and intersubjective normality' and in this context turn to the phenomenon of orthoesthetics, fit in better with the observation of the contrary use of language and thus with the general thesis of a certain intertwinement between normality and normativity.[14] Accordingly, in order to guarantee an intersubjective understanding between people at all, a 'certain continuous and exchangeable orthology [...] must of course exist'.[15]

It goes without saying that in the search for certain disruptive factors in relation to the seemingly clear separation of genesis and validity, the entire psychoanalytic tradition has to be considered, too.[16] Even more importantly, this consideration leads to another aspect. For the basic problem here at stake also becomes visible, but now to a certain extent from the other side, when normality is not understood as a simply given state, but as an intermediate, transitory condition within an ongoing social process, that is to say, when instead of enquiring simply about normality, one looks for the ever-present processes of normalisation underlying the situation called 'normal'. In this perspective, normality is not just the description of an empirical fact. It is an attribution with which a certain social state is to be imagined and by this imagination at the same time is produced as such. 'A norm, or rule,' as Georges Canguilhem formulates

---

[12] See, however, the interesting approach by M Potacs, 'The Fact of Norms' in Bersier Ladavac/Bezemek/Schauer (eds), *The Normative Force of the Factual* (n 3), 111, who argues that it is because norms are expressible in language that they can be addressed as a fact.

[13] See C Möllers, *Die Möglichkeit der Normen. Über eine Praxis jenseits von Moralität und Kausalität* (Berlin, Suhrkamp, 2015), 9, fn. 1.

[14] See E Husserl, 'Solipsistische und intersubjektive Normalität und Konstitution von Objektivität' in *Husserliana XIII: Zur Phänomenologie der Intersubjektivität. Erster Teil: 1905–1920*, ed. Iso Kern (Den Haag, Martinus Nijhoff, 1973), 360 ff. (379 ff.).

[15] Husserl, 'Solipsistische und intersubjektive Normalität und Konstitution von Objektivität' (n 14), 379.

[16] See S Freud, *Totem und Tabu. Gesammelte Werke, Bd. IX* (Frankfurt a.M., Fischer, 1961), 173.

it in his ground-breaking analyses of 'The Normal and the Pathological' (which were also to become a decisive impetus for Foucault's investigations into the 'Birth of the Clinic' and the 'History of Madness in the Age of Reason'[17])

> is what can be used to right, to square, to straighten. To set a norm (*normer*), to normalize, is to impose a requirement on an existence, a given whose variety, disparity, with regard to the requirement, present themselves as a hostile, even more than an unknown, indeterminant. It is, in effect, a polemical concept which negatively qualifies the sector of the given which does not enter into its extension while it depends on its comprehension.[18]

Bernhard Waldenfels takes up these considerations when, in his phenomenological analyses of the position of the foreigner, he calls into question the 'almost sacrosanct opposition of is and ought, of nature and freedom, of regularity and observance of rules'. In this perspective even

> functional disorders and diseases are not purely natural, but originate from processes of selective normalization. To a certain degree, health and illness, up to and including madness, present themselves as cultural products, too.[19]

Evidently, such an approach is not only based on a criticism of the classic prohibition of the so-called 'naturalistic fallacy'. Rather, this prohibition seems to be reversed into its radical opposite: into the commandment of a culturalistic inference or conclusion which – at least 'to a certain degree' – demonstrates that any talk about 'nature' or 'naturalness' is already a social construction. Thus, the process of de-naturalisations reveals the contingency of correlations which in times before this process started were always presented and perceived as natural necessities. The possibility of that process becomes particularly evident when a counter-perspective to the previously dominant model is successfully established. In an obvious homage to the *genius loci*, Luhmann's lecture at the Vienna City Hall in 1995 points to this context: 'If one really succeeds to switch to another form, for example to really produce atonal music, that which previously was considered to be valid and count becomes recognizable as the selection of a certain observer.'[20]

Finally, at the level of theory formation, the problem appears when Luhmann speaks of the fact that 'the legal system operates *normatively closed* and at the same time *cognitively open*'.[21] One can read this sentence, as Luhmann evidently intends it to be read through the respective italicization of the opposing determinations of the system, in the sense of emphasising this difference between

---

[17] Foucault explicitly thanks Canguilhem in the 'Préface' of his book *Folie et Déraison. Histoire de la folie à l'âge classique* (Paris, Plon, 1961, I–X). See on the complicated relationship between Foucault and Canguilhem in more detail D Eribon, *Michel Foucault*, trans Betsy Wing (Cambridge, MA, Harvard University Press, 1991).

[18] Canguilhem, *The Normal and the Pathlogical* (n 8), 239.

[19] B Waldenfels, *Ordnung im Zwielicht* (Frankfurt a.M., Suhrkamp, 1987), 72.

[20] Luhmann, *Die neuzeitlichen Wissenschaften und die Phänomenologie* (n 4), 57.

[21] Luhmann, *Das Recht der Gesellschaft* (n 1), 77.

cognitive and normative which, as I said before, in some way can be understood as a revenant of the is/ought-dichotomy. Yet one can also refer more strongly to the difficulty that implicitly appears in the expression 'at the same time', that is to say, of the simultaneity of this double operationality. In his Vienna City Hall lecture, in which Luhmann predominantly dealt with the precise analysis of a famous predecessor, Husserl's lectures on 'Philosophy in the Crisis of European Humanity', held almost exactly 60 years earlier at the invitation of the Vienna Cultural Association, Luhmann refers rather casually to certain

> distinctions with a built-in asymmetry, so that one side of the distinction simultaneously dominates the distinction itself. Thus moralists consider the distinction between good and evil to be good, and jurists have no doubt that courts are entitled to distinguish between right and wrong, provided it is only done lawfully.[22]

The description thus concerns a general problem also known from other contexts, such as the question of whether the difference between the practical and the theoretical faculty of reason itself constitutes a knowledge of theoretical rather than a commandment of practical reason, or whether the difference between dialectical and non-dialectical thinking is itself to be thought dialectically or non-dialectically.[23] The same would have to apply to a classification that considers the difference between cognitive and normative procedures to be a basically cognitive problem. In contrast, a dissolution of this asymmetry, ie a tentative re-symmetrisation of difference, would have to insist that the difference between facts and norms itself is not merely factual, ie that it does not designate a difference that is simply given as such. Rather, it would have to insist that – and above all – how difference as a process of active differentiation must be formed and endured within the law itself, while at the same time it nevertheless refers to an outside of the law that is more than a projection from within.

IV. INTERTWINEMENTS BETWEEN NORMALITY AND NORMATIVITY

Of course, this does not mean that normativity and normality are simply identical. As Waldenfels hastens to add to his explanations of normalisation, 'any arbitrary demarcation would soon be paid back painfully by nature. It would have to be a heroic relativism that would outlast the operating table.'[24] Yet the indications mentioned above suggest the assumption that one phenomenon cannot properly be understood without its relation to the other, or more precisely, that both can only be fully conceived as phenomena that have already been folded into or intertwined with each other in a certain way. A double perspective corresponding to this insight, which concedes the construedness of

---

[22] Luhmann, *Die neuzeitlichen Wissenschaften und die Phänomenologie* (n 4), 21.

[23] See on this difficulty, eg, F Ruda, *For Badiou. Idealism without Idealism* (Evanston/Ill.: Northwestern University Press, 2015), 70 f.

[24] Waldenfels, *Ordnung im Zwielicht* (n 19), 72.

the 'normal', while at the same time rejecting its possible claim to absolute-
ness, appears when Luhmann, again in his lecture at the Vienna City Hall, but
now with explicit reference to the 'experiences of the therapists', explains that
'"normality" cannot be defined as a better adaptation to an external reality, but
rather as a less painful construction, a construction that is easier to bear.'[25]

Such a stronger intertwinement of the cognitive and normative dimensions
in law can start at the level of the cognitive dimension of law. On this account,
it has to emphasise and elaborate on the already normatively pre-structured
form of cognitive procedures in the realm of law. As a kind of specifically legal
epistemology, its task consists in determining the amount of autonomy or epistemic independence which legal constructions have when they rely on concepts
like 'truth' or 'reality'. Although these legal concepts have to be fundamentally
compatible with alternative designs of reality, especially those developed by
natural sciences, they are not identical with them. Well known legal proverbs
such as 'Quod non est in actis non est in mundo' bear witness to this kind of
epistemic independence, indicating that this construction initially takes place
as a negative selection: the legal mechanisms exclude those aspects of reality
that do not fit into its schemes. Thus, the legal perception of the world is a
docta ignorantia, a deliberately trained ignorance, based on systematically integrated filter functions. However, other similarly well-known legal techniques,
particularly legal fictions, make it clear that legal constructions of reality are
not exhausted in such negative approaches. According to these additional techniques, the reality of the law is something other than merely an excerpt from an
assumed general, all-encompassing reality. In consequence, whenever someone
talks about the 'knowledge of law', what needs to be discussed is not only a
neutral knowledge of or about law. Rather, what is in question at the same time
is a legal, ie an also normatively relevant knowledge.[26]

On the other hand, constructivism must not be pushed so far that the entire
distinction between self-reference and external reference collapses, dissolving
on the side of self-reference.[27] The fact that the legal constructions of reality must be compatible with the other social models of reality, at least in their
basic features, refers on the one hand, as Luhmann explains with reference to
Gotthard Günther, to the necessity of so-called 'transjunctional' operations.
These operations are meant to make it possible 'to change from one contex-
ture (a positive/negative distinction) to another and in each case to mark which
signature one accepts or rejects for certain operations'.[28] On the other hand,

[25] Luhmann, *Die neuzeitlichen Wissenschaften und die Phänomenologie* (n 4), 44.
[26] See A Somek, *Wissen des Rechts* (Tübingen, Mohr Siebeck, 2018). On the idea of a juristic epistemology furthermore, I Augsberg, *Informationsverwaltungsrecht. Zur kognitiven Dimension der rechtlichen Steuerung von Verwaltungsentscheidungen* (Tübingen, Mohr Siebeck, 2014).
[27] See Luhmann, *Die neuzeitlichen Wissenschaften und die Phänomenologie* (n 4), 41.
[28] Luhmann, *Die neuzeitlichen Wissenschaften und die Phänomenologie* (n 4), 44, with reference to G Günther, 'Cybernetic Ontology and Transjunctional Operations' in id., *Beiträge zur Grundle-gung einer operationsfähigen Dialektik*, vol. 1 (Hamburg, Meiner, 1976), 249 ff.

however, it also refers to another, even more fundamental phenomenon: to a residual of 'reality' that is as indissoluble as it is beyond any further determination. The philosophical tradition has tried to grasp this phenomenon with the concepts of 'resistance' and 'resistiveness'.[29] In this perspective, the talk about 'pain' that appears both in Waldenfels and in Luhmann indicates a dimension of the problem that must be generalised beyond the anthropocentric perspective.

Perhaps even more interesting than the question outlined above which is addressed by legal epistemology is the intertwinement of the concept of normality and normativity that takes place at the level of the normative. Of course, normativity cannot be equated with normality. The entire necessity of the concept of normativity stems from the fact that what is dictated by normativity does not correspond to the actual normal state; in that case the concept of normativity would be simply superfluous. However, just as the so-called normality does not describe a mere fact, but is always already normatively preformed as a (self-)description of society, normativity does not only refer to alternative drafts of reality that simply deviate from the given status quo. The relationship is far more complex.

First of all, this part of the general topic refers to the dependence on a specific dimension of the construction of normative entities, a dimension which Vincent Descombes, in contrast to the well-known distinction by Sieyès between *pouvoir constituant* and *pouvoir constitué*, has described as *pouvoir instituant*.[30] What is meant by this neologism is that 'state law and its constitutional institutions [...] have always been interwoven in symbolic forms that are often ramified, in different forms of life and their webs of meaning, which in turn are linked to fluctuating sources of power, between which a variable network of relations stretches.'[31]

In the present context, however, another aspect of the intertwinement between normativity and normality is even more decisive: in this perspective, we have to recognise that the normatively imagined target state, that is to say, the ideal underlying a normative concept of order, at the same time, always and already, has to be imagined as a normal state.[32] Only in this way can it be internalised by those who are subject to the norm, and only because of this internalisation can the requirement of explicit sanctioning of norm-deviant behaviour be kept within limits. Since a permanent sanction practice rather weakens than strengthens a norm, as it implicitly admits that it is quite common

---

[29] See W Dilthey, 'Beiträge zur Lösung der Frage vom Ursprung unseres Glaubens an die Realität der Außenwelt und seinem Recht' in id., *Die geistige Welt. Einleitung in die Philosophie des Lebens. Erste Hälfte: Abhandlungen zur Grundlegung der Geisteswissenschaften, Gesammelte Schriften Bd. V* (Stuttgart/Göttingen: Vandenhoeck & Ruprecht, 1957), 90 ff. (esp. 98 ff.). Hereunto from a legal point of view Augsberg, *Informationsverwaltungsrecht* (n 26), 290 ff.

[30] See V Descombes, *Puzzling Identities* (Cambridge, MA, Harvard University Press, 2016), 174 ff., with reference to Cornelius Castoriadis.

[31] T Vesting, *Staatstheorie* (München: Beck, 2018), at 122, with reference to Descombes.

[32] See Bezemek, 'The 'Normative Force of the Factual'' (n 7), 71: 'The norm needs to resonate in normality, thereby ensuring that the lifeline connecting normality and normativity is not severed.'

not to follow a certain rule, normativity must fake itself as normality even where and when reality contradicts this claim. This account of normativity's dependence on normality (or rather: the image or idea of normality) is the result of Heinrich Popitz's sociological studies on the relevance of 'dark figures (of crime)'. According to these studies, the function of dark figures is not simply to conceal the real number of criminal cases which is indeed much higher than official statistics will make us believe. Read in this way, they only point to the fact that the normative system is unable to master certain social difficulties by relying on its own explicit counter-strategies. Viewed against a larger background, however, the masking of the system's inefficiencies no longer appears as an end in itself. Rather, what is decisive is its impact on society: the initially only fictitious state is to become a kind of self-fulfilling prophecy, because those subject to the norm orient themselves towards the pseudo-normality presented in this way and adapt their behaviour to the situation presented as a dominating social custom. In consequence, what used to be a pseudo-normality is gradually, step by step, transformed into an actual social condition.[33]

If we follow this idea, we can see that every normative expectation indeed operates with a conception that is not only two-fold but contradictory in itself. On the one side, it imagines a situation which does not (yet) correspond to the normal state of society. On the other side, co-instantaneously, it imagines that this correspondence between normality and normativity already exists. An observation by Alexander Somek apparently aims in at least a similar direction when he formulates: 'Legal validity requires us to treat a claim to validity as a social fact and in turn to endow this social fact with a claim to validity'.[34] Even more acutely observed, the contradictoriness of the conception means more than that the conceptions contradict each other. They are both contradictory in themselves. By *imagining* or *presenting* normality, law negates the implicit self-evidence that is normally associated with the concept of normality and that, in the present context, in order to achieve the intended effect, also has to be associated with it. According to this normal idea of normality, normality is not something that has to be presented in a certain way. It is simply there, naturally given. In turn, by presenting *normality*, law negates the act of representation as such. For normality, conceived of in the normal way, oppresses the technical aspect of its own existence. In consequence of this two-fold self-contradictory character, normativity, as a notion referring to a certain desired state of affairs, is a process of representation without the represented. It is a process simultaneously demonstrating and dissimulating its own inscrutability.[35]

---

[33] See H Popitz, 'Über die Präventivwirkung des Nichtwissens' in id., F Pohlmann and W Eßbach (eds) *Soziale Normen*, (Frankfurt a.M., Suhrkamp, 2006), 158 ff.

[34] Somek, *Wissen des Rechts* (n 26), 30.

[35] See for a parallel idea of presentation as a 'translation without original or as a representation without represented', with reference to 'the language of the unconscious, the unconscious as language', Samuel Weber, *Rückkehr zu Freud. Jacques Lacans Ent-stellung der Psychoanalyse* (Wien, Passagen, 1990), 16.

It is no coincidence that the movement is reminiscent of Hans Kelsen's perhaps most remarkable theoretical figure: the transition from the presentation of his 'basic norm' in the form of a 'hypothesis' in the sense of Hermann Cohen to its conception as a 'fiction' in the sense of Hans Vaihinger. In Kelsen's own view, this transition is not a merely incidental event.[36] On the contrary, he explicitly notes and comments on it, explaining its specific meaning. The reference to the hypothesis already contained a figure which no longer deals with the phenomenon of 'validity' as a structure necessarily given to our consciousness. Rather, the deliberately selected expression marks this phenomenon as an active prerequisite. Yet the transition to fiction moves beyond even this previous perspective. What is at stake now is – quite analogously to the idea of the normality of normativity – a double movement that does not merely assume a fact which, although possible in principle, does not exist in the specific case. Kelsen uses Vahinger's notion in order to refer to the more radical figure of an event that is 'contradictory in itself'. Only such an event corresponds to the special character of those fictions which Kelsen calls, using a terminology which appears almost like an ironic *contradictio in adiecto* and which is therefore so exactly fitting, the 'real' or 'actual' fiction.[37]

Against this background, it should have become clear that the intertwinement between normality and normativity is more than just a psychological phenomenon. It is a structural necessity. Yet what is more, the explanations given so far challenge the traditionally fiercest opponent of a merely psychological perspective: the claim that the dichotomy between Is and Ought is an unavoidable consequence of logic.[38] A system whose very core is said to be based on a necessarily self-contradictory movement obviously can no longer be determined by a logic grounded in the law of the excluded contradiction. It resists, rejects and indeed contradicts this law.

V. THE TEMPORAL STRUCTURE OF NORMATIVITY

At the very end of his book on *Das Recht der Gesellschaft*, Luhmann comes to speak of another, specific form in which normality and normativity or cognitive

---

[36] See on the general idea of the *Grundnorm* as a means of legal epistemology M Potacs, *Rechtstheorie* (Wien, Facultas, 2015), 83.

[37] See Kelsen, *Allgemeine Theorie der Normen* (n 3), 206 f.: 'The basic norm of a positive moral or legal order is [...] not a positive, but a merely imagined, and that is to say, a fictitious norm, the meaning not of a real, but of a merely fictitious act of will. As such, it is an authentic or "actual" fiction in the sense of Vaihinger's philosophy of the As-If, which is characterized by the fact that it not only contradicts reality, but is also contradictory in itself. For the assumption of a basic norm [...] is also contradictory in itself, since it represents the authorization of a supreme moral or legal authority, and thus proceeds from an authority that still stands above this authority – albeit only fictitious.'

[38] See for a most prominent representative of this view Kelsen, *Allgemeine Theorie der Normen* (n 3), 3. On the difference as well as on the relationship between logical and psychological attempts to explain the dichotomy in more detail Bezemek, 'The "Normative Force of the Factual"' (n 7).

12   *Ino Augsberg*

and normative expectations may become intertwined. The point at hand is the idea of how the current legal system might develop in the future. In question, therefore, is an attitude which, for its part, is more likely to be applied to the cognitive side. To be more precise, it is about the development of law in a society which, for Luhmann, is already a world society in decisive respects, but which, especially in the legal field, undermines purely functional differentiation by continuing predominantly nation-state based modes of justification. It is against this conceptual background that we have to understand these very last sentences of the book. They read as follows:

> It is quite possible [...] that the current prominence of the legal system and the dependence of society itself and most of its functional systems on the functioning of the legal code is nothing more than a European anomaly which will weaken in the evolution of a world society.[39]

This final point takes up an already much older insight. More than two decades earlier, at the beginning of the 1970s, in his central study on the emergence of the 'world society' Luhmann had already emphasised which alternative techniques could possibly replace the now so called anomaly. According to this previous position, the transition to world society is likely to be associated with a development in which social self-orientation switches more strongly from normative to cognitive expectations.[40]

At first glance, this outlook provides another, new perspective on the interdependence of the previously distinct levels, a perspective that is implied in the genitive construction of the 'normality of normativity' and which so far we seem to have ignored. Accordingly, the expression can now no longer be understood primarily as a *genitivus subiectivus*, but also as a *genitivus obiectivus*. Read in this way, it explains why neither the emergence nor the persistence of law are quite normal events in the sense of being largely self-evident for any form of society. On this account, the old idea of *ubi societas, ibi ius* is simply not true.

A second glance, however, makes it clear that in this very outlook Luhmann does not at all dismiss or at least relativise his previous distinction between the spheres of the cognitive and the normative. In contrast, he confirms and maintains the difference, even emphasising its importance in a new, specific way. Moreover, in doing so, by presenting the dominance of normative and cognitive expectations as successive phases in a historical course of events, he also demonstrates a specific understanding of time. In this view, time forms a kind of external framework for the social evolutionary processes taking place in it.

Strangely enough, with this approach to time Luhmann repeats exactly the kind of approach that he had accused Husserl of and blamed him for in his Viennese town hall lecture. According to this previous accusation, Husserl

---

[39] Luhmann, *Das Recht der Gesellschaft* (n 1), 585 f.
[40] See N Luhmann, 'Die Weltgesellschaft' in id., *Soziologische Aufklärung 2. Aufsätze zur Theorie der Gesellschaft* (Opladen, Westdeutscher Verlag, sec. ed. 1982), 51 ff. (esp. 55 ff.).

had 'localized the crisis of the European sciences in the historical period of the Western history of reason. In all this, time was thought of as a current, as a movement, as a process'.[41] In Luhmann's view, it is precisely at this point that a different, rather autologous thinking must take its wings, by beginning to develop a 'radically different relationship to time'.[42] This new and different relationship enables a different understanding of time: 'Time is now a certain form of observation, a world construction with the help of the difference between the infinite horizons of past and future.'[43] Following a Heideggerian differentiation, one could speak of a change of perspective from time to temporality qua temporisation. For a theory reoriented correspondingly, the following must apply: 'It understands its present as the difference between its past and future. It no longer articulates its position in time, but with the help of time'.[44]

In my opinion, the consequences that such a change of perspective could have can be demonstrated precisely by the intertwinement between normality and normativity. An appropriately sharpened view can emphasise normativity not only as a given condition, but a process, by elaborating on its very peculiar mode of temporalisation. Traditionally, legal normativity is primarily determined by its reference to the past. Thus, current decision-making practice is legitimised by referencing what has already been decided (be it in the form of general norms or of precedents).[45] In contrast, the above-mentioned recent study on the 'possibility of norms' is characterised by the fact that it breaks with this classical view and instead emphasises future orientation as the primary characteristic of the normative.[46] A closer look at the interdependence of normativity and normality now makes it possible, however, to take another step, moving beyond this broadening of perspective, and propose a further, somewhat more complex form of temporalisation. On this account, normativity takes place neither primarily with regard to the past nor to the future. Its most fundamental movement can be best characterised in the mode of a *futur antérieur*, that is to say, as the idea of a 'will have been'. Instead of a form of temporalisation which already in its designation as 'perfect' makes it clear that it is a movement which is regarded as completed and finalised and which therefore can only be continued through repetition, the *futur antérieur* describes a temporality which due to its futuristic component breaks with this idea of self-circling completion, yet without referring only to a completely undetermined open horizon.[47] The entity claimed in

---

[41] Luhmann, *Die neuzeitlichen Wissenschaften und die Phänomenologie* (n 4), 58.
[42] Ibid.
[43] Luhmann, *Die neuzeitlichen Wissenschaften und die Phänomenologie* (n 4), 59.
[44] Ibid.
[45] See, eg, Luhmann, *Das Recht der Gesellschaft* (n. 1), 237; G Teubner/P Zumbansen, 'Rechtsentfremdungen: Zum gesellschaftlichen Mehrwert des zwölften Kamels' in G Teubner (ed), *Die Rückgabe des zwölften Kamels: Niklas Luhmann in der Diskussion über Gerechtigkeit* (Stuttgart, Lucius & Lucius, 2000), 189 ff. (201 f.).
[46] See Möllers, *Die Möglichkeit der Normen* (n 13).
[47] See for a respective idea with regard to the constitution of the subject, Weber, *Rückkehr zu Freud* (n 35), 25 f.

this way denotes a past that was never present. Consequently, norms are not only about the present future instead of the future present, as one could say with reference to another helpful differentiation by Luhmann.[48] It is about the present future of having been. We can detect in this ambiguity of legal presence the temporal sense of that 'representation without representation' which the talk about the 'normality of normativity' is supposed to express.

VI. CONCLUSION

All explanations given so far allow for another, final perspective on our initial question. According to the idea presented here, legal normativity itself operates with different conceptions, each of which presents the imagined in the mode of an As-If. Thus, the most basic, constitutive operations of law have a fictional character. They do not only determine a concrete cognitive object by way of cognition. They themselves bring forth what they are concerned with. As Kelsen's differentiation between hypothesis and fiction precisely indicates, fiction in this context means something other than a process of mere mimesis. It is not only oriented on a model taken as an underlying general reality. By contrast, this fiction is more than the simple reproduction of something already existing elsewhere. The As-If appears in a double, twofold way. In a characteristic turn, it applies its own mechanisms on itself. The fictions used reflexively refer back to themselves. Yet the reflexivity that comes into play in this way does not mean a turning back of the gaze, in which what is taken into gaze closes into a circle. Rather, it refers to a necessary rupture, an unavoidable self-derision in the process of self-closure, which itself is experienced as a prerequisite of all self-constitution. The reflection is always and already a refraction. Thus, Kelsen's claim that the law is founded on the assumption of a fiction which is 'contradictory in itself' means that the law is based on the ability to contradict itself.

This perspective enables two final attempts to determine the 'normality of normativity'. On the one hand, if one describes irony with Friedrich Schlegel as a constant 'change of self-creation and self-destruction, of self-limitation and self-delimitation',[49] we may have to conceive of the intertwinement between normality and normativity in a fundamentally ironical procedure.[50] On the other hand, the normativity thus conceived is decisively based on an imagination that could, due to its characteristic operations, be called literary or even poetic. Viewed from this perspective, we might have a decisive starting point for

---

[48] See E Esposito, 'Zeitmodi' 12 *Soziale Systeme* (2016), 328.

[49] See M Frank, *Einführung in die frühromantische Ästhetik* (Frankfurt a.M., Suhrkamp, 1989), 344.

[50] See for a parallel idea regarding a self-critical and ironic concept of reason Luhmann, *Die neuzeitlichen Wissenschaften und die Phänomenologie* (n 4), 45 f. On the connection between legality and irony furthermore Somek, *Wissen des Rechts* (n 26), 17, 106 ff.

coming back to Jacob Grimm.[51] In consequence, the traditional problems and solutions of legal theory and legal philosophy not only have to be supplemented by a legal epistemology. What is more, they should be accompanied by a philology of law, too.

Against this background, we may conclude with one last remark. After all, perhaps Alexander Somek is, in contrast to his own assumption, not 'the only one – and thus probably also the last' – who still believes in a 'romantic project' in the field of jurisprudence.[52] However, what remains to be seen then, is whether the non-fulfilment of this expectation is also a frustrating disappointment.

[51] See in more detail, I Augsberg, 'Sätze Setzen Gesetz' in J Kersten/I Mülder-Bach/ M Zimmermann (eds), *Prosa schreiben. Literatur – Geschichte – Recht* (München, Wilhelm Fink, 2019) (forthcoming).

[52] See Somek, *Wissen des Rechts* (n 26), 3, with reference to C Schönberger, 'The German Approach'. *Die deutsche Staatsrechtslehre im Wissenschaftsvergleich* (Tübingen, Mohr Siebeck, 2015).

2

On the Significance of Virtues in Morality and Law

PETER KOLLER*

I. LAW, MORALITY AND THEIR FUNCTIONAL INTERRELATIONS

THE CONCEPTS OF law and morality in general and their relationships in particular have been the subject of ongoing dispute since antiquity. The main positions on this matter are known to be divided into two opposing camps: legal positivism on the one hand and natural law doctrine or legal moralism on the other. Whereas legal positivism advocates the view that law and morality are conceptually separated in the sense that the validity of legal norms does not depend on their compatibility with any principles of morality and justice, legal moralism maintains that law and morality are conceptually connected in the sense that valid legal norms must be in accordance with fundamental requirements of morality and justice at least to a certain degree.[1] In the present context, however, there is no need to enter in this debate, for it will suffice to focus on the *contingent empirical and functional interrelations* between law and morality, leaving their conceptual relationships aside. To this end it is nevertheless helpful to take a brief glance at the very concepts of law and morality.

As for the *concept of law*, I would like to propose the following definition: law is a collective social practice aiming at the provision of generally binding social norms which are characterised by the following features: (1) they are created and applied by authorised agents who are deemed to be empowered to do that; (2) if mandatory, they are backed by organised force, ie they may be enforced by authorised people in a determined way; and (3) they entail a two-sided claim to legitimacy, laid on the part of its authorities on the one hand

* Professor Emeritus of Legal and Social Philosophy and Sociology of Law at the Karl-Franzens-Universty of Graz.
[1] See P Koller, *Theorie des Rechts* 2nd edn (Vienna, Böhlau, 1997), 19 ff; idem, 'The Concept of Law and its Conceptions' (2006) 19 *Ratio Juris* 180–196.

and on the part of its addressees on the other.[2] I think that the first two features can be taken for granted and do not need any further elaboration. Taken together, they characterise the law as a *real social fact*, namely as a dynamic system of binding social norms that differs from other practices of social regulation, such as conventional morality and custom, by being based on authorised power whose effectiveness is warranted by means of force. Not so obvious, however, is the third feature, the law's claim to legitimacy, which is thought to explain the law's *normative force* and connects it in some way to morality and justice. So I should clarify this feature a bit.

Law's claim to legitimacy includes two claims, depending on the parties by whom it is laid, namely the authorities' claim and the addressees' claim. On the one hand, legal authorities must claim the legitimacy of their directives in order to maintain that these directives should be generally acknowledged by the addressees as binding. On the other hand, law's addresses also raise the claim that the legal directives to which they are subject must be legitimate in order to be acceptable as binding under proper consideration. In general, law's legitimacy may be assessed from three categories of normative principles: (i) *social efficiency*, ie the actual utility for the individuals concerned under the present circumstances; (ii) *the common good*, understood as the overall welfare of the particular collective under consideration; and (iii) *morality and justice*, requiring law's universal acceptability from an impartial perspective considering the relevant interests of all people concerned.[3] The question as to whether law's legitimacy depends on its moral acceptability will be settled later on.

A *morality* may be understood in general as a bundle of practical standards that (i) are autonomous in the sense that they are accepted freely and voluntarily by people who regard them as binding, (ii) claim universal validity in the sense that people who accept them regard them as binding for everybody, and (iii) have special weight in the sense that they are deemed to be more important than other guidelines of human conduct, in some cases even so important that they take absolute priority over other practical standards, like those of personal taste and prudence. On the basis of this general definition, which leaves room for a great variety of different conceptions of morality, I would like to introduce two more specific concepts of morality, namely those of a conventional morality on the one hand, and of a reasonable or critical morality on the other.[4]

---

[2] Cp Koller, *Theorie des Rechts* (n 1) 37 ff; idem, 'The Concept of Law and its Conceptions' (n 1) 192 f.

[3] This classification draws on Kant's distinction between technical, pragmatic and moral imperatives (standards) as guidelines of individual action. See P Koller, 'On the Legitimacy of Political Communities' in M Baurmann & B Lahno (eds), *Perspectives in Moral Science* (Frankfurt/Main, Frankfurt School Verlag 1009) 309–326, 310 ff. For a similar view see J Habermas, 'Vom pragmatischen, ethischen und moralischen Gebrauch der praktischen Vernunft' in idem, *Erläuterungen zur Diskursethik* (Frankfurt/Main, Suhrkamp, 1991) 100–118.

[4] See S Körner, *Experience and Conduct. A Philosophical Enquiry into Practical Thinking* (Cambridge, Cambridge University Press, 1976) 137 ff; Koller, *Theorie des Rechts* (n 1) 255 ff; idem, 'Law, Morality, and Virtue' in RL Walker & PJ Ivanhoe (eds), *Working Virtue. Virtue Ethics and Contemporary Moral Problems* (Oxford, Clarendon Press. 2007) 191–205, 193 f.

A *conventional* morality is a set of moral norms that are widely acknowledged by the members of a certain social aggregate (be it a social group, a society, a culture, or even mankind) as supreme standards of their conduct and, therefore, have effective validity in this aggregate. Such moral norms exert, within the respective social aggregate, a certain degree of social pressure resulting from the interplay of the individuals' informal reactions to the behaviour of others. Of course, the mere fact that moral norms are widely acknowledged in a collective doesn't imply that their recognition is based on good reason. So a conventional morality may be more or less reasonable or even rather unreasonable.

Moral standards are *reasonable* if there are sufficient reasons to assume that they should be unanimously accepted by all individuals possibly affected upon critical reflection, ie from an impartial point of view and in consideration of all relevant facts, because their general observance is deemed to be in everyone's best interest. It is true, however, that we can never be completely sure that a moral standard is justified, even if it is commonly accepted for the best reasons we know, since there could be other factors that would call it into question. Yet, this fact provides no ground for moral scepticism. Moral discourse is, like any other rational discourse, an ongoing enterprise in which we have to consider any moral standard under discussion in light of all reasons for and against it, in order to accept the standards that seem to be based on the best reasons available. Thus the idea of a reasonable morality can play a very important role in moral life, since it provides a critical viewpoint on individual moral consideration and public moral discourse, a viewpoint which helps us to reflect on our personal moral attitudes and scrutinise the standards of public morality.[5]

A comprehensive morality contains two levels of moral standards: interpersonal and institutional standards. The *interpersonal standards*, which refer to normal interactions among people, particularly face-to-face activities, may be divided into three sets: general morality, justice, and supererogation. First of all, *demands of general morality* are strictly universal, ie binding for all people vis-à-vis others regardless of their specific social relationships; they include two kinds of duties, namely, on the one hand, perfect duties of not harming others without justification, and, on the other, imperfect duties to render active assistance or beneficence to people in need, if this does not involve significant sacrifices.[6] Furthermore, there are *demands of justice* which differ from those of general morality insofar as they are only relatively universal; this means that they only apply to people who are involved in social relationships which impose particular associative obligations, such as communal relationships which call

---

[5] See K Baier, *The Moral Point of View. A Rational Basis of Ethics* (Ithaca, NY, Cornell University Press, 1958); idem, *The Rational and the Moral Order. The Social Roots of Reason and Morality* (Chicage, Open Court, 1995) 214 ff; J Habermas, *Erläuterungen zur Diskursethik* (n 3) 119 ff; idem, 'Eine genealogische Betrachtung zum kognitiven Gehalt der Moral', in idem, *Die Einbeziehung des Anderen* (Frankfurt/Main, Suhrkamp, 1996) 11–64, 59 f; J Rawls, *Political Liberalism* (New York, Columbia University Press, 1993) lectures II and VI.

[6] See W Kersting, ''Pflicht' and 'Pflichten, unvollkommene/vollkommene', in *Historisches Wörterbuch der Philosophie* vol 7 (Basel, Schwabe, 1989) 405–439.

for a just distribution of the communal benefits or burdens under consideration, or exchange relationships that require fair market transactions.[7] Lastly, *instructions of supererogation* are recommending ways of acting that appear highly desirable, but cannot be generally required of individuals, such as charitable activities for people in need that entail significant sacrifices, or heroic actions of political resistance against a despotic regime.[8]

In order to make these interpersonal standards effective, a morality needs *institutional standards*, which are concerned with the creation and preservation of a just social order.[9] These standards, the requirements of *social and political justice*, may again be divided up into three sorts according to their scope: local justice, focussing on particular small-scale arrangements; domestic justice referring to the basic structure of national societies; and international or global justice which extends to the international or global order.[10] The requirements of each of these kinds of justice are connected with at least two duties of the individuals concerned: (i) a strict moral duty to abide by the rules of an effective social order, provided that they are not clearly unjust; and (ii) a more indeterminate duty to contribute to a just social order to an extent which can be reasonably expected.[11]

On the basis of these conceptual considerations, it is possible to identify two conspicuous features of the functional interrelation between law and morality resulting from the fact that both morality and law are aiming at providing people with binding directives for a peaceful and flourishing social life, while neither of them is able to achieve this aim alone without the other: first, morality requires a legal order in order to become sufficiently determinate and effective, and, secondly, law must rely on the moral attitudes of its participants in order to meet its claim to legitimacy and function properly.

On the one hand, *morality requires a legal order*, because it alone is not capable of regulating social life in accordance with its own demands. And this applies all the more as the number of interacting people grows. In most social

---

[7] See P Koller, 'Zur Semantik der Gerechtigkeit' in P Koller (ed), *Gerechtigkeit im politischen Diskurs der Gegenwart* (Vienna, Passagen Verlag 2001) 19–46; idem, 'Economic Distributive Justice' in S Puntscher Riekmann, A Somek & D Wydra (eds), *Is there a European Common Good?* (Baden-Baden, Nomos, 2013) 64–84, 66 f.

[8] See JO Urmson, 'Saints and Heroes' in AI Melden (ed), *Essays in Moral Philosophy* (Seattle, University of Washington Press, 1958) 198–216; Rawls, *A Theory of Justice* (Cambridge, MA, Harvard University Press, 1971) 478 f.

[9] Cp I Kant, *Die Metaphysik der Sitten* (1797), Kant-Werkausgabe, ed W Weischedel, vol VIII (Frankfurt/Main, Suhrkamp 1968) part I (Rechtslehre) § 41 f A155 ff / B 154 ff (422 ff); O Höffe, *Politische Gerechtigkeit. Grundlegung einer kritischen Philosophie von Recht und Staat* (Frankfurt/Main, Suhrkamp 1987) 382 ff; J Habermas, *Faktizität und Geltung. Beiträge zur Diskurstheorie des Rechts und des demokratischen Rechtsstaats* (Frankfurt/Main, Suhrkamp 1992) 42 ff.

[10] See P Koller, 'On the Interrelations between Domestic and Global (In)Justice' (2010) 13 *Critical Review of International Social and Political Philosophy* 137–158; idem, 'International Law and Global Justice' in LH Meyer (ed), *Legitimacy, Justice and Public International Law* (Cambridge, Cambridge University Press, 2009) 186–206.

[11] Cp Rawls, *A Theory of Justice* (n 8) 333 ff.

communities, we find a widely acknowledged conventional morality, which appears to be indispensible for achieving a fairly peaceful and beneficial social order. Such a morality, however, does not suffice to ensure such an order, since it unavoidably suffers from a number of shortcomings, which increase along with a society's growing size and differentiation. For there is obviously a negative correlation between the extent of a social aggregate and the content of its conventional morality: the larger a social aggregate is, the smaller is the set of generally shared moral standards, which themselves become even more indeterminate, incomplete and ineffective, like the moral precepts to respect the possessions of others and not to cheat other people. Such standards are not only too indeterminate to guide people's conduct in most particular cases, but also incomplete in the sense that their application hinges on conditions about which morality keeps silent; and they are also highly ineffective, because the social pressure by which they were backed has lost its strength. These shortcomings apply particularly to imperfect moral duties and demands of justice which remain highly ineffective as long as they are not specified through an institutional order that assigns special obligations to particular agents. Consequently, larger societies will only succeed to achieve a fairly peaceful und generally beneficial social order, when their conventional morality is supplemented and supported by an appropriate legal order whose norms and practices fill the gaps which morality unavoidably leaves open.[12]

On the other hand, *law relies on the moral attitudes of its participants* in a twofold way. First of all, the claims of law's officials and addressees to its legitimacy presuppose normative principles which necessarily include moral standards. Even though the participants of a legal order may – and usually do – assess its legitimacy not only from the viewpoints of morality and justice, but also in light of social efficiency and the common good, their claims to the order's legitimacy necessarily include, at least implicitly, a claim to its *moral* acceptability because of the overriding stance of its directives backed by organised force. Consequently, legal authorities and officials must claim that their own legal decisions are in fact morally acceptable, while law's addressees have reason to claim that legal norms to which they are subject ought to be morally appropriate, either on the basis of widely shared standards of conventional morality or with reference to principles of critical morality which they deem to be defensible. Thus, law's legitimacy includes its moral acceptability, which, when taken seriously, is deemed to have normative priority over the other viewpoints.[13] A second

---

[12] See HLA Hart, *The Concept of Law* (1961) 2nd ed, ed by PA Bulloch & J Raz (Oxford, Clarendon Press, 1994) 79 ff; Habermas, *Faktizität und Geltung* (n 9) 41 ff; R Alexy, 'Legal Certainty and Correctness' (2015) 28 *Ratio Juris* 441–451.

[13] On this point, taken generally, there exists wide-spread agreement even among most advocates of the two main camps of philosophy of law, ie legal positivism and non-positivism (or legal moralism), in spite of their disagreement on other matters, including the interpretation of the idea of law's legitimacy. I only point to Joseph Raz, who maintains law's claim to legitimate authority, and Robert Alexy with the thesis that law claims correctness; see J Raz, 'On the Nature of Law' (1996) 82 *ARSP* 1–25; R Alexy, 'On the Concept and Nature of Law' (2008) 21 *Ratio Juris* 281–299.

reason why a legal order must rely on the moral attitudes of its participants is the fact that its proper functioning not only requires loyalty to its fundamental values and principles on the part of officials, but also depends on the voluntary support of its addressees. For a legal order with rules that are not taken seriously by its authorities or that deviate too far from the moral convictions of its subjects will operate poorly, and in the worst case may even collapse. I will return to this aspect later on, after the following considerations on the role of virtues in morality.

II. VIRTUES AND THEIR ROLE IN MORALITY

In the last decades, there has been a growing philosophical debate about the role of virtues in ethics and morality, particularly whether virtues are fundamental elements of ethics or merely instrumental devices for a flourishing moral practice.[14] Yet, this question will not be dealt with in this chapter, since I am mainly interested in the *contingent function* of virtues for morality and justice as a social practice. For this purpose, however, a few general remarks on the very notion of virtue are in order.

According to usual understanding, a *virtue* is conceived of as a lasting practical disposition or character trait that motivates people to behave in a way that is regarded as desirable. By contrast, a *vice* is a character trait driving people to bad conduct. There are, however, numerous dispositions that are widely regarded as virtues, as well as a great number of attitudes that count as vices. As to the former, most prominent are the so-called cardinal virtues, ie prudence, courage, moderation, and justice; further well-known examples are reasonableness, truthfulness, honesty, fairness, sincerity, benevolence, helpfulness, generosity, politeness, open-mindedness, tolerance, fidelity, loyalty, reliability, diligence, carefulness, humility, modesty, and the like.[15] When we look at this list, it becomes obvious that the assessment of an attitude as a virtue depends not only on the respective evaluative viewpoint, but also on the relevant social context. Hence a human attitude may be regarded as a virtue in one context, but a vice in a different context.

This observation makes it necessary to differentiate between different sorts of virtues in order to put their variety in a systematic order.[16] To this end, I want

---

[14] I just mention some collections among the abundance of literature about this matter: JW Chapman & WA Galston (eds), *Virtue* (New York, New York University Press, 1992); R Crisp & M Slote (eds), *Virtue Ethics* (Oxford, Oxford University Press, 1997); D Stratman (ed), *Virtue Ethics: A Critical Reader* (Edinburgh, Edinburgh University Press, 1997).

[15] Cp D Hume, *A Treatise of Human Nature* (1739/40) ed by TH Green & TH Grose (London, Longmans, Green & Co, 1882) II/III (238 ff); A Smith, *The Theory of Moral Sentiments* (1759) ed by DD Raphael & AL Macfie (Oxford, Oxford University Press, 1976) II/I+II (67 ff); Kant, *Metaphysik der Sitten* (n 9) II (Tugendlehre).

[16] For an interesting approach to a systematic classification of virtues and vices see C Halbig, *Der Begriff der Tugend und die Grenzen der Tugendethik* (Berlin, Suhrkamp 2013) 142 ff. In one respect,

to make use of three distinctions: intellectual and practical virtues, non-moral and moral virtues, and unconditional and conditional moral virtues. The first and most fundamental distinction is the one between intellectual and practical virtues, which goes back to Aristotle.[17] *Intellectual* virtues aim at true knowledge and theoretical insight, such as reasonableness, truthfulness, the habit of critical thinking and careful consideration.[18] By contrast, *practical* virtues have right conduct as their goal, such as the cardinal as well as most other virtues previously mentioned. This distinction is analytical and does not imply that intellectual and practical virtues are actually separate. In fact, they are often closely connected, as intellectual virtues are in most cases of great importance for the guidance to right conduct, and people's practical virtues may support their inclination to search for the truth. Moreover, it seems that there even exists an intermediate kind of virtue between them, namely the virtue of 'practical wisdom', understood as an excellence in practical deliberation.[19] I will mainly focus on practical virtues, which themselves can be divided up into two different sorts: non-moral and moral virtues.

Non-moral virtues are character traits that motivate individuals to behave in a way that is beneficial to themselves or the members of the social groups to which they belong, but not necessarily beneficial to other people too. So these virtues, such as diligence, perseverance, fidelity, and loyalty, are instrumental to the promotion of the good of particular individuals or collectives, though they may collide with moral demands. By contrast, *moral* virtues are directed to moral conduct, a conduct that appears to be required or desirable from a general and impartial point of view; such virtues include justice, benevolence, honesty, and tolerance.[20] There are, however, virtues that cannot be easily assigned to one category or may belong to both sorts. One such case is prudence, understood as the pursuit of one's reasonable self-interest: while some authors maintain that its proper exercise is always in accordance with the basic demands of morality, others think that it can also be directed to immoral ends.[21] Regardless, the following considerations will deal with moral virtues only.

A *moral virtue* can be conceived of as a character disposition that motivates individuals to conduct themselves in a way which, in light of the accepted moral

---

however, I have reservations about Halbig's treatise, because it neglects the difference between moral and non-moral virtues, which I deem to be fundamental for an appropriate conception of virtues.

[17] See Aristotle, *Nicomachean Ethics* (Oxford, Oxford University Press, 1998) 1103a; cp Halbig, *Begriff der Tugend* (n 16) 78 ff.

[18] See R Roberts & WJ Wood, *Intellectual Virtues* (Oxford, Oxford University Press, 2007).

[19] See D Wiggins, 'Deliberation and Practical Reasoning' in E Millgram (ed), *Varieties of Practical Reasoning* (Cambridge MA, MIT Press, 2001) 279–301, 293; A Amaya, 'Virtue and Reason in Law' in M Del Mar (ed), *New Waves in Philosophy of Law* (New York, Palgrave Macmillan, 2011) 123–143, 124 f.

[20] See B Gert, *Morality. Its Nature and Justification* (New York-Oxford, Oxford University Press, 1998) 283.

[21] Cp Smith, *Theory of Moral Sentiments* (n 15) VI/I (212 ff); Körner, *Experience and Conduct* (n 4) 163 ff.

standards, appears required or desirable.[22] This notion of virtue, which relies on its usual understanding from Aristotle to Adam Smith and Kant until Rawls,[23] is sufficiently narrow to be understood as a specific aspect of moral life, while it is also wide enough to be compatible with different conceptions of morality. If we look at the list of virtues which are considered to be moral, we will find that some of them are unambiguously directed to moral conduct, such as justice, fairness and honesty, whereas others may in certain cases also be supportive of the pursuit of morally dubious or even clearly immoral ends, eg helpfulness, generosity, and solidarity, if they extend to unjust social relationships. This observation suggests a distinction between two sorts of moral virtues, namely unconditional and conditional ones. *Unconditional* are moral virtues which motivate people to conduct that appears to be morally required, permissible or desirable in all social contexts, while *conditional* moral virtues are generally conducive to moral conduct, but may, under certain conditions, also lead to morally inacceptable results. Here, I will primarily deal with unconditional moral virtues with regard to their function in the practice of morality, and allude to conditional ones only if they serve to support unconditional moral virtues.

In my opinion, the most fundamental moral virtues are two human capacities which are often neglected, although they are constitutive for the very practice of morality in general: empathy and impartiality. *Empathy*, the capacity to share the emotions of other sentient beings, is a necessary precondition for taking the needs of others into consideration. It is certainly not an inborn property of people, but a mental disposition that human individuals usually acquire through a favourable socialisation and ought to cultivate during their lives.[24] By contrast, *impartiality* is the capacity to abstract from one's own special interests or sympathies and adopt a general and impersonal point of view, from which the respective needs or claims of all people concerned are considered. This capacity, which alongside empathy is a further constitutive ingredient of moral thinking, is also a mental disposition that is contingent upon individual education and social culture.[25] Thus, both empathy and impartiality are capacities that qualify as the most fundamental moral virtues by which morality as a social practice stands or falls. Without them people would neither have reason to consider the interests of other people, nor be able to weigh these interests, as well as one's own desires, against each other.

[22] Cp Koller, 'Law, Morality, and Virtue' (n 4) 192 f.

[23] See Aristotle, *Nicomachean Ethics* (n 17) 1105b; Smith, *Theory of Moral Sentiments* (n 15) I/I/V (23 ff); Kant, *Metaphysik der Sitten* (n 9) II (Tugendlehre) IX A 28 ff (525); Rawls, *A Theory of Justice* (n 8) 192.

[24] See Smith, *Theory of Moral Sentiments* (n 15) II/I (67 ff); M Hoffman, *Empathy and Moral Development: Implications for Caring and Justice* (Cambridge, Cambridge University Press, 2000); M Slote, 'Empathy. Law and Justice' in A Amaya & H Hock Lai (eds), *Law, Virtue and Justice* (Oxford – Portland, OR, Hart Publishing, 2013) 279–292; HL Maibom (ed), *Empathy and Morality* (Oxford, Oxford University Press, 2014).

[25] See Smith, *Theory of Moral Sentiments* (n 15) III (109 ff); T Nagel, *The View from Nowhere* (New York, Oxford University Press, 1986); Gert, *Morality* (n 20) 130 ff.

Apart from these capacities, virtues that clearly seem to be unconditionally desirable from the moral point of view are justice, fairness, benevolence, peacefulness, and honesty. *Justice*, understood as an individual attitude rather than a property of institutions or a set of standards of human conduct, means the habit of judging and acting in a way that appears morally required in contexts concerning interpersonal or social conflicts, such as the resolution of private litigations, the distribution of communal goods or burdens, the exchange of goods through contractual transactions, the use and exercise of social power, and the punishment of wrongs.[26] *Fairness* as a moral virtue of individuals is apparently closely related or even tantamount to justice, although there are various contexts where its notion appears to be preferable, such as in matters of sport or in some contexts where the procedural aspects of collective decision-making processes take on more importance than their results. In contrast to justice and fairness, *benevolence*, the disposition to do good, is often conceived of as an attitude which mainly applies to the weak moral demands of humanity and supererogatory activities.[27] I think, however, that benevolence is also supportive of or even requisite for the demands of general morality and justice, since these demands' target to promote everybody's well-being could certainly not be achieved without people's benevolence. Something similar is true of *peacefulness*, the striving for non-violent resolution of social conflicts, since it is built into the very idea of morality from the start. Last but not least, the virtue of *honesty*, according to its usual understanding, combines a number of attitudes, such as integrity, truthfulness and sincerity, which all appear to be mandatory both for moral discourse and moral conduct.

Regardless of the contested question whether virtues are fundamental elements of morality on which its principles and rules may be based or mere secondary qualities derived from moral principles or rules, there can be no doubt that virtues have an indispensable motivational function for the social practice of morality. In order to illuminate this function in detail, I want to distinguish between the general function of virtues for morality as a whole, and their special functions for various sorts of moral standards.[28]

Moral virtues have, first of all, the *general function* to strengthen the weak motivating force of moral standards, which often compete with our self-interested preferences and, therefore, are highly susceptible to defects, by creating internal and external sanctions in support of these standards. By creating *internal sanctions*, ie feelings of good or bad conscience, our internalised moral attitudes provide us with some additional, even though often rather weak reasons to comply with acknowledged moral standards even in cases where external

---

[26] See Koller, *Theorie des Rechts* (n 1) 295 ff idem, 'Zur Semantik der Gerechtigkeit' (n 7).

[27] See Smith, *Theory of Moral Sentiments* (n 15) II/II (78 ff); Kant, *Metaphysik der Sitten* (n 9) II (Tugendlehre) II 1 1 A §§ 29 ff (588 ff).

[28] See Baier, *The Rational and the Moral Order* (n 5) 7 ff, 89 ff; Gert, *Morality* (n 20) 277 ff.

social sanctions are insufficient or missing. In this way, virtues contribute to the effectiveness of moral practice, which, however, also needs a supportive social environment that reinforces and fosters it. And moral virtues are an important ingredient of such an environment, for they cause people to pay attention and react to the conduct of their fellows in a way that reinforces shared moral standards. Thus we are in the habit of acknowledging and praising persons who have behaved or are still behaving in a morally desirable way that exceeds the moral duties whose fulfilment may be expected of normal people as a matter of course. In this way, moral virtues exert external sanctions too.[29]

Beside this general function, moral virtues also have various *special functions* according to the different sorts of moral standards mentioned above. Let us take a look at *interpersonal* morality, which itself can be divided into general morality, justice and supererogation. (1) As for the demands of *general morality*, moral virtues have different functions in relation to the duties under consideration: (a) In relation to *perfect duties*, which, in general, are not only rather clear, but also not very demanding, virtues have the function of motivating individuals to regular and lasting compliance with these duties, even in cases where they could easily violate them without risking any social sanction. (b) With regard to *imperfect duties*, which are even more susceptible to defection, because they are generally more demanding and less precise, virtues can help to counteract the permanent and significant temptation of insufficient compliance; so we may feel moral shame, when we are confronted with the social injustices and evils that result from the fact that the uncoordinated behaviour of individuals fails to achieve a morally acceptable state of social affairs, a moral shame which itself may lead us to contribute to social reform.[30] (2) The demands of *justice* are even more in need of support by corresponding moral virtues in order to be fairly effective; for, on the one hand, they are deemed as rather strong moral demands which constitute individual rights and duties, while on the other hand, they are usually fairly indeterminate and controversial, so that people are often tempted to tailor them to their particular interests.[31] (3) As far as *supererogatory activities* are concerned, moral virtues serve the purpose to motivate people to act in ways that exceed their moral duties, but are desirable from a general point of view.[32]

Moral virtues also play an important role in *institutional* morality, which calls for political and legal arrangements enabling and fostering a peaceful and just social order. From the viewpoint of a critical political morality, such an order

---

[29] See Hume, *Treatise of Human of Human Nature* (n 15) II/I (75 ff; Smith; *Theory of Moral Sentiments* (n 15) II/II/II (82 ff), II/III (134 ff); S Bowles, *The Moral Economy. Why Good Incentives Are No Substitute for Good Citizens* (New Haven – London, Yale University Press, 2016) 39 ff.

[30] See Koller, 'Law, Morality, and Virtue' (n 4) 194 ff.

[31] See Rawls, *A Theory of Justice* (n 8) 496 ff.

[32] See Onora O'Neill, 'Duties and Virtues' in A Phillips Griffiths (ed), *Ethics* (Cambridge, Cambridge University Press, 1993) 107–120; B Gert, *Morality* (n 20) 285 ff.

ought to ensure the following principles: on the national level, legal equality, civil liberty, democratic participation, equality of opportunity, and socio-economic equity, together with appropriate procedural devices (eg fair trial, equal access to justice, separation of powers); and on the international or global level, equal political standing of nations, appropriate national self-determination, fair international division of labour and trade relationships, fair access to global natural resources, and peaceful conflict-resolution.[33] These institutional principles imply various duties for appropriate social cooperation on the part of the members of the social aggregates under consideration, namely a rather strict duty to comply with the rules of a fairly just social order and a more indeterminate duty to contribute to the establishment and preservation of a just social order as far as possible.[34] These duties are often not easy to fulfil and, therefore, need sufficient support from related moral virtues.

The functions of moral virtues not only vary with the type of moral demands, but also with individuals' moral conceptions. Some people may have strange moral views that bring them into opposition with the conventional morality widely shared in their social environment: for instance the view that any expression that makes fun of religious beliefs or rituals should be regarded as a severe moral wrong deserving death. If such a view goes hand in hand with the pronounced attitude of its advocates to defend it at any cost, this attitude will cause conflict rather than promote a peaceful and tolerant social life. Consequently, not every attitude that is deemed to be a moral virtue by those who hold it, will be regarded as a virtue by most other people. But in almost all societies we find a wide-spread consensus on a certain set of moral standards, ie a conventional morality backed by informal social pressure. Yet the fact that moral standards are actually agreed upon does not imply that these standards are also reasonably defensible from a critical perspective. So it may be that, upon critical reflection, some of these standards turn out to be highly erroneous or even immoral, and therefore, the individual moral attitudes that support their effectiveness may be erroneous too. As a result, the final authority for the assessment of whether the standards of an individual or conventional morality are reasonably defensible, is a *critical* morality whose standards appear to be generally acceptable for the best reasons available.[35] In the following, I will assume that most people are able to adopt the perspective of a critical morality and hold respective moral virtues in support of a legal order which by and large in in accord with its demands.

In my subsequent considerations, which are devoted to the role of moral virtues within the domain of law, I will proceed in two steps. First, I will focus

---

[33] See Koller, 'On the Interrelations between Domestic and Global (In)Justice' (n 10); idem, 'International Law and Global Justice' (n 10).

[34] See Rawls, *A Theory of Justice* (n 8) 350 ff; Joseph Raz, 'The Obligation to Obey the Law' in idem, *The Authority of Law* (Oxford, Oxford University Press, 1979) 233 ff.

[35] See HLA Hart, *Law, Liberty, and Morality* (Oxford – New York, Oxford University Press, 1963) 17 ff; Baier, *The Rational and the Moral Order* (n 5) 214 ff.

on the more general virtues of the participants of a legal order, ie its ruling authorities and its addressees, virtues that cause them to support a legitimate legal order as a whole. Thereafter, I will turn to the more specific virtues which the individual parties of legal practice in their related – professional or private – activities should exert in order to promote the successful functioning of this practice. It should be clear, however, that the virtues that we encounter in these two fields are not different in kind, but do often overlap and interact.[36]

III. MORAL VIRTUES IN SUPPORT OF LEGAL ORDER

This chapter deals with the significance of moral virtues for the formation and preservation of a well-functioning and legitimate legal order in general, ie the level of its basic institutional arrangement, including the constitution and legislation. To this end, it is necessary to make a few remarks on the moral aims and limits of a legal order from the viewpoint of a critical morality in advance.

As for the *aims of law*, a legal order firstly has to specify and enforce the fundamental rights and duties of its subjects which flow from well-founded and widely acknowledged *perfect demands of general morality and justice*, insofar as their enforcement serves the protection of essential interests of people which outweigh the negative consequences of legal force. In my view, these rights and duties not only include the familiar negative duties of non-interference and their correlative rights, but also a few modest positive duties, such as the duty to render help in case of emergency, if such help can be reasonably expected. Secondly, a legal order has to establish and enforce an arrangement of individual rights and duties that facilitates the cooperative fulfilment of those *imperfect moral demands whose satisfaction is of essential importance for individuals*, but can only be achieved by coordinating their behaviour in an appropriate way. This is also true of the demands of social justice which entail positive rights of individuals, such as the rights to legal equality, civil liberty, democratic participation, equal opportunity, and economic equity. And thirdly, a legal order has to issue and enforce individual rights and duties which are necessary for achieving *collective goals* that require cooperative interaction, if their pursuit has been decided on in an appropriate way, even though achieving these goals may not be morally required in itself. Thus the law may establish rights and duties in order to provide public goods to the citizens' common benefit.[37]

On the other hand, there are also definite *limits of law* constraining the legitimate tasks of a legitimate legal order. First of all, such an order must not

---

[36] For a broader and more general assessment of the role of virtues within law see the collections: C Farrelly & LB Solum (eds), *Virtue Jurisprudence* (Basingstoke, Palgrave MacMillan, 2008); Amaya & Hock Lai (eds), *Law, Virtue and Justice* (n 24), therein particularly the editors' article 'Of Law, Morality and Justice – An Introduction' 1–25.

[37] See Hart, *Concept of Law* (n 12), 124 ff; Koller, *Theorie des Rechts* (n 1) 288 ff.

enforce *erroneous or eccentric moral views* that are not aimed at the protection of important human interests, such as the prohibition of homosexual relationships, interracial marriages or blasphemous utterances. This constraint flows immediately from the law's ultimate aim to guarantee a just and generally advantageous social order, because the legal enforcement of eccentric views would create significant costs to those individuals who do not share them without serving the realisation of generally acceptable aims. Secondly, a legal order ought not to enforce *supererogatory moral ends* that exceed what can be reasonably expected of an average person from an impartial perspective. For even though moral acts, like donating a kidney or risking one's life to rescue another person, may appear generally desirable, it is not the law's job to enforce them, since this would create social affairs even less desirable than the continued occurrence of the dangers that could be diminished through the legal enforcement of those ends. And thirdly, a legal order must not force certain *inner convictions and attitudes* upon people even if they appear morally desirable, since this would unavoidably result in public hypocrisy or, even worse, a rigid repression of free thought. Consequently, legal force is not an appropriate means to bring forth moral virtues.[38]

Yet, although law must not enforce moral virtues directly, it certainly can and should contribute to their promotion by supporting them indirectly. There are at least two possible ways. First, a legal order should provide legal framing conditions of social interaction which make moral conduct beneficial to its subjects rather than disadvantageous, for instance, by preventing people from taking benefit from dishonest, corrupt or unfair activities.[39] Thus, a legitimate and functioning legal order actually contributes to the diffusion and cultivation of moral virtues, although it is not its job to enforce them. Second, a legal order may foster moral virtues by providing appropriate positive incentives, such as promoting fairness and solidarity in public education, supporting desirable social activities through public subsidies or the tax system, or offering special awards for laudable ways of conduct.[40]

Now, in order to figure out the particular moral virtues of law's participants which support a legitimate legal order, I would like to distinguish between three groups: a legal order's decisive political agents and superior public officials, subordinated legal officials, and ordinary people in their role as legal subjects. To identify the respective virtues, it will be useful in all cases to first ask what the tasks of the people under consideration are and then to contrast a state of affairs in which these people are led by certain virtues with a state in which they lack these virtues, ie a state in which they are pursuing only their respective individual preferences, especially their self-interest.

---

[38] See Hart, *Law, Liberty, and Morality* (n 35) 30 ff; Koller, 'Law, Morality, and Virtue' (n 4) 198 f.
[39] See Bowles, *The Moral Economy* (n 29) 151 ff.
[40] See G Brennan & A Hamlin, *Democratic Devices and Desires* (Cambridge, Cambridge University Press, 2000) 76 ff.

Which moral tasks fall to the *decisive political agents and superior public officials* of a legitimate legal order, including the ministers of government, members of legislative bodies, judges of high courts, powerful politicians, and influential political advisers, who bear particular responsibility for the shaping and operation of legal institutions, rules and procedures in general? Some of their tasks are obvious. First of all, all these persons are expected to stick with the *basic requirements of liberal democracy and social justice*, especially basic human rights, such as the rule of law, equality before the law, fair trial, civil and political liberty, and the like. Furthermore, we also expect that these people are led by a *publicly defensible conception of the common good* rather than pursuing the special interests of particular social groups, and that they exercise their powers impartially in accordance with what they deem the common good rather than in a corrupt way to the benefit of the political rulers or the rich. Yet, we have to bear in mind that it is hardly possible to enforce these demands through legal means, not only because they are highly abstract and open-textured, but also because of the fact that the individuals to whom they are addressed are often beyond legal control due to their position at the top of the legal system.[41] Therefore, these individuals will hardly comply with those demands sufficiently, unless they acknowledge them wholeheartedly as binding guidelines of their conduct and comply with them voluntarily even in absence of external pressure. If we imagine a legal order in which most leading authorities and officials are people mainly pursuing their own interests or private aims and only comply with the demands of their public function out of fear of negative consequences when they don't, it is quite clear that such a legal order would work very badly or even be in danger of collapsing. As a result, a well-functioning legal order requires that its leading authorities and officials possess moral virtues that motivate them to fulfil their functions in an appropriate way.[42] What are these moral virtues?

First and foremost, decisive political agents and superior public officials need a *sense of justice* that enables them to develop a reasonable conception of a generally acceptable legal order that provides guidelines for their conduct in shaping legal institutions, rules, and procedures. I suppose that, in the context of modern societies, this sense of justice entails a number of more special moral attitudes towards people who are subject to or affected by the legal order, such as *equal respect* for their fundamental dignity and autonomy, *sensitivity* for their individual needs, *solidarity* with individuals in serious difficulties, *tolerance* for the diversity of individual ways of life, and *courage* in defending the principles of justice against illiberal, anti-democratic or inhumane movements as well as in supporting unpopular measures for the common good against counteracting special interests.[43] In addition, the superiors of a legal order should also

---

[41] See Hart, *Concept of Law* (n 12); DE Thompson, *Political Ethics and Public Office* (Cambridge, MA – London, Harvard University Press, 1987) 66 ff.

[42] See Brennan & Hamlin, *Democratic Devices and Desires* (n 40) 51 ff.

[43] See Rawls, *Theory of Justice* (n 8) 567 ff; R Forst, *Toleranz im Konflikt. Geschichte, Gehalt und Gegenwart eines umstrittenen Begriffs* (Frankfurt/Main, Suhrkamp 2003) 656 ff.

distinguish themselves by various virtues related to their social roles, namely *integrity* in the sense that they are not susceptible to corruption, *responsibility* for the social effects, particularly potential costs and failures of their decisions, and, last but not least, *judgement and prudence* in the pursuit of their political goals or the exercise of their legal powers.[44] Even though it would be greatly naive to expect actual politicians or officials to fully act according to these virtues, it would be disastrous for a legal order if they completely lacked them and only pursued their own self-interest or the special interests of their faction.

Some of the virtues mentioned above also apply to subordinated *legal officials*, such as judges at intermediate and lower courts and officials in public administration, but their responsibilities appear to require other attitudes too. Their most important law-related moral attitudes – beside professional expertise – should be devotion to the rule of law, impartiality, a sense of justice, sound judgement and, of course, honesty. *Devotion to the rule of law* has two opposite aspects: on the one hand, *loyalty* and *obedience* to valid legal directives, whether based on legislation or flowing from precedents, as long as their application is not clearly in conflict with fundamental and evident requirements of morality or justice; on the other hand, *bravery* or *courage* in refusing to follow directives if their application appears to be incompatible with basic moral requirements. Unless legal officials have an attitude of loyalty and obedience to current laws, the rule of law will be built on sand, since otherwise they could hardly be brought to uphold these laws by the threat of legal sanctions alone. And if they never dare refuse to comply with legal rules that they regard as greatly unjust, the rule of law will degenerate to blind obedience so that law would lose an essential device of self-correction through paying attention to the critical views of those who are actually implementing it in social reality.[45]

In order to arrive at these views, however, legal officials should have a well-developed *sense of justice*, which they also need to impartially apply the relevant legal rules in all cases under consideration and to exercise the discretion these rules have left them in a fair and appropriate way. In this context, their reasoning should be guided by *sound judgement*, which requires both a solid knowledge of the relevant legal norms and a proper understanding of the affairs of social reality to which these norms apply.[46] Combined with justice, such an understanding should take particular care of actual social inequalities which may impair the legal subjects' equal access to law or their performance within legal litigations or proceedings. All these attitudes, however, would remain somehow incomplete without being supplemented and supported by legal officials' *honesty* or

---

[44] See M Matravers, *Responsibility and Justice* (Cambridge, Polity Press, 2007).

[45] See J Jovell, 'The Rule of Law and its Underlying Values' in J Jovell & D Oliver (eds), *The Changing Constitution* 7th edn (Oxford, Oxford University Press, 2011) 11–34.

[46] See N MacCormick, *Rhetoric and the Rule of Law. A Theory of Legal Reasoning* (Oxford, Oxford University Press, 2005); Amaya, 'Virtue and Reason in Law' (n 19); idem, 'Exemplarism and Judicial Virtue' (2013) 25 *Law and Literature* 428–445; and the following articles in Amaya & Hock Lai (eds), *Law, Virtue and Justice* (n 24): C Michelon, 'Practical Wisdom in Legal Decision Making' 29–49; A Amaya, 'The Role of Virtue in Legal Justification' 51–66.

integrity that strengthens their resistance to corruption by making them immune to the temptation of misusing their position for the advantage or disadvantage of certain subjects, as they do in cases of bribery or political interference.[47]

An important or even necessary condition for encouraging politicians and officials to develop and cultivate these virtues is certainly a *well-informed and critical public* that constantly scrutinises the superiors' activities for their legitimacy and puts appropriate pressure on these people to exercise their powers in a proper way.[48] Such a critical public, however, could hardly remain if most *ordinary people* lacked moral attitudes that support a proper shaping and operation of the legal order to which they are subjected. So such an order also requires supportive moral virtues on the part of a significant number of its subjects. Some of these virtues coincide with those of the superiors, such as justice, equal respect, solidarity and courage, while others are related to their subordinate position vis-à-vis political and legal powers. The latter include, in consideration of the general truth that power corrupts, three attitudes in particular: (1) *moderate scepticism* towards the projects, declarations and activities of the political and legal rulers which often are led by hidden partial ambitions rather than generally defensible reasons: (2) sufficient *political commitment* that motivates them to contribute to the public discourse on matters of common interest in general and their legal regulation in particular; and (3) *legal obedience*, even when legal directives do not fit with one's own preferences and could easily be violated without negative consequences, provided that they do not appear clearly immoral or unjust.[49]

Undoubtedly, there are various social conditions that either foster or impede the emergence and cultivation of moral virtues that help shape a legal order. These include, among others, the respective legal culture, political system, and economic structure.[50] In this context, I just want to point to one factor which seems to me of great importance, namely the degree of socio-economic inequalities.

I think that *large inequalities undermine the development and force of moral virtues*. Although I cannot offer solid empirical evidence for this thesis, I deem it very plausible both for general reasons and in light of everyday observations. A general reason is the conjecture that growing differences between the living conditions and interests of people make it more difficult for them to achieve moral impartiality as the basic prerequisite of justice and fairness, because

[47] See Kleinig, *Ethics and Criminal Justice. An Introduction* (Cambridge, Cambridge University Press, 2008) 166 ff.

[48] See Habermas, *Faktizität und Geltung* (n 9) ch VIII; A Gutmann & D Thompson, *Democracy and Disagreement* (Cambridge, MA – London, Harvard University Press, 1996) 95 ff.

[49] See O Höffe, *Wirtschaftsbürger Staatsbürger Weltbürger. Politische Ethik im Zeitalter der Globalisierung* (München, CH Beck 2004) 82 ff.

[50] See RE Goodin, *Motivating Political Morality* (Cambridge, MA – Oxford, Blackwell, 1992).

individuals will increasingly have problems putting themselves in the place of others with greatly different living conditions and, therefore, be inclined to tailor their moral views and attitudes to their own interests. And this conjecture seems to find confirmation by the observation of public debates on controversial issues of legal policy, like quarrels over taxation, welfare programmes, and public education. Hence I think that a society will have little success in fostering the moral virtues that are important for a well-functioning legal order, if it does not keep socio-economic inequalities within fairly reasonable limits.[51]

This concludes my section on moral virtues related to the general arrangements and institutions of a legal order. Yet, virtues also play an important role in everyday legal practice to which I would now like to turn.

IV. LEGAL PRACTICE AND ITS RELATED VIRTUES

The area of everyday legal practice, as I understand it here, includes a wide range of legal activities, such as the judicial proceedings in lower courts concerning particular cases, the execution of administrative regulations by government offices, the enforcement of legal rules by the police and other administrative bodies, the settlement of legal disputes by arbitral institutions, and the sphere of contractual transactions among private parties. In the following, I will take a glance at some of these activities in order to figure out why and in what respects their proper and fair performance requires certain moral attitudes on the part of their participants, be they legal officials, lawyers or private people. To this end, it will again be useful to consider a state of affairs in which individuals lack any moral virtues and are led exclusively by self-regarding interests and preferences.

There is a tradition of political thinking advocating the view that, in general, individuals are inclined to pursue – exclusively or, at least, primarily – their own interests within the respective limits of their conduct, set by natural constraints and social framing conditions. The latter include legal directives connected with negative and positive sanctions in the form of penalties and rewards that induce their addressees to abide by these directives in their own self-interest. As law has become the dominant means of social regulation in modern society, a peaceful and flourishing social life may be achieved by establishing a legal order whose norms, backed by appropriate sanctions, compel its participants to behave in a way that leads to the desired result. Thus, if law provides its participants, both legal officials and subjects, with firm and unequivocal directives backed by effective sanctions that compel them to fulfil their tasks and duties, it will enable a

[51] See J Stiglitz, *The Price of Inequality. How Today's Divided Society Endangers Our Future* (New York, Norton, 2012; AB Atkinson, *Inequality. What can be done?* (Cambridge, MA – London, Harvard University Press, 2015); B Milanovic, *Global Inequality. A new Approach for the Age of Globalization* (Cambridge, MA – London, Harvard University Press, 2016).

well-ordered social life without any supportive moral virtues on the part of its participants.[52]

Upon closer examination, however, this view turns out to be completely illusory for a multitude of reasons: (1) Every legal order, even a most complete and just one, unavoidably contains a great many rules which are highly indeterminate or abstract and, therefore, leave a high degree of discretion to officials in applying them to particular cases in various ways some of which may significantly deviate from moral demands. Examples are legal rules containing the notions of guilt, fault, negligence, emergency, self-defence, and the like.[53] (2) Every legal order is actually exposed to the danger that its rules are applied by its officials in a biased, distorted or even obviously incorrect way without providing the subjects concerned with appropriate means of remedy, as, for instance, certain ways of a concealed discrimination against individuals because of their ethnic origin or social position.[54] (3) Every legal order includes many rules whose effective enforcement depends on the voluntary cooperation and support of its subjects, including a sufficient number of those who themselves do not benefit from supporting legal enforcement. One example is people who take the time to give testimony in trials that do not affect them.[55] (4) Every legal order contains sets of rules, for instance, contract or tort law, whose requirements on lawful conduct must, for the sake of practicability, be kept lower than reasonable standards of morality. Consequently, they can easily lead to morally questionable outcomes, such as distorted contractual transactions or insufficient liability for risky enterprises.[56] (5) Every legal order operates in such a way that its actual results in particular cases depend not merely on its rules, but rather on their interplay with variable facts of social reality, such as the individuals' social position, economic situation, knowledge, power, reputation, ethnic origin, and

---

[52] This view, which combines a rational choice approach to human action with a conception of law as a system of coercive commands, can be traced back to Hobbes, Spinoza, Bentham and John Austin. Although it is rarely advocated in today's academic social and legal philosophy, it still enjoys some popularity in everyday public debates, eg when certain dubious practices in politics, business and law are at stake.

[53] See Hart, *Concept of Law* (n 12) 128 ff; J Kleinig, *Ethics and Criminal Justice* (n 47) 71 ff; F Schauer, 'On the Open Texture of Law' (2013) 87 *Grazer Philosophische Studien* 197–215.

[54] See D Kennedy, 'Form and Substance in Private Law Adjudication' (1975) 89 *Harvard Law Review* 1685–1778; DS Emmelman, 'The Effect of Social Class on the Adjudication of Criminal Cases: Class-linked Behavior Tendencies, Common Sense, and the Interpretive Procedures of Court-appointed Defense Attorneys' (1994) 17 *Symbolic Interaction* 1–20; E Golin, 'Solving the Problem of Gender and Racial Bias in Administrative Adjudication' (1995) 95 *Columbia Law Review* 1532–1567; M Chamallas, 'The Architecture of Bias Deep Structures in Tort Law' (1998) 146 *University of Pennsylvania Law Review* 463–531; CD Maxwell, AL Robinson & LA Post, 'The impact of race on the adjudication of sexual assault and other violent crimes' (2003) 31 *Journal of Criminal Justice* 523–538. JD Vendel, 'General Bias and Administrative Law Judges: Is There a Remedy for Social Security Disability Claimants' (2005) 90 *Cornell Law Review* 769–809.

[55] See Kleinig, *Ethics and Criminal Justice* (n 47) 60 ff.

[56] See, eg, JM Feinman, *Delay, Deny, Defend. Why Insurance Companies don't Pay Claims and What You Can Do about it* (New York, Penguin, 2010).

the like, which may cause significant inequalities in their opportunity to have access to law and to enforce their legal claims.[57] All these facts support the thesis that everyday legal practice must rely on supportive moral attitudes on the part of its participants to operate in a fair way.

In order to single out these virtues, I am going to differentiate between two groups of participants: first, lawyers, ie professional legal counsels or advisers on behalf of individuals or enterprises in litigations, contractual relationships or other legal affairs; and, second, ordinary people in their two roles as parties in legal transactions and as mere legal subjects.

An important function within everyday legal practice is assigned to *professional lawyers*, such as advocates, barristers, solicitors or legal counsellors whose job is to advise private people in legal matters and to represent or support them in legal proceedings. Although their particular functions and responsibilities are to a certain extent contingent upon the respective national legal system, they generally entail two kinds of duty: on the one hand, a lawyer's *duty to the client*, including confidentiality, expertise, perseverance, fidelity, reliability, and, on the other hand, the *duty to the rule of law* or the integrity of the legal order, which requires justice, honesty, courage and commitment to the common good. These two kinds of duty may not only come into conflict with one another, but also collide with the special interests of the lawyers or their law firms.[58]

For a closer inspection of lawyers' moral responsibilities and virtues, I can rely not only on abstract theoretical considerations and fragile intuitions as before, but also on a solid empirical study, the research report *Virtuous Character for the Practice of Law*, which extensively deals with the moral demands on lawyers in general and their performance in the face of ethical dilemmas in particular.[59] Participants in the study were divided into four groups, namely two groups of law students: first year undergraduates and advanced students, and two groups of experienced law professionals: solicitors and barristers. All of them were asked for their opinions concerning lawyers' performance by means of an e-survey and interviews. Although the study reflects some peculiarities of the British legal system, its main results quite obviously also apply by and large to other developed legal orders.

According to the study, there is widespread agreement on the most important character traits of an ideal lawyer among all groups in spite of slight differences between students and professionals, which obviously mirror their different

---

[57] See LM Friedman, *The Legal System: A Social Science Perspective* (New York, Russell Sage, 1975) 45 ff; S Baer, *Rechtssoziologie. Eine Einführung in die interdisziplinäre Rechtsforschung* (Baden-Baden, Nomos) 209 ff.

[58] See LR Patterson, 'The Function of a Code of Legal Ethics' (1981) 35 *University of Miami Law Review* 695–726; A Paterson, 'Lawyers' ethics and professional responsibility' (2016) 19 *Legal Ethics* 177–181.

[59] J Arthur, K Kristjánsson, H Thomas, M Holdsworth, L Badini Confalonieri & T Qiu, *Virtuous Character for the Practice of Law. Research Report* (Birmingham, University of Birmingham – Jubilee Centre for Character and Virtues, 2014).

levels of experience. Anyway, the top virtues include *judgement*, *perseverance*, *honesty*, *fairness* and *perspective*, which can all be certainly affirmed from the viewpoint of critical morality. Yet these virtues will hardly provide sufficient guidance for lawyers' conduct, as long as they remain that abstract. And since some of them are related to lawyers' duties to their clients, such as judgement and perseverance, while others have to do more with the duty to the legal order's integrity, such as honesty and fairness, they can easily come into conflict in cases where the lawyers' clients are exclusively interested in outcomes beneficial to themselves rather than in seeking justice. But even if lawyers are inclined to resolve such conflicts in a morally acceptable way, they may be subject to external pressures, possibly from their law firms, to refrain from doing so. The study offers interesting information about the range of opinions on how lawyers may cope with various ethical dilemmas which they frequently encounter. Here, I just want to mention two of these dilemmas.

One dilemma (named 'Divorce and Children Act Matter') concerns a conflict between a lawyer's duties to the client on the one hand and to the legal order on the other, or, in terms of virtues, between confidentiality and fidelity versus justice. A lawyer represents a mother of three children, who originally was seeking a divorce from her husband, but changed her mind. She instructs the lawyer to withdraw the legal proceedings, because she wants to move with her children back to her husband, although substantial evidence indicates that he brutally mistreated the children. Thus the lawyer has strong grounds to believe that the children will be at risk if the family is reunited. Interestingly, an overwhelming majority of students selected the option in favour of the lawyer's reporting the matter to the social services in order to protect the children, while more than a half of the professionals preferred to withdraw the proceedings as instructed. So it seems that legal experts give much more weight to virtues committing lawyers to their clients rather than considerations of justice and benevolence favoured by the less experienced.[60] This result raises two questions: first, what an appropriate balancing between the two competing duties should look like and second, whether the professional perspective of experienced lawyers tends to promote or distort proper balancing.

Another dilemma ('Rounding-up hours') differs from the former insofar as it is not about conflicting professional duties or virtues of lawyers, but about a conflict between lawyers' duties to their clients, namely honesty and courage, and pressure to work for their law firms' financial benefit. A young lawyer who works in a law firm is instructed by a senior partner to prepare some files for billing and to round up the hours spent on each file to the next hundred, saying this wouldn't matter to the clients. The young lawyer, however, feels uncomfortable with this instruction and asks advice from a different senior partner, who tells him that he does not want to be troubled with the matter, but says he would deal

---

[60] *Virtuous Character* (n 59) 21, 35.

with it, if the young colleague writes him a formal letter with his concerns. Thus our lawyer has the choice between rounding up the hours according to the first partner's instruction or writing a letter to the second partner. Although all four groups of participants exhibit a clear preference for the second option, namely that the young lawyer writes a letter, there are surprising differences between the groups, particularly between students and professionals. The students were significantly less in favour of this option than the professionals. While among the first-year undergraduates 31 per cent opted for carrying out the first partner's instructions, only 16 per cent of solicitors and 5 per cent of barristers found this appropriate. The study authors argue that this result partly reflects the commercial pressures on lawyers, partly the particular position of barristers.[61] This may be right, but it does not explain why so many students seem to have no problem with fraudulent conduct towards clients.

The Jubilee Centre's Report clearly shows tensions between the widely shared ideals about the moral attitudes of lawyers, on the one hand, and the actual professional routines of their everyday work, on the other hand. It comes as no surprise that in many cases those ideals are more or less sacrificed in favour of personal or business interests. Yet, the Report also shows that legal practice would not operate properly without lawyers' moral attitudes.[62]

Last but not least, a well-functioning legal practice also requires various moral attitudes on the part of *ordinary people*, who participate in a legal order in two different roles: as parties producing law and as individuals subject to law.

In virtually all legal systems, their addressees (or at least a part of them) have the status of *legal persons* who, usually only after they reach a certain age, are capable of entering into voluntary legal relationships leading to enforceable legal rights and obligations, such as concluding contracts, possessing and using property, entering into a marriage, founding a firm, and the like. The most prominent sphere of such relationships is the *market*, which itself is nothing more than an ongoing process of contractual transactions among legal persons, whether individuals or firms. It has been argued that a well-ordered market, ie one that approximately meets the conditions of perfect competition, represents a *morally free zone* in which parties are not bound by any moral standards (except those which are built in the market order) and, therefore, completely free to strive for the satisfaction of their own – selfish or other – preferences.[63] At first glance, this view may appear attractive, since it relieves us from moral

---

[61] *Virtuous Character* (n 59) 20, 32.

[62] For further information about problems of legal ethics, ie professional ethics of lawyers, see AT Kronman, *The Lost Layer: Failing Ideals of the Legal Profession* (Cambridge, MA, Harvard University Press, 1993); G Hanlon, *Lawyers, the State and the Market: Professionalism Revisited* (Basingstoke, Macmillan Press, 1999); A Paterson, *Lawyers and the Public Good. Democracy in Action?* (Cambridge, Cambridge University Press, 2012).

[63] See D Gauthier, *Morals by Agreement* (Oxford, Clarendon Press, 1986) IV 83 ff; similar K Homann, 'Wirtschaftsethik. Die Funktionen der Moral in der modernen Wirtschaft' in J Wieland (ed), *Wirtschaftsethik und Theorie der Gesellschaft* (Frankfurt/Main, Suhrkamp, 1993) 32–53.

burdens as long as we abide by the legal rules, assuming that these rules themselves regulate social life in a generally acceptable way. Upon closer inspection, however, this view turns out to be greatly mistaken. For it does not even apply to well-ordered markets that come close to perfection and applies even less to real markets, most of which are more or less flawed.

Even by and large well-ordered markets face a number of problems that may cause inefficient or unjust outcomes. One of these problems results from the fact that markets, including perfect ones, suffer from various *market failures*, in particular the incapability of providing a sufficient amount of public and merit goods. For private parties will likely abstain from producing these goods because the demand for them does not result in people's willingness or ability to pay for them, either because those who do not pay cannot be excluded from using such goods if they have been provided (eg public streets) or because many of those people who need them cannot afford them (eg appropriate health care in hospitals).[64] Another problem lies in the fact that most *contracts are incomplete*, ie they do not cover all possible aspects, which may give rise to unexpected costs or benefits to the parties involved. Due to this fact a contract's party may suffer disadvantages which, if foreseen, would have prevented her from entering into the respective contract.[65] The more real markets deviate from the ideal of perfect markets, the more they suffer defects that distort their outcomes, such as insufficient or asymmetric information, unequal access to markets as well as unequal exit options, manipulation of consumers' preferences, and the like.[66]

The main means of countering or correcting such market deficiencies are, of course, legal regulations that provide appropriate framing conditions of the market operation.[67] But these deficiencies can also be alleviated to a certain extent by the parties' moral attitudes that may cause them to abstain from taking advantage of all possible benefits available at the cost of others. Accordingly, moral virtues, such as honesty, fairness, consideration and benevolence, would support a proper functioning of market processes. This in turn raises the question of whether these processes themselves may have an impact on those virtues, either by fostering or by undermining them. In this respect, the results of empirical research are rather ambiguous. On the one hand, it has been plausibly argued that the market as a social practice may create and strengthen various virtues, such as the willingness to make mutually beneficial transactions with others on equal terms, respect for trading partners, trust, and responsibility

---

[64] See J Cassidy, *How Markets Fail. The Logic of Economic Calamities* (London, Penguin Books, 2009).

[65] See Bowles, *The Moral Economy* (n 29) 29 ff, 179 f: O Hart, 'Incomplete Contracts and Control' (2017) 107 *American Economic Review* 1731–1752.

[66] See R Kuttner, *Everything for Sale. The Virtues and Limits of Markets* 2nd edn (Chicago, University of Chicago Press 1997).

[67] See, ie, RJ Shiller, *Finance and the Good Society* (Princeton, NJ, Princeton University Press, 2012).

for ones' economic activities.[68] On the other hand, however, there is overwhelming evidence that markets, due to their competitive character and economic incentives, often promote selfish attitudes and, thereby, undermine or 'crowd out' moral motivations.[69]

Along with their role as law-producing parties, ordinary people are also *legal subjects under law's directives*. In this role, individuals can contribute to a well-functioning legal practice through certain moral attitudes, namely a balanced mixture of two opposite attitudes: on the one hand, the *affirmative* attitudes of legal obedience, tolerance for legal failures and inclination to support law enforcement; and, on the other hand, the *critical* attitudes of moderate distrust, commitment to struggle for rights, and courage to engage in civil disobedience.

In my opinion, there are conclusive reasons to believe that the subjects of a legal order have a moral duty to abide by its rules, as long as these rules are by and large fair or at least not grossly unfair. If this is true, they should have a moral attitude of *legal obedience*, which, however, should not be absolute and blind obedience, but rather a conditional willingness to abide by legal directives which, by and large, appear morally defensible or at least not grossly unjust. People should also exhibit relative *tolerance for legal failures and imperfections* which unavoidably occur in legal practice, for otherwise even a fairly well-functioning practice could be judged as greatly deficient.[70] This is particularly true of the official ways of enforcing mandatory legal rules through criminal prosecution and private litigation, since these are contingent on various social facts beyond the law's control, meaning that they are always to a certain extent deficient, accidental and biased. These defects will be diminished when people generally exhibit a sufficient *willingness to support law-enforcement* through their cooperation with the respective legal institutions, at least when they can do that without significant costs. Trivial kinds of such support include reporting an observed criminal act to the police and giving testimony in a court trial; more demanding are, for instance, sacrificing valuable time in sitting on a jury, supporting a victim of criminal violence in self-defence, or informing the public of corrupt practices in state institutions or private enterprises as a whistle-blower despite the risk of considerable costs in case of detection.

Yet these moral attitudes in favour of the current legal practice must go hand in hand with some attitudes that reflect a more critical view of this practice. One of them is a habit of *moderate distrust* towards the activities of legal authorities, a habit that should drive forward a lively public discourse submitting these

---

[68] See L Bruni & R Sugden, 'Reclaiming Virtue Ethics for Economics' (2013) 27 *Journal of Economic Perspectives* 141–164; I Pies (ed), *Die Tugenden des Marktes. Diskussionsmaterial zu einem Aufsatz von Luigino Bruni und Robert Sugden* (Freiburg – München, Alber, 2017); see, in this context, also M Baurmann, *Der Markt der Tugend. Recht und Moral in der liberalen Gesellschaft* (Tübingen, Mohr, 1996).

[69] See Bowles, *The Moral Economy* (n 29) 39 ff.

[70] See Rawls, *Theory of Justice* (n 8) 350 ff.

activities to public scrutiny and control. Furthermore, most activities of legal authorities must be initiated by private individuals who have a legal concern, whether they believe to have a legal claim against others who deny it, they were victims of criminal wrongdoing, they think that they were treated incorrectly by public officials, or were disadvantaged by other misdeeds. Consequently, a well-functioning legal practice needs people's *commitment to struggle for their rights* and quite possibly for the rights of neighbours who cannot help themselves.[71]

This leads to the question of how people should behave when they believe that the current legal practice suffers in a certain respect from a severe injustice that has survived any attempt to eliminate it through legal remedy and public protest, as, for instance, a clear racial bias in the treatment of people by the police or an ongoing habit of certain enterprises to violate basic social rights of their workers with the connivance of the authorities responsible for worker protection. While ordinary people, in my view, do not have a moral duty to put up illegal resistance to such injustices at the risk of punishment, I deem it a moral virtue of individuals who exhibit the *courage to engage in civil disobedience* in order to strengthen their protest against such a deplorable state of affairs. For, in a by and large liberal society, civil disobedience, ie committing non-violent offences under threat of penalty with the intent to draw public attention to unjust legal practices, may contribute to reforming the current legal practice.[72]

---

[71] See R v Jhering, *Der Kampf ums Recht* (1872) ed by H Klenner (Freiburg, Haufe, 1991); P Koller, 'Der Kampf um Recht und Gerechtigkeit' in J Estermann (ed), *Der Kampf ums Recht. Akteure und Interessen im Blick der interdisziplinären Rechtsforschung* (Wien-Beckenried, Lit Orlux, 2012) 13–32.

[72] See HA Bedau, 'On Civil Disobedience' (1961) 58 *Journal of Philosophy* 653–665; idem (ed), *Civil Disobedience in Focus* new edn (London, Routledge, 1991); Rawls, *Theory of Justice* (n 8) 363 ff.

3

The Basic Norm

STANLEY L PAULSON*

I. INTRODUCTION

T HE COURSE OF Kelsen's basic norm (*Grundnorm*) has been one of
notoriety. Churchill's line may be a tad shopworn, but it describes to a
tee the reception accorded the basic norm: 'a riddle wrapped in a mystery inside an enigma'. One way of contending with the basic norm is largely to
ignore it, a stance evident in certain circles favourably disposed to Kelsen's legal
philosophy. Kelsen himself, however, seems to place great stock in the notion,
writing that 'the *presuppositions* of legal cognition are implied in the sense of
the basic norm', that 'the normative import of all the material facts constituting
the legal system' is '[r]ooted in the basic norm', that 'the whole function of [the]
basic norm is to confer law-creating power', that the basic norm represents 'the
point of departure for a procedure: the procedure for creating positive law'.[1]
These quotations may strike the reader as bewildering, and rightly so. With
an eye to lending a modicum of comprehensibility to this most puzzling of all
the notions in Kelsen's conceptual répertoire, I look to various readings of the
basic norm.

* Visiting Research Fellow, Hermann Kantorowicz-Institut für juristische Grundlagenforschung,
Juristisches Seminar, Christian-Albrechts-Universität zu Kiel, formerly Professor of Philosophy and
William Gardiner Hammond Professor of Law, Washington University in St. Louis. I wish to thank
Brian H Bix, William A Edmundson, Jörg Kammerhofer, Hubert Rottleuthner, Brian Tamanaha,
Ewald Wiederin, and Kenneth Winston for a great variety of helpful suggestions. In addition, I am
indebted to my colleagues in Genoa, Pierluigi Chiassoni, Riccardo Guastini, Giovanni Battista Ratti,
and María Cristina Redondo for their generous support and stimulating criticism. I owe special
thanks to Bonnie Litschewski Paulson, whose insights – *sowohl sprachlich als auch sachlich* – were
invaluable, and to Robert Alexy for his gracious hospitality and many good conversations.
[1] These quotations are drawn, respectively, from H Kelsen, *Die philosophischen Grundlagen
der Naturrechtslehre und des Rechtspositivismus* (Charlottenburg, Pan-Verlag Rolf Heise,
1928) [hereafter: *PhG*] §12 (26); H Kelsen, *Introduction to the Problems of Legal Theory*, trans
B Litschewski Paulson and SL Paulson (Oxford, Clarendon Press, 1992) [hereafter: *LT*] §29 (58), a
translation of H Kelsen, *Reine Rechtslehre*, 1st edn (Vienna and Leipzig, Deuticke, 1934); H Kelsen,
General Theory of Law and State, trans A Wedberg (Cambridge, Mass, Harvard University Press,
1945) [hereafter: *GTLS*] 116; and H Kelsen, *Reine Rechtslehre*, 2nd edn (Vienna, Deuticke, 1960)
[hereafter: *RR 2*] §34(c) (202).

The greatest of the puzzles stems from Kelsen's effort to resolve, by appealing to the basic norm, the most fundamental problem of them all, to wit: the difficulty (the impossibility?) of moving from *Sein* to *Sollen*, from 'is' to 'ought'.[2] Kelsen, in considering the beginnings of a legal order, invariably resorts to the context of revolution.[3] That is, a legal order is up and running and is then challenged by revolutionary forces. Now to say, for example, that the revolutionary forces of community *B* prevail in a struggle with community *A* is to say that community *B* has proved to be more efficacious than community *A*. What is more, *B*'s efficacy is a *matter of fact*.[4] Kelsen moves straightaway from this factual state of affairs to the conclusion that community *B* is a *legal order*. How he moves from a matter of fact to a bona fide legal order is the problem he purports to resolve with the basic norm. This is, in a word, the basic norm problematic.

The function that Kelsen assigns to the basic norm is that of 'grounding' the law, of providing a normative foundation for the law. From the critic's standpoint, the ensuing puzzle – the basic norm problematic – might be conceptualised as a binary choice. Either the basic norm on its various readings provides nothing remotely like a foundation for the law, generating instead a *petitio principii*, a begging of the question. Or, despite an appeal to a neo-Kantian transcendental argument[5] as lending a grounding function to the basic norm, no such neo-Kantian transcendental argument proves to be sound.

With respect to the grounding function of the basic norm, why a neo-Kantian transcendental argument in the first place? Here Kelsen's purity thesis comes to the fore. It precludes every appeal to facts and to values, precluding, in other words, every argument reflecting either a naturalistic or a moral point of view. What remains, Kelsen would have us believe, is a neo-Kantian transcendental argument.

Immanuel Kant's judgement on the positions familiar from the philosophy of the seventeenth and eighteenth centuries offers an analogy. On the last page of the *Critique of Pure Reason*, Kant, referring to Christian Wolff and David Hume as the respective proponents of the competing positions of dogmatism

---

[2] See the lucid discussion of the basic norm in these terms, addressing the question of the move from 'is' to 'ought', in J Kammerhofer, *Uncertainty in International Law. A Kelsenian Perspective* (London and New York, Routledge, 2011) 250–59.

[3] See the references at n 38 below.

[4] See, eg, Kelsen, *RR* 2 (n 1) §6(c) (49). What does Kelsen mean when he describes community *B* as having prevailed by virtue of being 'more efficacious' than community *A*? If the question is addressed to the relation between the members of community *B* and those in community *B* who are in charge, the answer is straightforward: efficacy is understood in terms of compliance, namely, the community members' compliance with the directives of those in charge, never mind how compliance is brought about. See Kelsen, *LT* (n 1) §30(a) (59). The members of the community may be browbeaten into compliance, or, in a happier situation, they may accept the directives of the new regime as appropriate and comply for that reason.

[5] I take up the terminology 'transcendental' in section VII below.

and scepticism,[6] rejects both traditional positions.[7] But how can Kant do this if, as the proponents of one or the other of the traditional positions insist, these two positions are together exhaustive of the possibilities? Kant replies: 'The *critical* path alone is still open.'[8] His argument gives the lie to what had been the received opinion: *tertium non datur*.

Kelsen arguably proceeds in the same way, with natural law theory standing in for dogmatism (or rationalism) and with fact-based legal positivism representing scepticism (or empiricism).[9] In short, Kelsen offers an alternative to the jurisprudential tradition of natural law theory and fact-based legal positivism, two views that, when taken together, are believed to exhaust the possibilities.[10] Kelsen holds this belief to be mistaken, and, he contends, his neo-Kantian transcendental argument, in providing an account that relies on neither rationalism nor empiricism, shows why.

Other puzzles arise, although they pale by comparison with the basic norm problematic. There is, say, the adjective 'basic',[11] whose connotations are close to those of 'fundamental' and 'foundational'. In the legal arena, basic norms, basic laws, basic principles, and the like are understood not only as fundamental but as being fundamental by virtue of their content, for example, the opening articles of the post-War German Constitution or Basic Law (*Grundgesetz*), which address the fundamental or basic rights (*Grundrechte*) of dignity, liberty, and equality.[12] Kelsen's basic norm is different. It has no content. It has *form*, that is,

---

[6] Kant speaks of the Continental rationalists, eg, Descartes, Leibniz, and Wolff as 'dogmatists', and he refers to Locke and Hume with the expressions 'empiricism' and 'scepticism'.

[7] See, eg, Kant, *Critique of Pure Reason* [hereafter: CPuR] B xxxvi (on Wolff), A263/ B319–A276/ B332 (on Leibniz), A271/ B327 (on Locke), and A764/ B792–A769/ B797 (on Hume).

[8] Kant, *CPuR* (n 7) A 856/ B 884 (emphasis in original). PF Strawson, in *The Bounds of Sense* (London, Methuen, 1966) 12, captures neatly the idea of Kant's middle way, referring to the traditional views as exceeding the upper and lower bounds of sense: 'Dogmatic rationalism exceeds the upper bound of sense, as classical empiricism falls short of the lower.' On the middle way or third way in legal philosophy, see n 150 below.

[9] The terms 'dogmatism' and 'scepticism' are Kant's. I have added between parentheses the terms 'rationalism' and 'empiricism'. These latter terms are familiar as standard designations of the competing schools from the philosophy of the seventeenth and eighteenth centuries, continental rationalism and British empiricism.

[10] The nomenclature 'legal non-positivism', adopted by some writers in recent work, see, eg, R Alexy, 'The Dual Nature of Law' (2010) 23 *Ratio Juris* 67–82, is congenial in its emphasis on a generic reading of two altogether distinct types of legal philosophy – legal positivism and legal non-positivism – as they are embedded in claims that count as contradictories. The generic readings set out by Alexy and others presuppose, however, that a *single variable* is being read with distinct values, to wit: morality as playing – vis-à-vis legal validity – a necessary role in the case of legal non-positivism, and the absence of any such necessary role for morality in the case of legal positivism. As soon as one adds a *second variable* with its distinct values – naturalism and non-naturalism – as in Kelsen's legal philosophy, things become more complicated, and the generic reading no longer has any direct application.

[11] The expression 'basic' is the adjectival counterpart of Kelsen's substantive '*Grund*' (ground, basis, reason, foundation) in the expression '*Grundnorm*'.

[12] German Basic Law, arts 1, 2, and 3 respectively. On post-War German constitutional law generally, see DP Currie, *The Constitution of the Federal Republic of Germany* (Chicago, University of Chicago Press, 1995); in an appendix Currie sets out the provisions of the Basic Law. See also

it manifests on several of its most familiar readings one or another of the various forms of the legal norm, including the basic norm qua empowering norm or the basic norm qua command or obligation-imposing norm. Kelsen refers occasionally to 'the content' of the basic norm,[13] but these references simply amount to elliptical allusions to its form[14] or to the temporal and jurisdictional boundaries of the legal system vis-à-vis its basic norm.[15] Kelsen's disclaimer on content is no accident. His purity thesis dictates that the basic norm be without substantive content.

The present chapter comprises, in toto, ten sections, and, save for the introductory and concluding sections, I have broken them down into two groups. Sections II, III, IV, and V are textual, addressed to Kelsen's texts in tracing developments that lead to, and provide different readings of, the basic norm. In sections VI, VII, VIII, and IX, I take a more systematic approach to Kelsen's basic norm with an eye to different readings of what it comes to, including its grounding function and its explicative function.

Specifically, I explain in section II why Kelsen, in *Main Problems in the Theory of Public Law* (1911), his first major work, believes there to be no issue in legal theory that calls for a basic norm. The explanation turns on the distinction Kelsen draws between formal and material questions. Legal theory, he argues, is limited to formal questions, but a basic norm, however it might be understood, is pitched to material questions and therefore has no role to play in legal theory.

I devote section III to a first look into what I am calling the prehistory of the basic norm.[16] Kelsen, in a major paper of 1914, takes tentative steps in the direction

---

R Alexy, *A Theory of Constitutional Rights*, trans J Rivers (Oxford, Oxford University Press, 2002). Alexy, drawing on German public law, develops a system of constitutional rights from the standpoint of 'principles theory'; his work has enjoyed an international reception. See also in this genre: M Borowski, *Grundrechte als Prinzipien*, 3rd edn (Baden-Baden, Nomos, 2018); J Sieckmann, *Recht als normatives System. Die Prinzipientheorie des Rechts* (Baden-Baden, Nomos, 2009); J Sieckmann, *Rechtsphilosophie* (Tübingen, Mohr Siebeck, 2018) 275–300 *et passim*.

[13] See, eg, H Kelsen, *Allgemeine Staatslehre* (Berlin, Julius Springer, 1925) [hereafter: *ASL*] §36(b) (251), where he writes: '[T]he basic norm, which is countenanced – indeed required – in legal theory, has no absolute content, has *a priori* no content at all, but is directed to the material that is to be interpreted from a unified standpoint as law'. Understood in the reference to the material 'interpreted from a unified standpoint' is the idea that every legal system has its own basic norm, a point that Kelsen underscores with his talk about revolutionary change. See, eg, the quotation in the text at n 54 below.

[14] See, eg, Kelsen, *ASL* (n 13) §19(c) (99): 'The typical content of the basic norm or norm of origin, which establishes the system of the legal order (*das System der Rechtsordnung*), is that an authority, a legal source, is appointed whose expressions are to count as legally binding: behave as the legal authority – the monarch, the popular assembly, the parliament, etc. – commands. Simplified for the sake of clarity, so runs the basic norm.' Clear in the first lines of the quotation, the form of the basic norm depicted here is that of empowerment.

[15] See, eg, Kelsen, *PhG* (n 1) §35 (at 65): 'the content of the basic norm, that is, the particular historically given fact that is qualified through the basic norm as the original law-creating fact, is directed completely to the material that is to be comprehended as positive law'.

[16] I have adopted the expression 'prehistory' from GN Dias, *Rechtspositivismus und Rechtstheorie* (Tübingen, Mohr Siebeck, 2005) [hereafter: *RPRT*] 191.

of a basic norm. In particular, a formulation turning up here is recognisable –
at any rate from a later vantage point – as a statement of the basic norm.[17]
To be sure, Kelsen's focus in the 1914 paper lay elsewhere, not least of all with
the question of legal continuity in nineteenth-century Austrian constitutional
law. Kelsen's answer to the question of legal continuity has him unavoidably
resorting to politics, to matters of fact, a portentous move away from the purity
thesis, his hard-and-fast distinction between the legal and the factual. Also in
the 1914 paper, Kelsen introduces what he comes to acknowledge later as two
altogether distinct conceptions of the basic norm.

In section IV, I look at another aspect of the prehistory of the basic norm.
In a paper of 1915, Kelsen's focus this time around is on the notion of presupposition. The paper is a response to some of Eugen Ehrlich's arguments in his
influential treatise *Fundamental Principles of the Sociology of Law* (1913).
Kelsen's response makes extensive use of the notion of presupposition, which
figures centrally in many of his statements on the basic norm, in particular,
those during the 1920s.

In section V, I move beyond the prehistory. I begin with Kelsen's early statements on the basic norm, which are found in *The Problem of Sovereignty* (1920).
Here his characterisations reflect the role of the notion of presupposition and
point toward the grounding function as well. The same is true of statements in
other writings of the 1920s, up to his monograph *The Philosophical Foundations
of Natural Law Theory and Legal Positivism*, published in 1928. Two new developments are manifest. Kelsen builds into his concept of the basic norm certain
constraints on legal norms with an eye to meeting certain minimal but necessary requirements of legal cognition. And he takes steps in the direction of a
neo-Kantian transcendental argument with an eye to undergirding the basic
norm as his means of grounding the legal order – grounding, that is to say, the
objective validity of legal norms. I trace these developments up to and including
the second edition of the *Pure Theory of Law* (1960).

Then, in section VI, I turn to the various forms of the basic norm, which
follow in some instances the forms of legal norms in Kelsenian norm theory.
I identify five arguably distinct forms, two turning on empowerment, two on
legal validity, and one that records the shift from the subjective sense of an act
of will to its objective sense, the legal norm. I have drawn these distinct forms
from a greater, decidedly heterogeneous group of Kelsen's glosses on the basic
norm.[18]

In the case of the basic norm qua ultimate empowerment to impose sanctions, Kelsen presents the basic norm in a well-nigh canonical formulation,
very much the exception to the rule in his work. And he makes an important

---

[17] See the quotation in the text at n 61 below.
[18] See the different groups of basic norm characterisations to which I allude in section VI, at
nn 112–18 below.

connection between the basic norm and the 'reconstructed legal norm' found at the very heart of his norm theory. In the case of the basic norm qua ultimate basis of legal validity, where 'validity' refers to 'bindingness' (*Verbindlichkeit*), I argue – an unorthodox view – that the formulation gives expression to Kelsen's 'legal vernacular' and is not a part of his mature norm theory, which in its most complete form begins with developments in the 1930s.

Sections VII and VIII, addressed to the grounding function of the basic norm, count for many purposes as the core of the present chapter. In much of what Kelsen says on the issue of support for the objectivity of legal norms – and for normativism generally – he refers to doctrines in Kant's first *Critique*. Kant's question about the possibility of metaphysics and, in his recasting of the question, the possibility of synthetic *a priori* judgments has a counterpart in Kelsen's question about the very possibility of the positive law qua object of cognition.

In section VIII, I turn to issues stemming from the complexity of the neo-Kantian argument and the intractable problems it presents. I begin with notes on transcendental arguments generally, distinguishing between progressive and regressive forms of the argument. I follow this with a closer look at the regressive form as the neo-Kantians understand it, and then I turn to Kelsen's transcendental category. With this machinery in place, I show how the argument unfolds and then assess the argument as employed in Kelsenian legal science.

In section IX, I turn to what I am calling the explicative function of the basic norm. It represents Kelsen's effort to explain how jurists can, without appealing to natural law or morality, treat the positive law as normative. Here the avowed task of the basic norm is, in a word, explanatory, and whether or not Kelsen succeeds in providing the required explanation remains open. I argue, however, that even if one were to grant that Kelsen has an explanation here, nothing in it turns on a basic norm.

Finally, in the concluding section, I add a remark on the status of Kelsen's legal theory in light of the difficulties he encounters with the basic norm.

Before I turn to section II, I might add a handful of remarks in the spirit of a smorgasbord, an approach that is appropriate where there is nothing approximating a received opinion on the issues in question. Thus, in section II, the first of the sections devoted to Kelsen's texts, I look to *Main Problems* (1911), inviting attention to the arguments adduced there *against* the idea of a basic norm. In sections III and IV, turning to the papers of 1914 and 1915, I trace factors that lead Kelsen in the direction of a basic norm. In section V, the last of the sections devoted, *sensu stricto*, to Kelsen's texts, I trace the evolution of his ideas on the basic norm, taking the enquiry to 1960, which marks the end of his classical or neo-Kantian period. In the later sections of the chapter, I adopt a more systematic point of view. In section VI, I set out a range of different forms or characterisations of the basic norm. The following sections, VII, VIII, and IX, are devoted to the grounding and explicative functions of the basic norm along with some details of a neo-Kantian transcendental argument that might be adduced in support of the grounding function. In short, the idea behind the smorgasbord is to cover a good bit of ground, with different emphases, with an eye to factors that arguably played a role in Kelsen's reflections on the basic norm.

In his first major work, *Main Problems in the Theory of Public Law* (1911), Kelsen is not yet wedded to the notion of presupposition, let alone to a basic norm. His argument here, to the effect that no basic norm is required or even possible, is nevertheless of interest in light of his later commitment to and preoccupation with the basic norm.

II. LEGAL THEORY *SANS* THE BASIC NORM: KELSEN'S *MAIN PROBLEMS* (1911)

The notion of presupposition, which figures centrally in Kelsen's work on the basic norm, is not entirely absent in *Main Problems*. In the foreword to the initial printing, Kelsen writes that presuppositions serve as his point of departure in addressing the problems of legal science, presuppositions 'ultimately rooted in a *Weltanschauung* and therefore subjective and not open to discussion'.[19] Later, in the body of the text, he writes that, for the jurist, the 'normative character of the legal norm is an unshakeable presupposition, beyond all discussion'.[20] Arguably, presupposition is of some significance in Kelsen's text here, possibly counting as an anticipation of his introduction of the basic norm qua presupposition. Still, in *Main Problems* as a whole, Kelsen develops a framework that suggests pretty clearly the absence of any role for a basic norm.

What is this framework? It amounts to a systematic distinction between 'how'-questions and 'why'-questions, with the jurist being restricted to the 'how' questions.[21] The jurist, then, is properly addressing such questions as *how* legal norms are applied,[22] *how* they are 'cognized' or known,[23] *how* their form is to be determined,[24] *how* their legal validity is to be understood and ascertained,[25] *how* the law functions as a means to whatever ends are given,[26] and so forth. In good Kelsenian parlance, these issues pose *formal* questions and so fall within the bailiwick of jurisprudence.

---

[19] H Kelsen, *Hauptprobleme der Staatsrechtslehre* (Tübingen, JCB Mohr, 1911) [hereafter: *HP*] v, in *Hans Kelsen Werke*, ed M Jestaedt (Tübingen, Mohr Siebeck, 2007 ff) [hereafter: *HKW* with vol no], thus *HKW* 2 54.

[20] See the quotation in the text at n 30 below.

[21] See Kelsen, *HP* (n 19) 353, in *HKW* 2 (n 19) 482.

[22] See Kelsen, *HP* (n 19) 36, in *HKW* 2 (n 19) 121.

[23] See, eg, H Kelsen, *Das Problem der Souveränität* (Tübingen: JCB Mohr, 1920) [hereafter: *PS*] §6 (24).

[24] See, eg, Kelsen, *HP* (n 19) 237, also 238, 274–5, 279, in *HKW* 2 (n 19) 353, also 354, 394–5, 399–400.

[25] See, eg, Kelsen, *HP* (n 19) 13–18, in *HKW* 2 (n 19) 93–8.

[26] See, eg, Kelsen, *HP* (n 19) 272, in *HKW* 2 (n 19) 392.

Kelsen contends that, in sharp contrast to these 'how'-questions, the 'why'-questions are off limits for the jurist. As we know from the history of philosophy, the overriding 'why'-question – the question of one's obligation to obey the law – was first raised in Plato's *Crito*. Crito, an elderly gentleman and a friend, urges Socrates to permit a circle of friends to arrange for his escape from prison. Socrates sets himself against their plan, countering Crito's arguments and going on to adduce arguments of his own on why one ought to obey the law, even if it is unjust.[27]

Not only does Kelsen dismiss this overriding 'why'-question, he argues in *Main Problems* that from the standpoint of jurisprudence, it is nonsense to pose the question. 'Why *ought* the legal norm be complied with and applied?' Kelsen replies that 'the very posing of the question seems on first glance to be absurd' – absurd, that is, from the standpoint of jurisprudence.

> Intrinsic to the concept of the legal norm from the outset is that the legal norm *ought* to be complied with and applied. The idea of the legal norm qua "norm" already contains this qualification that a norm *ought* to be complied with and applied, so that the question of why ought a norm be complied with would be tantamount to asking, say, why ought a norm that ought to be complied with be complied with?[28]

The punch line at the end of the quotation underscores Kelsen's view that this line of enquiry is nonsense. It is the result of proceeding as though jurisprudence, with its distinctly formal stance, could sensibly pose and answer the overriding 'why'-question, which is by its very nature a material question.

What if everything is now turned upside down? What if the formal stance of jurisprudence is set aside and, with it, the idea that the legal norm is a formal concept? Only then, from the standpoint of a 'more general, higher norm', can one make sense of the question of obligation:

> If one does not assume the normative character of the legal norm to be a self-sufficient, independent, non-derivative quality, then the question of why a legal norm ought to be complied with can be understood as a question about the more general, higher norm that is superior to the legal norm at issue. For according to this higher norm, behaviour complying with the legal norm appears to be commanded, to be obligatory.[29]

This 'more general, higher norm' assumes a normative system superior to the legal system, a system, say, of morality. From this standpoint, the question of obligation can of course be posed as a material issue, as a genuine 'why'-question.

---

[27] Plato, *Crito* 43–54e, trans GMA Grube, in Plato, *Complete Works*, ed JM Cooper and DS Hutchinson (Indianapolis, Hackett, 1997) 37–48. See also AD Woozley, *Law and Obedience: The Arguments of Plato's Crito* (London, Duckworth, 1979); in the appendix, Woozley provides his own translation of the dialogue.
[28] Kelsen, *HP* (n 19) 352, in *HKW* 2 (n 19) 481.
[29] Ibid.

Without turning everything upside down, however, the jurist will not have this freedom. It is for the moral philosopher to weigh critically an answer to the question of obligation, while for the *jurist*

> the normative character of the legal norm is an unshakeable presupposition, beyond all discussion. For the jurist, knowing that a legal norm conflicts with a moral norm cannot in any way change the fact that he recognizes even this legal norm as a norm, that is, the jurist does not doubt that it ought to be complied with and applied. Any other reaction would have the jurist sawing off the very branch on which he sits.[30]

The concept of presupposition, the predominant motif in all that Kelsen writes on the basic norm, already turns up here. Still, despite Kelsen's claim that the presupposition of normativity is 'unshakeable' and 'beyond all discussion', he is not prepared to pursue the matter in *Main Problems*. Indeed, he goes off in the other direction, remarking that it is not the task of the jurist to determine 'the basis' of the validity of the law.[31] This takes us full circle, back to Kelsen's distinction between material and formal questions.

The pertinent text turns up in Kelsen's pursuit of the figure of speech, 'sawing off the branch'. What if the jurist does saw off the very branch on which he sits?

> Resorting to a higher, moral order would mean the surrender of a self-sufficient legal system, the abandonment of an independent legal science and its disappearance without a trace into ethics. The jurist is not to question the *material* basis of the validity of the legal system. The only question the jurist is competent to pose is a *formal* question. The jurist is to determine not the basis, not the "why", but, rather, only the "how".[32]

In fact, in *Main Problems*, Kelsen recognises and rejects both species of material question – explanatory questions and justificatory questions.

> [T]he question of the basis of the validity of the law on each of the two possible [material] readings turns out to be legally irrelevant. Either the question addresses the motive for lawful behaviour and is therefore a psychologico-sociological problem, or the question aims at moral justification and is therefore a question that has a place only in ethics.[33]

Explanatory questions – addressing, say, the causal factors associated with legal norms – can be answered only by appeal to psychology or sociology, while justificatory questions can be dealt with, if at all, only by appeal to morality.

In summary, all 'why'-questions are off limits for the jurist. By the same token, a basic norm is off limits in that it, too, would amount to the answer to a 'why'-question pitched to justification. Legal theory confines itself to questions posing formal issues, the 'how'-questions.

---

[30] Kelsen, *HP* (n 19) 353, in *HKW* 2 (n 19) 481, see also Kelsen's use of the verb 'to presuppose' in *HP* (n 19) 352, in *HKW* 2 (n 19) 481.

[31] See the quotation in the text at n 33 below.

[32] Kelsen, *HP* (n 19) 353, in *HKW* 2 (n 19) 481–2.

[33] Ibid, 482.

Still, is Kelsen not left in a quandary? Simply to say that the 'normative character of the legal norm' is absolute and 'beyond all discussion'[34] is a bit scanty for a thinker as astute as Kelsen. And he does not leave the matter there.

In the next two sections, both devoted to the prehistory of the basic norm, I look at two early papers of Kelsen's. In a lengthy paper of 1914, my focus in section III, Kelsen poses the question of legal continuity and how it is established. The paper is of special interest in underscoring a major problem faced by Kelsen – his need, at certain junctures, to appeal to matters of fact, with all that that portends for the purity thesis. The paper is also of interest as representing Kelsen's anticipation of the basic norm doctrine, with, as Kelsen notes later, two altogether different conceptions of the basic norm.

III. THE PREHISTORY OF THE BASIC NORM, 1914

Kelsen's first intimation of the basic norm comes in a lengthy article of 1914, 'Federal Law and State Law according to the Austrian Constitution'.[35] The article takes up, inter alia, a problem in nineteenth-century Austrian constitutional law, the problem of legal continuity.[36] Kelsen acknowledges only later that the 'Archimedean Point', described in the 1914 article as the point of departure 'from which the world of legal cognition is set into motion',[37] counts as a bona fide statement of the basic norm.

On the question of legal continuity, Kelsen is asking how long the Austrian legal system has existed without interruption, 'without interruption' meaning, for Kelsen, *without a constitutional break*.[38] Kelsen also puts the question

---

[34] See the quotation in the text at n 30 above.

[35] H Kelsen, 'Reichsgesetz und Landesgesetz nach österreichischer Verfassung' (1914) 32 *Archiv des öffentlichen Rechts* §§1–12 (202–45, 390–438) [hereafter: 'RGLG'], in *HKW* 3 (n 19) 359–425, and see, for some details on the publication of the paper, the 'Editorischer Bericht ("Reichsgesetz und Landesgesetz")', in *HKW* 3 (n 19) 723–9.

[36] At various points in my work on Kelsen's 1914 article and on certain nineteenth-century developments in Austrian constitutional law, I have received valuable advice from Jörg Kammerhofer, Theo Öhlinger, and, most recently, Ewald Wiederin. The usual disclaimer applies: these three friends are of course in no way responsible for what I have done with their good advice. Also, here just as elsewhere in my work on the paper, Bonnie Litschewski Paulson has been an unusually insightful and discerning conversation partner.

[37] See the quotation in the text at n 51 below.

[38] Kelsen invariably presents his criterion in the context of revolutionary change, giving rise to a constitutional break. In municipal law, this criterion has served as Kelsen's standard over a long period of time, see, eg, Kelsen, 'RGLG' (n 35) §3 (217), in *HKW* 3 (n 19) 371, quoted in the text below, at n 54; Kelsen, *PS* (n 23) §24 (96), in *HKW* 4 (n 19) 362; Kelsen, *ASL* (n 13) §23(a) (128–9), §29 (148), §46(c) (338); Kelsen, *LT* (n 1) §30(a) (59); Kelsen, *GTLS* (n 1) 117–19, 219–20, 368–9; H Kelsen, 'The Legal Status of Germany according to the Declaration of Berlin' (1945) 39 *American Journal of International Law* 518–26, at 522; Kelsen, *RR* 2 (n 1) §34(f) (212). It might be noted, *en passant*, that where the nation state is being considered from the standpoint of public international law, Kelsen has a different analysis, see, eg, H Kelsen, *Principles of International Law* (New York, Rinehart, 1952) 264, 415–19.

in other ways. When did the current legal system begin? Or, drawing on a well-known phrase of Kelsen's: what counts as the 'historically first constitution'?

I begin with legal continuity and its interruption by means of a constitutional break, be it the December Constitution of 1867 in Austria, be it the United States Constitution of 1787. I turn then to Kelsen's statement of the Archimedean Point in the 1914 text, which he later acknowledges as an early statement of the basic norm. I pay special attention to the import of the Archimedean Point vis-à-vis politics. This is followed by attention to the dilemma that, according to Kelsen, is faced by those representing the later nineteenth-century received opinion on federal and state powers in Austria. In an unusually abstract statement of their view, Kelsen writes that they would have it both ways, a power of derogation in both directions – namely, *Land* laws derogated by the *Reich* and *Reich* laws derogated by one or another of the *Länder*. After setting out this dilemma, I turn directly to basic norm issues. In the foreword to the second printing of *Main Problems* in 1923, Kelsen identifies two conceptions of the basic norm, which, he adds, reach back *expressis verbis* to the 1914 paper. In drafting that paper, Kelsen did not expressly recognise a basic norm, but now, informed by a fair bit of work in the meantime on the basic norm, he acknowledges that there are indeed two conceptions of the basic norm in the early paper. Finally, I pose the problem inherent in Kelsen's need to appeal to matters of fact, to politics, in defending his position on legal continuity. It is a problem that he confronts throughout his constructive and classical periods.[39] And Kelsen's means of resolving the problem in the early paper is arguably just the tip of the iceberg, for in resorting to matters of fact, he undermines the import of his purity thesis.

A. The Question of Legal Continuity

The complex of Austrian constitutional documents – in short, constitutions – that are in play comprises the October Diploma of 1860, the February Patent of 1861, and – of fundamental significance in all that follows here – the December Constitution of 1867.[40] Language in the February Patent of 1861 holds that

[39] Elsewhere in my work I have provided a sketch of a three-fold periodisation of the phases of development in Kelsen's legal theory: the early phase, critical constructivism, runs from 1911 up to circa 1920, then the classical or neo-Kantian phase from there up to 1960, and finally the late phase (*Spätlehre*) from 1960 up to 1971. For a richly detailed periodisation, see Dias, RPRT (n 16) 129–256.

[40] For the provisions of these constitutions, see F Bernatzik, *Die österreichischen Verfassungsgesetze*, 2nd edn (Vienna, Manz, 1911). The February Patent of 1861 gave effect to the provisions of the October Diploma of 1860. The expression 'documents' in my text invites attention to the fact that the third constitution, the December Constitution of 1867, is not a constitutional tract in the usual sense. Rather, it consists of an assemblage of laws brought together under the name 'December Constitution', including the catalogue of basic rights that have remained Austria's 'bill of rights' to this day, namely: Staatsgrundgesetz vom 21. Dezember 1867, RGBl Nr 142, in Bernatzik, *Die österreichischen Verfassungsgesetze* (above) 422–7, and see generally Th Öhlinger, *Verfassungsrecht*, 8th edn (Vienna, Facultas, 2009) 298–452.

certain provisions respecting the *Länder* can be altered in the parliament of the *Land* in question only by means of a qualified majority,[41] but the December Constitution of 1867 does not recognise this restriction.[42] If the earlier document is assumed to count as Austria's constitution and thereby to serve as the standard, then the 1867 Constitution has come about unconstitutionally.

The parallel in late eighteenth-century America is direct and illuminating. America's first constitution, the Articles of Confederation, was submitted to the emancipated colonies in 1777 and ratified in 1781. It specified that a change in the constitution, an amendment, required the agreement of every one of the 13 States.[43] Profoundly dissatisfied with the Articles of Confederation, the constitutional framers took matters in hand at a meeting in Philadelphia, the Constitutional Convention, running from 25 May to 17 September 1787. They drafted an entirely new constitution[44] and specified that its ratification would be complete as soon as nine of the 13 States in their ratifying conventions had registered agreement to its terms.[45] Ratification by nine States was completed in less than two years, and the Federal Constitution of 1787 was born. From the standpoint of the earlier Articles of Confederation, the undertaking was of course unconstitutional, but did that matter? Not at all if, as was the case, the Articles of Confederation had been set aside.[46]

But, Kelsen asks, how is that to be determined? Not by appealing to the law, neither in the American case nor in the Austrian case, for in both, the continuity of the law is precisely what is in question. Answering the question of continuity requires an appeal to something independent of the law, an appeal to politics.[47]

---

[41] February Patent of 1861 §§18, 38, see Bernatzik, *Die österreichischen Verfassungsgesetze* (n 40) 273 and 280 respectively.

[42] In the December Constitution of 1867, see the Gesetz vom 21. Dezember 1867, RGBl Nr 141, in Bernatzik, *Die österreichischen Verfassungsgesetze* (n 40) 390–403, and see Kelsen, 'RGLG' (n 35) §9 (414–18), in *HKW 3* (n 19) 409–12.

[43] See art XIII, Articles of Confederation, which reads (in part): 'And the Articles of this Confederation shall be inviolably observed by every State, and the Union shall be perpetual; nor shall any alternation at any time hereafter be made in any of them; unless such alteration be agreed to in a Congress of the United States, and be afterwards confirmed by the legislatures of every State.'

[44] Joseph J Ellis, awardee of the Pulitzer Prize, writes about these developments with verve in his recent book, *The Quartet. Orchestrating the Second American Revolution 1783–1789* (New York, Knopf, 2015).

[45] See art VII, US Constitution, which reads: 'The Ratification of the Conventions of nine States, shall be sufficient for the Establishment of this Constitution between the States so ratifying the Same.'

[46] To be sure, as Ewald Wiederin has pointed out to me, there would have been no issue of unconstitutionality if the requirement set out in the Articles of Confederation had in fact been met, to wit: ratification in all 13 States before the Constitution of 1787 took effect. That development would have represented constitutional continuity rather than unconstitutionality.

[47] The need for an appeal here to politics is of course obvious. And, equally obvious, one can arrive at very different political positions. Kelsen's comments on the question of legal continuity with respect to Germany in the immediate post-World War II period are instructive. Kelsen argued that the point from which the continuity of a new, post-War German state ought to begin is post-1945. The post-War Germans defended a diametrically opposed position, arguing that the continuity of the German state ought to take the *Reichsverfassung* of 1871 as the point of departure. Each side reflected a political position: Kelsen's interest in an altogether new beginning for the German state,

Kelsen is keenly aware of this and remarks several times in the 1914 paper that, from a juridical standpoint, answers to the question of continuity have the trappings of arbitrariness.[48]

With these notes on the background in place, we can pick up Kelsen's narrative in the 1914 paper, where he treats what appears to be an early statement of the basic norm in terms that are expressly political.

B. The Archimedian Point as an Early Statement of the Basic Norm?

Here Kelsen begins with remarks on legal construction. Every juridical construction, he writes, reflects one of two distinct tasks. The task is either to look to legal norms in taking judgments on 'real material facts in the external world'[49] or to consider '*legal norms* and *nothing* but legal norms' in their relation to each other.[50] For both tasks, the point of departure is 'some ultimate norm' that is presupposed as valid.

> Every juridical construction must proceed from certain norms as valid legal norms. Whether this amounts to judging concrete material facts or certain norms themselves in their relation to each other, the point of departure must always be some ultimate norm (or system of norms) that is itself finally presupposed as valid. The question of the validity of this final norm, adopted as the presupposition of all legal cognition, lies then beyond legal cognition. This norm, presupposed in the end as the ultimate norm, is therefore the Archimedean Point, so to speak, from which the world of legal cognition is set into motion.[51]

and the interest of the post-War Germans in preserving territorial claims. See H Kelsen, 'The International Legal Status of Germany to be Established Immediately upon Termination of the War' (1944) 38 *American Journal of International Law* 689–94; Kelsen, 'The Legal Status of Germany according to the Declaration of Berlin' (n 38 above); Kelsen, 'Is a Peace Treaty with Germany Legally Possible and Politically Desirable?' (1947) 41 *American Political Science Review* 1188–93; H Kelsen, 'German Peace Terms', *New York Times* (letter to the editor), 7 September 1947. See also H Nawiasky, *Die Grundgedanken des Grundgesetzes für die Bundesrepublik Deutschland* (Stuttgart and Cologne, W. Kohlhammer, 1950) 3–17. The vast literature on both sides of the issue is helpfully summarised, up to 1979, in H-J Bücking, *Der Rechtsstatus des Deutschen Reiches* (Berlin, Berlin Verlag, 1979). For a more recent and detailed account, see, eg, M Stolleis, 'Besatzungsherrschaft und Wiederaufbau deutscher Staatlichkeit 1945–1949', in *Handbuch des Staatsrechts*, ed J Isensee and P Kirchhof, 3rd edn (Heidelberg, C. F. Müller, 2003) vol 1: *Grundlagen von Staat und Verfassung* 269–313.

[48] See Kelsen, 'RGLG' (n 35) §3 (217), in *HKW 3* (n 19) 371, quoted in the text at n 52 below; see also §9 (413), in *HKW 3* (n 19) 408, quoted in the text at n 59 below; and see §9 (415, 417), in *HKW 3* (n 19) 410, 411.

[49] Kelsen, 'RGLG' (n 35) §3 (215), in *HKW 3* (n 19) 370.

[50] Kelsen, 'RGLG' (n 35) §3 (216), in *HKW 3* (n 19) 370. (As always in these quotations from Kelsen and others, the emphasis is there in the original text unless otherwise indicated.)

[51] Kelsen, 'RGLG' (n 35) §3 (216–17), in *HKW 3* (n 19) 371. On construction, Rudolf von Jhering writes that '[t]he expression "juridical construction" belongs to the most practicable (*gangbarsten*) terms of art in contemporary jurisprudence.' R Jhering, *Der Geist des römischen Rechts*, vol 2, pt 2, 3rd printing (Leipzig, Breitkopf und Härtel, 1875) 357. Kelsen, in *Main Problems*, striving towards 'a revision of the methodological foundations' of public law theory, remarks that 'the system thereby recognizes the *legal norm* as a central concept of legal construction'. The formulation of this

Drawing on knowledge of Kelsen's development of the basic norm in later writings, one easily recognises 'this final norm' as a statement of the basic norm. This norm is 'presupposed [as] the Archimedean Point ... from which the world of legal cognition is set into motion'. And the Archimedean Point, the ultimate norm, is the basic norm, serving to insulate the legal world from politics, from matters of fact.

If this is Kelsen's view in 1914, then what follows in his text comes as a surprise. For in the immediately following passage, he goes on to say that the issue at hand is political, not legal.

> The choice of this point of departure is in principle a political question, not a legal question, and so, from the standpoint of legal cognition, it must always appear to be arbitrary.[52]

The point of departure, according to Kelsen, represents a choice, which is to say that the ultimate norm – the standpoint for assessing the political question – stems from a choice. And the norm chosen, informed by accouterments of the Archimedean Point, is beyond legal cognition. More straightforwardly, the ultimate norm actually chosen is the 'final point' described by Kelsen in addressing the dilemma faced by proponents of the received opinion.[53] That is, the ultimate norm is arrived at as an answer to a political question.

In fact, everything in this long paragraph in the 1914 paper is addressed to politics. Kelsen's reference to revolution is one example.

> Almost all legal systems that are valid today rest on a revolutionary foundation, beginning their development with a break from the older system, from whose standpoint all the later norms would appear to be invalid.[54]

Later in the paper, Kelsen returns to the question of legal continuity, and here he poses a dilemma that underscores the problem he sees in the received opinion.

C. The Received Opinion Faces a Dilemma

Kelsen begins with an abstract statement of the problem stemming from the received opinion, from its interest in, so to speak, having it both ways.

> It is an obvious contradiction when the received opinion, on the one hand, claims the reciprocal competence of *Reich* laws and *Land* laws to derogate each other and, on the other hand, grants sovereign competence to the *Reich* alone.[55]

---

concept, he continues, 'is the condition for the solution to a number of specific problems'. Kelsen, *HP* (n 19) iii, in *HKW 2* (n 19) 51–2. Here Kelsen understands 'construction' as *Begriffsbildung*, that is, concept formation. In the present quotation, however, Kelsen's use of 'construction' appears simply to have reference to legal interpretation.

[52] Kelsen, 'RGLG' (n 35) §3 (217), in *HKW 3* (n 19) 371.

[53] See the quotation in the text at n 59 below.

[54] Kelsen, 'RGLG' (n 35) §3 (217), in *HKW 3* (n 19) 371.

[55] Kelsen, 'RGLG' (n 35) §8 (401), in *HKW 3* (n 19) 399.

Kelsen goes to considerable lengths to spell out the contradictory character of the views represented by the received opinion, including those of no less a figure than Georg Jellinek.[56] Jellinek's defence is to appeal to 'the nature of things' (*die Natur der Sache*), which prompts a blistering critique from Kelsen.

> On "the nature of things", one might well say that this oft misused, empty argument cannot be more obviously misused, is never emptier than in the present case. Only if one presupposes the universality of the result desired from the standpoint of a particular political conviction – namely centralism – can one claim it to be in "the nature of things" that "only the *Reich* parliament is legally competent" [Jellinek]. Correspondingly, there is from the standpoint of federalism most certainly the opposite of the nature of things, namely, the exclusive, sovereign competence of the *Länder*! So, Jellinek's argument is really an example of the unacceptable determining of legal construction by way of political value judgments.[57]

The only acceptable way to resolve the problem, Kelsen argues, is to implement intended limits between the competence of the *Reich* parliament and that of the *Länder* parliaments by means of mutually corresponding provisions.[58] But this was not done.

Instead, the received opinion takes the unacceptable tack, as Kelsen notes in his reply to Jellinek, of arriving at legal construction by means of political value judgements. But the received opinion cannot have it both ways. The one and only escape from this dilemma is to abandon the notion that the February Patent of 1861 is still law. If it were still recognised as law, then the later constitution, the December Constitution of 1867, in representing a break in continuity, would yield the incoherent state of affairs that embodies the dilemma faced by the received opinion. As Kelsen writes:

> An escape from this dilemma between the law and politics appears to emerge if the point of departure for the juridical view is not taken to be the February Patent of 1861 with its provisions, but is instead – as the ultimate, *not further derivable* constitutional norm – the basic law of the Constitution of December 1867. As stated earlier, the point at which the continuity of the juridical construction begins is always more or less arbitrary. The question is always meta-juridical, in principle a political question, as to which norm one chooses so to regard as final or ultimate that one dispenses with a further juridical justification of its validity. Every juridical view must arrive at a final point somewhere or other on which the entire system of the juridical construction rests, supported so to speak from outside.[59]

The December Constitution of 1867 is the 'final point', supported 'from outside', that is to say, by politics. And it was recognised over its lifetime of a half century

---

[56] See Kelsen, 'RGLG' (n 35) §8 (401–2), in *HKW 3* (n 19) 399–400, referring here to G Jellinek, *Ein Verfassungsgerichtshof für Österreich* (Vienna, Alfred Hölder, 1885), at 27, 28, and 36.

[57] Kelsen, 'RGLG' (n 35) §8 (401–2) in *HKW 3* (n 19) 400, referring to Jellinek, *Ein Verfassungsgerichtshof für Österreich* (n 56), at 28.

[58] See Kelsen, 'RGLG' (n 35) §6 (241–2) and §8 (410), in *HKW 3* (n 19) 389 and 406.

[59] Kelsen, 'RGLG' (n 35) §9 (413–14), in *HKW 3* (n 19) 408.

as the Austrian constitution. That its beginnings were inevitably tainted in some circles with the charge of unconstitutionality did not prove to be a problem. The rejoinder to unconstitutionality might well run: *ex injuria jus oritur*.[60]

D. Two Conceptions of the Basic Norm

Returning now to basic norm issues, I address the new foreword that Kelsen introduces in the second printing of *Main Problems* in 1923. There he comments on the basic norm language of the 1914 paper and distinguishes two conceptions of the basic norm.

> [I]n an article of 1914, I clearly presented the concept of the *basic norm* qua presupposition establishing the unity of the legal [system] – albeit without the distinction, developed only later, between the basic norm qua constitution in the juridico-logical sense and the basic norm qua constitution in terms of the positive law.[61]

From the later vantage point of 1923, 'the basic norm qua constitution in the juridico-logical sense' is a standard formulation of the prevailing conception of the basic norm. From this vantage point, one sees Kelsen's Archimedean Point in the 1914 paper as a clear statement of the basic norm. While Kelsen claims in the quotation just above that he made no distinction in the 1914 article between two conceptions of the basic norm, two conceptions are in fact found there. The second conception turns up in the earlier quotation that gives expression to the dilemma between the law and politics. There the line on 'which norm one chooses ... to regard as final or ultimate'[62] counts as Kelsen's reference to the basic norm qua positive law constitution, as he puts it now in the foreword of 1923. Kelsen does not pursue this latter conception, but it has had a life of its own in a series of cases addressing revolution in the African states, most prominently in Rhodesia.[63]

---

[60] From illegality law may emerge.

[61] Kelsen, *HP*(n 19), Foreword to the 2nd printing (1923) xv, in *Normativity and Norms*, ed B Litschewski Paulson and SL Paulson (Oxford, Clarendon Press, 1998) [hereafter: NN] 13. (The substitution of 'system' for Kelsen's '*Rechtsnorm*' in the original text simply corrects what is either a slip or a typographical error.).

[62] See the quotation in the text at n 59 above.

[63] On the Rhodesian case, see *Madzimbamuto v Lardner-Burke and others; Baron v Ayre N.O. and others*, Appellate Division: 1968 (2) SA 284 (29 January 1968). And there is a handful of comparable cases, see T Mahmud, 'Jurisprudence of Successful Treason: Coup d'État and Common Law' (1994) 27 *Cornell International Law Journal* 49–140. I am indebted to Iain Stewart for inviting my attention to Mahmud's paper. In these cases, the concern, couched in the language of a *Grundnorm*, is directed to competing *positive law constitutions*. On the issues to which the Rhodesian case, in particular, gave rise, see, eg, JM Eekelaar, 'Splitting the Grundnorm' (1967) 30 *Modern Law Review* 156–75; RWM Dias, 'Legal Politics: Norms behind the *Grundnorm*' (1968) 26 *Cambridge Law Journal* 233–59; JM Finnis, 'Revolutions and Continuity of Law', in *Oxford Essays in Jurisprudence (Second Series)*, ed AWB Simpson (Oxford, Clarendon Press, 1973) 44–76, repr in Finnis, *The Philosophy of Law* (Oxford, Oxford University Press, 2011) 407–35.

E. The Problem Faced by Kelsen

Finally, I turn to the problem that I believe Kelsen faces. I am distinguishing, this time around, not two conceptions of the basic norm but simply two different sorts of statement of the basic norm, one earlier and the others later. Specifically, my attention here is directed to the basic norm qua Archimedean Point. The contrast between it and Kelsen's later statements of the basic norm will be obvious.

Kelsen introduces the Archimedean Point in 1914, but he moves quickly to the political sphere, which is indispensable in answering the question of continuity. By contrast, in later statements of the basic norm, right up to the end of the classical or neo-Kantian period and culminating in the publication of the second edition of the *Pure Theory of Law* in 1960, Kelsen gives the distinct impression that the basic norm is serving *in place of* his earlier, candid appeal to politics, as if these later statements were serving simply to shroud politics from view.

Kelsen, in resolving the dilemma he has posed to the received opinion, takes his cues from the efficacy of the December Constitution of 1867 over a period of nearly 50 years, during which it had largely been complied with and applied.[64] Its social efficacy dictates that the December Constitution be the point of departure. But then, as Rainer Lippold writes in a powerful statement of the problem faced by Kelsen: 'Why should we not then also accept every other break in the law, so long as it is widely accepted in society?'[65]

IV. THE PREHISTORY OF THE BASIC NORM, 1915

My statement on the prehistory of the basic norm continues with an examination of Kelsen's paper of 1915, in which he responds to Eugen Ehrlich. While presupposition plays a barely discernible role in Kelsen's *Main Problems* (1911), he takes up the concept of presupposition in a serious way in the 1915 paper.

Eugen Ehrlich (1862–1922)[66] published *Fundamental Principles of the Sociology of Law* in 1913.[67] As time would tell, the treatise proved to be an

---

[64] This reflects Kelsen's standard line on efficacy in what might be dubbed his statement in the vernacular, namely, the norm is either complied with or applied.

[65] R Lippold, *Recht und Ordnung* (Vienna, Manz, 2000) 249, see also 213–16, 248–55, 504; Dias, *RPRT* (n 16) 160–3, 169–75.

[66] Ehrlich was born in Cernowitz. He studied law in Vienna, and the faculty, in 1894, recognised Ehrlich's early monograph, *Die stillschweigende Willenserklärung* (Berlin, Carl Heymann, 1893), as qualifying him for the *Habilitation*. Beginning in 1896, he taught as an associate professor of Roman law at the Franz-Josephs-University in Cernowitz, and as full professor from 1900. As early as 1888, he published a series of papers on gaps in the law (see n 69 below). His monograph *Freie Rechtsfindung und freie Rechtswissenschaft* (Leipzig, CL Hirschfeld, 1903), then the major work of 1913 (see n 67 below), and, finally, *Die juristische Logik* (Tübingen, JCB Mohr, 1918), count as contributions to legal sociology that established Ehrlich as a pioneering figure. See generally M Rehbinder, *Die Begründung der Rechtssoziologie durch Eugen Ehrlich*, 2nd edn (Berlin, Duncker & Humblot, 1986).

[67] E Ehrlich, *Grundlegung der Soziologie des Rechts* (Munich and Berlin, Duncker & Humblot, 1913) [hereafter: *GSR*], trans WL Moll under the title *Fundamental Principles of the Sociology of Law*,

unusually significant contribution to the field, underscoring in the name of the 'living law' the idea, as Paul Vinogradoff puts it, that 'the law applied by the courts is entirely insufficient to explain the juridical relations current in social intercourse'.[68] Ehrlich was writing in this vein as early as the 1880s.[69] He would eventually be recognised as the first of the Young Turks associated with the Free Law Movement, as it came to be known.[70] Ehrlich, later Hermann Kantorowicz, and, still later, Ernst Fuchs earned notoriety for their scathing criticism of traditional legal science. Kelsen responds to Ehrlich in acerbic terms, insisting that Ehrlich's 'living law', too, must be understood in terms of a presupposed norm.[71] And he anticipates, even if he does not expressly state, the basic norm doctrine.

At the beginning of *Fundamental Principles*, Ehrlich writes that traditional legal science proceeds by way of abstraction and deduction,

> as if the human mind were incapable of any higher attainment than the creation of bloodless forms that lose contact with reality in proportion to their level of abstraction. Legal science is thereby in sharp contrast to all genuine science, whose prevailing method is inductive and which seeks to enhance our insight into the essence of things through the observation of facts and the accumulation of experience.[72]

Kelsen replies in kind:

> Ehrlich is obviously of the naïve opinion that all science can only proceed *inductively*, and he seems to be completely unaware of the possibility of scientific knowledge attained *deductively*. He also seems to forget, with his aversion to "bloodless" abstractions, that knowledge cannot dispense with abstractions or concepts, which in relation to the individual, concrete phenomenon must necessarily be "bloodless".[73]

---

with an introduction by Roscoe Pound (Cambridge, Mass., Harvard University Press, 1936). Page references are to the original German-language edition, followed by references to the English edition. Where the translation has been amended, this is indicated in the corresponding footnote.

[68] P Vinogradoff, 'The Crisis of Modern Jurisprudence' (1919/20) 29 *Yale Law Journal* 312–20, at 313, in Vinogradoff, *Collected Papers*, 2 vols (Oxford, Clarendon Press, 1928) vol 2, 215–25, at 216.

[69] See E Ehrlich, 'Über Lücken im Recht' (1888) 17 *Juristische Blätter* 447–630 (16 intermittently published installments), repr in Ehrlich, *Recht und Leben*, ed M Rehbinder (Berlin, Duncker & Humblot, 1967) 80–169.

[70] Kantorowicz uses the expression 'Free Law Movement' to invite attention to his radical departure from the received opinion, but there was no greater movement in any very meaningful sense.

[71] H Kelsen, 'Eine Grundlegung der Rechtssoziologie' (1915) 39 *Archiv für Sozialwissenschaft und Sozialpolitik* 839–76 [hereafter: 'Rechtssoziologie'], in *HKW* 3 (n 19) 359–425. The *locus classicus* on the exchange is H Rottleuthner, 'Rechtstheoretische Probleme der Soziologie des Rechts. Die Kontroverse zwischen Hans Kelsen und Eugen Ehrlich (1915/1917)', in *Rechtssystem und gesellschaftliche Basis bei Hans Kelsen*, ed W Krawietz and H Schelske (Berlin, Duncker & Humblot, 1984) 521–51. See also B van Klink, 'Facts and Norms: the Unfinished Debate between Eugen Ehrlich and Hans Kelsen', in *Living Law. Reconsidering Eugen Ehrlich*, ed M Hertogh (Oxford, Hart Publishing, 2009) 127–55.

[72] Ehrlich, *GSR* (n 67) 6, Engl 9 (trans amended).

[73] Kelsen, 'Rechtssoziologie' (n 71) 843, in *HKW* 3 (n 19) 322. Kelsen's adverb '*deductively*' does not warrant the claim that he is proceeding 'formalistically'. Here the term refers to concept formation.

Ehrlich's focus is on early law, the law of associations – that is, the law of clans, families, households, and the like. He argues:

> The law of contracts is based solely upon the content of the contracts being entered into. There is an utter absence of general legal norms (*allgemeine Rechtssätze*) governing contracts, of all those rules on compulsion, supplementation, and interpretation that fill the *corpus iuris* and modern statute books.[74]

Thus far, one might well have the impression that Ehrlich is confining himself to customary law, that is to say, law that antedates the 'double institutionalisation' familiar from modern legal systems.[75] Customary law, so the argument goes, has no second dimension, no secondary rules in Hart's sense. If Ehrlich is addressing customary law whereas Kelsen is addressing the modern legal system, then the controversy between them can be set aside as uninteresting.

This view of the matter will scarcely do, however, for Ehrlich argues that what is true of the law of associations in early times is also true today.

> Even today, just as in primitive times, the fate of man is determined to an incomparably greater extent by the inner order of associations than by legal norms. This truth is hidden from the jurist … owing solely to habits of purely juridical thinking. The state existed before the state constitution, the family is older than the order of the family, possession antedates ownership, there were contracts before there was a law of contracts, and even the testament, where it is of native origin, is older than the law of last wills and testaments. If jurists think that before a binding contract was entered into, before a binding testament was made, there must have been a legal norm according to which contracts or testaments are binding, then they are putting the abstract ahead of the concrete.[76]

In his reply, Kelsen insists that Ehrlich is mistaken in *both* contexts – the law of associations and the modern legal system. The mistake, Kelsen would have us believe, is simple and obvious: Ehrlich has confused the temporal with the logical.

> No reasonable man has ever claimed that legal norms must *temporally* precede the material facts that are legally qualified by these norms! *Logically*, however, a legal norm must be *presupposed* if a concrete material fact is to have legal *significance*.[77]

---

[74] Ehrlich, *GSR* (n 67) 23, Engl 29 (trans amended). The English translation renders *Rechtssatz* (plural *Rechtssätze*) as 'legal proposition', but this is a mistake. There is nothing in Ehrlich's work that would justify attributing a doctrine of legal propositions to him, as the doctrine is understood, for example, by Bulygin (see below, this note), or by Kelsen himself, beginning in 1941. In traditional, German-language legal science, *Rechtssatz* and *Rechtsnorm* are treated – with occasional exceptions made in the field of customary law – as synonyms. On the doctrine of legal propositions generally, see, eg, E Bulygin, *Essays in Legal Philosophy*, ed C Bernal et al (Oxford, Oxford University Press, 2015) 188–206.

[75] I have drawn the expression 'double institutionalisation' from P Bohannan, 'The Differing Realms of the Law' (1965) 67 *American Anthropologist* 33–42, at 34–7. HLA Hart speaks of the intersection or 'union of primary rules of obligation with … secondary rules' as marking 'what is indisputably a legal system'. This, too, is of course a development of double institutionalisation, no doubt the most prominent in the literature. See HLA Hart, *The Concept of Law*, 3rd edn (Oxford, Oxford University Press, 2012) 94.

[76] Ehrlich, *GSR* (n 67) 27–8, Engl 35–6 (trans amended).

[77] Kelsen, 'Rechtssoziologie' (n 71) 849, in *HKW 3* (n 19) 329.

It is not clear that Kelsen is invoking the basic norm here, for the context is set by the law of contracts, and one can read the passage as his plea that a general legal norm from the law of contracts be presupposed, lest there be no basis for the validity of the individual norm. Still, in light of what follows in the text, it might well be thought that Kelsen is anticipating the basic norm here. He proceeds, first, by posing a question:

> Why ... is one legally obligated to do what one has promised another party to do, that is, why ought one to behave, legally speaking, in a certain way? Following the *epistemic basis* of this "ought" judgment, the question at hand is not directed to a temporally prior *cause*. There is a *binding contract* only in so far as, and only because, the promise was given and was accepted as the condition of an "ought", was thought of as an obligation. And this "ought" is not to be understood in factual terms – as the material fact of a contract – but as something drawn from a judgment of fact.[78]

Here, too, Kelsen's plea is addressed to a norm drawn from the law of contracts. If so, it falls short of what would count as a fully general answer to the question he poses above – the question, namely, of why one is legally obligated to do what one has promised to do. A fully general answer to the question requires a further step.

Arguably, Kelsen takes this step:

> It is only if I *presuppose* a norm to the effect that under certain conditions, certain persons *ought* to conduct themselves in a certain way ... that I can arrive at the claim of an obligation, and therefore arrive at the assumption of a binding contract.[79]

Three properties emerge here. First, the familiar point: the norm in question is understood as a *presupposed* norm (and I return to this in the next paragraph). Second, the requirement that the norm be presupposed is *necessary* ('[i]t is *only if* I presuppose ...'). Third, the motif to which the presupposed norm is addressed in these statements is *legal obligation*.

Does the presupposed norm in the text quoted above count as a basic norm? The answer, I think, turns on what Kelsen would have us understand by 'presupposed norm'. Is the presupposed norm a 'thought' (*gedachte*) norm, and not, then, a norm of the positive law? If so, it is reasonable to suppose that he has arrived, here, at a statement of the basic norm. In any case, the second and third properties that I list here, drawn from the quoted text, will be true of much of what Kelsen goes on to say about the basic norm, in particular, in writings up to 1928.

To be sure, a critic of Kelsenian legal philosophy will not have reason to see much progress over the view that Kelsen had set out initially, in *Main Problems*, where he writes that the 'normative character of the legal norm is an

---

[78] Ibid.
[79] Ibid, 329–30.

unshakeable presupposition'.[80] Here, in Kelsen's reply to Ehrlich, one can argue that the normative character of the transaction – the presence of an obligation, the binding force of the contract – turns, just as in *Main Problems*, on a presupposition, an 'assumption' as Kelsen sometimes puts it.[81] The critic can surely conclude that Kelsen's reply to Ehrlich does not represent marked progress over the state of affairs in *Main Problems*.

In section V, I turn to Kelsen's statements of the basic norm, beginning with his panoply of statements in *The Problem of Sovereignty* (1920) and following with the narrative up to and including the second edition of the *Pure Theory of Law* (1960). Major developments in Kelsen's treatise of 1928, *The Philosophical Foundations of Natural Law Theory and Legal Positivism*, serve as a line of demarcation between the early statements that rely largely on presupposition and the later statements that reflect something of Kelsen's neo-Kantianism.

V. BASIC NORM DEVELOPMENTS IN KELSEN'S TEXTS: 1920 UP TO 1960

Kelsen's statements on the basic norm, beginning in *The Problem of Sovereignty* (1920) and running up to *Philosophical Foundations* (1928), are pretty much of a piece. Although he makes an effort, albeit scarcely a systematic effort, to fill in some details, the outlines of the basic norm as a doctrinal statement on the role of presupposition remain constant.

In a number of the earlier writings, he dubs the basic norm the 'norm of origin' (*Ursprungsnorm* or *Ursprungsrechtssatz*).[82] For example, in the Foreword to *The Problem of Sovereignty* (1920), Kelsen gives expression to his newly won endorsement of neo-Kantianism[83] and offers what would become a staple in later work, the altogether familiar tracing exercise.[84] Here the basic norm is expressed as the 'norm of origin'.

> If I trace the individual legal norm of a judicial decision, an administrative act, or a
> legal transaction to the general norm of a statute, and trace the statute, in turn, to

---

[80] See the quotation in the text at n 30 above.

[81] See Kelsen, *PhG* (n 1) §3 (11–12), quoted in the text at n 90 below; see also, eg, Kelsen, *GTLS* (n 1) 116. As early as *Main Problems* (1911), one finds the verb 'to assume' alongside 'to presuppose', see Kelsen, *HP* (n 19) 352, in *HKW 2* (n 19) 481.

[82] See, eg, the text quoted at n 85 below.

[83] In the Foreword, Kelsen refers to the 'relative *a priori*' and adds that in pursuing this notion, he has the support of Kant's transcendental philosophy. In this connection, he notes his debt to Rudolf Stammler, who, Kelsen adds, brought the transcendental philosophy to legal science, see Kelsen, *PS* (n 23) Vorrede vi, in *HKW 4* (n 19) at 267. Elsewhere Kelsen criticises Stammler harshly, see Kelsen, *HP* (n 19) 58–62, in *HKW 2* (n 19) 147–52; H Kelsen, *Der soziologische und der juristische Staatsbegriff* (Tübingen, JCB Mohr, 1920)) [hereafter: *SJSB*] §25 (143–9). (Kelsen is in good company here; a number of major figures in early twentieth-century philosophy, academic law, and social theory engaged in trenchant criticism of Stammler, among others Hermann Cohen, Hermann Kantorowicz, and Max Weber.)

[84] In analytical jurisprudence, the tracing exercise is doubtlessly familiar, above all, from Hart, see *The Concept of Law* (n 75) 107.

the still more general norms of the constitution, and, finally, trace the constitutional norms to a general, highest (*höchste*) norm, representing the logical origin [of the process], which introduces as a legal hypothesis (*juristische Hypothese*) the authority setting down the constitution, I am conscious of the fact that the constitution acquires its validity from the presupposed norm of origin (*Ursprungsnorm*).[85]

In the treatise of 1922, *Sociological and Legal Concept of the State*, he distinguishes between facticity and normativity.

> [M]any legal theorists have been prompted to equate power and law, to consider the law and the state not from the standpoint of the "ought" (*Sollen*) but from that of the "is" (*Sein*), not as a system of norms but as a sum of rules for what in fact happens. Thereby, however, one completely overlooks the *autonomy* ... of the legal or state order whose *normative* system first *begins* with the basic norm or norm of origin. Once this norm, whose normative character is beyond doubt, is presupposed – never mind how and where – then the pure sphere of validity is attained and every incursion of facticity is rules out.[86]

The expression 'autonomy', given its well-known Kantian connotations, is an imperfect rendition of Kelsen's *Eigengesetzlichkeit*, which he understands in terms of laws – 'law' in the nomological sense – that arguably serve to undergird the law. Kelsen's most illuminating text on the issue is perhaps §34 of *Philosophical Foundations*,[87] even if, to be sure, he never really comes to terms with what he sometimes appears to envisage as nomological underpinnings of the positive law.

Finally in this early group of basic norm statements, Kelsen in the lengthy treatise of 1925, *Constitutional and Political Theory*, speaks of the basic norm as a hypothesis.

> Commensurate with the field of normative cognition, this hypothesis (*Hypothese*) takes the form of a hypothetical *norm*, a norm that is not properly within the system of positive legal norms but that instead establishes this very system, a norm that is not *issued* but *presupposed*, a norm that simply constitutes the unity of issued norms, underscoring the positivity of the system. It is the basic norm or norm of origin, which must be introduced – as hypothesis – by legal cognition in order to comprehend as elements of one and the same system "law", in order to understand the material as law and to interpret the material facts as legal acts. Just as this presupposition (*Hypothesis*) is determined, then, in accordance with the material it is to comprehend, so the material is determined according to the presupposition. It is a

---

[85] Kelsen, *PS* (n 23) Vorrede v, in *HKW 4* (n 19) 266.

[86] Kelsen, *SJSB* (n 83) §17 (99–101).

[87] See Kelsen, *PhG* (n 1) §34 (62–3). Kant's notion of autonomy (*Autonomie*) is familiar from the *Groundwork for the Metaphysics of Morals*, namely, his 'autonomous principle' of self-legislation, see Kant, *Akademie Ausgabe* (Berlin, Walter de Gruyter and predecessors, 1902) [hereafter: *Ak Ausg* with vol no] vol 4, at 432–3 (English translations of the *Groundwork* carry this pagination). For an unusually broad-based study of autonomy, see J-R Sieckmann, *The Logic of Autonomy* (Oxford, Hart Publishing, 2012); see also Sieckmann, *Rechtsphilosophie* (n 12) 217–44.

relation of correlation, just like the relation between fact and hypothesis (*Hypothese*) in the realm of cognition in the natural sciences.[88]

In this statement Kelsen seems to have the cart before the horse. The 'hypothesis', the presupposed basic norm, is a necessary condition of the possibility of legal cognition – and not, as Kelsen seems to have it here, the other way around (the basic norm 'must be introduced ... by legal cognition').[89]

Where the basic norm is concerned, these treatises from the 1920s, as noted above, are of a piece. That is, the notion of presupposition is the factor that prevails. In *Philosophical Foundations* (1928), however, Kelsen takes two steps that distinguish his work on the basic norm from everything that came earlier.

First, he would have the basic norm understood as imposing certain constraints on what counts as law, this with an eye to coherence and for the sake of legal cognition. Second, he takes steps in the direction of a Kantian or neo-Kantian transcendental argument as a means of undergirding the legal order.

To be sure, Kelsen begins in *Philosophical Foundations* in an altogether unassuming way. As he writes at an early point in the treatise:

> On the presupposition that one is to obey the commands of a certain monarch or that one is to behave in accordance with a certain people's assembly, a certain parliament, then what this monarch commands, what this people's assembly, this parliament decides, is law. The norms that have been issued in this way are "valid", the content of these norms "ought" to be carried out. Just as the absolute corresponds to the idea of natural law, so likewise a merely hypothetico-relative validity corresponds to the norms of the positive law, that is: its norms are valid *only on the presupposition*, only on the assumption, of an ultimate (*oberste*) basic norm that sets down the authority creating the law, and whose validity is not itself established within the sphere of the positive law and cannot be established.[90]

---

[88] Kelsen, *ASL* (n 13) §20(b) (103–4). It is of interest that Kelsen uses two different expressions for 'presupposition', namely, *Voraussetzung* and *Hypothesis*. The German counterpart of 'hypothesis' is *Hypothese*, whereas *Hypothesis* in the German (plural: *Hypotheseis*) stands for 'presupposition'. This expression is familiar from translations of Plato and in modern works from, eg, H Cohen, *Logik der reinen Erkenntnis*, 2nd edn (Berlin, Bruno Cassirer, 1914) 430–1, 504, 601, *et passim*. It is not obvious, however, that Kelsen's use of the two terms reflects any systematic distinction. A remark of Kelsen's at the end of the quotation in the text also calls for attention. There he says that the relation of correlation established by the presupposition is 'just like' the relation of correlation between fact and hypothesis in the natural sciences. One can grant that the one is just like the other in that there is a correlation in both instances. Beyond this trivial point, however, the claim seems to go off the track. The material of the law, contrary to what Kelsen says here, is not 'determined according to the presupposition' of the basic norm. There are, as Kelsen often remarks, no constraints whatever set by legal theory on the content of the law. See Kelsen, *PS* (n 23) § 11 (45); Kelsen, *LT* (n 1) §28 (56); Kelsen, *RR 2* (n 1) §34(e) (201). Indeed, it is the difference between the two correlations that stands out. As Verdross observed many years ago, whereas hypotheses in the sciences lend themselves to verification, there is of course nothing remotely comparable in the case of Kelsen's hypothesis, his presupposed basic norm. See Alfred Verdross, 'Die Rechtstheorie Hans Kelsens' (1930) 59 *Juristische Blätter* 421–3, at 423.

[89] For the correction, see, eg, Kelsen, *PhG* (n 1) §11 (25), §12 (26).

[90] Kelsen, *PhG* (n 1) §3 (11–12).

Here, just as in the earlier, pre-1928 phase, presupposition is predominant. A bit further on in the treatise, however, Kelsen embarks on something new. He begins by noting that the basic norm cannot be understood as lending 'justice' to the norms of the legal order, an idea, as he argues here, that would fly in the face of the 'principle of positivity'.[91] But, he continues, the basic norm can – indeed, must – be understood as providing for the intelligibility, the coherence, of the legal system.

> If the system of positive legal norms, constructed on the foundation of the basic norm, is to be a meaningful whole (*ein sinnvolles Ganze*), an intelligible construct (*ein verstehbares Gebilde*), a possible object of cognition – and this must be presupposed from the standpoint of a legal science that has as its aim the comprehension of its object, indeed, with this aim it looks to the presupposition (*Hypothesis*) of a basic norm – then the basic norm must offer the guarantee therefore.[92]

What does this mean in concrete terms? The answer is two-fold. First, Kelsen recognises that legal cognition will be limited to what is coherent, following the familiar adage: where 'p' stands for a proposition, if I know that p, then 'p' is true.[93] Carried over to the normative sphere (at a point in time antedating Kelsen's introduction of legal propositions in the technical sense),[94] and employing Kelsen's verb 'to cognise', this reads: if I am able to cognise norm N, then N is valid.

The constraint that Kelsen introduces here pertains to valid legal norms, that is, norms free from conflict. If I claim correctly to cognise norms N_1, N_2, and N_3, then these norms do not conflict. They are consistent. And this brings Kelsen to his second point: norm conflicts are eliminable if the *lex posterior* rule is built into the legal order. And he proceeds to do just that.

> If the legal material given to cognition exhibits a contradiction, undermining the sense of the material, then, where legal acts appear with their subjective meaning, this contradiction ... must be resolved. A self-contradictory subjective meaning cannot become an objective meaning.

> In fact, legal cognition in its interpretation of its object takes as its point of departure the presupposition that such contradictions lend themselves to resolution. If the norms whose content stands in a relation of contradictoriness are distinguished by

---

[91] The expression 'positivity' has several readings. It flags the fact that legal norms are issued (*gesetzt*), and in its 'negative meaning', as here, it precludes natural law. See, eg, Kelsen, *ASL* (n 13) §20(b) (103), where he writes: 'In so far as the principle of the positivity of the law in its negative meaning is directed against the principle of natural law, ... the positivity of the law and the sovereignty of the state are addressed to the same problem.'

[92] Kelsen, *PhG* (n 1) §10 (21).

[93] Kelsen's reference to the tie between cognition and truth is well hidden in his brief argument against the notion that justice might be rendered as an object of cognition. Still, the reference is there, see Kelsen, *PhG* (n 1) §37 (at 69).

[94] Their introduction is found in H Kelsen, 'The Pure Theory of Law and Analytical Jurisprudence' (1941/2) 55 *Harvard Law Review* 44–70.

distinct points in time vis-à-vis their issuance, then the principle *lex posterior derogat priori* applies.[95]

Here Kelsen refers to conflicting norms issued at distinct points in time. What about norm conflicts arising between norms issued at the same point in time? This is an issue that Kelsen struggled with in the 1950s, but without a satisfactory resolution. Along with other factors, it led, in 1960 and the years immediately following, to his throwing overboard the entire classical or neo-Kantian legal theory, supplanting it with a version of 'legal empiricism'.[96]

In the present context, there is more to say on *Philosophical Foundations*, Kelsen's treatise of 1928. In the first of the two developments to which I referred above, Kelsen builds the *lex posterior* principle into the basic norm – and he also refers in this connection to the principles *lex superior derogat legi inferiori* and *lex specialis derogat legi generali*.

> [They] all have no other purpose than to lend to the material of the positive law a meaningful interpretation, and they do this by bringing the principle of non-contradiction to bear on material within the normative sphere. These principles are for the most part not norms issued by the positive law, but *presuppositions* of legal cognition, that is, they are a part of the sense of the basic norm, and [...] serve to guarantee a system that is, then, at least *meaningful*, and therefore qua complex of norms an *order*.[97]

This is one development, namely, the constraints imposed by the basic norm for the sake of legal cognition – or, more generally, for the sake of coherence.

There is a second development. Kelsen makes a direct comparison between the laws of cognition qua conditions of experience in the transcendental philosophy of Kant's first *Critique* and the conditions of our experience of the positive law. The latter reflect the role of the basic norm.

> [W]e have already become acquainted with what is, from the standpoint of positivism, the final, highest presupposition, the basic norm qua hypothetical basis of every positive legal order. By means of it, [power is] delegated to the ultimate norm-issuing authority. Just as the transcendental laws of cognition are not empirical laws but are only the conditions of experience (*Erfahrung*), the basic norm itself is no positive legal norm, no statute of the positive law, for it is not itself issued but is only presupposed: the condition of all positive law norms. And just as one does not comprehend the empirical world from the transcendental laws, but only *by means of* them, so likewise one cannot derive the positive law, say, from the basic norm but can only comprehend it by means of the basic norm.[98]

---

[95] Kelsen, *PhG* (n 1) §10 (21–2).

[96] The expression 'legal empiricism' with reference to Kelsen's late period, 1960–71, is justified by the role Hume played in Kelsen's sceptical turn, first, *expressis verbis*, at the end of the 1930s, and then, implicitly, in 1960 and following. See SL Paulson, 'Metamorphosis in Hans Kelsen's Legal Philosophy' (2017) 80 *Modern Law Review* 860–94.

[97] Kelsen, *PhG* (n 1) §12 (26).

[98] Kelsen, *PhG* (n 1) §35 (64).

This passage in *Philosophical Foundations*, along with a passage on cognition in the same work that runs parallel to it,[99] represents Kelsen's most ambitious statement on the Kantian dimension of the Pure Theory of Law in his *œuvre* up to this point in time. It reflects some of the hints found in his work as early as 1922,[100] and it culminates in statements of Kelsen's in the treatises of 1953 and 1960.[101] The statement here, coupled with the later statements, gives rise to the question: is it possible to adduce a counterpart to Kant's transcendental argument that has application in the standing disciplines, here legal science? In effect, the question asks whether the attribution of a 'grounding function' to the basic norm is defensible. The grounding function presupposes, as a means of support that is commensurate with the purity thesis, a Kantian or neo-Kantian transcendental argument. I take up this question at some length in sections VII and VIII below.

Here, however, I am tracing Kelsen's texts on the basic norm up to and including the second edition of the *Pure Theory of Law* (1960). The first significant statement after the developments in *Philosophical Foundations* (1928) is found in the first edition of the *Pure Theory of Law* (1934). There, in section 29 of the treatise, Kelsen writes:

> The basic norm confers on the act of the first legislator – and thus on all other acts of the legal system resting on this first act – the sense of "ought", that specific sense in which legal condition is linked with legal consequence in the reconstructed legal norm, the paradigmatic form in which it must be possible to represent all the data of the positive law. Rooted in the basic norm, ultimately, is the normative import of all the material facts constituting the legal system. The empirical data given to legal interpretation can be interpreted as law, that is, as a system of legal norms, only if a basic norm is presupposed.

At the end of section 29, Kelsen adds:

> With the doctrine of the basic norm, the Pure Theory analyses the actual process of the long-standing method of cognizing positive law, in an attempt simply to reveal the transcendental logical conditions of that method.[102]

Of special interest here is the tacit reference to the peculiarly juridical category, that of imputation (*Zurechnung*), which serves to link legal condition with legal consequence. And, one scarcely need add, the category is a Kantian or neo-Kantian notion. Kelsen tends to confirm this reading in the last lines of the quotation immediately above, where he points explicitly to the 'transcendental logical conditions' of the method of cognising positive law.[103] This, in

---

[99] See Kelsen, *PhG* (n 1) §34 (62).

[100] See H Kelsen, 'Rechtswissenschaft und Recht' (1922) 3 *Zeitschrift für öffentliches Recht* 103–235.

[101] See H Kelsen, *Théorie pure du droit*, trans H Thévenaz (Boudry-Neuchâtel, Editions de la Baconniére, 1953) 53–4, and Kelsen, *RR* 2 (n 1) §16 (74–5).

[102] Kelsen, *LT* (n 1) §29 (58).

[103] To be sure, there is also language in Kelsen, *LT* (n 1) §29, that goes off in a different direction. See, on this, the explicative function of the basic norm, discussed in section IX below.

shorthand form, follows up on Kelsen's remarks on a Kantian inspired notion of legal cognition in *Philosophical Foundations* (1928), quoted above, and anticipates the more ambitious statements on legal cognition found in the treatises of 1953 and 1960.

It is of interest that in *General Theory of Law and State* (1945), Kelsen presents the basic norm without the Kantian trappings. Here his emphasis, to be understood heuristically, is on the distinction between the basic norm in a static norm system, say, morality or theology, and in a dynamic norm system, the legal order. In the former case, lower-level norms are arrived at deductively. As he writes, the norms stemming from the natural law, like the norms of morality, are 'deduced from a presupposed self-evident basic norm'.[104]

By contrast, the basic norm of a dynamic norm system, the legal order, serves not as the point of departure in a deduction but as the ultimate empowering norm.

> The ultimate hypothesis of positivism is the norm authorizing the historically first legislator. The whole function of this basic norm is to confer law-creating power on the act of the first legislator and on all the other acts based on the first act. To interpret these acts of human beings as legal acts and their products as binding norms, and that means to interpret the empirical material which presents itself as law as such, is possible only on the condition that the basic norm is presupposed. ... [It is] this necessary presupposition of any positivistic interpretation of the legal material.[105]

Why, in *General Theory of Law and State*, does Kelsen take leave of the Kantian dimension of the basic norm? One can only speculate. My best guess is that Kelsen's flirtation with empiricism, indeed, his endorsement of David Hume's philosophy at the end of the 1930s together with the abandonment, *expressis verbis*, of Kant,[106] was still very much a part of, so to speak, Kelsen's mind-set in the early 1940s, when he drafted what we know, in translation, as the *General Theory of Law and State*. These developments of the late 1930s culminate in Kelsen's treatise, *Vergeltung und Kausalität*, completed in 1940.

Less than a decade after *General Theory of Law and State*, the restoration of the old order, Kelsen's neo-Kantian legal theory, is nearly complete. In an unusually important paper, 'What is the Pure Theory of Law?' (1953), Kelsen is once again depicting the basic norm as the condition of legal cognition, this time directing the basic norm to the question of the unity of the legal order.

> Among the logical problems taken up by the Pure Theory of Law, there is, in particular, the question of what constitutes the unity in a plurality of legal norms, that is, what constitutes the unity designated as a legal system or a legal order. To answer

---

[104] Kelsen, *GTLS* (n 1) 114.

[105] Ibid, 116.

[106] On these developments, see Paulson, 'Metamorphosis in Hans Kelsen's Legal Philosophy' (n 96).

this question, the Pure Theory of Law has arrived at the idea of the *basic norm* as the hypothetical presupposition of all legal cognition. The basic norm represents the basis of the validity of all those norms that belong to the same legal order.[107]

And, for good measure, Kelsen quotes from the leading figure in the Marburg School of Neo-Kantianism, Hermann Cohen.[108]

The restoration is then completed in the second edition of the *Pure Theory of Law* (1960), where Kelsen gives the neo-Kantian dimension of his theory a good bit of attention. Indeed, this work counts, alongside *Philosophical Foundations* (1928), as Kelsen's most outspoken text on behalf of neo-Kantianism. In section 16 of *Pure Theory*, we find his ambitious statement on the constitutive role of legal science,[109] and in section 34(d), his outspoken language giving expression to the Kantian inspired basic norm.[110]

In section VII, I return to the case Kelsen makes on behalf of a neo-Kantian argument. First, however, I want to turn to the basic norm generally with an eye to a systematic approach that draws on the possible forms of the basic norm. This is my focus in section VI.

VI. THE FORMS OF THE BASIC NORM: A SYSTEMATIC APPROACH

From Kelsen's myriad statements on the basic norm, found in his writings from 1914 up to and including the second edition of the *Pure Theory of Law* (1960),[111] it is possible to draw out, arguably, seven different groups of basic

---

[107] H Kelsen, 'Was ist die Reine Rechtslehre?', in *Demokratie und Rechtsstaat. Festgabe zum 60. Geburtstag von Zaccaria Giacometti* (Zurich, Polygraphischer Verlag, 1953) [hereafter: 'WRR'] 143–62, at 148.

[108] See Kelsen, 'WRR' (n 107) 160, quoting Cohen, *Logik der reinen Erkenntnis* (n 88) at 587.

[109] See Kelsen, RR 2 (n 1) § 16 (74–5).

[110] See the quotations in the text at nn 165–6 below.

[111] See Kelsen, *RR 2* (n 1) §6(a) (32), §6(c)(d) (47, 51, 54–5), §26 (110), §34(a) (197), §34(b) (198–200), §34(c) (201–4), §34(d) (204–9), §34(e) (209, 211–12), §34(f) (214), §34(g) (219), §34(h) (221–3), §34(i) (223–6), §34(j) (226–7), §35(a) (228–9), §35(b) (232–3), §35(e) (239), §35(f) (239–40, 242), §41(d) (317), §42(c) (325), §42(d) (339), and in the appendices to *RR 2*, 355–444, at 404, 443. It would not be entirely accurate to claim that the second edition of the *Pure Theory of Law* marks the end of Kelsen's work on the basic norm as he understood it during his lengthy classical or neo-Kantian period. There is an exception. During the 1960s, in replies to critics, Kelsen reverts back to the doctrines of the classical or neo-Kantian period, including his doctrine of the basic norm. See, eg, H Kelsen, 'Professor Stone on the Pure Theory of Law' (1964/5) 17 *Stanford Law Review* 1130–57, at 1141–9. The same is true of Kelsen's replies, during the 1960s, to other critics. This aside, Kelsen speaks of the basic norm in his last period, 1960–71, as a 'fictitious norm', see H Kelsen, *General Theory of Norms,* trans M Hartney (Oxford, Clarendon Press, 1991) ch 59, §I, at D (236), where he writes that the basic norm has 'the meaning of a merely fictitious, and not a real act of will.' As such, 'it is a genuine or "proper" fiction … whose characteristic is that it is not only contrary to reality, but self-contradictory' (footnote omitted). I take up the issue briefly in section IX below.

norm characterisations, including empowerment and legal validity,[112] the unity of the legal system,[113] normativity,[114] definitions of the law,[115] normative meaning (*Sinn*), coherence or meaningfulness, and 'normative consistency'.[116] In addition, certain basic norm characterisations speak to the neo-Kantian dimension of Kelsen's legal philosophy, in particular, characterisations that hint at the possibility of establishing, transcendentally, the conditions of 'legal experience'[117] – in other words, the conditions of the 'objective validity of legal norms'.[118] An example of a transcendental characterisation of the basic norm is found in the last of the quotations from *Philosophical Foundations* that I set out in section V above.[119] Still another characterisation purports to explicate what jurists are doing when they 'understand the positive law as a valid system, that is, as norm, and not merely as factual contingencies of motivation'.[120] I term this the 'explicative function' of the basic norm. (I return to the language of 'function' in section VI below.)

By themselves, these groups of basic norm characterisations do not take us very far. The characterisations are too heterogeneous and too ill-sorted to lend themselves to a single overriding explanation. There is, however, a strategy that makes it possible to impose a semblance of order on the basic norm, namely, to treat it, following Kelsen's characterisations in his texts, as a signpost that directs one's enquiry. The basic norm serves as a signpost most clearly with respect to form, where the idea of form is taken from Kelsenian norm theory. Thus, the basic norm qua ultimate empowerment to issue legal norms reflects the form of an empowering norm. And this is the first of five basic norm forms that I have drawn from Kelsen's texts, to wit: two forms drawn from empowerment, two from legal validity, and one from the move from the subjective sense of an act of will to its objective or legal counterpart, a legal norm. The criterion for inclusion in the list, with one exception, is quantitative. That is, if the basic norm form in question occurs frequently in Kelsen's writings, it finds its way

---

[112] See the forms of basic norms, replicating empowerment and validity, in the text at nn 121–4 below.

[113] See, eg, Kelsen, *PS* (n 23) §23 (93); Kelsen, *ASL* (n 13) §17(c) (84), §20(b) (104), §27(a) (165), §36(a) (249), §38(a) (263); Kelsen, *PhG* (n 1) §7 (17); Kelsen, *LT* (n 1) §27 (55), §31(a) (64); Kelsen, *GTLS* (n 1) 111, 124; Kelsen, *RR* 2 (n 1) §6(a) (32), §34(a) (196), §34(e) (209), §35(a) (228).

[114] See. eg, Kelsen, *SJSB* (n 83) §17 (99–101); Kelsen, *PhG* (n 1) §4 (13).

[115] See, eg, Kelsen, *RR* 2 (n 1) §6(d) (51–2).

[116] See, eg, Kelsen, *PhG* (n 1) §4 (12), §10 (21), §11 (23–5), §12 (25–6), §36 (66), §37 (68, 70), see also Kelsen, *RR* 2 (n 1) §34(e) (212).

[117] See, in particular, F Sander, 'Die transzendentale Methode der Philosophie und der Begriff der Rechtserfahrung' (1919/20) 1 *Zeitschrift für öffentliches Recht* 468–507.

[118] See, eg, Kelsen, *PS* (n 23) §24 (97 n 1), in *HKW* 4 (n 19) 362 n 1; Kelsen, *SJSB* (n 83) §17 (94).

[119] See the quotation in the text at n 98 above.

[120] Kelsen, *LT* (n 1) §29 (58).

onto my list. The one exception is basic norm (2), to which I return below. First, however, the list:

(1)   the basic norm qua ultimate basis of the empowerment to issue legal norms;[121]

(2)   the basic norm qua ultimate basis of the empowerment to impose sanctions;[122]

(3)   the basic norm qua ultimate basis of legal validity where the 'validity' of a legal norm refers to its membership in a legal system, in other words, refers to its belonging (*gehören*) to a legal system;[123]

(4)   the basic norm qua ultimate basis of legal validity where 'validity' refers to bindingness (*Verbindlichkeit*), the idea that one ought to obey the commands of the law;[124]

(5)   the basic norm qua presupposition of the move from the merely subjective sense of an act to its objective or legal sense.[125]

I devote the first of three subsections to the basic norm forms that I list here.[126] Then, in a separate subsection, I single out the second basic norm form, the basic norm qua empowerment to impose sanctions. It fails to meet my criterion, for it does not appear all that frequently in Kelsen's writings. It is, however, the closest Kelsen comes to offering a canonical formulation of the basic norm – he speaks here of a 'schematic formulation'[127] – and this suggests that Kelsen lends significance to it. What is more, the significance that Kelsen attributes to this formulation is, I believe, no accident. For it reflects, in Kelsenian parlance, the 'basic form' (*Grundform*) of the reconstructed legal norm. It, in turn, is at the heart of Kelsen's norm theory, understood above all in terms of his effort to steer clear of imperative theories of law. Finally, in still another subsection I take up the fourth of the basic norm forms on the list, the basic norm qua ultimate basis of legal validity where 'validity' refers to bindingness (*Verbindlichkeit*).

---

[121] See, eg, Kelsen, *SJSB* (n 83) §17 (101 n); Kelsen, *ASL* (n 13) §19(c) (99), §36(a)(b) (249, 251); Kelsen; *PhG* (n 1) §8 (19), §9 (20), §10 (21), §11 (24–5), §35 (64–5); Kelsen, *LT* (n 1) §30(a) (59); Kelsen, *GTLS* (n 1) 113, 116; Kelsen, *RR 2* (n 1) §34(b)(c)(g) (199, 202–3, 219). These references to Kelsen's texts on his characterisations of the basic norm are meant to be representative, but they are of course by no means exhaustive.

[122] See, eg, Kelsen, *SJSB* (n 83) §12 (84); Kelsen, *PhG* (n 1) §12 (25); Kelsen, *LT* (n 1) §28 (57); Kelsen, *GTLS* (n 1) 116.

[123] See, eg, Kelsen, *ASL* (n 13) §20 (104); Kelsen, *PhG* (n 1) §4 (12–13), §7 (17); Kelsen, *LT* (n 1) §28 (57); Kelsen, *GTLS* (n 1) 111, 113–14, 115; Kelsen, *RR 2* (n 1) §34(a)(b) (196–7, 199), §35(a) (228), §35(f) (239–40).

[124] See Kelsen, *ASL* (n 13) §19(c) (99); Kelsen, *GTLS* (n 1) 115–16; Kelsen, *RR 2* (n 1) §4(b) (8), §34(a)(c) (196, 203–4).

[125] See, eg, Kelsen, *PhG* (n 1) §4 (12), §11 (23–5), §35 (65); Kelsen, *RR 2* (n 1) §6(c) (46–7), §34(d) (204–9).

[126] The form of the empowering norm is clear enough in (1) and (2). Basic norm form (4) has a corresponding norm form in the positive law, namely, the imperative or obligation-imposing norm. It is not obvious that (3) and (5) reflect legal norm forms.

[127] See the quotation in the text at n 139 below.

'Bindingness' turns out to be a problematic notion in Kelsen's legal theory. The problem, as he sees it, stems from the imperative theories of law.

I have drawn these forms of the basic norm from the first of the different groups of basic norm characterisations that I list above. My warrant for confining the discussion to these five basic norm forms is two-fold. First, three of these basic norm forms, namely, (1), (3), and (5), are altogether representative of Kelsen's work, both from the standpoint of the frequency of their appearance in his writings and from the standpoint of coherence, that is to say, making sense of the basic norm as a part of a single whole that reflects his legal philosophy generally. The basic norm forms modelled after empowerment and legal validity count, in Kelsen's work, as two sides of a single coin. They address the status of the legal norm qua process, that is, the empowerment to issue a legal norm, and they address the status of the legal norm qua product, the ensuing legally valid norm, in short, the notion of legal validity.

One other basic norm form ought to be mentioned here. It, too, meets the criteria I have set out – frequency of appearance in Kelsen's texts and coherence, that is, a reflection of a dominant strand in Kelsen's legal philosophy generally. This is the basic norm qua ultimate basis of the unity of law. Kantian support for this basic norm form stems from a different section of Kant's first *Critique*, not the Transcendental Analytic but the Transcendental Dialectic, specifically the section on systematicity. I have therefore deferred discussion of this basic norm form to other work of mine on Kelsen.[128]

Turning for just a moment from basic norm forms to their counterparts in the positive law, empowerment as the underlying modality of the legal norm in Kelsen's norm theory stems from his adoption of the *Stufenbau*, which represents the outlines of his legal system. In the Vienna School of Legal Theory, the legal system is represented by the *Stufenbau*, and empowering norms at the various *Stufen* or levels are front and centre. Thus, as Alfred Verdross correctly suggests in a paper of 1930, the legal system determines the form of the legal norm, and not the other way around.[129] This motif is worthy of mention in underscoring the significance of empowerment in Kelsen's work generally.

Basic norm form (4) is the exception to all of this, ostensibly addressing legal validity from the altogether different standpoint of bindingness. I shall be arguing, on the basis of substantial textual support, that it reflects Kelsen's 'legal vernacular'.

---

[128] See ch 4, §5, of my monograph, *Kelsen's Legal Philosophy* (forthcoming).

[129] See Verdross, 'Die Rechtstheorie Hans Kelsens' (n 88) 421–2. A recent statement that compares, in part, with what Verdross has argued is Pablo Navarro, 'Normative Systems and Legal Positivism. Eugenio Bulygin and the Philosophy of Law', in Bulygin, *Essays in Legal Philosophy* (n 74) 1–21, at 3–4. One will want to take issue, however, with Navarro's tacit endorsement of John Gardner's lumping Kelsen together with John Austin on their common failing with respect to this issue. See J Gardner, *Law as a Leap of Faith* (Oxford, Oxford University Press, 2012) 178, 181. In fact, Verdross represents Kelsen on the issue, and the distance between Kelsen and Austin could not be greater.

First, however, I take up a handful of details in basic norm forms (1), (2), (3), and (5).

A. The Forms of the Basic Norm

Empowerment is, *expressis verbis*, the motif of (1) and (2). In the short treatise of 1928, *The Philosophical Foundations of Natural Law Theory and Legal Positivism*, Kelsen offers a representative and highly compressed statement of (1):

> [A dynamic system] is at hand if the basic norm confines itself to empowering a certain human will to issue norms.[130]

Here Kelsen is contrasting the dynamic system with a static system, whose basic norm – say, an overriding moral precept – has content.[131] By contrast, the basic norm of a dynamic system has, as noted above, no substantive content at all.[132]

In *General Theory of Law and State* (1945), Kelsen provides a more expansive reading of (1):

> The basic norm merely establishes a certain authority, which may well in turn vest norm-creating power in some other authorities. The norms of a dynamic system have to be created through acts of will by those individuals who have been authorized to create norms by some higher norm. This authorization is a delegation. Norm-creating power is delegated from one authority to another authority; the former is the higher, the latter the lower authority. The basic norm of a dynamic system is the fundamental rule according to which the norms of the system are to be created.[133]

The basic norm qua ultimate basis of the empowerment to issue norms empowers a certain individual or body, thereby creating a law-making authority. Once created, this authority can of course empower other authorities, that is, can authorise, delegate power to, or vest power in other individuals or bodies.

The other basic norm form that speaks to empowerment, the basic norm qua ultimate basis of the empowerment to impose sanctions, is, as noted, something I take up in a separate subsection below.

---

[130] Kelsen, *PhG* (n 1) §8 (19). The dynamic character of the legal system is given effective expression by P Koller, *Theorie des Rechts*, 2nd edn (Vienna, Böhlau, 1997) 106–17, and by M Jestaedt, 'Einführung', in H Kelsen, *Reine Rechtslehre*, 1st edn (n 1), Studienausgabe, ed Jestaedt (Tübingen, Mohr Siebeck, 2008) xi–lxvi, at xxxvii–xl.

[131] See Kelsen, *PhG* (n 1) §8 (18–20); Kelsen, *GTLS* (n 1) 39, 122–3. Aquinas's 'first command of law', namely that 'good is to be sought and done, evil to be avoided', is a prominent example of an overriding moral precept that serves, in Kelsenian nomenclature, as the basic norm of a static system. Aquinas, *Summa Theologiae I-II*, q. 94, art 2, see also J Finnis, *Aquinas. Moral, Political, and Legal Theory* (Oxford, Oxford University Press, 1998) 82–4 *et passim*.

[132] See nn 13–15 above.

[133] Kelsen, *GTLS* (n 1) 113.

Basic norm form (3) addresses legal validity qua membership. In *General Theory of Law and State*, Kelsen writes:

> That a norm belongs to a certain system of norms, to a certain normative order, can be tested only by ascertaining that it derives its validity from the basic norm constituting the order.[134]

The notion that the validity of a legal norm rests on its belonging to a certain legal system dovetails neatly with basic norm form (1), on empowerment. Kelsen invites attention to the tie with an example he draws from America's unfortunate experiment with 'prohibition': 'One who manufactures or sells alcoholic beverages is liable to punishment.' This norm-formulation gives expression to a valid legal norm if, as Kelsen puts it, the norm 'belongs to' a certain legal order. And it belongs to that legal order if it has been issued in a way that is ultimately determined by the basic norm of that order.[135] Thus, issuance – by means of the exercise of powers conferred by the appropriate empowering norm – is sufficient for membership, and membership, in turn, is sufficient to establish legal validity.[136]

Rounding out the picture in this first group of basic norm forms, there is form (5), on the basic norm as the warrant for the move from the subjective sense of an act to its objective sense. In the second edition of the *Pure Theory of Law*, Kelsen writes:

> One can interpret the subjective sense of the act giving rise to the constitution and of the acts carried out in accordance with the constitution as their objective sense, that is, as objectively valid legal norms, ... only if one presupposes a basic norm referring to this constitution.[137]

This statement of Kelsen's on basic norm form (5) is correctly seen as a restatement of (3), on legal validity qua membership. That is, a subjective expression of will counts as an objective expression only if the latter counts, in turn, as a valid legal norm. Basic norm form (5) leads back to form (3), on legal validity qua membership, and (3), in turn, is explicated in terms of (1), on empowerment.

It goes without saying that a subjective expression of will may have no objective counterpart. Indeed, this phenomenon represents a good part of the business of the law. Kelsen offers an example in the first edition of the *Pure Theory of Law*, inviting attention to the famous case of the Captain of Köpenick.[138] In 1906, a

---

[134] Ibid, 111.

[135] Ibid, 113.

[136] Sufficient but not necessary. That is, even if the legal norm in question is defective, say, for failing to fall within the scope of the applicable empowering norm, Kelsen regards it as nevertheless valid – unless and until it is overturned. This, in a word, is Kelsen's doctrine of 'invalidatability' (*Vernichtbarkeit*).

[137] Kelsen, *RR 2* (n 1) §34(d) (204).

[138] See Kelsen, *LT* (n 1) §3 (9–10).

shoemaker, Wilhelm Voigt, dons the uniform of a captain of the guard and, with the help of several unsuspecting soldiers, occupies the city hall at Köpenick, near Berlin, arrests the mayor, and seizes the city treasury. Subjectively, Voigt intends to create the appearance of an administrative directive, but objectively, his expression of will is a delict.

To summarise thus far: basic norm forms (1), (2), (3), and (5) fit together tidily, offering, from the standpoint of the basic norm, different approaches to the status of the legal norm. Whereas basic norm forms (1) and (2) address the issuance of legal norms by means of empowerment, form (3) takes the issued norm as its point of departure. Here the form is in terms of membership: A legal norm is valid if it is a member of a system of norms, the legal order, and it is a member of the legal order if it has been issued in the appropriate way, namely, by the exercise of powers drawn from the empowering norm, which is specified, ultimately, by the basic norm. Finally, form (5) is simply a variation on the theme of legal validity: The subjective sense of an act of will counts as its objective sense only if the latter counts, in turn, as a valid legal norm. Basic norm forms (1), (3), and (5) appear frequently in Kelsen's writings, and, together with (2), they offer a coherent account of the basic norm in terms of empowerment and validity. Basic norm form (2) requires, however, additional attention.

B. The Basic Norm qua Ultimate Basis of the Empowerment to Impose Sanctions: Basic Norms and 'Basic Form'

Basic norm form (2), on the empowerment to impose sanctions, is correctly seen as an application or instantiation of (1). Here is Kelsen's formulation of (2) in the first edition of the *Pure Theory of Law*:

> What is to be valid as norm is whatever the framers of the first constitution have expressed as their will – this is the basic presupposition of all cognition of the legal system resting on this constitution. Coercion is to be applied under certain conditions and in a certain way, namely, as determined by the framers of the first constitution or by the authorities to whom they have delegated appropriate powers – this is the schematic formulation of the basic norm of a legal system (a single-state legal system, which is our sole concern here).[139]

This formulation is of interest for two reasons. First, as noted above, it offers something close to a canonical formulation ('the schematic formulation') of the basic norm, a canonical formulation as distinct from a mere characterisation.[140] This may well be Kelsen's way of lending special significance to a basic norm

---

[139] Ibid, § 28 (57).
[140] Riccardo Guastini has given me helpful advice on this distinction.

formulation that brings together the sanction theory and the doctrine of empowerment.

Second, at several points Kelsen addresses the 'basic form' of the legal norm, as he puts it, that is to say, the reconstructed legal norm. He argues that the basic norm has this form. The point is worth explaining.

As Kelsen puts it in *Philosophical Foundations*, the basic form (*Grundform*) of a positive law norm, its reconstructed form, is that 'a particular coercive act is linked to particular conditions'.[141] Here he refers to the notion of the 'basic form' of positive laws:

> The basic norm has the form of the reconstructed legal norm, the basic form (*Grundform*) of the law of normativity (*Rechtsgesetz*).[142]

He spells out the motif at greater length in the first edition of *Pure Theory of Law*:

> The Pure Theory of Law does not [understand] the legal norm, like the moral norm, as an imperative – the usual approach of traditional theory – but as a hypothetical judgment that expresses the specific linking of a conditioning material fact with a conditioned consequence. The legal norm becomes the reconstructed legal norm, which exhibits the basic form (*Grundform*) of positive laws. Just as the law of nature (*Naturgesetz*) links a certain material fact as cause with another as effect, so the law of normativity (*Rechtsgesetz*) links legal condition with legal consequence (the consequence of a so-called unlawful act).[143]

In describing the 'law of normativity' (*Rechtsgesetz*) alongside the law of nature (*Naturgesetz*), Kelsen invites attention to the parallel, as he sees it, between causation in the natural world and imputation in the legal world.

Finally, one form of the basic norm in my list of five forms is, from the standpoint of its place in Kelsen's legal theory, problematic. This is the basic norm that refers to bindingness.

C. The Basic Norm Form (4) qua Ultimate Basis of Legal Validity Where 'Validity' Refers to Bindingness

One of Kelsen's most expansive statements of basic norm form (4) is found in *Constitutional and Political Theory*, his major treatise of 1925:

> The characteristic content of the basic norm (*Grund- oder Ursprungsnorm*), providing a foundation for the legal system, is that an authority, a source of law, is established whose expressions are to count as legally binding (*rechtsverbindlich*). The basic norm

---

[141] Kelsen, *PhG* (n 1) §11 (23).

[142] Ibid, §12 (25), reading *Rechtsgesetz* as running parallel to *Naturgesetz*, as per the parallel in Kelsen, *LT* (n 1) §11(b); see the quotation in the text at n 143 below. On this parallel, see also Kelsen, *HP*, Foreword (1923) (n 61) vi, in *NN* (n 61) at 4–5.

[143] Kelsen, *LT* (n 1) §11(b) (23) (trans amended).

says, simplified for the sake of clarity: conduct yourself as the legal authority – the monarch, the popular assembly, the parliament, etc. – commands.[144]

Early in the quotation one finds still another instance of basic norm form (1), on empowerment ('an authority ... is established'). Further on in the quotation, questions arise in connection with the notion that 'expressions are to count as legally binding'. Bindingness, found in passages like this, has been given a life of its own in Kelsen's legal theory, most prominently in Raz's contention that Kelsen 'uses the natural law concept of normativity' in his understanding of obligation.[145]

Of overriding importance in coming to terms with Kelsen's statement is the fact that his talk of '[c]onducting yourself as the legal authority ... commands' is a simplification. Kelsen says as much, to wit: the quoted formulation is 'simplified for the sake of clarity'.

What does Kelsen's view come to once the 'simplified' formulation is replaced by a full explanation? He speaks to the issue in *Philosophical Foundations*:

> With an eye to the actual shaping (*Gestaltung*) of the material that, with the help of the basic norm, is to be rendered comprehensible as law, the coercive character of the law must be given expression in the basic norm itself. Here it will not do to proceed with the abbreviated formula of the basic norm, which runs: what the highest authority issues [as law] ought to take place. Rather, and more precisely, the formula must run: coercion ought to be imposed according to the conditions determined by the highest authority and only according to these conditions.[146]

Here Kelsen's 'abbreviated formula' takes the place of the 'simplified' formulation in the earlier statement. And his 'ought to take place' in this quotation is the compressed version of '[c]onduct yourself as the legal authority ... commands' in the earlier statement.

In the second edition of the *Pure Theory of Law*, Kelsen offers another statement of his alternative to the 'simplified' formulation found in the treatise of 1925, *Constitutional and Political Theory*:

> [T]he legal obligation is not or at any rate is not directly the behaviour laid down in the norm [and addressed to the legal subject] as obligatory. Only the coercive act functioning as a sanction is obligatory. When one says: Whoever is legally obligated to behave in a certain way "ought" by law so to behave, what is thereby being expressed is that the coercive act laid down as the consequence of the opposite behaviour and functioning as a sanction is obligatory – and that means it is commanded ... or that one is empowered to carry it out.[147]

---

[144] Kelsen, *ASL* (n 13) §19(c) (99).

[145] See J Raz, 'Kelsen's Theory of the Basic Norm' (1974) 19 *American Journal of Jurisprudence* 94–111, at 110–11, see also at 103, 105, in J Raz, *The Authority of Law*, 2nd edn (Oxford, Oxford University Press, 2009) 122–45, at 144, see also at 134, 137.

[146] Kelsen, *PhG* (n 1) §12 (25).

[147] Kelsen, *RR 2* (n 1) §28(b) (124), and see §5(a) (26).

Several points emerge from this text. Unlike the 'simplified' formulation of basic norm form (4) in the first of the quotations in this subsection – a statement that has Kelsen attributing obligations to legal subjects – Kelsen's present explanation of legal obligation has him resorting to the hypothetically formulated sanction-norm addressed to the legal official. If an obligation is in question, it is found here.

To be sure, there is an ambiguity in the quotation. Kelsen begins in an altogether traditional way, as though he were still wedded to his early norm-theoretic view according to which the official's imposition of the coercive act is obligatory. But the ambiguity in the quotation lends itself to clarification. In Kelsen's writings from the mid-1930s up to and including the second edition of the *Pure Theory of Law*, the language to the effect that one 'ought' to impose a sanction is not to be understood as an obligation in the familiar sense at all. Rather, the modal auxiliary 'ought' in Kelsen's later writings, most prominently the second edition of the *Pure Theory of Law*, serves as a placemarker, functioning akin to a variable.[148] In this instance, as Kelsen makes explicit in the quotation, the readings of the variable 'ought' are either an empowerment to impose the sanction or an obligation to do so where the obligation is explicated in terms of paired empowerments. If, as Kelsen writes in the first quotation of this sub-section, this representation of basic norm form (4) is a 'simplified' statement, the full statement, as Kelsen develops it in the second edition of the *Pure Theory of Law*, serves to eliminate basic norm form (4) altogether, the formulation in terms of bindingness. Of course, talk of bindingness is there in the 'legal vernacular', but the notion is not a part of Kelsen's Pure Theory of Law in its mature form.

I turn, in the next two sections, to the grounding function. First, in section VII, I ask whether Kelsen has moved in the direction of a neo-Kantian argument on behalf of the grounding function. Thus, section VII is largely textual in nature. Then, in section VIII, I turn to the neo-Kantian argument on the merits, setting out aspects of its form and concluding with an assessment.

VII. THE GROUNDING FUNCTION: DOES KELSEN ADDUCE A NEO-KANTIAN ARGUMENT?

As Horst Dreier neatly puts it, Kelsen employs a 'two-front strategy' that has him dismissing both natural law theory and fact-based legal positivism.[149]

---

[148] See SL Paulson, 'A "Justified Normativity" Thesis in Hans Kelsen's Pure Theory of Law? Rejoinders to Robert Alexy and Joseph Raz', in *Institutionalized Reason. The Jurisprudence of Robert Alexy*, ed M Klatt (Oxford, Oxford University Press, 2012) 61–111, at 84–5.

[149] See H Dreier, *Rechtslehre, Staatssoziologie und Demokratietheorie bei Hans Kelsen,* 2nd edn (Baden-Baden, Nomos, 1990) 27–42. From the very beginning, the two-front strategy is evident in Kelsen's work, see Kelsen, *HP* (n 19) 33–57, 142–88, *et passim,* in *HKW* 2 (n 19) 117–44, 248–300,

Kelsen's alternative is a 'third way', and it is well to begin, in this section, with the assumption that he is indeed concerned to develop a third way, a distinct kind of legal philosophy.[150] The assumption directs attention to Kelsen's development of an argument to establish, as he puts it, 'a system of objectively valid legal norms'.[151]

What sort of argument might he adduce? He begins with an understanding of legal positivism and natural law theory in *generic* terms.[152] Thus understood, the theories appear to be not only mutually exclusive but also jointly exhaustive of the possibilities: *tertium non datur*. Kelsen's quest for a third way, giving the lie to *tertium non datur*, will have to take the form of a Kantian or neo-Kantian transcendental argument; every other species of argument is precluded by the purity thesis.

'Transcendental' is a distinctly Kantian notion, representing a radical departure from the medieval use of the notion, where 'the transcendentals', *unum*, *bonum*, *verum*, counted as general features of being that transcend classification into genera and species. 'Transcendental' in Kant's writings refers to the conditions for the possibility of cognition or knowledge. In a justly famous passage, Kant writes that he is using the expression 'transcendental' to speak of knowledge that is 'occupied not so much with objects as with the mode of our knowledge of objects in so far as this mode of knowledge is to be possible *a priori*.'[153] Thus, the transcendental grounding of knowledge includes an *a priori* component, and Kant speaks of the categories of the understanding as 'the *a priori* conditions upon which the possibility of experience rests'.[154]

et passim. The two-front strategy is also an overriding motif in Raz's work on Kelsen, see, eg, J Raz, 'The Purity of the Pure Theory' (1981) 35 *Revue international de philosophie* 441–59, at 442, repr in Raz, *The Authority of Law* (n 145) 293–312, at 294.

[150] To be sure, the claim to have arrived at a 'third way', a distinct kind of legal philosophy, is by no means limited to Kelsen. John Mackie makes this claim on behalf of Dworkin, expressly contrasting Dworkin's theory with legal positivism and natural law theory. See J Mackie, 'The Third Theory of Law' (1977/8) 7 *Philosophy & Public Affairs* 3–16. Hermann Kantorowicz refers to a 'middle way', contrasting it with natural law theory and the historical school. See H Kantorowicz, 'Zur Lehre vom Richtigen Recht' (1908/9) 2 *Archiv für Rechts- und Wirtschaftsphilosophie* 42–74, at 45. In the monograph *Auf der Suche nach einem 'dritten Weg'. Die Rechtsphilosophie Arthur Kaufmanns* (Baden-Baden, Nomos, 2006) 60–7 *et passim*, Stefan Grote speaks of a host of figures who defend a 'third way' in one form or another. Important in distinguishing Kelsen's 'third way' from other efforts is the fact that he takes his cues on this front from Kant's first *Critique*. Peter Strawson, drawing on the title of his celebrated treatise *The Bounds of Sense* (n 8) 12, prepares the ground for an examination of Kant's third way, see n 8 above. On Kant's view, see the text at nn 6–9 above.

[151] On this language, see the quotation in the text at n 166 below.

[152] On the generic distinction, see n 10 above. For an unusually lucid statement of various legal theories, grouped generically under the 'positivist' and 'non-positivist' rubrics, see AP d'Entrèves, 'Two Questions about Law', in *Existenz und Ordnung. Festschrift für Erik Wolf zum 60. Geburtstag*, ed Th Würtenberger et al (Frankfurt, Klostermann, 1962) 309–20, repr in AP d'Entrèves, *Natural Law*, 2nd edn (London, Hutchinson, 1970) 173–84.

[153] Kant, *CPuR* (n 7) B 25.

[154] Ibid, A 96.

'Transcendent', the contrary expression, refers to that which goes beyond cognition or knowledge.[155] Kelsen, in the first edition of the *Pure Theory of Law*, follows Kant's distinction to the letter. Specifically, the transcendental category of the law, Kelsen's 'relative *a priori*' category,[156] purportedly serves to make experience possible, here 'legal experience'.[157] And the 'transcendent idea of law', going beyond experience,[158] is dismissed by Kelsen as 'metaphysics'.[159]

Another aspect of the Kantian notion of 'transcendental' can be drawn from Kant's transcendental questions, which he poses in terms of possibility. In a letter of 21 February 1772 to Marcus Herz, a decade before the publication of the first *Critique*, Kant anticipates the issue. He speaks of 'the pure concepts of the understanding' and poses the question of their *possibility*. What is at stake, Kant says, is how one's

> understanding may formulate real principles concerning the possibility of such concepts, with which principles experience must be in exact agreement and which nevertheless are independent of experience.[160]

In the first *Critique*, Kant returns to the question of possibility. He begins with a reference to traditional metaphysics, which, he remarks, has been more a 'combat zone' than a field 'entering upon the secure path of a science'.[161] The puzzles of metaphysics give rise to Kant's transcendental question, which is, as always, about *possibility*.

> One has already gained a great deal if one can bring a multitude of investigations under the formula of a single problem. For one thereby not only lightens one's own task, by determining it precisely, but also the judgment of anyone else who wants to examine whether we have satisfied our plan or not. The real problem of pure reason is contained in the question: How are synthetic judgments *a priori* possible?[162]

---

[155] On the distinction, see Kant, *CPuR* (n 7) A296/ B351, and on 'transcendent' A308/ B365.

[156] See Kelsen, *LT* (n 1) §11(b) (at 24), also Kelsen, *PS* (n 23) Vorrede vi (printing of 1920), in *HKW 4* (n 19) 267. In both of these texts, *LT* and the earlier *PS*, one encounters a 'relative *a priori*' category, a notion that Felix Somló had employed in *Juristische Grundlehre* (Leipzig, Felix Meiner, 1917) 127. On the issue, see R Alexy, 'Hans Kelsens Begriff des relativen Apriori', in *Neukantianismus und Rechtsphilosophie*, ed R Alexy et al. (Baden-Baden, Nomos, 2002) 179–202.

[157] The notion of 'legal experience' is prominent in Fritz Sander's early work. Sander sought to carry over to legal philosophy virtually the whole of the Transcendental Analytic of Kant's first *Critique*, going much further in this direction than anyone else in Kelsen's Vienna School of Legal Theory.

[158] Kelsen, *LT* (n 1) §11(b) (25).

[159] See Kelsen, *LT* (n 1) §11(b)(c) (25–6). For what appears on first glance to be a comparable position, see G Jellinek, *Allgemeine Staatslehre*, 3rd edn (Berlin, O. Häring, 1914) 332. Jellinek's legal theory proves, however, to be psychologistic through and through, a point that was not lost on Kelsen, see Kelsen, *SJSB* (n 83) §§ 20–1 (114–32).

[160] Kant, in *Ak Ausg* (n 87) vol 10, 129–35, at 131, Engl in Kant, *Correspondence*, ed and trans A Zweig (Cambridge, Cambridge University Press, 1999) 132–8, at 134.

[161] Kant, *CPuR* (n 7) B xiv–xv.

[162] Ibid, B 19.

Kant anticipates the pursuit of the issue with the queries he poses respecting pure mathematics and pure natural science.

> In solving the problem above, we solve at the same time another problem, that concerning the possibility of the pure use of reason in establishing and carrying out all sciences that contain theoretical *a priori* cognition of objects, that is, we have also to answer the questions:
>   How is pure mathematics possible?
>   How is pure natural science possible?[163]

Kelsen, in *Philosophical Foundations* (1928), poses his own transcendental question, identified by the characteristic Kantian language of possibility:

> How is positive law qua object of cognition, qua object of cognitive legal science, possible?[164]

And he poses the question anew in the second edition of the *Pure Theory of Law* (1960), this time at greater length:

> Just as Kant asks: How without appealing to metyphasics, is it possible that the facts perceived by our senses can be interpreted in the laws of nature, as these are formulated by natural science? In the same way, the Pure Theory of Law asks: How, without appeal to meta-legal authorities such as God or nature, is it possible that the subjective sense of certain material facts can be interpreted as a system of objectively valid legal norms that are describable in legal propositions?[165]

Kelsen answers his transcendental question by appealing to the basic norm:

> Provided that it is only the presupposition of the basic norm that makes possible the interpretation of the subjective sense of [certain material facts] as their objective sense, that is, as objectively valid legal norms, the basic norm can be described in its characterization by legal science – applying by analogy a concept of Kant's theory of knowledge – as the logico-transcendental condition for this interpretation.[166]

Here Kelsen in effect commits himself to a transcendental argument. Such an argument, lending support to Kelsen's third way, would be in conformity with his purity thesis, that is to say, it would be an argument altogether distinct from any argument that reflects either a naturalistic standpoint or a moral point of view.

It remains – my focus in section VIII – to examine the argument more closely and to offer an assessment. It goes without saying that the argument presented here is a reconstruction.

---

[163] Ibid, B 20.
[164] Kelsen, *PhG* (n 1) §36 (66).
[165] Kelsen, *RR* 2 (n 1) §34(d) (205).
[166] Ibid, §34(d) (204–5).

VIII. THE NEO-KANTIAN ARGUMENT: FORM AND ASSESSMENT

The Kantian-inspired argument is a transcendental argument, suitably modified to apply in the standing disciplines, here legal science.[167] In what follows, I divide the discussion on transcendental arguments and the philosophical problem that stems from them into seven sub-sections, namely: (A) notes on transcendental arguments generally, (B) Kant's progressive and regressive forms of argument, (C) the neo-Kantians' transcendental argument in its regressive form, (D) the neo-Kantians 'neo-Kantians' 'fact of science', 'fact of science', (E) Kelsen's transcendental category, (F) the unfolding of the argument, and (G) an assessment of the argument.

A. Transcendental Arguments Generally

Transcendental arguments are not straightforward proofs in logic; rather, they proceed indirectly. One can contrast the Kantian version of the argument with the neo-Kantian version by looking at their respective points of departure. The element that is common to both is *something given*. In Kant's case, what is given are states of consciousness, whereas for the neo-Kantians, what is given is the fact of science. For example, the neo-Kantian Hermann Cohen (1842–1918) interprets experience (*Erfahrung*) as scientific experience or, quite simply, as science.[168] Cohen's 'fact of science' is a familiar motif in the work of a number of *fin-de-siècle* neo-Kantians.[169] Both Cohen and Kelsen provide illustrations, and I return to the motif below.[170] I also take up, below, Kant's distinction between progressive and regressive forms of the transcendental argument and the neo-Kantian counterpart to Kant's regressive form. This sheds more light on their respective points of departure.

First, however, I might note *en passant* that there have been no fewer than three rounds on transcendental arguments in what is, broadly speaking, the Kantian

---

[167] On the problems in applying the transcendental argument within one or another of the standing disciplines, see my essay 'The Great Puzzle: Kelsen's Basic Norm', in *Kelsen Revisited* ed LD d'Almeida et al. (Oxford, Hart Publishing, 2013) 43–61, at 53–7.

[168] See H Cohen, *Kants Theorie der Erfahrung* (Berlin, Ferd. Dümmler, 1871) 206.

[169] See, eg, E Cassirer, 'Zur Frage nach der Methode der Erkenntniskritik' (1907) 31 *Vierteljahrsschrift für wissenschaftliche Philosophie und Soziologie* 441–65, at 457–8, repr in E Cassirer, *Gesammelte Werke. Hamburger Ausgabe*, vol 9: *Aufsätze und kleine Schriften 1902–1921*, ed M Simon (Hamburg, Meiner, 2001) 83–103, at 97; F Kaufmann, 'Kant und die reine Rechtslehre' (1924) 29 *Kant-Studien* 233–43, at 237, repr in *33 Beiträge zur Reinen Rechtslehre*, ed RA Métall (Vienna, Europaverlag, 1974) 141–51, at 145. See generally A Richardson, '"The Fact of Science" and Critique of Knowledge: Exact Science as Problem and Resource in Marburg Neo-Kantianism', in *The Kantian Legacy in Nineteenth-Century Science*, ed M Friedman and A Nordmann (Cambridge, Mass., MIT Press, 2006) 211–26.

[170] See the quotations in the text at nn 176–7 below. See also my essay 'Das regulative Prinzip als Rettung der Reinen Rechtslehre Hans Kelsens?', in *Wissenschaftsphilosophie im Neukantianismus*, ed C Krijnen and KW Zeidler (Würzburg, Königshausen & Neumann, 2014) 259–88, at 265–73.

tradition. First and foremost, there is Kant's own transcendental argument, the notoriously difficult and prolix 'transcendental deduction' in the transcendental analytic of the first *Critique*. Second, there are various transcendental arguments collected under the rubric of the 'transcendental method'[171] in the work of the *fin-de-siècle* neo-Kantians. While Kant's overriding concern with his transcendental argument was to make the critical idealist philosopher's case on behalf of the existence of the phenomenal world, the neo-Kantians, Kelsen among them, presuppose the phenomenal world and proceed by applying aspects of the transcendental philosophy in the standing disciplines (*Einzelwissenschaften*). And, in a third round, there are the initiatives of Peter F Strawson, which have given rise to a cottage industry on transcendental arguments in analytic philosophy over the past half-century.[172]

The neo-Kantian argument that might be attributed to Kelsen on a suitable reconstruction of his work reflects what is called, in the literature, the neo-Kantians' regressive form of the transcendental argument. I return to Kant for a general explication of progressive and regressive forms of the transcendental argument, and I then turn to the distinction between Kantian and neo-Kantian versions of the regressive form.

B. Kant's Progressive and Regressive Forms of Argument

Kant's transcendental argument is found in both progressive and regressive forms.[173] As he develops the argument in the first *Critique*, it reflects the progressive form, which begins with a strikingly weak premise, the data of consciousness, and moves ultimately to the existence of the phenomenal world. Where Kant's transcendental argument is understood as a response to the sceptic,[174] the argument, if sound, shows that the sceptic cannot help but undermine his own position in the course of defending it. For the sceptic, too, must

[171] The *locus classicus* on the 'transcendental method' is Paul Natorp; see his paper 'Kant und die Marburger Schule' (1912) 17 *Kant-Studien* 193–221, repr. in *Erkenntnistheorie und Logik im Neukantianismus*, ed W Flach and H Holzhey (Hildesheim, Gerstenberg, 1980) 197–225. It is generally recognised that the expression 'transcendental method' does not occur in Kant's writings.

[172] See PF Strawson, *Individuals. An Essay in Descriptive Metaphysics* (London, Methuen, 1959), at 35–6; Strawson, *The Bounds of Sense* (n 8). The volume *Transcendental Arguments*, ed R Stern (Oxford, Oxford University Press, 1999), is a representative collection of papers and includes a lengthy bibliography.

[173] Kant regards the regressive form of the argument as a summary statement of the progressive form. In the *Prolegomena to Any Future Metaphysics* (first published 1783), Ak Ausg (n 87) 277 (note) (English editions of the *Prolegomena* carry the Ak Ausg pagination), Kant alludes to the regressive form of the argument. On the distinction between the two forms of the argument, see my essay 'The Neo-Kantian Dimension in Kelsen's Pure Theory of Law' (1992) 12 *Oxford Journal of Legal Studies* 311–32, at 322–32.

[174] On Kant's transcendental argument as a reply to the sceptic, see, eg, MN Forster, *Kant and Skepticism* (Princeton, Princeton University Press, 2008).

begin with the data of consciousness, and he is then drawn ineluctably along into the further reaches of the argument against him.

Contrariwise, the starting point of Kant's transcendental argument in its regressive form is a very strong premise, the fact of experience (*Erfahrung*) and so the existence of the phenomenal world. But there is a catch: the regressive form of Kant's transcendental argument presupposes the progressive form, and Kant simply offers it as a heuristic device. Otherwise, the very strong initial premise of the argument in its regressive form would be question-begging.

Everything changes as soon as we turn to the neo-Kantians, including Kelsen. The transcendental argument that turns up in their work reflects something of the regressive form of Kant's argument, but *without* a progressive counterpart.

C. The Neo-Kantians' Transcendental Argument in its Regressive Form

The form of their argument looks like this.

1. P (given).
2. P is possible only if Q (transcendental premise).
3. Therefore, Q (transcendental conclusion).

In the first premise, 'P' stands for the material that is given, and, in the second premise and the conclusion, 'Q' stands for the presupposed category.[175] From what is given, we 'regress' to the transcendental category without which what is given would not be possible.

A strong initial premise – the 'fact of science', as the neo-Kantians put it – is given. The task, then, is to make the case for the *very possibility* of P by showing that P implies Q, the transcendental category.

D. The 'Fact of Science'

As noted, the fact of science is the point of departure in the argument of the neo-Kantians, and it is instructive to have a closer look. Hermann Cohen writes:

> If … I take cognition not as a form and manner of consciousness, but as a *fact* that has established itself in *science* and that continues to establish itself *on given foundations*, then the enquiry is no longer directed to a subjective fact; it is directed instead to a fact that, *to whatever extent* self-propagating, is *nevertheless* objectively given, a fact *grounded in principles*. In other words, the enquiry is directed not to the process

---

[175] The argument is rendered formally valid by adding the trivial premise – call it premise *1a* – to the effect that if P is given, as in premise *1*, then P is possible.

and apparatus of cognition, but to its result, to science itself. Then the unequivocal question arises: from *which presuppositions* does this fact of science derive its certainty?[176]

In the treatise of Kelsen's that comes closest to shedding light on how, exactly, the reconstructed transcendental argument attributed to him is to be understood, the point of departure is the 'fact of legal science', the very point of departure found in the work of the Marburg neo-Kantians, who speak *expressis verbis* of the 'fact of science'. Kelsen writes:

> The possibility and the necessity of a normative theory of law is shown by the very fact of legal science over a millennium, which, in the guise of dogmatic jurisprudence, serves – so long as there is law at all – the intellectual requirements of those who concern themselves with the law.[177]

E. Kelsen's Transcendental Category

Kelsen writes that the legal 'ought' designates 'a transcendental category',[178] but he does not pursue the idea. Instead, his most effective expression of the idea of a transcendental category in legal science is imputation (*Zurechnung*).[179] By appeal to imputation, he is in a position to set out, between material fact and legal consequence, a connection, he contends, that runs parallel to the causal connection between facts.

> If the mode of linking material facts is causality in the one case, it is imputation in the other, and imputation is recognized in the Pure Theory of Law as the particular lawfulness, the autonomy, of the law. Just as an effect is traced back to its cause, so a legal consequence is traced back to its legal condition. The legal consequence, however, cannot be regarded as having been caused by the legal condition. Rather, the legal consequence (the consequence of an unlawful act) is linked by imputation to the legal condition.[180]

---

[176] H Cohen, *Das Prinzip der Infinitesimal-Methode und seine Geschichte* (Berlin, Ferd. Dümmler, 1883) §7 (5), and see §89 (128). See also H Cohen, *Ethik des reinen Willens*, 2nd edn (Berlin, Bruno Cassirer, 1907) 65–6; H Cohen, *Kants Theorie der Erfahrung*, 3rd edn (Berlin, Bruno Cassirer, 1918) 41, 79, 108, 637. An early statement on the fact of science is found in H Cohen, *Von Kants Einfluß auf die deutsche Kultur* (Marburg celebratory lecture) (Berlin, Ferd. Dümmler, 1883) 7. Presumably Cohen's notion of the fact of science is traceable to Adolf Trendelenburg, although research on the Cohen-Trendelenburg tie is still awaiting attention. See A Trendelenburg, *Logische Untersuchungen*, 2nd edn, 2 vols (Leipzig, S. Hirzel, 1862) vol 1, 130–1, 268, 306.

[177] H Kelsen, *Reine Rechtslehre*, 1st edn (n 1) §16 (37); Kelsen, *RR 2* (n 1) §26 (111). See also Kelsen, *SJSB* (n 83) §35 (at 218); Kelsen, *ASL* (n 13) §1 (5); Kelsen, *PhG* (n 1) §40 (75); Kelsen, 'Letter to Treves', in *NN* (n 61) 173; Kelsen, 'WRR' (n 107) 144.

[178] In Kelsen, *LT* (n 1) §11(b) (23), heading of the sub-section.

[179] Support is lent to the rendering of *Zurechnung* as 'imputation' by Kelsen's own occasional use of the Latin *imputatio* in place of *Zurechnung*; see Kelsen, *HP* (n 19) 138, 194, 209, 503, in *HKW 2* (n 19) 244, 306, 322, 650.

[180] Kelsen, *LT* (n 1) §11(b) (23–4).

Thus, imputation is to be understood by analogy to causation, and imputation serves as the presupposed juridical category, corresponding to 'Q' in the second premise and the conclusion of Kelsen's transcendental argument.

F. The Unfolding of the Argument

Some of the machinery of the reconstructed transcendental argument attributable to Kelsen is now in place. How exactly does the argument unfold? I begin with the state of affairs that would obtain if the argument were sound, taking Kelsen's purity thesis as the point of departure.[181] It precludes every appeal to fact-based legal positivism and to natural law theory, the traditional views on the 'nature of law' question. In other words, it precludes every appeal to facts and to values. The purity thesis, according to some of Kelsen's critics, gives rise to a dilemma. They assume that the two traditional views, taken together from a suitably abstract standpoint,[182] exhaust the field: *tertium non datur*. And, the critics continue, the purity thesis, in ruling out both traditional views, goes too far. Kelsen faces the dilemma of either abandoning the purity thesis or confronting nihilism, the result of adhering to the purity thesis. Kelsen appeals to Kant and thereby escapes the dilemma. More precisely, he appeals to the category of imputation, which he can draw from the reconstructed neo-Kantian argument. The category of imputation, evaluated from the standpoint of the purity thesis, withstands scrutiny. Or so Kelsen contends.

G. An Assessment of Kelsen's Argument

The sketch above is roughly the picture we would have if Kelsen's argument were sound. But it is not sound. It fails to comport with a basic requirement of all transcendental arguments, namely, that every alternative explanation of the fact of science, every explanation that would undermine the second premise in the reconstructed transcendental argument attributable to Kelsen, be eliminated. Kelsen believes he has accomplished this, but he has not. Even if we were to recognise Kelsen's arguments against naturalism and psychologism as sufficient for the elimination of fact-based legal positivism, these arguments do not address natural law theory, which Kelsen all too often simply dismisses out of hand. At this juncture in Kelsen's work, cogent argument is conspicuous by its

---

[181] See my essay 'The Great Puzzle: Kelsen's Basic Norm' (n 167) 45–9.

[182] I would have 'suitably abstract standpoint' understood as saying, inter alia, that legal realism counts as a species of fact-based legal positivism. In short, I use 'fact-based legal positivism' as a generic term. This tack receives welcome support from Brian Leiter. See his recent paper 'Legal Positivism about the Artifact Law', in *Law as an Artifact*, ed Luka Burazin et al (Oxford, Oxford University Press, 2018) 3–28.

absence. Natural law theory – for purposes of the transcendental argument – remains a viable alternative to Kelsen's Pure Theory of Law. The presence of a viable alternative undermines the truth of the second premise in Kelsen's transcendental argument and, therefore, its soundness.[183]

Another factor, completely overlooked by Kelsen, is the problem of *quartum non datur*. Kelsen introduces *two* complexes as a means of representing his version of legal positivism – first, his stance against naturalism, reflected in the neo-Kantians' fact-value distinction, and, second, his stance against morality and politics, reflected in the legal positivist's separability principle. These two complexes generate *four* distinct species of legal theory. Thus, even if Kelsen's dismissal of fact-based legal positivism and natural law theory were granted, he would not have, without further ado, an argument addressing the issue posed by *quartum non datur*.

In concluding this section, one might ask: how is it that Kelsen can be assumed to have defended the trappings of a transcendental argument if the argument is clearly seen to be unsound? The deceptively simple answer is this. Kelsen *believes* that neither of the traditional theories, fact-based legal positivism and natural law theory, is defensible. He rejects fact-based legal positivism on the grounds that legal norms yield, on the fact-based positivist's analysis, causal claims (one thinks, most obviously here, of 'will' theories of law), and he rejects natural law theory on the grounds that it is nothing more than ideology. Thus, he reasons, there are no alternatives to his Pure Theory of Law – or, more precisely, no alternatives to a neo-Kantian theory of law. This does not, however, account for the second objection to the transcendental argument in Kelsen's hands, that posed by appeal to *quartum non datur*.

I want now to leave to one side the grounding function, with its discouraging outcome, and turn to what I am calling the explicative function of the basic norm.

IX. THE EXPLICATIVE FUNCTION: AN OUTLIER?

Kelsen offers a useful statement of what I am calling the explicative function of Kelsen's basic norm. The statement stems from the first edition of the *Pure Theory of Law*.

> In formulating the basic norm, the Pure Theory of Law is not aiming to inaugurate a new method for jurisprudence. The Pure Theory aims simply to raise to the level of consciousness what all jurists are doing (for the most part unwittingly) when, in conceptualizing their object of enquiry, they reject natural law as the basis of the

---

[183] See my essay 'A "Justified Normativity" Thesis in Hans Kelsen's Pure Theory of Law? Rejoinders to Robert Alexy and Joseph Raz', in *Institutionalized Reason. The Jurisprudence of Robert Alexy* (n 148) 75–8.

validity of positive law, but nevertheless understand the positive law as a valid system, that is, as norm, and not merely as factual contingencies of motivation.[184]

In the same work, two short sections later, Kelsen alludes to this passage, and writes that 'analysing positive law raised to the level of consciousness [is] the same analysis that reveals the function of the basic norm'.[185]

A comparable, though not identical, statement of what I am calling the explicative function of the basic norm is found in the second edition of the *Pure Theory of Law* (1960).[186] Elsewhere, too, in *Philosophical Foundations* (1928),[187] in *General Theory of Law and State* (1945),[188] and in *Théorie pure du droit* (1953),[189] which is Kelsen's initial revision of *Reine Rechtslehre*, one finds statements that closely resemble the statement I have quoted above. These five treatises, ranging from 1928 to 1960, cover the greater part of Kelsen's classical or neo-Kantian period, and it is, then, not implausible to suggest that they establish a prima facie case on behalf of the explicative function. As noted above, the question arises: does the basic norm from the standpoint of its explicative function explain anything?

It is significant that the explicative function seems clearly to dovetail with what Kelsen says about the validity of legal norms in terms of an *assumption*. An example is found in the passage in *General Theory of Law and State* (1945) that reflects the explicative function:

> By formulating the basic norm, we do not introduce into the science of law any new method. We merely make explicit what all jurists, mostly unconsciously, assume when they consider positive law as a system of valid norms and not only as a complex of facts, and at the same time repudiate any natural law from which positive law would receive its validity. That the basic norm really exists in the juristic consciousness is the result of a simple analysis of actual juristic statements.[190]

If, however, an assumption is all that is at stake, there is no need to invoke a basic norm. It is for this reason that I suggest, in the title of the present section, that

---

[184] Kelsen, *LT* (n 1) §29 (58). To be sure, what I am quoting here from the first edition of the *Pure Theory of Law* is, in an important respect, incomplete. The last line in the paragraph from which I quote reads: 'With the doctrine of the basic norm, the Pure Theory analyses the actual process of the long-standing method of cognizing positive law, in an attempt simply to reveal the transcendental-logical conditions of that method.' Arguably, this line raises doubts about whether the text can be seen as an expression of the explicative function. Still, the other texts that give expression to the explicative function, see nn 186–9 below, do not raise doubts on this score.

[185] Kelsen, *LT* (n 1) §31(a) (63).

[186] See Kelsen, *RR 2* (n 1) §34(d) (209).

[187] See Kelsen, *PhG* (n 1) §4 (12).

[188] See Kelsen, *GTLS* (n 1) 116, quoted in the text at n 190 below.

[189] See Kelsen, *Théorie pure du droit* (n 101) ch VIII, §3 (125).

[190] Kelsen, *GTLS* (n 1) 116. To be sure, one could raise questions about whether 'assume' is not simply the translator's language rather than Kelsen's. Still, 20 years earlier, Kelsen, in *ASL* (n 13) §36(b) (251), is using the language of assumption, albeit in a different context; there he speaks of the basic norm as 'a hypothetical assumption (*hypothetische Annahme*) that serves to establish the unity of the legal or state system'. See also the occurrence of 'assumption' in Kelsen, *PhG* (n 1) §4 (12).

the explicative function may be little more than an outlier. Not everyone will agree. Robert Walter, in his interpretation of the basic norm, takes the idea of an assumption altogether seriously:

> Kelsen also speaks of a "hypothesis that refers to the material of the positive law, by analogy to the hypotheses in the natural sciences". It is a matter of an *assumption*, which Kelsen calls "hypothetical" because it is *not coerced*. It does not have to be made; it is simply that it can be made.[191]

Walter, addressing what I am calling the explicative function, moves from the assumption found in Kelsen's classical period to the basic norm qua fiction in Kelsen's late period,[192] as though this move were obvious. Here, too, the talk of an assumption is prominent. As Walter writes:

> Now the basic norm can certainly be interpreted – as Kelsen does in the late period – as a fiction in the sense of Vaihinger's philosophy. For the basic norm does not really exist but is only assumed to exist. This is, therefore, a counterfactual assumption.[193]

Elsewhere, Walter puts a sharp edge on it:

> The basic norm is nothing other than an *assumption*. It permits the interpretation, the description of efficacious coercive systems as normative systems, [or,] more precisely, *as if* they were normative systems.[194]

Walter's statements suggest that two issues are now on the table. One issue is the status of the explicative function during Kelsen's classical or neo-Kantian period. As I have argued, all is well and good if the explicative function turns simply on an assumption about what jurists understand in the name of normativism. But there is no reason to adorn this tack with the label 'basic norm', that is, the jurist's assumption or belief stands as it is. Adding an appeal to a basic norm adds no explanatory force.

The second issue is the status of the basic norm qua fiction in the late period. In both of these last quotations from Walter, he is giving expression to the fictitious basic norm. It is well known that Kelsen, in his late period, rejects the basic norm qua presupposition and *a fortiori* the basic norm as inspired

---

[191] R Walter, 'Entstehung und Entwicklung des Gedankens der Grundnorm', in *Schwerpunkte der Reinen Rechtslehre*, ed R Walter (Vienna, Manz, 1992) 47–59, at 54–5. Walter is quoting from Kelsen, *HP*, Foreword (1923) (n 61) xv, in *NN* (n 61) 13. Walter continues by remarking that 'it remains an open question whether any purpose is served by [Kelsen's] speaking also of a *Hypothese* and not always of a *Hypothesis*.' It is regrettable that Walter chose not to pursue this question, for he may have been able to shed light on Kelsen's usage. The German *Hypothese* means 'hypothesis', but the other German expression, *Hypothesis*, is used in the philosophical literature to mean 'presupposition'. See the discussion at n 88 above.

[192] The so-called late period (*Spätlehre*), from 1960 to 1971, marks the last of three periods in Kelsen's stages of development.

[193] Walter, 'Entstehung und Entwicklung des Gedankens der Grundnorm' (n 191) 56.

[194] R Walter, 'Der gegenwärtige Stand der Reinen Rechtslehre' (1970) 1 *Rechtstheorie* 69–95, 80 (emphasis in original), see also at 73 (here, too, Walter writes 'als ob' in italics).

by Kant (the latter as the prominent reading of Kelsen's basic norm during the period 1928–60). Kelsen rejects the basic norm, thus understood, at a conference that took place in 1962:

> In my earlier writings ... I characterized my entire doctrine of the basic norm in terms of a norm that is not the sense of an act of will but is, rather, a norm that is presupposed. Now, gentlemen, I must unfortunately confess that I am no longer able to maintain this doctrine. I have had to abandon it. You can believe me when I say that it was anything but easy to abandon this doctrine, which I had defended for decades. I have abandoned it in the knowledge that an "ought" has to be the correlate of a will. My basic norm is a *fictitious* norm, which presupposes a *fictitious* act of will that sets down this norm.[195]

Kelsen replaces his presupposed basic norm with a fictitious basic norm. What is more, the fiction in question is the more demanding of the two readings of 'fiction' set out by Hans Vaihinger, whom Kelsen is following here. This stronger reading of 'fiction', Vaihinger's fiction in the 'proper' sense of the word, not only contradicts reality but is self-contradictory.[196] Kelsen, far from shying away from Vaihinger's reading, expressly endorses it:

> [T]he basic norm of a positive moral or legal system ... is not a positive norm, but a merely thought norm, that is, a fictitious norm, the meaning of a merely fictitious, not a real, act of will. As such it is, in the sense of Vaihinger's philosophy of *as if*, a genuine or "proper" fiction, which is characterized not only as contradicting reality but also as being self-contradictory.[197]

Does this count as a new version of Kelsen's explicative function? In any case, just as with the explicative function he introduced in the classical period, nothing is added by bringing the basic norm to bear on the issue.

X. CONCLUSION

It is generally conceded in Kelsenian circles that the basic norm is the Achilles' heel of the Pure Theory of Law. My own work on the problem tends to confirm the received opinion. The effort to provide the basic norm with a grounding function fails because the argument that would be required, a neo-Kantian transcendental argument, cannot be made to work. The explicative function, seen

---

[195] H Kelsen et al., 'Diskussionen', in *Das Naturrecht in der politischen Theorie*, ed F-M Schmölz (Vienna, Springer, 1963) 117–62, at 119–20.

[196] See H Vaihinger, *Die Philosophie des Als-Ob* (first published 1911, written 1876–9) 9th and 10th printings (Leipzig, Felix Meiner, 1927) 24; this edition is identical to the 7th and 8th printings (of 1922) used by Kelsen, trans CK Ogden as *The Philosophy of 'As-If'* (first published 1924), 2nd edn (London, Kegan Paul, Trench, Trübner, 1935) 16.

[197] H Kelsen, *General Theory of Norms*, trans Michael Hartney (Oxford, Clarendon Press, 1991) ch 59, § 1, at D (256) (emphasis added) (trans amended).

as an explanation of jurists' normative conception of the law, rests on their assumption or presupposition of normativity. A basic norm has no role to play.

Wilhelm Windelband, the leader of the Baden neo-Kantians, argued that you cannot prove the basic principles of logic or ethics – or those of the law – without presupposing them.[198] If Windelband is right, are we then chasing a will-o'-the-wisp?

---

[198] See, eg, W Windelband, 'Kritische oder genetische Methode?', in Windelband, *Präludien* (Freiburg and Tübingen, JCB Mohr, 1884) 247–79, at 259, and in Windelband, *Präludien*, 9th edn, 2 vols (Tübingen, JCB Mohr, 1924) vol 2, 99–135, at 111–12.

4

Normativity at Large: On Moral Absolutism, Legal Relativism and Social Systems Anti-Normativism

JIŘÍ PŘIBÁŇ

H UMANITY IS THE capacity to distinguish between good and evil. Society is the capacity to protect people from evil even if pursued in the name of good. People strive for good and meaningful lives but society has to keep distance from this struggle and find other distinctions beyond good and evil to constitute itself.

In this chapter, I discuss the process of universal declarations of morality enforced by particular laws which recursively draw on universal legitimacy of moral claims of humanity or cosmopolitanism while constituting the particular rule of law and its enforcement institutions. The idea of meaningful existence anchored in universal humanity and its moral order is confronted by the autopoietic systems theoretical conceptualisation of meaning and critique of normativity as the constituent basis of positive law. Instead, the autopoietic systems concept of meaning is used to explain the circularity of absolute and relative validity claims in the system of positive law which paradoxically makes the value-free rule of law a repository and enforcement mechanism of societal values and the constituent value itself.

In the opening sections, I discuss the classic tension between moral absolutism and legal relativism, formal legalist responses to the substantive moral claims and their recent criticisms in post-positivist legal theory. I subsequently analyse the difference between philosophical and sociological conceptualisations of meaning and use the autopoietic social systems theory to critically analyse both legal and moral normativist theories of the legal system. I conclude by arguing that universality of moral claims in positive legal norms is a matter of social contingency and not metaphysical necessity.

I. MORALITY AT LARGE: MODERN SOCIETY BETWEEN THE *ICY*
SELF-CONSTITUTION AND THE *HOT* SELF-DESTRUCTION

Basic philosophical, ethical, social, political and legal theoretical questions may
be approached by either a highly abstracted language and arguments, or concrete
story-telling and literature. Before embracing the conceptual framework of a
sociological theory of constitutional values and normativity, I, therefore, want
to introduce the problem of political constitutionalism and its value legitimation by briefly revisiting the works of modern art and literature.

Modernity and modernist avant-gardes were anti-moralist and aimed their
hammer blows at societal values. Marinetti's *Futurist Manifesto* summarised
it in the following words: 'We intend to destroy museums, libraries, academies
of every sort, and to fight against moralism, feminism, and every utilitarian or
opportunistic cowardice.'[1]

The manifesto was a first salvo in the avant-gardes' attack on conventional
morality in the name of humanity's new order. However, this attack, rather than
denying the place of morality in modern society speeding up towards its future,
merely represents alternative moralism building on the destructive potential and
constructive promises of moral judgements. It actually had little in common
with the Nietzschean hammer of philosophy because of merely presenting
utopian moral and political alternatives to the existing order.

Marinetti's manifesto thus inadvertently proved the explosive nature of all
modern morality described so powerfully by the Czech novelist Karel Čapek in
his dystopian science-fiction novel *The Absolute at Large* written in 1922.

In this book, Čapek depicts a modern society which invented a reactor that,
apart from providing cheap energy, produces the absolute as a by-product. As a
spiritual essence, the industrially produced absolute appears in many different
forms of industrial production and therefore turns people into the agents of the
good in many different forms. It subsequently leads to the moral disaster and the
most horrible global war driven by nationalist and religious fundamentalisms,
each of them fighting for their different versions of the good.

Soberly commenting on the pitiful state of things and the real God, the
entrepreneur Bondy, who first industrially produced the absolute, grasped the
paradox of moral absolutism in the following words:

> This true God is far too big. ... He is infinite. That's just where the trouble lies.
> You see, everyone measures off a certain amount of Him and then thinks it is the
> entire God. Each one appropriates a little fringe or fragment of Him and then thinks
> he possesses the whole of Him ... In order to convince himself that God is wholly
> his, he has to go and kill all the others. Just for that very reason, because it means so
> much to him to have the whole of God and the whole of the truth. That's why he can't

---

[1] FT Marinetti, 'The Founding and Manifesto of Futurism' in L Rainey, C Poggi, L Wittman (eds),
Futurism: an anthology (New Haven, Yale University Press, 2009) 49–53, at 51.

bear anyone else to have any other God or any other truth. If he once allowed that, he would have to admit that he himself has only a few wretched metres or gallons or sackloads of divine truth.[2]

Čapek's reflection on morality and fanaticism shows as much the destructive potential of morality as its impossibility to integrate into modern society. Moral values and arguments represent the *hot* dramatic aspect in modern society and its politics. However, the permanent process of transvaluation of values and the process's value itself haunt modern individuals and society in which absolute values become extremely explosive and can only be presented as relative normative expectations.

Čapek's story reveals the other side because it also shows that objective validity of the scientific reason and its legitimation capacity are weakened due to the reason's loss of subjective meaning. What Max Weber famously called *stahlhartes Gehäuse*, commonly referred to as the iron cage of increased rationalisation of modern life driven by efficiency, calculation, industrial production and bureaucratic control, constitutes the *icy* world[3] in which human action and interaction are deprived of their existential value. It is exactly this cage of rationality and utilitarianism that Marinetti wanted to destroy in his futuristic vision.

Drawing on Čapek's dystopian vision of the modern industrial world, it is possible to say that hot moral fanaticism and icy rational functionalism both respond to the situation of humankind after its murder of God. Friedrich Nietzsche's notorious and tirelessly quoted and misinterpreted comment on the death of God does not merely depict an ontological condition of modernity. 'God is dead! God remains dead! And we have killed him! How can we console ourselves, the murderers of all murderers!'[4] – these four crucial sentences in Nietzsche's *Gay Science* actually describe the actively self-imposed loss of the absolute meaning and validity of being which constitutes existential and moral discontents.

Divine mercy is substituted for by moral fanaticism constituting what Zygmunt Bauman called 'explosive communities'[5] pursuing mutually exclusive and conflicting moral absolutes and hot universals in the relative and pluralistic modern social condition.

II. THE LAW'S SELF-VALIDATION: A COMMENT ON NORMATIVISM

Modern humanity has been profoundly shaken in the course of its short history and philosophers, political and legal theorists and moralists of all kinds have

---

[2] K Čapek, *The Absolute at Large* (New York, Macmillan, 1927) 266 (ch 27).

[3] Weber spoke of 'the polar night of icy darkness'. See M Weber, *Political Writings* [ed Peter Lassman; trans Ronald Speirs] (Cambridge, Cambridge University Press, 1994) xvi.

[4] F Nietzsche, *The Gay Science: With a Prelude in Rhymes and an Appendix of Songs* (Cambridge, Cambridge University Press, 2001 [originally published in German in 1887]) 120 (s 125).

[5] Z Bauman, *Liquid Modernity* (London, Polity, 2000) 193–4.

been looking for the possibility of ethical bonds and solidarity in this situation.[6] Legalist normativism was born out of societal risks of *hot* moralism and promised the *icy* value-free and objectively valid legality and its scientific reflection – the pure theory of law.[7]

In Kelsen's theory, deontology was strictly separated from ontology of law. The Kantian notion of 'pure' science[8] was used to separate a priori pure science of legal concepts and norms from empirical sciences of law, such as sociology, anthropology and history of law. Description of positive law was distinguished from its evaluation by philosophical and sociological notions of natural law, social justice etc. The pure legal theory was to treat norms as deontic data preceding their interpretation and application by legal agents. It was to objectively describe what jurists do when they make, interpret and apply statutes, precedents, administrative regulations and other sources of legal norms.

The pure theory's normativism can be summarised as *no values, no facts, no cognitions, only norms*. Positive law and its theory were to be purified of natural and social justice and normatively separated from its social and intellectual environment.[9] Instead of the limited law and morality separation thesis typical of modern legal positivism drawing on the classic liberal difference between private views of the good and public views of the right, Kelsen's normativist theory radically expanded the separation thesis to politics, economy, religion, philosophy and other external evaluations and critical assessments of positive law.[10]

According to this expanded separation thesis, law is to be purified from everything that is not law and has to be theorised from its internal sources of normativity. It is exactly in this sense that Kelsen's functionalism, despite all criticisms of Weber's sociology, heavily draws on the Weberian distinction between the sociological and juridical method.[11] Positive law and its theory were to be not only value-free but also fact-free and operating through the legal system's normative self-closure.

In the spirit of modern liberalism, Kelsen argued that law's function was not to enforce moral values and virtues but normatively organise society.

---

[6] For comparison, see Jan Patočka's elaboration on the concept of 'solidarity of the shaken' as a response to Nietzsche's modernity after deicide. J Patočka, *Heretical Essays in the Philosophy of History* (Chicago IL, Open Court, 1999), 130.

[7] H Kelsen, *Pure Theory of Law* (Berkeley CA, University of California Press, 1967) 1; for recent theoretical assessments of Kelsen's theory, see, ie, L Vinx, *Kelsen's Pure Theory of Law. Legality and Legitimacy* (Oxford, Oxford University Press, 2007) 10; C Kletzer, *The Idea of a Pure Theory of Law: An Interpretation and Defence* (Oxford, Hart Publishing, 2018) 11.

[8] SL Paulson, 'The Neo-Kantian Dimension in Kelsen's Theory of Law' (1992) 12 *Oxford Journal of Legal Studies*, 311–32.

[9] For critical assessment, see SL Paulson (2019): Hans Kelsen on legal interpretation, legal cognition, and legal science, *Jurisprudence*, DOI: 10.1080/20403313.2019.1604887.

[10] C Kletzer, (n 7), 120.

[11] For further analysis, see J Přibáň, *Sovereignty in Post-Sovereign Society: A Systems Theory of European Constitutionalism* (London, Routledge, 2015) 67–91.

Law as a normative order also was not to be treated as a political instrument and a matter of individual or collective will because political decisions and judgements already depend on normative conditions and constraints of legality.

In this respect, Kelsen's separation of legal and moral normativity followed the common structural disentanglement of the value-neutral facts of social institutions or human action from the values attached to these facts by legitimation narratives or individual agents. Moral values are not sources of legal normativity and legal obligations are not specific forms of moral obligations. The binding force of law does not derive from its moral substance.

In modern society, values often compete and conflict with each other and legality is considered a force neutralising these conflicts. A pluralistic value structure is thus contained by a monistic system of positive law in which legality is the only and ultimate source of validity.[12] The value neutrality of legality as an intrinsic value of law and 'legal morality' but only in the functional sense because it, rather than legitimising legal rules by substantive moral values, effectively leads to the societal goal of subjecting humans and their conduct to the governance by general rules and principles.[13]

The separation of law and morality is important for political liberals because legality can be functionalised as a guarantor of societal order in the modern pluralistic situation in which the classic view of society integrated by one set of moral values and principles looks increasingly counterfactual and politically dangerous. It is equally important for legal theorists realising that the positive law's functionality and existence is neither guaranteed, nor created by a higher normative order or will.

The separation of legal and moral normativity, therefore, does not necessarily lead to the cynical reduction of law as a mere systemically organised force channelling political interests and protecting social privileges of powerful elites. Law is neither morality, nor politics and the most challenging question of legal theory becomes the positive law's self-creation and normative self-governance.[14] In this sense, Hart's formulation of the rule of recognition is no different from Fuller's older inquiry into 'the law in quest of itself'[15] and subsequent definition of internal morality of law which, rather than focusing on the law's moral substance, defines conditions of law's societal functionality and operative force.[16]

---

[12] P Gragl, *Legal Monism: Law, Philosophy, and Politics* (Oxford, Oxford University Press, 2018).

[13] See especially Fuller's definition of the morality of law as 'the enterprise of subjecting human conduct to the governance of rules.' LL Fuller, *The Morality of Law. Revised edition* (New Haven, Yale University Press, 1969) 96.

[14] B van Roermund, 'Norm-claims, Validity and Self-Reference' in LD d'Almeida, J Gardner, L Green (eds), *Kelsen Revisited: New Essays on the Pure Theory of Law* (Oxford, Oxford University Press, 2013) 11–42.

[15] LL Fuller, *The Law in Quest of Itself* (Chicago IL, The Foundation Press, 1940).

[16] LL Fuller, (n 13). Fuller interchangeably speaks of 'the inner morality of the law' (p 42) and 'the internal morality of law' (p 4).

III. DEMOCRACY AND RELATIVISM

Unlike many political liberals and legal theorists, Kelsen, however, did not believe in the capacity of reason to establish what is right and just and advanced the separation of normative and cognitive elements in law and politics. Criticising moral and cognitive universalism, he considered democracy a political settlement fitting the relativistic and pluralistic condition of modern society.[17]

Instead of the possibility of a reasoned and consensually constituted common good pursued and protected through the popular will, Kelsen argued that democracy merely means a government of direct or indirect participation of the people on the basis of majority decisions. Against strong political and moral intuitions, he separated value judgements from democratic decision-making and stated:

> That value judgments have only relative validity-one of the basic principles of philo-sophical relativism-implies that opposite value judgments are neither logically nor morally excluded. One of the fundamental principles of democracy is that everybody has to respect the political opinion of everybody else, since all are equal and free. Tolerance, minority rights, freedom of speech, and freedom of thought, so charac-teristic of democracy, have no place within a political system based on the belief in absolute values.[18]

Kelsen's concept of democracy draws on moral relativism ruling out the possibility of constituting the objectively reasoned and absolutely valid common good. This is consistent with his critique of all metaphysical foundations of democracy. According to Kelsen, freedom and equality are not normative foundations and preconditions of polity but materialise through political procedures of direct or indirect participation. Democracy thus 'designates a government in which the people directly or indirectly participate, that is to say, a government exercised by majority decisions of a popular assembly or of a body or bodies of individuals or even by a single individual elected by the people.'[19]

Closely associated with the relativistic and procedural concept of democracy is Kelsen's critique of the state as 'a mysterious substance ... and ... a transcendental reality beyond rational, empirical cognition'.[20] Instead of this absolutist notion of statehood as the ultimate meaning of human existence, Kelsen promotes the relativist concept of the state as 'a specific normative order regulating the mutual behavior of men'.[21] The state does not constitute a higher sphere of human existence. It does not have a collective essence which could claim absolute sovereignty over its relative subjects. It, rather, treats individuals as subjects of legally enforceable rights and obligations.

---

[17] See L Vinx, (n 7), 134.
[18] H Kelsen, 'Foundations of Democracy' (1955) 66(1) *Ethics*, 1–101, at 38–39.
[19] Ibid, 2–3.
[20] Ibid, 33.
[21] Ibid.

The state is defined through its law.[22] Like other legal concepts, the objective juridical concept of the state has to be strictly separated from the intersubjective sociological and cultural or moral conceptualisations of the state and normative order.[23] Interaction among individuals and their subjective and intersubjective meanings attributed to the state authority must not be confused with the objective scientific 'purity' of legal concepts and their theoretical meaning.

According to Kelsen, moral absolutism is the foundation of totalitarianism. Democracy, however, flourishes in moral relativism. His relativist critique of the absolute notion of political sovereignty[24] was an intrinsic part of the normativist perspective illuminated by the concept of *the Grundnorm – the basic norm*. The basic norm is self-referential in the sense that it authorises all law as its internal, non-cognitive and ultimate source of normativity. While the law-making process integrates political and ethical debates as external inputs, the internal outcome is always law represented by its pure normativity.[25] The normative character of law can be explained by the positive law's basic assumption of bindingness operating independently of some higher normativity of classic laws of nature, eternal rules of morality, divine will or its modern equivalent of general will of the people.

This internal constitution of law's meaning through its basic norm was to be used for the purposes of legal science formulating the basic assumption of law's content as a normative social system. The basic norm is an epistemological foundation of Kelsen's pure legal theory. However, it is exposed to the infinite regress embedded in the question of authorising a more basic norm authorising the basic norm's authority etc. The basic norm as a legal fiction cannot be used as the source of real authorisation of positive law. Its transcendental-logical character[26] is incommensurable with immanent reality of positive law and its enforcement. The strict separation of 'ought' of norms from 'is' of facts plus factual non-existence of the basic norm, therefore, make it impossible to answer the question of power and obedience of law and its legitimacy.

IV. SYNCRETISM OF POST-POSITIVIST LEGAL THEORY

Historical developments, political ideologies and total war disasters of the twentieth century are typically used as a starting point of fundamental criticisms of the value-free concept of legality, formalist normativism and legal

---

[22] H Kelsen, (n 7), 286–290.
[23] Ibid, 66.
[24] See J Přibáň, (n 11), 75.
[25] See H Kelsen, (n 7), 198.
[26] Ibid, 201.

science as well as the positivistic separation of law and morality. Once again, positivist ideas and concepts of law critically meet the principle of natural or non-legal justice.[27]

Distinctions between external and internal perspectives of law, legal formalism and realism or norms and values of positive law have been challenged and criticised as 'ideological positivism'.[28] Meaning of law, rather than inside the legal system, is searched for beyond its normative limits in 'real life' and legal self-validation is criticised and replaced by external validation by universal values and normativity of cosmopolitan rights and ethics. As Ronald Dworkin reminded us, '[V]alue and content have become entangled.'[29]

In an essay commenting on the anniversary of the US Declaration of Independence, HLA Hart even critically contemplated the possibility of the end of an epoch of legal positivism informed by Bentham's philosophy of utilitarianism and the coming age of legal theory founded in the concept of rights representing 'a new form of the ancient theory that there are vital conceptual connections between law and principles of justice which justify the law, to which, it is said, positivism has been blind and blinded its victims.'[30]

Current legal theories certainly enjoy a renaissance of moralism and return to the discourse of ethics, values and principles of human rights and dignity. Described as 'post-positivist',[31] these theories abandon both the law and morality separation and the scientific purity of legal research conducted independently of positive law as its object.[32]

Legal theorists, otherwise methodologically drawing on the tradition of positivism, normativism and analytical jurisprudence, commonly accept that the validity of laws depends on the negative principle or requirement of avoiding gross injustice which is institutionalised through the protection of human rights. They believe that post-positivist legal theories are on the right track as regards 'the rendering of objectivity in terms of moral justifiability.'[33]

Instead of purism and normativism, post-positivist theories are typical of syncretism justifying non-positive legal principles as moral validations of

---

[27] For an example of recent polemics between positivism and post-positivism or supra-positivist legal theories, see, ie, G Pavlakos (ed), *Law, Rights and Discourse: The Legal Philosophy of Robert Alexy* (Oxford, Hart Publishing, 2007); see also NE Simmonds, *Law as a Moral Idea* (Oxford, Oxford University Press, 2007); S Taekema, *The Concept of Ideals in Legal Theory* (The Hague, Kluwer, 2003).

[28] The concept of 'ideological positivism' was introduced by Norberto Bobbio.

[29] R Dworkin, *Law's Empire* (London, Fontana Press, 1986) 48.

[30] HLA Hart, '1776–1976: Law in the Perspective of Philosophy' in HLA Hart, *Essays in Jurisprudence and Philosophy* (Oxford, Clarendon Press, 1983) 145–58, at 148.

[31] See, ie, N MacCormick, *Institutions of Law: An Essay in Legal Theory* (Oxford, Oxford University Press, 2007) 5.

[32] K Füsser, 'Farewell to 'legal positivism': The separation thesis unravelling', in RP George (ed.), *The Autonomy of Law: Essays on Legal Positivism* (Oxford, Oxford University Press, 1996) 119–62.

[33] A Somek, *The Legal Relation: Legal theory After Legal Positivism* (Cambridge, Cambridge University Press, 2017) 4.

legal normativity.[34] Even theories profoundly influenced by both legal and sociological positivism, such as institutionalist theory of law, return to the Enlightenment, its moral aspirations and liberal traditions blending political, moral and legal philosophies with proto-theories of modern society.[35]

This re-anthropologising view of both the individual and collective subjects is summarised by Neil MacCormick in the following words:

> Human societies are societies of persons with a capacity to realize moral autonomy in their lives. This can occur in conditions of civil society (perhaps in others as well, but certainly in civil society), where civil interaction of persons is possible. Civil society requires some form of law, and the legal order of a constitutional state, or law-state, is certainly a key element in securing civility. But other key elements are economic relations and politics.[36]

The concept of society as the sum of interacting individuals pursuing their moral existence under the law's protection still appears attractive to jurists and legal theorists despite all its structural simplifications, theoretical inadequacies and methodological eclecticism. Similarly, Dworkinian versions of the moral unity of law and politics formulated by the concept of rights continue to be favoured by those who are tempted to act and judge as if they were Dworkin's judge-Hercules or, at least, his doctrinal advisors and intellectual leaders lecturing on 'sovereign virtue'.[37] Instead of protecting the public from moral explosions, it is the system of positive law that is expected to enforce particular visions of the right and public morality on the totality of society.[38]

While attracted by a number of thoughts and concepts elaborated by the post-Enlightenment and post-humanist autopoietic social systems theory, such as the autonomy of legal reason, MacCormick and other theorists of contemporary legal institutionalism and post-positivism remain ambivalent as regards the self-validation of law as well as the relativisation and marginalisation of values in law and other social systems.[39] The ambivalence of embracing systemic autonomy of the functionally differentiated system of positive law and refusing to accept the anti-essentialist nature of the cultural subsystem of values is a typical mark of contemporary theories of the legal system.

---

[34] J Waldron, 'Normative (or Ethical) Positivism' in J Coleman (ed), *Hart's Postscript* (Oxford, Oxford University Press, 2001) 411–33; W Waluchow, 'The Many Faces of Legal Positivism' (1998) 48 *University of Toronto Law Journal,* 387–449.

[35] M La Torre, 'Institutional Theories and Institutions of Law: On Neil MacCormick's Savoury Blend of Legal Institutionalism' in M Del Mar and Z Bankowski (eds) *Law as Institutional Normative Order* (Aldershot, Ashgate, 2009) 67–82.

[36] N MacCormick, (n 31), 303.

[37] R Dworkin, *Sovereign Virtue: The Theory and Practice of Equality* (Cambridge MS, Harvard University Press, 2000).

[38] J Simmons, *Moral Principles and Political Obligations* (Princeton NJ, Princeton University Press, 1979).

[39] N MacCormick, (ed) *Constructing Legal Systems* (Dordrecht, Kluwer, 1997).

In short, legal theorists find it hard to accept the uncertainty and contingency of values and continue to treat society as what Zygmunt Bauman called 'a factory of morality'[40] and see the legal system as its central machine.

V. A FACTORY OF MORALITY, OR DIGITAL IRONY
FOR THE COSMOPOLITAN AGE?

There are many diverse arguments fuelling this machine of morality's overproduction but most of them address the problem of legal principles and values in the context of globalisation and transnationalisation of law which opens new routes for arguments of cosmopolitanism, global governance and constitutionalism. The classic questions of how and why people obey rules and respect principles and accompanying doctrines of practical reason and rights are now confronted by the emergence of powerful and often even coercive institutions at transnational and global levels. Legal reasoning thus gets framed by transnational operations recursively calling for the global rule of law and cosmopolitan rights.[41]

Cosmopolitan philosophy typically contrasts the universal validity of reason to the particular validity of patriotic and group bonds and sentiments.[42] However, cosmopolitan ethics have also been promoted by social sciences and sociology which always perceived modernisation as a global process of worldwide social integration, organisation and association. According to sociologists from Emile Durkheim[43] to Ulrich Beck,[44] the economic, political and technological unification of industrial and post-industrial societies leads to the critique of methodological nationalism and corresponding constitution of global ethics, cosmopolitan law and polity.[45]

In this philosophical and social theoretical context, normative legal theories of global cosmopolitanism represent a middle ground between prescriptive philosophies of cosmopolitan law and descriptive theories of global society. As Alexander Somek puts it, the cosmopolitan constitution is expected 'to reconcile the particularity of political communities with the universal values of freedom and equality.'[46] This, however, requires going beyond normative limits of

---

[40] Z Bauman, *Modernity and the Holocaust* (Cambridge, Polity Press, 1989) 170.

[41] V Rodriguez-Blanco, 'What Makes a Transnational Rule of Law? Understanding the Logos and Values of Human Action in Transnational Law' in KE Himma, M Jovanovic, B Spaic (eds) *Unpacking Normativity: Conceptual, Normative and Descriptive Issues*, (Oxford, Hart Publishing, 2018) 209–26.

[42] M Nussbaum, 'Kant and Cosmopolitanism' in J Bohman and M. Lutz-Bachmann (eds) *Perpetual Peace: essays on Kant's cosmopolitan ideal* (Cambridge, Mass, The MIT Press, 1997) 25–58.

[43] E Durkheim, *Professional Ethics and Civic Morals* (London, Routledge, 1957), chs 6 and 9.

[44] U Beck, 'The Cosmopolitan Perspective: sociology of the second age of modernity' (2000) 51(1) *British Journal of Sociology*, 79–105.

[45] R Fine, *Cosmopolitanism* (London, Routledge, 2007) 6–14.

[46] A Somek, *The Cosmopolitan Constitution* (Oxford, Oxford University Press, 2014) 281.

legalism and embracing global politics with its rapidly evolving and transforming forces and powers.

Some scholars argue that legalism and liberal constitutionalism driven by the goal of removing rights out of politics and legally enforcing them as part of substantive public morality actually both undermines democratic legitimacy and gives rise to arbitrary rule.[47] Others, like Somek, aim at reconstructing cosmopolitan values, politics and legal theory in the global societal constellation. Announcing the eventual demise of both legal positivism and natural law theories, a new theoretical framework of legal constructivism drawing on the typology of law as a social relation is formulated to address traditional jurisprudential problems of polity, authority, technocracy and coercion in the context of both moral universalism beyond particular legal institutions and legal particularisms of universal rights and obligations.

The use of social theoretical imaginary and concept of *relationship*[48] helps to reformulate the law's institutional and intellectual autonomy by declaring the difference between traditional doctrines of positivism and natural law obsolete and relegating them to the status of ironical judgements constituted at globalised meeting points of legal and moral reasoning. Morality persists in positive law because it resolves matters of right and wrong. Nevertheless, the relationship between law and morality becomes a matter of 'serene irony' because moral reasoning and its universalism cannot remain unaffected by particular legal institutions and context.[49]

The post-positivist distinction and theoretical conflicts between positivist legalism and supra-positivist moralism actually signify the societal circularity of particularism and universalism. The moral factory of positive law is transformed to the digital processing of ironic meanings and forces Dworkin's Hercules to laugh at his folly of objectivism.

VI. FROM PURE LAW AND SOVEREIGN VIRTUES TO THE DIRTY LIFE-WORLD: ON THE CRISIS OF THE SCIENTIFIC REASON

This brief sketch of recent post-positivist legal theories, their value foundations and conceptual syncretism shows that the relationship between legal and moral normativity hardly can be resolved within a normative theory of legal principles, values and moral justifications. Instead, it is necessary to philosophically

---

[47] R Bellamy, *Political Constitutionalism: A Republican Defence of the Constitutionality of Democracy* (Cambridge, Cambridge University Press, 2007) 8.

[48] For sociological and phenomenological analysis of social relationships, see especially classic works of Alfred Schutz. A Schutz, *On Phenomenology and Social Relations. Selected Writings* [edited by HR Wagner] (Chicago IL, University of Chicago Press, 1970) 163–235.

[49] A Somek (n 33), 128–9.

examine the complex relationship between normativity, validity and reasoning and question its social and legal theoretical meaning.[50]

To move beyond the simplicity of the law and morality separation theses and understand the above shifts and developments in legal theory beyond conventional schematisations, argumentative frameworks and conceptual clichés surrounding different schools of legal positivism, supra-positivism and post-positivism, it is helpful to recall the following historical paradox: exactly at the time when Hans Kelsen synthesised his earlier theoretical views and published them in *Pure Theory of Law* in 1934, Edmund Husserl criticaly revised his earlier philosophical views and idea of 'pure phenomenology'.[51]

This paradox was driven by different assessments of the scientific reason and its capacity to objectively validate conditions of our social existence. While Kelsen elaborated on the Kantian notion of pure science in the context of law and chose the philosophical position promising to uphold the objective validity of legal science by its methodological and conceptual self-insulation from the relativistic universe of social facts and moral values, Husserl abandoned his earlier phenomenological critique of positivism and engaged in a more general critique of objectivity of the scientific reason by adopting the concept of the intersubjectively shared life-world.

Reflecting on the modern paradoxes of reason, science and moral existence and paraphrasing Goethe's Faust, Edmund Husserl described as *crisis* the absence of the higher meaning in the world in which everything supposedly unconditional and absolute turns out to be relative and conditioned by history, society and culture. He grasped the crisis in the following question:

> But can the world, and human existence in it, truthfully have a meaning if the sciences recognize as true only what is objectively established in this fashion, and if history has nothing more to teach us than that all the shapes of the spiritual world, all the conditions of life, ideals, norms upon which man relies, form and dissolve themselves like fleeting waves, that it always was and ever will be so, that again and again reason must turn into nonsense, and well-being into misery?[52]

Husserl's late and unfinished book *The Crisis of European Sciences and Transcendental Phenomenology* drew on lectures delivered in Vienna and Prague in May and November 1935. In this work, Husserl focused on expansive tendencies of the modern science, its particular historical and social success and capacity to dissolve the philosophy's claim of universal validity and ideals.[53] Instead of insisting on a philosophically rigorous reason and objective validity of pure phenomenology, he, however, elaborated on the alternative concept of

---

[50] B Tamanaha, 'The Contemporary Relevance of Legal Positivism' (2007) 32 *Australian Journal of Legal Philosophy*, 1–38.

[51] E Husserl, *Ideas: General Introduction to Pure Phenomenology* (London, Routledge, 2012) 44.

[52] E Husserl, *The Crisis of European Sciences and Transcendental Phenomenology: An Introduction to Phenomenological Philosophy* (Evanston, Northwestern University Press, 1970) 6–7.

[53] Ibid, 11.

the life-world (*Lebenswelt*) – the world of intersubjective experiences and activities and the pre-theoretical meaning of life countering the critical expansion of the scientific reason.

Husserl's shift from pure phenomenology to the life-world philosophy was driven by urgent feelings of societal and cultural crisis and the questions of what modern science can teach us about the distinction between reason and nonsense or rationality and irrationality and what it has to say about the humankind and its freedom to make such distinction. In this respect, one can also ask what the modern scientific reason can say about society in which this freedom is operationalised and where the power of rational judgements and social engineering increases coevally with the power of irrational feelings of togetherness and communal bonds.

Husserl's defence of philosophy as a spiritual 'struggle for the meaning of man'[54] at modern times dominated by the scientific and instrumental reason represents a critique of both naive rationalisms of the Enlightenment and irrational responses to the modern process of rationalisation. Calling modern irrationalism 'the rationality of "lazy reason"',[55] Husserl famously described philosophers as 'functionaries of mankind'[56] unlimited in their searches and struggles for the meaning and true being of man and humanity by private or cultural goals. According to him, such a new philosophy leading to the authentic self-understanding of humanity is impossible to formulate as just another philosophical conceptualisation of the crisis of modernity. It becomes possible only through its execution.[57] Theoretical scepticism thus meets the hope of a new philosophy validated outside its domain in structures and experiences of the life-world.

Husserl's critical response to the modernity caged in instrumental rationality and the scientific reason was echoed in a great number of philosophical, social, political and legal theoretical works from Martin Heidegger, Max Scheler and Alfred Schutz to Maurice Merleau-Ponty, Jan Patočka and Edith Stein. His philosophy influenced both Jürgen Habermas and Niklas Luhmann and thus informed debates about the role of social theory and its contribution to the legitimacy of modern society in the last five decades.[58]

These highly influential and well documented debates gradually evolved and incorporated a number of legal theoretical and philosophical themes and problems.[59] Habermas integrated the concept of the life-world into his

---

[54] Ibid, 14.
[55] Ibid, 16.
[56] Ibid, 17.
[57] Ibid, 18.
[58] J Habermas and N Luhmann, *Theorie der Gesellschaft oder Sozialtechnologie – was leistet die Systemforschung?* (Frankfurt am Main, Suhrkamp Verlag, 1971).
[59] PF Kjaer, 'Systems in Context: On the Outcome of the Habermas/Luhmann-Debate' (2006) *Ancilla Iuris*, 66–77.

communicative action and the systemic rationality of constitutional democracy[60] and Luhmann responded to this normative critique by reinterpreting Husserl's concept of the life-world within the framework of his autopoietic social systems theory.[61] While Habermas pursued the goal of constituting the discourse ethics 'between facts and norms' as a superstructure of the legal system,[62] Luhmann remained sceptical of the possibility of constituting any foundations of modern society by critical reason and theoretical knowledge. Instead, he considered legal theory the subsystem of positive law's normative self-description. According to this view, the philosophical or theoretical concept of legitimacy of law is redundant because what Husserl and many others before and after him would call 'life', 'spirit', 'morality' or 'political integrity' of law is already operating in the self-validating and self-legitimising system of positive law.

VII. NORMATIVITY AND MEANING: A SYSTEMS THEORETICAL VIEW

These philosophical and social theoretical encounters with the life-world and their historical developments and transformations are very important for legal theory because they show that problems of legitimation and its crisis are part of the more general problem of meaning unlimited by questions of legal normativity and value pluralism.

Luhmann's autopoietic social systems reformulates the difference between normative and cognitive elements in positive law as the difference between the legal system's internal self-closure and external openness to the social environment. It thus radicalises both legal and sociological positivism and offers transvaluation of the life-world beyond the humanist concepts of understanding, consensus, reason, its authority and normative force. The quest for truth as the meaningful and authentic life of subjective and intersubjective experiences is replaced by the systemic concept of meaning as temporal stabilisation of contingent societal expectations.

While using Husserl's notion of meaning as the horizon of possibilities and the difference between the possible and the actual, Luhmann abandoned the transcendental subject and intersubjectivity of experiences and defined meaning in the context of immanent operations of self-referential social systems:

> [T]he phenomenon of meaning appears as a surplus of references to other possibilities of experience and action. Something stands in the focal point, at the center of intention, and all else is indicated marginally as the horizon of an "and so forth" of experience and action. In this form, everything that is intended holds open to itself the world as a whole, thus guaranteeing the actuality of the world in the form of

---

[60] J Habermas, *The Theory of Communicative Action*, 2 vols (Cambridge, Polity Press, 1987).

[61] N Luhmann, 'Die Lebenswelt – nach Rücksprache mit Phänomenologen' (1986) 72(2) *Archiv für Rechts- und Sozialphilosophie*, 176–94.

[62] J Habermas, *Between Facts and Norms* (Cambridge, Polity Press, 1996).

accessibility. Reference actualizes itself as the standpoint of reality. It refers, however, not only to what is real (or presumably real), but also to what is possible (conditionally real) and what is negative (unreal, impossible). The totality of the references presented by a meaningfully intended object offers more to hand than can in fact be actualized at any moment. Thus the form of meaning, through its referential structure, forces the next step, to selection.[63]

Luhmann critically engaged with Husserl's *Fifth Cartesian Meditation* and the problem of consciousness as the parallel self-referential knowledge of itself and external reference to phenomena. For Luhmann, this proves that the problem of reference has to be treated as the problem of 'the operative processing of the difference between self-reference and reference to others'[64] – something requiring a critique of the naively sociological treatment of key concepts, such as the subject, intersubjectivity, social action etc.

Luhmann critically praised Husserl for teaching us that to answer the question 'How is social order possible?' one cannot succeed 'by beginning with the concept of the subject.'[65] However, his theory of society represents a radical break with the humanist sociological tradition drawing on the phenomenological and hermeneutical methods inspired by Husserl's philosophy.

It is also noteworthy that Luhmann used positive law as a test case for his general theory of social systems and particularly used it to show actual meaning evolving in social systems. He criticised both doctrinal concepts of law as a static form and older biological metaphors treating the legal system as an organic whole following general laws of societal evolution.[66] According to him, all social systems including the system of positive law are constituted as normative orders not through some a priori normativity but through internal meaning constituted by 'expectations of expectations'. Social systems, therefore, cannot be identified with their normative structures.[67]

Furthermore, like legalist positivism, Luhmann's autopoietic systems theory is critical of all doctrines and theories or sociologies of law looking for external sources of positive law in natural justice, societal traditions and morality. Positivity of law means that the sources of law are intrinsic to its system.

Luhmann's theory draws on the assumption that understanding law in society assumes understanding the positivity of law as a social phenomenon. A sociological theory of law, therefore, needs to get beyond the legal theoretical debates 'restricted to the immediate legal problem of the legitimating bases of positive law.'[68] While the legal system exchanges information with its environment and communicates political, religious, moral, scientific and other societal

---

[63] N Luhmann, *Social Systems* (Stanford CA, Stanford University Press, 1995) 60.
[64] Ibid, xli.
[65] Ibid.
[66] N Luhmann, *A Sociological Theory of Law. Second Edition* (London, Routledge, 2014) 20–21.
[67] Ibid, 62.
[68] Ibid, 20.

facts, it remains normatively closed and its internal operations are independent of these external facts.

This autopoiesis is not a unique feature of law but something common to all systems in modern society as they evolve through self-constitution, self-description and self-validation. Legal positivism is just a specific example of sociological positivism describing all social subsystems as internally constituted, functionally differentiated from each other and evolving through normative self-reference.

Nevertheless, there is a profound difference between legal positivism and the autopoietic systems theory's understanding of norms and normativity. Luhmann admits that the world can be experienced only through meaning but adds that it cannot be guaranteed by the transcendental reason and morality or political consensus and equal participation. Normativity can be neither an external, nor internal guarantor of the system's validity and functioning. Instead of relying on the transcendentally anchored basic norm, the system of positive law operationalises its normativity as a counterfactual stabilisation and generalisation of meaning.

The basic norm is replaced by the basic process of functional differentiation. The obvious fact that social systems produce norms does not mean that they are normative structures. Normativity is a variable with different systems and norms function only as immanent responses to generalizstions of meaning which counterfactually stabilise these generalisations to the extent that they become necessary. According to Luhmann, the basic problem of social systems, their structure and temporality subsequently shifts 'from the concept of norms to the concept of generalization.'[69]

VIII. SYSTEMIC MEANING OF LEGAL NORMATIVITY: A CRITIQUE OF ONTOLOGY AND DEONTOLOGY

Luhmann reinterpreted Husserl's phenomenological notions of meaning and intention and offered the systems theoretical definition of meaning as a referential context of potential alternatives related to societal intentions and their expectations. It is the system that constitutes its environment as a horizon of meaning for itself and there is no chance of constituting one universal environment because there are only many system-relative environments and a plurality of multiple system-environment differences. There is no environment 'in itself/an sich' because specific systems only have specific contacts with the environment constituted by them.[70] Only in this sense, 'the closure of the self-referential order is synonymous here with *the infinite openness of the world*',[71]

---

[69] N Luhmann, (n 63), 326.
[70] Ibid, 101.
[71] Ibid, 62.

yet this universal is validated by the blind process of societal evolution and differentiation and not the insightful philosophical reason.

According to Luhmann, the old metaphysical identity of the true and the good has been lost in modern society and its functional differentiation makes the issue of rational validation both more urgent and insoluble. An ultimate unity of societal differences guaranteed by the scientific or theoretical reason is impossible because society in its totality cannot gain normative distance from itself. Functional differentiation rules out the possibility of a rational identity of modern society. The autopoietic systems theory is a radical critique of both ontology and deontology and the long philosophical tradition drawing on the notions of being, truth and reason.

To some, like Jürgen Habermas, this amounts to the liquidation of reason as irrational by systems rationality and a condition in which '[F]unctionalist reason expresses itself in the ironic self-denial of a reason shrunk down to the reduction of complexity.'[72] Habermas then adds that '… with a concept of meaning conceived in functionalist terms, the internal connection between meaning and validity dissolves',[73] but Luhmann dryly states that 'some people would like to mount a simplistic attack here using ethics'[74] while others would be recalling metaphysical concepts of the state, revolution and so on to generalise and externally validate internal meaning generated by specific social systems.

According to him, it is impossible to constitute modern society by a single principle. Social systems are not preconditions of this order and norms are not the ultimate explanation of this order's facticity – a theoretical position Luhmann described as 'the skeptical abstinence vis-á-vis norm-centered theory' while ironically commenting that '[T]he recently erected temples of emancipation are already overgrown with weeds, and the faithful appear to have abandoned the cult.'[75]

Legal and any other social meaning is constituted by neither the objective theoretical reason, nor the life-world of intersubjectively shared intentions. Meaning, rather, is considered the contingent expectation of other people's intentions. The constitution of social systems evolves as the self-referential constitution of internal systemic meaning independent of its empirical societal environment.

In the context of positive law, Luhmann showed little interest in legal theory enclosed in norms, concepts and their interpretation. Instead, he addressed the problem of systemic meaning of legal normativity. In his view, normativity does not constitute the legal system. The system is not determined by higher societal norms or transcendental principles, but by its relation to society. This is a relation of functional differentiation in which the legal system and its social

---

[72] J Habermas, *The Philosophical Discourse of Modernity* (Cambridge, Polity Press, 1987) 373.
[73] Ibid.
[74] N Luhmann, (n 63), 442.
[75] Ibid, 325.

environment become richer in possibilities and law, therefore, must be structurally compatible with the growing complexity of society. This compatibility is achieved by the positive law's autonomy and autopoiesis of its terminology, methodology and dogma.[76]

The sociological theory of law's job is then to externally observe and explain how this autopoietic legal system constitutes its positive methods and dogma, functions and internally differentiates roles, professions, expertise etc. The difference between 'ought' and 'is', so central for legal positivists, subsequently can be reformulated as the difference between two forms of societal expectations, namely norms and cognitions.[77] The difference between fulfilment and disappointment of expectations thus translates as the normative difference between conformity and deviance and the cognitive difference between knowledge and ignorance.

As Luhmann comments,

> structural formation is not preformed in a principle, an *arché*, nor does it occur according to objective historical laws that establish how state A is transformed into state B. Instead, the decisive point seems to be the translation of problems in system formation into differences.[78]

Meaning of a legal norm is then generated as much by factual conformity as by counterfactual deviance. It is a matter of the paradoxical necessity to include the difference between such opposites which is radically different from the Kelsenian theoretical approach based on the strict separation of norms and cognitions and the methodological supremacy of normative expectations over factual deviances.

Furthermore, the autopoietic systems theory represents a radical critique of the philosophical tradition of the morally and intellectually autonomous subject as well as the notion of society as a common sphere normatively constituted by rational intersubjective communication. Luhmann stated that:

> Binding oneself to norms or values is a pervasive aspect of social life. It does not, however, come about because human beings value living in a social order and honor this through a kind of constitutional consensus.[79]

As regards the system of positive law, the consensus theories of truth and political legitimacy cannot explain the social fact that in functionally differentiated societies, meaning verified in one system can be negated in other systems and negations in some systems do not necessarily imply negations in the other systems.[80] For instance, legal or political negations of certain forms of scientific research do not necessarily negate its scientific verification or technological potential.

---

[76] Ibid, 18–19.
[77] Ibid, 320–321.
[78] Ibid, 324.
[79] Ibid, 326.
[80] Ibid, 91.

IX. LEGALITY OF VALUES AND LEGALITY AS A VALUE:
CONCLUDING REMARKS ON THE CIRCULARITY OF MORAL
UNIVERSALISM AND LEGAL PARTICULARISM

Comparing contemporary sociological and legal theory, it is possible to detect a
similar asymmetry like the one between Husserl's critical reflections on the scientific reason and pure phenomenology and Kelsen's quest of pure legal science.
While social systems theory engages in a post-humanist critique of normative
reason and critical theory to address the complexity of contemporary societies, post-positivist legal and sociological theories openly adopt the humanist
position and reductively draw on principles and norms of cosmopolitanism,
liberalism, socialism and other ideological formulas of justice.[81]

   In the section on post-positivist legal theory, I critically focused on the latest
reformulations of the ancient and classic conflict between legal positivism
and natural law and concluded that they are part of the law's quest of its self-
constitution and self-referential governance of its own creation and evolution.
According to positivists, law may be expressing moral ideals and values, yet the
system of positive law requires internal legal justification of its operative power.
Against this view, post-positivists claim that law incorporates moral ideas and
justifications which cannot be ignored by legality and represent the internal part
of the law's self-constitution.

   Critics of positivism argue that positive law can claim moral authority
and aspire to the ideal of justice even in modern society and thus functions
as a counterforce legislating one official system of values enforceable even in
the otherwise pluralistic condition of modernity. This position, however, is
denounced by legal positivists as an example of 'the romantic optimism'[82] which
ignores the societal pluralism of values and naively believes that compromises
and conflicts can be ultimately resolved if the system of positive law assumes the
role of a moral legislator and civiliser of peoples and their cultures in the spirit
of Rousseau's philosophical idealism.

   These contradictory claims of positivists and their critics actually do not
have any final solution and have to be relegated to the level of ironical judgements communicating the paradoxes evolving from conflicts between moral
absolutism and legal relativism or universal supra-positive principles and particular positive legal rules. The question whether law as a social institution can
also incorporate a moral ideal of justice and happiness does not have a definite
answer beyond the conceptual framework of legal theories and philosophies.

   The circularity of absolute and universal moral claims enforceable only
through relative and particular legal reasoning is well documented in classic legal

---

[81] For a globalised and complex overview, see, ie, KE Himma (ed), *Law, Morality, and Legal
Positivism: Proceedings of the 21st World Congress of the International Association for Philosophy
of Law and Social Philosophy. Vol. 3* (Stuttgart, Franz Steiner Verlag, 2004).
[82] HLA Hart, 'Problems of the Philosophy of Law' in HLS Hart, (n 30), 49–87, at 77.

philosophies as well as modern and post-modern legal theories. Positive law's capacity to internalise all sorts of societal facts, feelings, fictions and philosophies and qualify them by legality as solid principles, values and norms already fascinated citizens, politicians and lawyers of ancient Rome who protected such capacity as one of the most important values and ethical virtues – the rule of law and the public respect for it. Since those ancient times, the substantive value of justice and formal techniques of legality thus enjoy mutual enforcement and legitimation.

According to the critical legalist perspective, law is an autonomous system with specific ways of reasoning and arguing what is true and false, yet completely different from scientific, moral and any other social truths, arguments and reasoning. Law is typical of homeostasis[83] and has its specific regime of truth exclusively defined in terms of legality and illegality which, however, is considered societal value exactly due to its capacity of self-validation independent of moral, religious, scientific, economic and any other meanings and truths.

As Bruno Latour comments, lawyers use the adjective 'legal' to 'qualify everything they say … without even realizing that they are caught up in a tautology!'[84] because these tautologies exclude any other societal explanations and keep the strict distinction between the law's inside and the societal outside. Law is thus paradoxical because its autonomy and insulation from morality and values makes it 'a repository or warehouse for all endangered values.'[85] An ethnographic and ethnological inquiry into the making of law shows how even legally untrained politicians and junior clerks quickly adopt the formalist language and arguments of legality to insulate it from the social environment.[86]

If value is an imposition of the will upon morally divided and pluralistic modern society, lawyers and judges, like any other human beings, are constantly confronted by the problem of value-creation which always depends upon societal expectations and selection. Moral judgements claiming universal validity are thus always confronted by the particular choice of certain values and rejection of other possibilities. Ethics subsequently becomes a matter of responsibility for these choices for which there is no pre-existent moral law, code or template.

In these circumstances, interpreters will have to dominate over legislators not only in the moral domain but also in the system of positive law. As Isaiah Berlin knew, moral values may have an objective status but their plurality and incommensurability mean that they will often be controversial and conflictual and therefore require the acknowledgment of social costs of moral judgements and their universal claims in any particular system of positive law.

---

[83] B Latour, *An Inquiry into Modes of Existence: An Anthropology of the Moderns* (Cambridge Mass, Harvard University Press, 2013) 365.
[84] Ibid, 359.
[85] Ibid, 363.
[86] B Latour, *The Making of Law: An Ethnography of the Conseil d'Etat* (Cambridge, Polity Press, 2010) 32.

Furthermore, this classic structural coupling between law and morality reveals the imaginary of the rule of law itself as both a particular political technique and a universal moral ideal. Returning to Čapek's *Absolute at Large*, this moral ideality of the positive rule of law's reality shows that the system of positive law, like any other social system, actually operates in a manner similar to the reactor and, apart from an energy manifested in societal evolution, produces a by-product of its absolute value. Social systems in general and the legal system in particular can thus be observed as self-constituting its internal relative meaning while constituting external absolute values at the same time. Environment constituted by the social system's self-reference also can recursively describe the system in absolute terms as a carrier of transcendental truths and universal values despite the fact that these can only be internalised as immanent operations of specific systemic procedures.

I opened this chapter by summarising the difference between humans and societies in terms of good and evil. I want to conclude by returning to the question of whether the rule of law can be perceived as a moral ideal and universal value. One of the strongest adherents of legal positivism, Joseph Raz, argues that the rule of law hardly can be treated as an ideal because its virtue is purely negative in the sense that it 'does not cause good except through avoiding evil and the evil which is avoided is evil which could only have been caused by the law itself.'[87]

Raz correctly identifies the basic sociological fact that legality operates both as a limitation and enhancement of power and the risk of arbitrariness does not come from outside the legal system but from within its internal operations. The rule of law, therefore, is a technique of self-containment and self-restraint protecting law from its social expansionism.

One example of this expansionism is then the legality's claim of operating as a vessel of moral unity. This is why the rule of law, apart from being the legality's self-constituted power limitation, cannot claim any virtue as its moral legitimation.

Universality of moral claims in particular legal norms is a matter of social contingency, not metaphysical necessity. To this conclusion, critics of positivism, however, respond by claiming that the rule of law's value may be purely negative, yet it still is a value and not just some indifferent technique of social steering and engineering. The paradox of moral universalism enforced by particular laws thus can be endlessly constituted and reconstituted, replicated and communicated in many different forms, contexts and regimes of positive law within and beyond political constitutionalism and statehood.

---

[87] J Raz, *The Authority of Law: Essays on Law and Morality. Second Edition* (Oxford, Oxford University Press, 2009) 224.

5

Legal Realism and Legal Reasoning: A Quasi-Realist Approach

TORBEN SPAAK*

I. INTRODUCTION

LEGAL PHILOSOPHERS WHO espouse an expressivist (or non-cognitivist) meta-ethics may fairly be said to have adopted an anti-normativist position in law. This is so because they hold that moral statements do not aim to report (moral) facts or to describe the (moral) world, but aim instead to express the speaker's attitudes, preferences, or emotions and thereby to influence the audience, and because they typically also hold that there simply is no normativity in the world. Scandinavian realist Karl Olivecrona, for example, maintains that legal rules are best conceived as independent imperatives, which cannot establish legal relations but which can cause human behaviour, and that they can do this because the citizens respect the constitution and so are disposed to obey rules that can be traced back to the constitution. He also maintains that there is no such thing as the binding force of law, arguing that the reason why so many people nevertheless believe in the binding force of law is that they misunderstand the nature of legal statements and fail to see that they do nothing more than express the attitudes (preferences, emotions) of the speaker.

One could, however, object to Olivecrona's position, and to the expressivist position more generally, that it cannot account for our practice of discussing questions of legal interpretation and application. For it is clear that we often make use of fact-stating language and assume that in many cases there are right and wrong answers to legal questions. Although I accept moral anti-realism and

* Professor of Jurisprudence, Department of Law, Stockholm University. I would like to thank the audience at the Vienna Lecture of Legal Philosophy on 21 July 2018 for helpful comments on my presentation of the main ideas in this article and the participants in the advanced seminar in practical philosophy at Uppsala University for a number of very helpful comments on an earlier version of this article. I would also like to thank Robert Carroll for checking my English. As always, the responsibility for any remaining errors and imperfections in the text rests with the author alone.

am sympathetic to Olivecrona's position, I agree with the critics that the expressivist position in general is a bit problematic in this sense; and I would therefore like to consider in this chapter Simon Blackburn's quasi-realism, which aims to account, on the basis of expressivism, for any objectivist (or realist) features of moral (or legal) discourse and to earn in this way the right to discuss moral (or legal) questions using fact-stating language.

I am going to argue (1) that in order to understand legal reasoning one needs to distinguish between first-order and second-order legal statements and between two types of first-order legal statements, namely, between committed statements and detached statements, and to be clear about which type of statement one is concerned with; and (2) that, on an expressivist analysis, first-order legal statements are not normative at all. I am also going to argue (3) that Scandinavian realist Karl Olivecrona's anti-normativism is indeed problematic, (4) that expressivism in general is problematic, too, and (5) that Simon Blackburn's quasi-realism can provide us with an interesting, and in many ways attractive, account of our practice(s) of legal reasoning, conceived as resting on an expressivist foundation. However, I am also going to argue (6) that the modest version of quasi-realism is problematic, because it assumes that clashing attitudes (which are assumed to lack truth-value) are inconsistent; and (7) that ambitious quasi-realism is even more problematic, primarily (i) because it assumes that there is such a thing as a best possible set of attitudes, but also (ii) because it might be self-defeating.

I begin by saying a few words about legal statements (Section II), about expressivism (Section III), about Karl Olivecrona's anti-normativism (Section IV), and about some problems with expressivism in general (Section V). I then introduce Blackburn's quasi-realism (Sections VI–VIII) and proceed to discuss some objections to the quasi-realist analysis (Sections IX–XIV). I reiterate my conclusion in Section XV.

II. LEGAL STATEMENTS

When judges and others engage in legal reasoning, they make legal statements, that is, statements of or about the law. Typically, they maintain that a person has a legal obligation, or a legal right, or legal power, or that a statute or a precedent should or should not be interpreted and applied in a certain way, etc. They might maintain, for example, that one should decide the case in accordance with the plain meaning of the statute, unless doing so would yield an absurd or manifestly unjust result, or that one should focus on the intent of the legislature when interpreting statutes, or that like cases should be treated alike, etc. Not all legal statements are of the same type, however. As I see it, there are two main types of legal statements, namely, (i) first-order statements, which are normative (or evaluative), and (ii) second-order statements, which are descriptive, and two different types of first-order statements, namely, (ia) committed statements and (ib) detached statements:

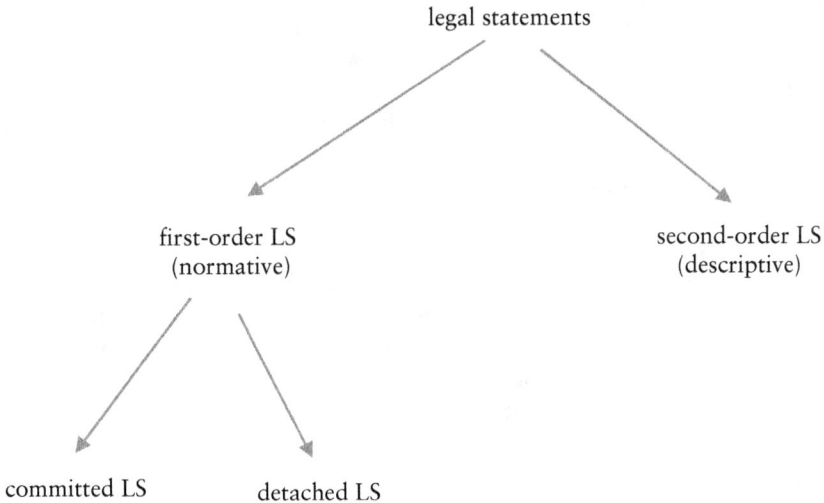

legal statements

first-order LS
(normative)

second-order LS
(descriptive)

committed LS   detached LS

Whereas a first-order legal statement is a normative (or evaluative) statement *of* law, a second-order legal statement is a descriptive statement *about* law.[1] Thus, to make a first-order legal statement is to *prescribe* (or evaluate) a course of action, or *evaluate* an action, an event, or a state of affairs, X, whereas to make a second-order legal statement is to *describe* the stance of a normative system towards X. The distinction between first-order and second-order legal statements is clearly important to legal (and moral) thinking; and even though it may seem obvious in the abstract, it may be difficult to maintain the distinction consistently when analysing legal or moral problems.

As I said, I believe there are two different types of first-order legal statements, namely committed statements and detached statements. One who makes a *committed* statement, such as 'one ought to drive on the right-hand side of the road', or 'I sentence you to 25 years in prison for aggravated murder', makes a genuine normative claim in the sense that he seriously means what he says.

---

[1] On this, see I Hedenius, *Om rätt och moral* [*On Law and Morality*] (Tidens förlag, 1941) 60–66; E Bulygin, 'Norms, Normative Propositions, and Legal Statements' in E Bulygin, *Essays in Legal Philosophy*, eds C Bernal, C Huerta, T Mazzarese, JJ Moreso, PE Navarro, and SL Paulson (Oxford, Oxford University Press, 2015) 188–194 (Originally published 1982 in G Fløistad (ed) *Contemporary Philosophy. A New Survey. Vol 3: Philosophy of Action*, 127–52. The Hague: Martinus Nijhoff; H Kelsen, *General Theory of Law and State*. Trans. Anders Wedberg (The Lawbook Exchange, 1999) (Originally published by Harvard University Press, 1945.) 162–164; GH von Wright, *Norm and Action. A Logical Inquiry* (Routledge & Kegan Paul, 1963) 103–105.

What, then, is a *detached* legal statement?[2] In an effort to understand Kelsen's theory of the basic norm, Joseph Raz introduces the concept of the legal man – the legal man accepts the law of the land as his personal morality – and explains that, on Kelsen's analysis, legal scholars adopt the point of view of the legal man, albeit in a *detached*, not a committed, way.[3] The reason is that they wish to be able to conceive of the law as a system of valid (binding) norms for the purely intellectual purpose of discussing its correct interpretation and application. As Raz puts it, '[l]egal science is not committed to regarding the law as just. It adopts this point of view in a special sense of "adopt". It is professional and uncommitted adoption. Legal science presupposes the basic norm not as individuals do – i.e. by accepting it as just – but in this special professional and uncommitted sense.'[4] What this means is that, on Raz's (and Kelsen's) analysis, a person who maintains that Smith has a legal obligation to do X, is typically speaking from a point of view that he does not share, namely, that of someone who believes that the legal order has moral authority – if he had shared this point of view, he would have been making a committed statement.

We see here that a detached legal statement is a first-order, albeit a detached, legal statement. As Raz points out elsewhere, to make a detached legal statement is *not* to make a conditional legal statement, such as 'If you want to achieve Y, you ought to do X.'[5] To make a detached legal statement is instead to state that you ought to do X, on the *assumption* that you want to achieve Y, without being committed to that assumption. The difference between a conditional legal statement and a detached legal statement, then, is that in the former case the assumption that you want to achieve Y is part of the statement, whereas in the latter case it functions as a tacit presupposition. Clearly, this is not a substantive, but a *semantic* (or perhaps a pragmatic) difference, that is, a difference in the *meaning* (or use) of the two types of statements: whereas a conditional legal statement is *descriptive*, a detached legal statement is *normative* (evaluative), albeit detached.

Let us note, finally, that the above division of legal statements into first-order and second-order statements, committed statements and detached statements, does not rest on a common distinction criterion. Whereas the distinction between first-order and second-order statements concerns the *content* of the statements, in the sense that first-order statements are normative and second-order statements are descriptive, the distinction between committed statements and detached statements concerns the speaker's *propositional attitude* in regard to the statements, in the sense that he has a committed attitude to committed statements and a detached attitude to detached statements.

---

[2] The following paragraphs can be found, more or less verbatim, in T Spaak, 'Legal Positivism, Conventionalism, and the Normativity of Law' (2018) 9 *Jurisprudence* 331–3.

[3] J Raz, *Between Authority and Interpretation* (Oxford, Oxford University Press, 2009) 140–3.

[4] Ibid, 142–3.

[5] J Raz *Practical Reasons and Norms* 2nd edn (Oxford, Oxford University Press, 1999) 170–7.

III. KARL OLIVECRONA'S ANTI-NORMATIVISM[6]

Karl Olivecrona rejects the view that law has binding force. The problem, he explains, is that the (alleged) binding force is such a peculiar property that one must locate legal rules that have binding force in some sort of supernatural world, where this property can make sense, and that there can be no connection between such a world and the world of time and space. He also maintains that since legal rules do not and cannot have binding force, they cannot confer rights and impose duties, or more generally, establish legal relations. And since he maintains that legal rules cannot have binding force and cannot establish legal relations, he cannot maintain that their function is to guide human behaviour by establishing legal relations. Instead, he argues that the function of legal rules is to cause human behaviour, and that legal rules can fulfil this function because they have (what he calls) a suggestive character.

The *content* of a legal rule, he explains, is an idea of an action by a person in an imaginary situation.[7] The *form* of legal rules, he continues, is *imperative*, because the lawmakers aim to impress a certain behaviour on us: 'Their aim is not to tell us which are the ideas in their minds but to impress a certain behaviour on people. To this end the imaginary actions are put before the eyes of the people in such a way as to call up the idea that this line of action must, unconditionally, be followed. Therefore the *imperative* form is used.'[8]

Pointing out that the *command* is the prototype of the imperative, he explains that a command *works directly on the will* of the recipient of the command, and that this means that it must have a *suggestive character*.[9] As Olivecrona sees it, if a command takes effect there arises in the addressee's mind a *value-neutral intention* to perform the commanded action, that is, an intention that is not motivated by the addressee's own wishes, and he adds that in some cases a command may actually trigger an action without the addressee's having had any intervening value-neutral intention.[10]

Olivecrona proceeds to explain that legal rules are *not* commands.[11] He explains that in addition to commands, there is a class of imperatives that we may refer to as *independent imperatives*, and points out that legal rules are precisely such independent imperatives.[12] On his analysis, there are three important differences between commands and independent imperatives. First, whereas a command is always *issued* by a certain person, an independent imperative is

---

[6] The text in this section can be found, more or less verbatim, in T Spaak, *A Critical Appraisal of Karl Olivecrona's Legal Philosophy* (Cham, Springer, 2014) 127–39.

[7] K Olivecrona, *Law as Fact* (Munksgaard & Humphrey Milford, 1939) 28–29.

[8] Ibid, 31.

[9] Ibid, 33–4.

[10] K Olivecrona, *Lagens imperativ* [*The Imperative of the Law*] (Gleerup, 1942) 7, 10–1.

[11] Olivecrona, *Law as Fact* (n 7) 35–40.

[12] Ibid, 42–9.

not issued by anyone in particular.[13] Second, whereas a command is always *addressed* to a certain person or persons and concerns a particular action or actions, an independent imperative, although it concerns a *kind* of action, is not addressed to anyone in particular.[14] Third, whereas a command is in no way equivalent to a judgment, an independent imperative *can sometimes be replaced by a sentence that expresses a judgment.*[15] Olivecrona objects, however, that there are no real judgments behind the sentences that (appear to) express such judgments, but only a *psychological connection*, viz. a connection in a person's mind between the imperative expression and the idea of an action.[16]

Olivecrona's central claim about legal rules, then, is that they can influence human beings because they have a suggestive character, and that this in turn means that they can cause human behaviour. This claim is, of course, very important to Olivecrona's analysis – if legal rules were not psychologically effective in this way, the analysis would be incomplete, since on Olivecrona's analysis, as we have seen, there are no legal relations the knowledge of which could motivate the citizens to act accordingly.

IV. EXPRESSIVISM

Like the other Scandinavian realists, Olivecrona is an expressivist, and his account of the function of legal rules is based on his expressivism. But what, exactly, is expressivism? Expressivism is a species of *moral anti-realism*, where the latter type of theory comes in least four main forms: (i) error theory, (ii) fictionalism, (iii) expressivism, and (iv) relativist and non-relativist constructivism. In what follows, I shall say a few words about (i) and (ii) but shall focus on (iii).

Error theorists believe that moral statements assert something about something, that there are no moral facts, and that therefore moral statements are always false. John Mackie, for example, denies the existence of objective moral values and maintains that ordinary moral statements include a claim to objectivity, that this claim has been incorporated into the conventional meaning of moral terms, and that therefore the denial of objective moral values has to be put forward as an error theory.[17] *Fictionalists*, on the other hand, insist that one who makes a (committed) moral statement is not literally asserting what he seems to be asserting (given the semantic meaning of the words he utters, say, that a certain action is morally required), but is instead expressing an *attitude* to the relevant moral system, say, that acting in conformity with it will be beneficial

---

[13] Ibid, 43.
[14] Ibid, 44–5.
[15] Ibid, 45–6.
[16] Ibid, 46.
[17] JL Mackie, *Ethics. Inventing Right and Wrong* (London, Penguin Books, 1977) 35.

to us all in one (non-moral) way or other. The idea of fictionalism, then, is that what is characteristic of moral discourse is to be found not in the semantics, but in the *pragmatics*, of moral language.[18]

Like error theorists, *expressivists* typically maintain that there is no moral reality or moral knowledge, but unlike error theorists, they maintain that moral statements do not assert anything about anything, and that therefore they cannot be true or false. Instead, they maintain that a person who makes a moral statement is simply expressing his feelings, attitudes or preferences.[19] On this type of analysis, the function of moral statements is to *influence* people. Russ Shafer-Landau offers the following characterisation of non-cognitivism (or, as I call it here, expressivism):[20]

> As non-cognitivists see it, the point of moral discourse is not to report some fact about oneself, one's group, or the larger world, but instead to give vent to one's feelings and to persuade others to share them ... prescribe some rule of conduct for oneself and others ... or express one's commitment to norms regulating guilt and anger. ... Such judgments do not ... admit of truth and falsity – indeed, there is nothing that could make them true. There is no world of moral facts against which the truth of a moral judgment can be checked. There are no moral properties whose instantiations can determine the qualities of persons, traits, actions, practices, or institutions. There is the familiar world that science speaks of. And there is us, responding to that world. And that is it.[21]

This also means that, on the expressivist analysis, terms like 'right,' 'duty,' and 'ought' are non-referential, although they are said to have so-called emotive meaning.[22] As a result, on the expressivist analysis, such terms express no *concepts* when they occur in first-order statements, and this means that there is nothing there to analyse. For example, the word 'duty' in a committed statement, such as 'It is your duty to help your neighbour,' does not express a concept of duty.

---

[18] On fictionalism, see, eg, M van Roojen, *Metaethics. A Contemporary Introduction* (London, Routledge, 2015) 176–179.

[19] AJ Ayer, *Language, Truth and Logic* 2nd edn (Victor Gollancz Ltd., 1947) Ch 6; S Blackburn, *Ruling Passions* (Oxford, Oxford University Press, 1998); A Gibbard, *Wise Choices, Apt Feelings. A Theory of Normative Judgment* (Oxford, Oxford University Press, 1990); A Hägerström, *Philosophy and Religion* (Muirhead Library of Philosophy, gen ed. HD Lewis, transl. RT Sandin, Humanities Press, 1964); Hedenius, *Om rätt och moral* (n 1) 14–38; CL Stevenson, *Ethics and Language* (Yale, Yale University Press, 1944).

[20] Strictly speaking, non-cognitivism and expressivism are not the same thing: The class of non-cognitivist theories includes not only expressivist theories, but also the universal prescriptivism advocated by RM Hare. See RM Hare, *The Language of Morals* (Oxford, Oxford University Press, 1952); RM Hare, *Moral Thinking* (Oxford, Oxford University Press, 1981). However, since emotivism, which Olivecrona embraces, is a version of both non-cognitivism and expressivism, the differences are not important in this context. For more on this, see, eg, van Roojen, *Metaethics* (n 18) 5.

[21] R Shafer-Landau, *Moral Realism. A Defence* (Oxford, Oxford University Press, 2003) 20.

[22] On this, see CL Stevenson, 'The Emotive Meaning of Ethical Terms' (1937) 46 *Mind, New Series* 14–31.

Finally, as Shafer-Landau points out (in the quotation above), expressivism is very much in keeping with a natural-scientific world-view, in that it does not assume the existence of moral values or standards. Moreover, it explains in a straightforward manner a rather widespread, if somewhat controversial, view, often called *motivational internalism*, according to which moral judgements are necessarily motivating.[23] Since, on the expressivist analysis, a person who makes a moral judgement expresses his feelings or attitudes, expressivism easily explains the view that moral judgements are necessarily motivating.

V. EXPRESSIVISM: SOME DIFFICULTIES

As I have said, Olivecrona is an expressivist, though not all expressivists would accept his account of the function of legal rules. For example, HLA Hart,[24] is an expressivist, too, although his expressivism is a bit more subtle than Olivecrona's.[25] Nevertheless, any account of legal rules that is based on a version of expressivism would seem to suffer from the same problems that mar expressivism in general. To be sure, from the standpoints of metaphysics and epistemology, expressivism appears quite attractive. For, as we have seen, expressivism does not assert or presuppose the existence of moral properties, which would have to be located somewhere; nor does it assert or presuppose the existence of moral knowledge, which would have to be accounted for in some way. However, it has been objected to expressivism, that it cannot account for our practices of moral and legal thinking and argumentation. Let me point to three such difficulties for expressivists.

First, there is the problem that the participants in the above-mentioned practices appear to assume that there are legal or moral properties and facts, in the sense that in some cases they appear to assume that there is a right answer to the legal or moral question at issue. To be sure, I have some doubts about this claim as regards the moral case. For one thing, one might object that there are no, or very few, objectivist features of moral discourse. Secondly, one might object that such features – assuming they exist – do not support moral objectivism. My own doubts concern mainly the first point.[26] I shall, however, proceed in this chapter assuming that the assumption is well founded.

---

[23] What I call motivational internalism comes in several forms. On this, see van Roojen, *Metaethics* (n 18) 55–9.

[24] HLA Hart, *Essays on Bentham. Jurisprudence and Political Theory* (Oxford, Oxford University Press, 1982) 159–61.

[25] On this, see J Raz, 'H. L. A Hart (1907–1992)' (1993) 5 *Utilitas* 45.

[26] For an illuminating discussion of this general question, see G Björnsson, 'Do "Objectivist" Features of Moral Discourse and Thinking Support Moral Objectivism?' (2012) 16 *The Journal of Ethics* 367–393.

Second, there is the problem of explaining how legal or moral inferences can be logically valid, given that the laws of logic are said to apply only to entities (such as statements) that are true or false, and that, on the expressivist analysis, first-order legal or moral statements cannot be true or false. True, in some cases, we make inferences that do seem to be logically valid, even though we are dealing with normative or evaluative statements. For example, if I say to Linda (P1) 'you should take all the suitcases to the station' and add (P2) 'the blue suitcase in the corner is one of the suitcases', then Linda will surely conclude that she should take the blue suitcase in the corner to the station; and we will all agree that she is right in drawing that conclusion. However, this does not mean that we have a good *explanation* of wherein the validity of this inference consists. We take it to be logically valid, but it seems we cannot explain why this is so. However, this difficulty has been much discussed in the logical and philosophical literature,[27] and I shall not discuss it any further in this chapter.

Third, there is the so-called Frege-Geach problem (or the problem of embedding), which has been much discussed by moral philosophers since Peter Geach drew our attention to it in the early 1960's.[28] This is a more specific logical problem than the above-mentioned, general problem of logical validity. The problem, which has to do with *ambiguity*, is that, on the expressivist analysis, normative and evaluative terms like 'right,' 'obligation,' 'ought,' and 'good' do not have the same meaning (sense) in asserted and unasserted contexts, and that therefore, on this analysis, an inference such as the following – (P1) lying is wrong, (P2) if lying is wrong, it is wrong to get little brother to lie; therefore (C) it is wrong to get little brother to lie – involves the fallacy of equivocation (*quaternio terminorum*). And this is surprising, to say the least. Specifically, the problem is that whereas in (P1) and (C), the word 'wrong' occurs in a statement that is asserted; in (P2) it occurs in the antecedent of a conditional statement, where the antecedent itself is not asserted but is simply entertained – what is asserted is the whole conditional; and that, on the expressivist analysis words like 'wrong' have cognitive meaning when they occur in a second-order statement, but have no cognitive meaning when they occur in asserted first-order statements. Hence they do not have the same meaning in first-order and second-order statements. Thus, the person reasoning appears to have committed the fallacy of equivocation.

---

[27] See, eg, A Ross, 'Imperatives and Logic' (1944) 11 *Philosophy of Science* 30–46; A Ross, *Directives and Norms* (Routledge & Kegan Paul, 1968) 139–143; CE Alchourròn and AA Martino, 'Logic Without Truth' (1990) 3 *Ratio Juris* 46–67; Shafer-Landau, *Moral Realism* (n 21) 22–6.

[28] See PT Geach, 'Ascriptivism' (1960) 69 *The Philosophical Review* 221–225; PT Geach, 'Assertion' (1965) 74 *The Philosophical Review* 449–465; S Blackburn, *Spreading the Word* (Oxford, Oxford University Press, 1984); S Blackburn, *Essays on Quasi-Realism* (Oxford, Oxford University Press, 1993); Gibbard, *Wise Choices* (n 18); W Sinnott-Armstrong, 'Expressivism and Embedding' (2000) 61 *Philosophy and Phenomenological Research* 677–93; D Stoljar, 'Emotivism and Truth Conditions' (1993) 70 *Philosophical Studies* 81–101; N Unwin, 'Quasi-Realism, Negation, and the Frege-Geach Problem' (1999) 49 *Philosophical Quarterly* 337–52.

VI. QUASI-REALISM: THE AIM

Given these difficulties, one may well wonder how anyone could reasonably espouse an expressivist account of first-order legal statements. Isn't the natural conclusion that expressivism is a non-starter? Simon Blackburn does not think so, however, arguing as he does that expressivists can in good conscience mimic the talk and reasoning of moral realists and other cognitivists and speak and reason as if there were moral and legal facts, as if legal and moral questions had correct answers, and so on. The idea, then, is that the quasi-realist aims to account for the realist (or objectivist) features on the surface level of legal and moral discourse, while espousing expressivism about normative and evaluative statements on the deep level of such discourse.[29] Blackburn labels the enterprise of showing 'that even on anti-realist grounds there is nothing improper, nothing "diseased" in projected predicates ... *quasi-realism.*'[30] The quasi-realist, he explains,[31] 'tries to earn, on the slender basis, the features of moral language (or of the other commitments to which a projective theory might apply) which tempt people to realism.'

Blackburn thus thinks of expressivism and error theory as two different versions of projectivism and sees the quasi-realist enterprise as an attempt to vindicate a projectivist account of morality (and of some other fields). Note that projectivism thus conceived is very much in keeping with ontological (or metaphysical) *naturalism*, according to which there is nothing but natural properties in the world. As Blackburn puts it, '[t]he projective theory intends to ask no more from the world than what we know is there – the ordinary features of things on the basis of which we make decisions about them, like or dislike them, fear them and avoid them, desire them and seek them out.'[32]

As we have seen, expressivists do not believe that there are moral or legal properties, which could account for the truth or falsity of our moral or legal statements. But, Blackburn points out,[33] we do have attitudes, emotions, etc, and we do wish to work out the implications of our attitudes (emotions, etc); and this means that our moral language needs the resources of ordinary fact-stating language. The standard view of the semantics of predicates, including evaluative predicates, he points out, is that a predicate – say, 'is tall' or 'is good' – is used to refer to a certain property, and that a statement involving a predicate is true if (and only if) the relevant object has that property and false if (and only if) it does not.[34] The quasi-realist view, on the other hand, is that we should anchor

---

[29] S Blackburn, *Spreading the Word* (n 28) 196.
[30] Ibid, 170–1.
[31] Ibid, 170–1.
[32] Ibid, 182.
[33] Ibid, 191–2.
[34] S Blackburn, 'Quasi-Realism' in H LaFolette (ed), *The International Encyclopedia of Ethics* (Chichester, Blackwell Publishing, 2013) 4263–4270. Available at www.https://onlinelibrary.wiley.com pp 1–8.

the semantics of evaluative predicates not in the property or properties to which the predicate would, on a realist analysis, be used to refer, because there are no such properties, but in the *attitudes* of the speaker, and say that a person who makes a value judgement speaks truly if (and only if) he has the attitude that corresponds to the relevant predicate and falsely if (and only if) he does not. As Blackburn points out,[35] this means that the question for the quasi-realist is not what the world is like, but under what conditions it is *semantically appropriate* to say that an action or a state of affairs is good or bad; and this in turn means that, on the quasi-realist analysis, there is a shift away from truth and reference towards the *use* of evaluative predicates in practical reasoning, that is, towards pragmatism.

In my discussion of quasi-realism below, I shall follow Alexander Miller,[36] who makes a distinction between modest and ambitious quasi-realism. Whereas a *modest* quasi-realist maintains that although there are no moral facts and no moral truths, one may earn, on a projectivist basis, the right to think and speak *as if there were* moral facts and moral truths, an *ambitious* quasi-realist maintains that *there really are* moral facts and moral truths, but insists they can be accounted for (only) on a projectivist basis. Let us now turn to consider these two versions of quasi-realism in that order.

VII. MODEST QUASI-REALISM

Blackburn begins his account of quasi-realism with a discussion of the above-mentioned (in Section V) Frege-Geach difficulty, concerning the meaning of evaluative predicates in asserted and unasserted contexts. The question, he explains,[37] is, how can an expressivist account for the sameness of meaning of evaluative predicates in asserted and unasserted contexts that we take for granted? He proposes a two-step solution to the problem.[38] First, he gives an account of *what we are up to* when we make evaluative conditionals, such as 'if lying is wrong, it is wrong to get little brother to lie.' What we are doing, he explains, is *working out the implications of our commitments*. But, one wonders, can attitudes – as distinguished from beliefs – have implications at all? Blackburn answers this question in the affirmative. On the projective picture,[39] he explains, a person's *moral sensibility* is that person's set of attitudes, emotions, preferences, and the like; and, he continues, since a person's behaviour can be explained by his moral sensibility, it is important to rank sensibilities, to endorse some and reject others. On this analysis, to utter the above evaluative conditional

---

[35] Ibid, 4.
[36] A Miller, *An Introduction to Contemporary Metaethics* (Oxford, Polity Press, 2003) 278.
[37] Blackburn, *Spreading the Word* (n 28) 190.
[38] Ibid, 191–6.
[39] Ibid, 192.

is to express a positive attitude to the *coupling* of a negative attitude to lying and a negative attitude towards getting little brother to lie.

Secondly, he offers a *semantic theory* intended to underpin the quasi-realist use of evaluative predicates. He imagines an expressive language, E_{ex}, that contains no evaluative predicates, but contains instead a hooray operator, (H!), and a boo operator, (B!), both of which may be attached to descriptions of actions or events. For example, one might say H!(truth-telling) and B!(lying), that is, hooray for truth-telling and boo for lying. In addition, he explains, E_{ex} needs a notation for endorsing or rejecting *couplings* of attitudes, or couplings of beliefs and attitudes, in order for the speakers of the language to be able to work out the implications of their commitments. Thus, to continue with the example in the above paragraph, one might want to say: H!([B!(lying)];[B!(getting little brother to lie)]), that is, hooray for the coupling of 'boo for lying' and 'boo for getting little brother to lie'.

Blackburn proceeds to point out that a person who has a negative attitude to lying (premise 1) and a positive attitude to the coupling of a negative attitude to lying and a negative attitude to getting little brother to lie (premise 2) *must*, if he is to reason *logically*, also have a negative attitude to getting little brother to lie (the conclusion). If such a person doesn't have a negative attitude to getting little brother to lie, he has a *fractured* sensibility, that is, a sensibility that includes *clashing attitudes*; and, Blackburn points out,[40] one cannot approve of a fractured sensibility, because such a sensibility cannot fulfil the practical purposes for which we evaluate things.

Blackburn maintains in conclusion (i) that we need to make E_{ex} an instrument that we can use in a serious, reflective, evaluative practice, in which we are concerned to express 'improvements, clashes, implications, and coherence of attitudes', (ii) that E_{ex} can achieve this by becoming like ordinary English and including evaluative predicates, and (iii) that this makes it clear that our use of indirect contexts does not show that expressivism in the field of morality is wrong; 'it merely proves us to have adopted a form of expression adequate to our needs. *This is what is meant by 'projecting' attitudes onto the world.*'[41]

VIII. AMBITIOUS QUASI-REALISM

Having come this far, Blackburn takes a further step and proposes that we proceed and develop a projectivist account of *truth*, too.[42] As he puts it,[43] 'given attitudes, given constraints upon them, given a notion of improvement and of possible fault in any sensibility including our own, we can construct a

[40] Ibid, 195.
[41] Ibid, 195.
[42] Ibid, 197–202.
[43] Ibid, 198.

notion of truth.' Focusing on the notion of improvement and of possible fault in a sensibility, he introduces the concept of a *best possible set of attitudes*, where such a set is a set of attitudes that is the result of the person whose set it is taking all opportunities to improve it. If we have such a set, we may say that holding a value statement to be true is to say that the attitude it expresses is a member of, or is implied by, the set. If we call the best possible set of attitudes M^*, and if we say that m is a value judgement that expresses an attitude, a, we may say that m is true if, and only if, a is a member of M^*.[44]

To show that we may plausibly assume the existence of such a thing as a best possible set of attitudes, Blackburn considers David Hume's discussion of two literary critics, one young and one old, who disagree about the merits of two different writers, Tacitus and Ovid.[45] The younger critic prefers Ovid and holds that Ovid is better than Tacitus, whereas the older critic prefers Tacitus and holds that Tacitus is better than Ovid. The question, then, is whether the set of attitudes, M^*_O, or the set of attitudes, M^*_T, or both, can be improved, or whether there is no possible improvement of either M^*_O or M^*_T. Blackburn illustrates the situation with the help of a tree-structure (see below), in which (moving from left to right) each node (place where there is a branching) indicates two different but equally good ways of improving the set:

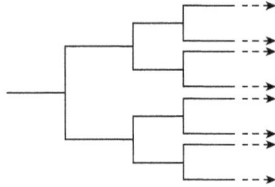

The tree-structure, he explains, illustrates the *relativist* position, which is that a moral judgement can be true only in light of a given moral framework, and that there is no such framework that is privileged as the objectively true framework; and, he continues,[46] such relativism undermines one's '... right to think of [one's] own sensibility as true, which is equivalent to unsettling [one's] commitments.' He argues, however, that it is obvious that there *is* room for improvement in at least one of the competing sets of attitudes, pointing out that already *awareness* of the competing system, *B*, on the part of the proponent of the first system, *A*, and vice versa, constitutes an improvement. For such awareness, he continues, will bring with it a more nuanced way of looking at the opposition between the two systems, according to which one might say that the systems are of equal merit, or have features that appeal to different people, etc.[47]

---

[44] Ibid, 198.
[45] Ibid, 199–202.
[46] Ibid, 199.
[47] Ibid, 200.

Blackburn concludes from his discussion of the two critics that we are constrained to argue and practice *as though truth is single*, and that therefore an evaluative system should contain resources to transcend the tree-structure: '... in practice evidence that there is a node is just treated as a signal that the truth is not yet finally argued, and it does go into discussions as part of the evidence.'[48] Of course, even if this is true, it does not tell us exactly where the mistake is to be found. Blackburn proceeds, however, to argue that when two competing systems of norms or values conflict, it is typically *obligations*, not permissions, that will have to yield. For example, if *OA* means that one is obligated to do *A* and *P-A* means that one is permitted to do -*A*, if one system, M^*_1, includes *OA* and another system, M^*_2, includes *P-A*, and if there is no possible way of improving either M^*_1 or M^*_2, then one must be permitted to choose M^*_1 or M^*_2, as one pleases. One might then reason that if it is permitted to choose M^*_2, it is permitted to permit the doing of -*A* (PP-A), that this means that it is permitted to do -*A* (P-A), and that therefore M^*_1, which conflicts with M^*_2, must be rejected. We thus assume here a reduction principle (as Blackburn calls it), according to which it is permitted to do -*A* if it is permitted to permit doing -*A*, that is, (PP-A→ P-A). One might, however, reason instead that if one is permitted to choose M^*_1, it is permitted to make it obligatory to do *A* (POA), that this means that it is obligatory to do *A* (OA), and that therefore M^*_2, which conflicts with M^*_1, must be rejected. Clearly, we have here adopted a different reduction principle, namely, one according to which it is obligatory to do *A* if it is permitted to make it obligatory to do *A*, that is, (POA) → (OA). But, Blackburn argues, the latter reduction principle is not as plausible as the former: 'Evidence of a permissible system which permits -A is evidence that -A is permissible; evidence of a permissible system which obligates A is not so plausibly thought of as evidence that A is obligatory.'[49]

IX. MODEST QR: THE PURPOSE OF EVALUATION

Blackburn's theory is highly interesting, but also problematic. One difficulty concerns Blackburn's underdeveloped view of the purposes for which we evaluate things. Blackburn holds, as we have seen, that a fractured sensibility – a sensibility that includes clashing attitudes – cannot itself be an object of approval, and that 'cannot' here means that such a sensibility cannot fulfil the practical purposes for which we evaluate things. The idea thus appears to be that a fractured sensibility cannot be a *means* to the *end* of evaluating human behaviour for a certain purpose or certain purposes.

Blackburn does not explain, however, what the relevant practical purposes are, or why they would be undermined by the existence of a fractured sensibility. It does, however, seem clear that a fractured sensibility might undermine the

[48] Ibid, 201.
[49] Ibid, 202.

action-guiding capacity of moral and legal norms. Whatever else law and morality aim to do, and whatever their precise purpose or function may be, they aim to
guide human behaviour, and this action-guiding capacity could be undermined
by the existence of fractured sensibilities. For example, a person cannot on the
same occasion *act* both on the attitude that lying (abortion, capital punishment,
war, etc) is wrong and the attitude that it is not wrong, although he can certainly
act on the one attitude today and on the other tomorrow. One may, however,
wonder whether *all* fractured sensibilities would undermine the action-guiding
capacity of law and morality. I am inclined to answer this question in the affirmative. But, as I shall argue below (in Section X), not all situations in which a
person cannot satisfy his attitudes simultaneously should count as situations in
which he has a fractured sensibility.

X. MODEST QR: CLASHING ATTITUDES[50]

Consider again Blackburn's claim that a person who disapproves of lying, and
who approves of the coupling of disapproval of lying and disapproval of getting
little brother to lie, but who does not disapprove of getting little brother to lie,
has attitudes that clash and has in this sense a fractured sensibility. As we have
seen, Blackburn holds that the existence of clashing attitudes constitutes a logical fault, an inconsistency (a contradiction). But is it really a *logical* fault? Could
it be that Blackburn is here helping himself to the concept of an inconsistency
between attitudes, although he is not justified in doing so?

   Bob Hale has objected to Blackburn's analysis, that Blackburn is not entitled to take the idea of a coupling (or a combination) of value judgements,
such as [H!(A;B)] as meaning that *B follows* upon *A*, because this would be to
assume precisely what he is supposed to explain, and that therefore he has to be
content with the simpler idea of a *coupling* of attitudes.[51] But, Hale continues,[52]
on this analysis, it is unclear in what sense clashing attitudes are inconsistent:
'Certainly an inconsistency could be located if we could appeal to a principle
of inference such as: from "B!(x), H!([B!(x);B!(y)])" *infer* B!(y)". But to appeal to
any such principle at this stage would be to assume clear precisely what was to
be explained, i.e., how principles of inference get a grip on expressives.' Hale
proposes to solve the problem by introducing an alternative way of formalising
evaluative conditionals. Instead of following Blackburn and conceiving of the
deep structure of such conditionals as H!([B!(lying)];[B!(getting little brother to
lie)]), we can introduce a kind of negation sign and conceive of the deep structure as B!([B!(lying)];[-B! (getting little brother to lie)]).[53] If we do, he points out,
we have an inconsistency of sorts between [B!(lying)], [B!(B!(lying));[-B!(getting

[50] My discussion in this section follows Alexander Miller's discussion of these issues in Miller,
Contemporary Metaethics (n 36), ch 4.
[51] Bob Hale, 'The Complete Projectivist' (1986) 36 *The Philosophical Quarterly* 73–4.
[52] Ibid, 73–4.
[53] Ibid, 74.

little brother to lie)], and [-B!(getting little brother to lie)]. He points out, however, that this does not amount to an inconsistency in the logical sense, but *in a failure to adjust one's actions to one's attitudes*. What it does is to give expression to a general principle of moral inconsistency, according to which you should not do what you boo: B!(B!(x);x).[54]

Blackburn has responded to the objection that his theory cannot explain that clashes of attitudes are logical, as distinguished from moral, failings, by introducing the concept of a *tree of commitments* (roughly, the concept of a truth tree that concerns commitments, not statements or propositions), to which the speaker ties himself.[55] The idea is that such a tree of commitments will make it clear that a person who *believes* (in the case of factual premises) or *accepts* (in the case of evaluative premises) the premises of an argument, while not believing or accepting the conclusion, is guilty of an inconsistency. Let us consider first an example of an obviously valid factual modus ponens inference:

(P1) *B* is in Minnetonka.

(P2) If *B* is in Minnetonka, *B* is in Minnesota.

(C) *B* is in Minnesota.

As should be clear, there are two different ways in which (P2) can be true: if *B* is not in Minnetonka, or if *B* is in Minnesota. Thus, assuming that the premises are true and the conclusion false, we get the following two branches of our tree of commitments. As we will see, both branches contain a contradiction, namely *A* & -*A* and *B* & -*B*, respectively; and this means that the argument is logically valid. Here are the premises and the conclusion and (in the rectangle) the tree:

Premises and Conclusion		*Tree*
(P1)	Bel. T	(P1) Bel. T
(P2)	Bel. T $\longrightarrow$ Bel. S	(P2) Bel. T $\longrightarrow$ Bel. S
(C)	Bel. S	(C) -Bel. S
		↙ ↘
		-Bel. T Bel. S
		X X

<hr>

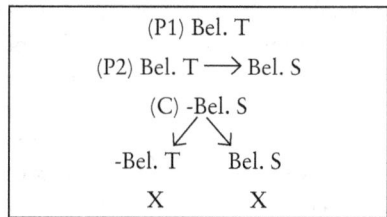

[54] Crispin Wright, too, has objected that, on Blackburn's account, a person who accepts the premises but not the conclusion in the above inference is guilty of a *moral*, not a logical, failing. As Wright sees it, a person with a fractured sensibility simply has a set of attitudes that he himself does not approve of, which means that he has failed to adjust his *actions* to his attitudes; and this is a moral, not a logical, failing. See C Wright, 'Realism, Antirealism, Irrealism, Quasi-Realism' (1988) XII *Midwest Studies in Philosophy* 33.

[55] Blackburn, *Ruling Passions* (n 19) ch 3. For an introduction to the truth-tree method, see, eg, R Jeffrey, *Formal Logic. Its Scope and Limits* 3rd edn (New York, McGraw-Hill Education, 1991); E Lepore, *Meaning and Argument. An Introduction to Logic Through Language* (with S Cumming) 2nd edn (Chichester, Wiley-Blackwell, 2009).

Branch 1

(A) Believing that *B* is in Minnetonka.	BT
(-A) Not believing that *B* is in Minnesota.	-BS
(-B) Not believing that *B* is in Minnetonka.	-BT

Branch 2

(A) Believing that *B* is in Minnetonka.	BT
(B) Not believing that *B* is in Minnesota.	-BS
(-B) Believing that *B* is in Minnesota.	BS

We see that the contradictions in Branch 1 and Branch 2, respectively, are between believing and not believing that *B* is in Minnetonka (BT&-BT) and between believing and not believing that *B* is in Minnesota (BS&-BS). Thus, the contradictions in this tree of commitments are not between statements, but between *beliefs*.

The question now arises whether we can expand the tree of commitments to include value judgements understood along the lines of expressivism. Blackburn thinks so. Consider again our running example:

(P1) Lying is wrong.

(P2) If lying is wrong, getting little brother to lie is wrong.

--

(C) Getting little brother to lie is wrong.

If we take the view that (P2) can be accepted by one who does not accept that lying is wrong, or accepts that getting little brother to lie is wrong, we see that this tree, too, has two branches. And, as we shall see, here, too, both branches contain a contradiction, namely *C* & -*C* and *D* & -*D*, respectively; and this means that the argument is logically valid. Below are the premises and the conclusion and (in the rectangle) the tree:

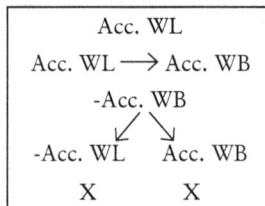

Premises and Conclusion		*Tree*
(P1)	WL	Acc. WL
(P2)	WL $\longrightarrow$ WB	Acc. WL $\longrightarrow$ Acc. WB
(C)	WB	-Acc. WB
		-Acc. WL Acc. WB
		X X

Branch 1

(C) Accepting that lying is wrong.

(-D) Not accepting that getting little brother to lie is wrong.

(-C) Not accepting that lying is wrong.

Branch 2

(C) Accepting that lying is wrong.

(-D) Not accepting that getting little brother to lie is wrong.

(D) Accepting that getting little brother to lie is wrong.

We see that the contradictions in Branch 1 and Branch 2, respectively, are between accepting and not accepting that lying is wrong and between accepting and not accepting that getting little brother to lie is wrong. Thus the contradictions in this tree of commitments are not between attitudes, but between *acceptances*.

As Blackburn sees it, the evaluative tree of commitments makes it clear that a person who accepts the premises but not the conclusion in the above inference is guilty of an inconsistency. He puts it as follows:

> There has been some skepticism about whether this approach can deliver the mighty "musts" of logic. But we see now that it can do so perfectly well. Consider the example made famous by Geach, of inference according to the pattern of *modus ponens*. Someone saying each of "p" and "if p then q" has the premises of a *modus ponens* whose conclusion is "q". He is logically committed to q, if he is committed to the premises. To put it another way, if anyone represented themselves as holding the combination of "p" and "if p then q" and "not-q" we would not know what to make of them. Logical breakdown means failure of understanding. Is this result secured, on my account, for an evaluative antecedent, p? Yes, because the person represent themselves as tied to a tree of possible combinations of belief and attitude, but at the same time represent themselves as holding a combination that the tree excludes. So what is given at one moment is taken away at the next, and we can make no intelligible interpretation of them.[56]

One may, however, wonder with Hale (see above) whether Blackburn does not tacitly assume precisely what he is supposed to prove when he without comment maintains that one can accept the evaluative conditional 'if lying is wrong, getting little brother to lie is wrong' by not accepting that lying is wrong, or by accepting that getting little brother to lie is wrong (or both). For this seems to me to be tantamount to assuming that evaluative conditionals *are* truth-conditional, so that they are false if the antecedent is true and the consequent false, and true otherwise. But, I wonder, can one coherently take this view, if one also holds that value-statements lack truth-value? I am skeptical.

Moreover, if an attitude towards lying lacks truth-value, why can't a person both accept and not accept such an attitude? The natural answer, in my view, is that a person cannot *satisfy* such a combination of attitudes at the same time,

---

[56] Blackburn, *Ruling Passions* (n 19) 72.

although he can certainly change his mind from accepting *A* to not accepting *A*, and vice versa. The problem with such a logic of satisfaction, however, is that in some cases it will be a *contingent* matter which attitudes (commands, norms, etc) can be satisfied together and which cannot; and logical validity is about *necessity* in the sense that, necessarily, if the premises are true, then the conclusion is true. Suppose, for example, that I have a positive attitude to giving to two different and reputable charity organisations, one concerning the environment and the other concerning animal welfare. Suppose also that my financial situation is such that I simply cannot afford to support both charities, but have to choose the one over the other, at least if I also have a positive attitude to my own well-being. To be sure, I do seem to have clashing attitudes in such a situation, but not in the strong sense of a fractured sensibility. Following Risto Hilpinen, we might say that what we have in such a situation is a normative conflict, but not a normative inconsistency.[57] My view, then, is that in order to count as a clash of attitudes in the strong sense, the clash has to be necessary.[58]

XI. MODEST QR: QUASI-REALISM AND MORAL FICTIONALISM?

As we have seen (in Section III), error theorists maintain that moral judgements are genuine but systematically false judgements, because they attribute properties to actions and states of affairs – such as the property of being a right or a wrong action – that they do not, and perhaps cannot, have. On this analysis, to maintain, say, that a certain action is a moral duty is to describe the (moral) world incorrectly and thus to state a falsehood. So if one is an error theorist, the following question arises: given that I believe our moral judgements are systematically false, should I give up on morality altogether and cease making moral judgements (eliminativism), or should I rather continue to think and speak about moral matters on the assumption that doing so is likely to have beneficial, although non-moral, consequences (moral fictionalism)?

As we have seen (in Section IV), the idea behind moral fictionalism is that one accepts non-cognitivism about moral *thought* and cognitivism about moral *language*, while insisting that one who makes a (committed) moral statement is not literally asserting what he seems to be asserting (given the semantic meaning of the words he utters, say, that a certain action is morally required), but is instead expressing an *attitude* to the relevant moral system, say, that acting in conformity with it will be beneficial to us all in one (non-moral) way or other. According to van Roojen,[59] moral fictionalism thus conceived is a moral

---

[57] As Hilpinen sees it, whereas a normative conflict depends on contingent circumstances, a normative inconsistency does not. R Hilpinen, 'Conflict and Change in Norm Systems' in Å Frändberg and M Van Hoecke (eds), *The Structure of Law* (Iustus förlag, Uppsala, 1987) 37–49.

[58] I would like to thank Karl Petterson for helpful comments on this section.

[59] van Roojen, *Metaethics* (n 18) 182–4.

analogue to so-called constructive empiricism in the philosophy of science. For constructive empiricists do not take a scientist's claim about unobservable particles, say, that there is a proton in the cloud chamber, to express the belief that there is a proton in the cloud chamber, but to express the belief that the claim in question is empirically adequate, in the sense that it can be used to predict observable phenomena. We see, then, that, on the fictionalist analysis, moral entities and properties are fictions, in the sense that we (seemingly) assert their existence, yet we do not believe they exist.

It is common in the literature on fictionalism to distinguish between revolutionary and hermeneutic fictionalism: whereas revolutionary fictionalists are error theorists, who believe that our moral statements are systematically false and recommend that we *become* moral fictionalists, hermeneutic fictionalists hold that fictionalism offers a true description of moral discourse as it actually proceeds today, because (they argue) no one takes moral discourse seriously.[60] The distinction between revolutionary and hermeneutic fictionalism is of some interest in this context, because Blackburn's quasi-realism is an attempt to account for moral discourse as it actually proceeds today, and it should therefore be compared to hermeneutic, not revolutionary, fictionalism.

Against this background, we may ask, is quasi-realism a species of moral fictionalism, or is moral fictionalism a species of quasi-realism, or are quasi-realism and moral fictionalism two distinct types of theory? David Lewis maintains that Blackburn's quasi-realism is indeed a species of moral fictionalism. As Lewis sees it, moral fictionalists make all the claims moral realists make, but they preface these claims with a disclaimer, such as 'Let's make believe that moral realism is true, though it isn't.'[61] He argues, more specifically, that moral fictionalists are willing to say everything moral realists are saying, provided that they have first introduced such a disowning preface (or disclaimer), and that this means that they are not asserting what they seem to be asserting, but are quasi-asserting it.[62] On the basis of this account of fictionalism, Lewis maintains that quasi-realism is a species of moral fictionalism. The reason, he explains, is that Blackburn's discussion of projectivism, which is what motivates Blackburn's quasi-realism, plays the same *role* in the quasi-realist program as the fictionalist's disowning preface does in the fictionalist program, that is, it turns assertions into quasi-assertions – the only difference being that whereas the fictionalist is explicit about this, the quasi-realist is not.[63]

Blackburn has considered and rejected Lewis's claim that quasi-realism is a species of fictionalism.[64] First, he objects to moral fictionalism that it is unclear

[60] See, eg, ibid, 177–94.

[61] D Lewis, 'Quasi-Realism is Fictionalism' in M Kalderon (ed), *Fictionalism in Metaphysics* (Oxford, Oxford University Press, 2005) 314–321.

[62] Ibid, 319.

[63] Ibid, 319.

[64] S Blackburn, 'Quasi-Realism no Fictionalism' in ME Kalderon (ed), *Fictionalism in Metaphysics* (Oxford, Oxford University Press, 2005) 322–338.

what it *means* to treat morality as something that is a fact, though it is not really a fact. He considers as an example John Locke's theory of colours, according to which we talk as if there were colours, although there are in fact no colours. And, he points out, in order to understand this theory, we need to understand what it means to say, first, that our world is not a world of colour and, secondly, what it would mean for it to be a world of colour. If we do not understand this, we do not understand fictionalism about colours. And he believes the same type of objection can be levelled against moral fictionalism.[65]

I am, however, not sure that Blackburn's objection is successful, because I am inclined to think the moral fictionalist could argue successfully that the difference between our world, in which it is, say, not wrong to neglect children, and a world in which it *is* wrong to neglect children, is simply that whereas the latter world is so constituted that acts of neglecting children have the (mind-independent) property of being morally wrong, our world is not so constituted. This, I take it, is the view of moral realists, and even if it is mistaken, I do not think it is incomprehensible.

Secondly, Blackburn argues that unlike the moral fictionalist, the quasi-realist does *not* have to explain what it would mean for our world to not be a world of moral entities and properties and for some other world to be a world of moral entities and properties, because quasi-realism does not require us to make sense of such claims.[66] I assume that Blackburn has in mind here ambitious, not modest, quasi-realism. For while *ambitious* quasi-realists do *not* purport to say that they have earned the right to speak as if moral realism were true, although it is not, the aim of *modest* quasi-realism does seem to be precisely that of earning the right to speak as if moral realism were true, although it is not (on this, see Sections VI–VII above). I therefore conclude that if successful, Blackburn's objection to moral fictionalism would also undermine modest, though not ambitious, quasi-realism.

XII. AMBITIOUS QR: A BEST POSSIBLE SET OF ATTITUDES

Blackburn maintains, as we have seen, that we may assume the existence of a best possible set of attitudes and say that a moral judgement is true if, and only if, it expresses an attitude that is a member of this set of attitudes. One may well wonder, however, whether it makes sense to speak of a best possible set of attitudes at all. The argument that Blackburn adduces in support of the claim that we are entitled to assume the existence of such a set is not without merit, though it is, in my view, ultimately unconvincing.

Blackburn considers, as the reader will remember, David Hume's discussion of two literary critics who disagree about the merits of two different writers.

[65] Ibid, 325.
[66] Ibid, 323.

The younger critic prefers Ovid and holds that Ovid is better than Tacitus, whereas the older critic prefers Tacitus and holds that Tacitus is better than Ovid. Blackburn argues, as we have seen, that it is obvious that there is room for improvement of one or both of the competing sets of attitudes, inter alia, because each person involved may improve his own set of attitudes simply by becoming *aware* of the other critic's set of attitudes; and he also argues, more specifically, in the case of the systems M^*_1 and M^*_2, that one reduction principle is more plausible than the other, and that this means that there is room for improvement of at least one of the systems. As the reader will remember, the choice was between the reduction principle (PP-A → P-A) and the reduction principle (POA → OA), and Blackburn's view was that the former is more plausible than the latter.

I am not convinced by Blackburn's reasoning, however. To be sure, I agree with Blackburn that a critic who becomes aware of a different and incompatible view will gain something in the process, and that such awareness means that if he insists on his own view, in spite of his being aware of the competing view, he now holds a view that has been better grounded. However, it does not follow from the fact that both critics in our example now hold views that are better grounded, that the views themselves have been improved (except in the minimal sense that they are now better grounded); and still less does it follow that the one view has been improved more than the other.

As for Blackburn's discussion of the competing reduction principles, I believe this yields a more substantial recommendation, one that could be of practical use. I am not, however, convinced that Blackburn's preferred reduction principle is more plausible than the competing one. For I can see no good reason to hold that in case of a conflict between two competing normative systems, it is always the more demanding system that is in need of improvement; and I cannot see that Blackburn offers any real argument in support of his claim. Moreover, I am not convinced of Blackburn's tacit assumption, that in a situation where neither of the competing normative systems can be improved, one is *permitted* to choose between them as one pleases. Can we really deduce a *normative* conclusion from the premise that we cannot improve either normative system? If the premise is *not* normative, we run into Hume's law; if it is normative, and if Blackburn's logic of prescriptions works out, we can perhaps deduce a normative conclusion. If, however, the premise is normative, then it presupposes precisely what Blackburn is aiming to prove, namely, that there is a best possible set of attitudes one of which is (or entails) that neither system is better than the other.

Finally, given that Blackburn holds, as we have seen, that evaluative truth is single and that therefore meta-ethical relativism is not a viable option, it is difficult to see how one could find oneself in a situation whether neither system can be improved. Blackburn thus appears to be arguing that if neither system can be improved, then at least one of the systems can be improved. If instead he means to say that if it *seems to the agent* that neither system can be improved, then at least one of the systems can be improved; then the question arises how the agent's impression could possibly yield the relevant conclusion.

XIII. AMBITIOUS QR: FUNDAMENTAL MORAL ERROR

We have seen that expressivism has it that on the deep level of moral and legal discourse our value judgements do not express beliefs and are not truth-apt, but simply express the speaker's attitudes, preferences, emotions, etc, and that quasi-realism is a theory that aims to account, on the basis of expressivism, for the realist (or objectivist) features on the surface-level of moral and legal discourse. The problem of moral error arises (i) because the quasi-realist aims to account for our ordinary moral talk as it actually proceeds, (ii) because our ordinary moral talk assumes, or appears to assume, that there is such a thing as moral error, and (iii) because it is difficult to understand, on the quasi-realist picture, wherein such error is supposed to consist – if there are no moral properties and thus no moral facts, and if value judgements do not even aim to report such facts, but only express our attitudes, what could it mean to say that such a judgement is false?

Blackburn has argued that, on the quasi-realist analysis, a person who is contemplating the possibility of moral error is really contemplating a hypothetical situation in which his or her set of attitudes has been improved through a correction of a defect of information, sensitivity, maturity, imagination or coherence, or something along those lines:

> How can I make sense of fears of my own fallibility? Well, there are a number of things I admire: for instance, information, sensitivity, maturity, imagination, coherence. I know that other people show defects in these respects, and that these defects lead to bad opinions. But can I exempt myself from the same possibility? Of course not (that would be unpardonably smug). So I can think that some of my opinions are due to defects of information, sensitivity, maturity, imagination, and coherence. If I really set out to investigate if this is true, I stand on one part of the (Neurath) boat and inspect the other parts.[67]

Although this account of moral error appears to presuppose that the agent in question already *has* a positive attitude to information, maturity, etc, Andy Egan finds the account satisfactory as regards moral error in general, but argues that it is not satisfactory as regards (what he refers to as) *fundamental* moral error.[68] Having explained that the problem of moral error concerns first-person error about the present time, not third-person error, or first-person error at some other time than the present,[69] he makes a distinction between stable and unstable moral beliefs and explains that, on the quasi-realist analysis, a moral belief is *stable* if, and only if, the believer would not abandon it whatever changes to his set of beliefs he would endorse and *unstable* if, and only if, it is not stable. Next, he contemplates a situation in which two persons disagree about some moral

---

[67] Blackburn, *Ruling Passions* (n 18) 318.

[68] A Egan, 'Quasi-Realism and Fundamental Moral Error' (2007) 85 *Australasian Journal of Philosophy* 205–219.

[69] Ibid, 208–10.

matter and points out that the reason why there is such disagreement might be that they started out from very different substantive starting points, or that they accept very different standards of improvement as regards their sets of attitudes, or both. In such a situation, he points out, the incompatible views may well be *stable* in the sense that no matter what changes in their sets of beliefs the persons involved would endorse, they would not abandon the relevant beliefs. What we are faced with in such a case, he explains,[70] is a matter of *fundamental disagreement*; and, he points out, where there is fundamental disagreement, there is also *fundamental error*. For, he reasons, if we accept that there might be fundamental disagreement without fundamental error, we would (tacitly) be accepting that (meta-ethical) relativism is a live option, and this would not be in keeping with ordinary moral practice, which is what the quasi-realist aims to explain.

Egan argues, more specifically, that the quasi-realist is committed to accepting three incompatible theses, namely, (1) the no smugness thesis, (2) the thesis of fundamental fallibility, and (3) the thesis of first-person immunity.[71] According to the no smugness thesis, as we have already seen (in the Blackburn quotation), there is no sort of moral error to which others are subject, but against which I myself am immune; according to the thesis of fundamental fallibility, as we have just seen, it is possible for people's stable moral beliefs to be mistaken;[72] and according to the thesis of first-person immunity, I have an *a priori* guarantee against fundamental moral error.[73] The problem for Blackburn, Egan points out, is that he is committed to all three theses, which are incompatible.[74]

Why are they incompatible? Egan reasons that, on Blackburn's account of moral error, for a person, Smith, to be fundamentally in error, she must have a moral view that is both stable *and* mistaken, but given Blackburn's account, this simply cannot happen.[75] For, on this account, Smith's moral belief that *P* is stable if, and only if, it would survive any improving change of her set of beliefs, and it is mistaken if, and only if, it would *not* survive any improving change of her belief set, that is, if, and only if, it is not stable. If Egan is right, Blackburn has to admit that, on his analysis, a person *cannot* have a view that is both stable and mistaken, and this is to say that one has an *a priori* guarantee against fundamental moral error.

Egan argues that the quasi-realist must not abandon the no smugness thesis, because doing so would mean giving up the attempt to account for our moral practice, which is a central quasi-realist idea.[76] Similarly, abandoning the thesis of fundamental fallibility would involve giving up on a central component of the quasi-realist enterprise, namely, that it aims to account for ordinary moral

[70] Ibid, 212.
[71] These are my labels. Egan does not use precisely the same labels.
[72] Egan, 'Quasi-Realism' (n 68) 213.
[73] Ibid, 214.
[74] Ibid, 215.
[75] Ibid, 214.
[76] Ibid, 216.

practice.[77] Finally, abandoning the thesis of first-person immunity would be
very difficult. Egan concludes that the quasi-realist must come up with a different account of moral error, one that avoids commitment to either the thesis
of fundamental fallibility or the thesis of first-person immunity.[78] He does not
believe that the quasi-realist can do this, however.

Blackburn has considered Egan's objections and has countered that the
attribution to him (Blackburn) of the first-person immunity thesis rests on a
conflation of two similar but different views about what it means for a belief
to be stable.[79] He points out that whereas Egan attributes to quasi-realists the
view (EQR) that a belief is stable if, and only if, it would survive anything that
is an improvement, the quasi-realist view (QR) is that a belief is stable if, and
only if, it would survive anything that the person whose belief it is *would regard*
as an improvement; and he concludes that without this conflation Egan cannot
force upon the quasi-realist the view that it is *a priori* that a stable belief cannot
be mistaken. The reason, Blackburn explains, is that while one might plausibly
argue that (EQR) is *a priori*, it does not introduce any asymmetry between the
agent and others, and that while (QR) does introduce an asymmetry between the
agent and others, it is not *a priori*.[80] Having (QR) in mind, he reasons as follows:
'What you regard as an improvement might be a deterioration, and vice versa.
And if I can think this about you, then equally you will be able to think it about
me, and it cannot be *a priori* that you are wrong.'[81]

I find Blackburn's line of reasoning convincing and conclude that the quasi-
realist does not have to worry about the problem of fundamental moral error.
I should add that I also doubt that the quasi-realist has to accept the thesis of
fundamental fallibility, for it is not clear to me that people in general presuppose
that there are correct answers to the moral questions they debate. It is worth
noting here that Gilbert Harman adopts a quasi-realist stance in defending a
version of meta-ethical relativism, namely, in order to account for the existence
of basic moral disagreement on the basis of such relativism.[82] Clearly, Harman
does not believe that quasi-realism is incompatible with meta-ethical relativism.

XIV. AMBITIOUS QR: DOOMED IF YOU DO AND DOOMED IF YOU DON'T?

Crispin Wright objects to Blackburn's quasi-realist programme, that it confronts
a serious dilemma: either it fails, which means that Blackburn's projectivism is

---

[77] Ibid.
[78] Ibid.
[79] S Blackburn, 'Truth and *A Priori* Possibility: Egan's Charge Against Quasi-Realism' (2008) 87
Australasian Journal of Philosophy 205–8.
[80] Ibid, 206
[81] Ibid.
[82] G Harman, 'Moral Relativism' in G Harman and JJ Thomson, *Moral Relativism and Moral
Objectivity* (Oxford, Blackwell, 1996) 32–44.

not able to account for our linguistic practices, or it succeeds, which means that Blackburn has managed to explain that our linguistic practices *are* assertoric and truth-apt, which is what he began by denying. So if Wright is right, the quasi-realist is doomed if he succeeds (p→⊥) and doomed if he doesn't succeed (–p →⊥). Here is Wright:

> The goal of the quasi-realist is to explain how *all* the features of some problematic region of discourse that might inspire a realist construal of it can be harmonized with objectivism. But if this program succeeds, and provides inter alia – as Blackburn himself anticipates – an account of what appears to be ascription of truth and falsity to statements in the region, then we shall wind up – running the connection between truth and assertion in the other direction – with a rehabilitation of the notion that such statements rank as assertions, with truth-conditions, after all. Blackburn's quasi-realist thus confronts a rather obvious dilemma. Either his program fails – in which case he does not, after all, explain how the projectivism that inspires it can satisfactorily account for the linguistic practices in question – or it succeeds, in which case it makes good all the things the projectivist started out wanting to deny: that the discourse in question is genuinely assertoric, aimed at truth, and so on.[83]

Wright notes that Blackburn might want to object to the proposed dilemma, that his (Blackburn's) idea is precisely that it is *only the quasi-realist account*, of, say, moral reasoning and moral statements that gives us the right to speak of moral matters in an objectivist way. Wright objects, however, that if this is so, the quasi-realist program is actually a *detour* on the way to what counts, namely, the notion of *truth*:

> Working with that idea, and pursuit of the quasi-realist program on its basis, may help us to focus on the notion of truth that is appropriate to the statements in question. But once that focus is achieved, we have to drop the idea – and it hardly seems credible that only by this somewhat circuitous route can the requisite focus be gained.[84]

I find Wright's objection well worth thinking about, though I also find the proposed alternative, that the notion of truth is not uniform across all regions of assertoric discourse, somewhat difficult to understand.[85] I shall not, however, pursue the very difficult subject matter of truth here.

XV. CONCLUSION

I have argued (1) that in order to understand legal reasoning one needs to distinguish between first-order and second-order legal statements and between two types of first-order legal statements, namely, committed legal statements and detached legal statements, and to be clear about which type of legal statement

---

[83] Wright, 'Realism' (n 54) 35.
[84] Ibid, 35.
[85] For Wright's discussion of the matter, see ibid, 35–42.

one is concerned with; and (2) that, on an expressivist analysis, first-order legal statements are not normative at all. I have also argued (3) that Scandinavian realist Karl Olivecrona's anti-normativism is indeed problematic, (4) that expressivism in general is problematic, too, and (5) that Simon Blackburn's quasi-realism can provide us with an interesting, and in many ways attractive, account of our practice(s) of legal reasoning, conceived as resting on an expressivist foundation. However, I have also argued (6) that the modest version of quasi-realism is problematic, because it assumes that clashing attitudes (which are assumed to lack truth-value) are inconsistent; and (7) that ambitious quasi-realism is even more problematic, primarily (i) because it assumes that there is such a thing as a best possible set of attitudes, but also (ii) because it might be self-defeating.

6

On the Boundaries
of Normativity in Law

ADITI BAGCHI[1]

D EBATES ABOUT NORMATIVISM tend to take law and legal systems as a phenomena about which we can speak generally. That is, whether law is normative is not usually a question that we ask about a given legal system except by way of example or to test the limits of a theory. There is certainly much we can learn from thinking about law in this way.

My question here, though, is different from the primary scholarly question in that I will explore whether features of history and institutional context might inform our thinking about the nature and extent of law's claim to normativity. In particular, I will suggest that the operation of the common law, as distinct from the civil law, might do some work and that the claims of law on private citizens might be more expansive in some ways, in common law countries. The common law is replete with soft legal norms that derive from the public justifications behind hard legal norms. While there are clearly other kinds of soft norms in civil law countries, and probably in civil law, theories of justification probably do not give rise to legal reasons that apply to private citizens in the way that I will argue that they do in common law. The resulting conclusion that common law effectively generates large categories of content-independent reasons that are not however usually exclusionary reasons might be surprising.

The common law has a few features of immediate relevance. First, it is precedential. Cases are binding on judges in the same jurisdiction that decide cases that present the same question. Here we must distinguish between the holding of a case, which is binding, and dicta, the legal status of which is less clear. While there is disagreement on the weight future judges should give dicta, dicta is at least not binding in the formal sense of the legal rule.[2]

[1] Many thanks to Professors Alexander Somek, Michael Potacs and Christoph Bezemek for the invitation to present this lecture at the University of Vienna, and to participate in this edited volume.
[2] *Kokkonen v Guardian Life Ins. Co.*, 511 U.S. 375, 379 (1994) ('It is to the holdings of our cases, rather than their dicta, that we must attend.').

What exactly is dicta?[3] Dicta amounts to what judges say in order to reach their conclusions. It may include commentary on other cases, as in a comparison of the facts of the case at hand and the facts of another. But it can broadly include other kinds of judicial reasoning. Of course, it can include good old-fashioned interpretation of case law or statutes. But especially notable for our purposes, it can include any reason, including straight up moral, economic or functional reasons for preferring the legal rule ultimately adopted over other possible rules.

This brings us to two other features of common law. First, judges make law.[4] Hans Kelsen argued that this is true everywhere, and rejected the theory that judges merely apply law created by legislatures.[5] But in the operation of the common law it can be said that there is a more transparent (or openly acknowledged) background norm that invests judges with law-making authority. Of course, the democratic credentials of judges is a controversial matter unto itself, but their authority to create new legal norms is not inconsistent with a picture in which all legal norms derive their authority from a foundational constitutional norm that delineates law-making procedures.

The other less-discussed feature we have already observed is the practice by which judges explain their reasons. Again, this explication is not limited to identifying existing norms and interpreting them. It self-consciously and transparently includes original law-making. There are largely two scenarios that might prompt a judge to state a new legal rule. First, existing case law might not speak to the facts of a case. Normally, a judge will attempt to link her new rule with existing rules. For example, she might cast the new rule as an extension of the existing rule. But sometimes judges will just distinguish the facts of previous cases with the facts of the case at hand and articulate a new rule tailored to the new facts.

In other cases, a judge will overturn precedent. The weight assigned to precedent is the US system is of special salience today as the political composition of the Supreme Court makes it possible to overturn a great many critical cases of constitutional significance. Judges of comparable substantive political

---

[3] *See* JM Stinson, 'Why Dicta Becomes Holding and Why It Matters', (2010) 76 *Brookly Law Review* 219, 264; T Fowler, 'Holding, Dictum ... Whatever', (2003) 25 *North Carolina Central Law Journal* 139; M Dorf, 'Dicta and Article III', (1994) 142 *University of Pennsylvania Law Review* 1997; K Greenawalt, 'Reflections on Holding and Dictum', (1989) 39 *Journal of Legal Education* 431; HJ Friendly, 'In Praise of Erie--and of the New Federal Common Law', (1964) 39 *New York University Law Review* 383; D Coale & W Couture, 'Dictum Revisited', (1952) 4 *Stanford Law Review* 509; A Goodhart, 'Determining the Ratio Decidendi of a Case', (1930) 40 *Yale Law Journal* 161.

[4] See A Barak, 'Foreward: A Judge on Judging: The Role of a Supreme Court in a Democracy', (2002) 116 *Harvard Law Review* 16, 62; CJ Peters, 'Adjudication as Representation', (1997) 97 *Columbia Law Review* 312, 315; F Schauer, 'Opinions as Rules', (1986) 53 University of Chicago Law Review 682, 684.

[5] H Kelsen, *Pure Theory of Law* (Max Knight trans., 1967) (Lawbrook Exchange Ltd, 2009) 255.

inclination appear differentially willing to depart from precedent.[6] But of course their dilemma as judges derives from the fact that they are understood both to be bound by precedent and also to be authorised to depart from it. There is no hard legal norm that dictates when they may overturn a case.[7]

Whether they are adopting an altogether new rule or overturning an existing rule, judges can be more or less open about the fact of their lawmaking. One might take this to reflect some discomfort with this power. But while exercising the power in a given case removes cover for a judge – both from appellate courts and in the court of public opinion – there is little doubt that judges are invested with authority to make law when they decide cases. It is presumably for this reason that it is especially important that their reasoning be detailed and transparent.

Of course, judges are not entitled to make any law, at any time. Most obviously, they cannot overturn norms that derive, or appear to derive, directly from a written constitution. Nor can they overturn statutes, unless the statute is unconstitutional. The subjects in which judges have the most substantial role in making law are in the private law. This is why the examples I will talk about today are from three pillars of private law-common law: namely, contract, tort and property. By now, every state in the US has a host of statutes in these subject areas. But they do not purport to set out the law exhaustively. The common law, by which I mean a substantial case law, is the primary source for many if not most legal norms in common law subjects.

With those preliminaries out of the way, I would now like to turn to my primary subject: the peculiar status of public justifications for private law norms in a common law system. Do judicial and perhaps even other public reasons behind common law rules have normative status? That is, do reasons behind rules give people reasons to act in addition to reasons that derive from the rules themselves? Are these reasons that derive from justifications exclusionary, as law ordinarily claims its norms to be for persons subject to its norms?

I will not attempt to argue that the 'standard' justifications for rules are legal norms themselves, at least in the sense of hard legal norms. I do not mean by hard legal norm a 'rule' as opposed to a standard. I am referring to the weight of the norm rather than its clarity. The line between hard and soft legal norms can be variously described and the concept of soft law most often arises with respect to international law.[8] For my purposes here, allow only that a soft legal

---

[6] See J Knight & L Epstein, 'The Norm of Stare Decisis', (1996) 40 *American Journal of Political Science* 1018, 1029 (showing that many judges adhere to precedent at expense of their ideology).

[7] See DA Farber, 'The Rule of Law and the Law of Precedents', (2006) 90 *Minnesota Law Review* 1173 (discussing disagreement on weight of values that cut in favour of and against, respectively, rigorous application of stare decisis).

[8] See GC Shaffer & MA Pollack, 'Hard vs. Soft Law: Alternatives, Complements, and Antagonists in International Governance', (2010) 94 *Minnesota Law Review* 706, 707 (describing legal positivist, rationalist, and constructivist conceptions of hard and soft law).

norm does not give rise to material consequence upon breach, standing alone or in the ordinary operation of the law. Breach of a soft legal norm might have consequence where there is *also* a breach of a related hard legal norm. In that case, it might result in a greater or different penalty, for example. And sometimes, as in international law or in the extraordinary context of impeachment, political bodies are charged with enforcement. Such bodies are not restricted to enforcement of hard legal norms.

If that were all that could be said of soft legal norms, they might not be of great interest to scholars of private law. But soft legal norms can be important even where they do limited doctrinal work on their own. Specifically, they may have some normative effect on private actors. That is, even when a soft norm does not usually direct legal officials, it may address private citizens. This is especially true where there is no hard legal norm that occupies the space. For example, imagine a hypothetical world where there is no legal rule that entitles a person to damages when specific performance is unavailable for breach of contract, but there is a soft legal norm that a court is more likely to award specific performance or some other injunctive relief if no compensation has been offered to the non-breaching party. We could say there is a soft legal norm that favours compensation. But even if an offer of compensation did just the same work under the doctrine of specific performance, where there is a hard legal rule entitling the nonbreaching party to compensation by way of legal damages, private actors will not look to the soft norm favouring voluntary compensation for guidance.

Of concern in this chapter is a very special kind of soft norm. These are norms that seem to logically follow from the justification behind a legal rule, but have never been anointed as hard law. I will explore three examples in greater depth shortly but consider Learned Hand's formula. Learned Hand was a well-respected judge who stated the following formula to justify liability: if the probability of harm multiplied by the magnitude of the harm exceeds the cost of the precaution taken, the defendant should be liable (B less than PL).[9] This is not a legal rule. However, many people have found it compelling and it is at the heart of legal economic treatment of torts.[10] One cannot say now that it is the law that a person must undertake any precaution that costs less than the magnitude of harm it is intended to prevent, discounted for probability. But arguably, the soft norms do generate a reason for individuals to take such precautions – and this is key – a reason that does not depend on the merits of the formulation. It is not just that Hand identified a reason that applied to private actors already. Nor is it that he offers expert guidance, such that he acts as expert authority on the scope of the hard legal rules that constitute the law of negligence. Nor is it merely that the formula predicts when a person will be held liable, and thus

---

[9] *U.S. v Carroll Towing*, 159 F.2d 169 (2d Cir. 1947).
[10] See RJ Allen, 'Two Aspects of Law and Theory', (2000) 37 SAN DIEGO LAW REVIEW 743, 749 (observing that legal economists treat the Learned Hand formula as essential to tort law).

generates reasons of self-interest for compliance. My contention, or at least the one I wish to explore, is that the Hand formula – at least if it were widely cited and regarded as the justification for liability under negligence law – gives rise to content-independent reasons for taking certain precautions. It would have normative effect in just the manner of a legal norm, even if its effect was not the same as a case rule that directed boat operators to provide life jackets to all passengers.

The common law context of Hand's pronouncement is doing a lot of work. A civil law opinion is unlikely to offer such a formula in passing. There would also be a code that purports to state fully the conditions of liability and it cannot be amended by the dicta in a judicial opinion. And other judges would not be bound by anything Hand said, in a civil law system, so it would be peculiar to elevate language outside of the holding.

That a soft legal norm could have normative effect in a common law system is perhaps more plausible if we consider the particular normative shortfalls of a common law system. Arguably, one of the disadvantages of the common law method from a rule of law perspective is that it seems to operate ex post.[11] Liability conditions are not stated clearly up front. We do no worry too much about this because, after all, no one is going to jail (on the basis of private law claims) so liberty is not at stake. And just as important, even new rules are supposed to be responsive to custom and evolving social facts; so there is usually no great element of surprise. It is also important to observe, however, that the normative status of legal justifications and their status as soft legal norms functions to shrink to a substantially smaller set those cases where private actors do not have appropriate legal guidance with respect to their conduct. The normative status of justifications effectively means people who are found liable usually failed to do something they *ought to have done* given the set of legal norms in place, even in those cases where judges appear to be issuing new legal norms. While it is implausible that every hard legal norm stated by a common law judge (and perhaps also by a civil law judge) is determined by prior hard law, it is very plausible that almost all new hard law is supported by justificatory theories that are already out there and already enjoy legal status.

Notwithstanding the non-binding status of dicta, justifications are already (and properly) understood to be normatively consequential for legal officials charged with applying and interpreting the law. Although it is not clear exactly how past judicial reasons should inform subsequent judicial reasoning, that question is different from the one here, which is how justifications should alter conduct by private persons. Private law is a particularly interesting domain in which to ask this question because it directly and indirectly delegates legal power to private persons. Common law on private law does this work by way

[11] Cf. S Issacharoff, 'Regulating After the Fact', (2007) 56 *DePaul Law Review* 375, 377 (discussing this feature as a virtue).

of judicial opinions that do not cleanly bind legal norms. I will study public justifications in three areas of private law that illustrate the challenges of delineating the boundaries of normativity in law. It turns out that normativity is not so easily contained as more modest (or defensive) accounts of legal normativity would imply.

I. NORMATIVISM AND PUBLIC JUSTIFICATION

I will now try to situate my claim in the landscape of the extensive literature on legal normativism.

Normativists argue that certain practices are normative for their participants.[12] Legal normativists make this claim on behalf of legal systems.[13] My aim is not to advance the debate between normativists and anti-normativists but instead to study one dimension of the picture painted by normativists, that is, that the legal system has boundaries within which norms are binding. The claim that law is obligatory is bolstered, or at least it is less radical, if the domain within which its claims are binding is neatly bound.

The primary target of anti-normativists has been the potential problem of infinite regress, in which legal norms are valid by virtue of other legal norms but ultimately rely on a foundational norm of allegedly mysterious origin.[14] Short of escaping into an epistemological construct that has no independent normative force, we can try to solve the mystery of origin by way of democratic theory – the foundational norm derives its authority from the collective decision-making of the population subject to it. I am sympathetic to that solution, notwithstanding the difficulties in explaining how the particular decision-making procedures deployed gain their legitimacy. Certainly, I am happy to sacrifice any claim to total insularity on the part of legal normativity. My focus here, though, is a problem at the opposite end of the so-called hierarchy of norms: the porous boundaries of the legal system that make it difficult to identify those legal norms which purport to bind.

The status of public justification can be broken down along two lines. We can distinguish between justifications offered by lawmakers, such as those stated

---

[12] For a critical take on the claims of normativists across fields of application, *see* S Turner, *EXPLAINING THE NORMATIVE* (Oxford, Polity Press, 2010).

[13] See, eg, RM Dworkin, 'The Model of Rules', (1967) 35 *UNIVERSITY OF CHICAGO LAW REVIEW* 14; HLA Hart, *THE CONCEPT OF LAW* (Oxford, Oxford University Press, 1961). Although Dworkin and Hart disagreed over how legal norms are constituted, they both treat law as a normative system. For a summary of the reasons that drive the view that law has its own distinct normativity, as well as a rejection of that conclusion, see S Hershovitz, 'The End of Jurisprudence', (2015) 124 *YALE LAW JOURNAL* 1160, 1187.

[14] See M La Torre, 'The Hierarchical Model and H. L. A. Hart's Concept of Law', (2013) 21 Revus – *Journal for Constitutional Theory and Philosophy of Law* 141 (summarising the problem of infinite regress).

in the preface to legislation or in judicial opinions, and justifications offered in public discourse about legal norms, whether in the press or in academic scholarship. And then again we can distinguish between the normative effect of a justificatory theory on the judgment of other legal officials, on the one hand, and on the decision-making of private persons, on the other.

Because my interest is in the special questions raised by common-law private law (which I will usually refer to simply as common law), I will say little about the status of justifications offered by lawmakers. Notable for my purposes is that the status of legislative reasons should be understood to turn on a variety of institutional features, including the functional relationship between the legislative and judicial branches. Thus, aspects of the common law probably have implications for how we should regard even the kinds of legislative reasons we might also observe in civilian systems.

I am concerned primarily with justifications offered by judges in the course of adjudicating disputes in common law. I am interested in other public justifications, such as those in legal scholarship, only inasmuch as they are given some credence in judicial opinions. A theory proposed to explain a legal rule, that has never been acknowledged by courts is unlikely to have any law-like status. But public justifications that have been 'picked up' by courts can be incorporated into what we I have called the 'soft legal norms' that should figure into decision-making about the law.

Again, I am also primarily interested in decision-making by private actors rather than by legal officials. But again, we can learn some lessons from the status of public justifications as they are directed to other legal officials. It is a useful case because their status has been addressed: dicta is not binding. But the line between the legal judgment and its supporting dicta is unclear and because reasoning is predictive, on some theories of precedent, it should be binding. It is plausible to say that dicta has a normative effect on decision-making by future judges even if it is not strictly speaking binding, a concept we might reserve for hard legal norms.

My interest here in the status of public justifications for legal officials extends insofar as it informs my main inquiry, which is whether public justifications as soft legal norms can make private conduct permissible or impermissible from the standpoint of law where the hard legal norm is silent. (The soft norm cannot contradict the hard norm because the former is a justification for the latter, and would fail as a justification if there was contradiction.) Any legal status for the soft norm derives from the hard norm – the actual legal rule – in the way that normativists expect lower norms to derive authority from higher norms.

II. COMMON LAW JUSTIFICATIONS

Let us think through the status of public justifications, as contained in judicial opinions, for private persons in three areas. My examples are from tort, contract and property, respectively. In the tort case, the justification is robustly developed in judicial reasoning. In the contracts case, there is a tight fit but no consistent endorsement. Finally, in the property example, the justification is in controversy. No justification can presently motivate private conduct. However, the controversy allows us to consider whether the rule could be understood to operate differently were one justification to be referenced repeatedly in judicial decisions. I argue that it would.

A. Tort

Consider first whether a court that finds conduct unreasonable in the context of a tort claim in part because it is inconsistent with professional standards gives professionals reason to comply with a revised professional standard before it has been specifically endorsed by a court. Judicial reasoning in this case expands the realm of normativity beyond legal norms that are the product of recognised procedures for generating law – unless we say there is actually a background norm that gives justification legal status.

The most typical example of professional negligence is a claim for medical malpractice. Imagine a judicial decision that holds a surgeon is not liable because a professional body has not issued any official recommendation that a different procedure be used than the one that the surgeon actually used. The professional body is not self-regulating – that is, it has not been delegated lawmaking authority. Its recommendations are merely guidance to courts as to what the prevailing standard of care is. Moreover, the court never declares that the standard of care is just what the professional body recommends, such that it is just a rule that one must comply with its recommendations (which in that case, would of course cease to be recommendations). Subsequent to the case that determines there is no liability, the professional association issues just that recommendation which the court observed was absent at the time of its decision. On these facts, I would posit that though it is not generally true that doctors are legally required to comply with the recommendations of certain professional associations, it is nevertheless required of a surgeon deciding whether to use the new procedure at issue in the earlier case that she comply with the newly issued recommendation.

B. Contract

Next, consider the status of efficient breach theory. That theory purports to explain why expectation damages, which aim to put the plaintiff where she would have been economically had the contract been performed, are usually the best remedy for breach of contract. (As opposed to, say, reliance damages, which put the plaintiff where she was at the time of contract, or specific performance, which entitles the plaintiff to actual performance). Efficient breach theory observes that expectation damages motivate a potential breacher to breach if and only if the benefit to herself from breaching exceeds the loss she will impose on the other party.[15] This is not a legal principle. Nevertheless, it does imply that the remedial scheme offered by contract contemplates breach by a party of her first-order contractual obligations when her gain exceeds the loss borne by the other party. It appropriately informs private reasoning as well.[16] Although it does not give rise to an exclusionary reason, it generates a justificatory reason for private conduct that derives from a legal norm. Efficient breach theory would generate a soft norm permitting breach where it is efficient to do so.

As a public justification for the rule of expectation damages, the theory allows parties merely to pay or perform (ie, not simply to perform). Although the soft norm does not give rise to any direct consequence separate from the doctrine of expectation damages, it could be important to the application of hard norms. It limits the conditions under which breach of contract is a legal wrong to those where no compensation is paid. It speaks to whether specific performance would be made available, or whether restitution should be available. It might affect whether we read a contract as one for alternative performance or whether it is better read as specifying liquidated damages or conditions for cancellation. The public justification for the expectation damages rule alters the normative status of the breacher's conduct within the law *even if* we continue to regard breach of the contractual commitment a moral wrong or imprudent for other reasons.

C. Property

Finally, consider the doctrine of adverse possession, which transfers title to a person who uses someone else's property as if it were her own for more than some specified period. It has been argued that, though the doctrine does not openly require 'good faith' on the part of the adverse possessor (that is, a belief that it is already her property), it effectively requires an 'innocent' mental state.[17] Others resist and argue that the adverse possessor's state of mind should be irrelevant.[18] Here too, if the latter justifications for the doctrine of adverse

---

[15] RL Birmingham, 'Breach of Contract, Damage Measures, and Economic Efficiency', (1970) 24 *RUTGERS LAW REVIEW* 273, 284; R Posner, *ECONOMIC ANALYSIS OF LAW* (Wolters Kluwer, 1972) 57.

[16] See SV Shiffrin, 'The Divergence of Contract and Promise', (2007) 120 *HARVARD LAW REVIEW* 708, 731 (criticising the conflict between the apparent guidance of that doctrine and the requirements of morality).

[17] See RH Helmholz, 'Adverse Possession and Subjective Intent', (1983) 61 *WASHINGTON UNIVERSITY LAW QUARTERLY* 331, 331–32.

[18] AJ Casner, (1952) 3 *AMERICAN LAW OF PROPERTY* § 15.4 (characterising objective standard as majority rule in the US). See also LA Fennell, 'Efficient Trespass: The Case for 'Bad Faith' Adverse Possession', (2006) 100 *NORTHWESTERN LAW REVIEW* 1037 (arguing that intentional overstep should be not only tolerated but required).

possession came to dominate public discourse about the rule, those justifications should be understood to justify private conduct in a way that a rule that is merely silent about mental states would not. Indeed, the prospect of justifying strategic behaviour is among the significant considerations in weighing the merits of a theory of adverse possession that is indifferent to the intention of an adverse possessor. Such a theory cannot rely on acoustic separation between those who will apply the rule and those that will profit from it. Otherwise, we are left with a legal regime that cannot meet rule of law requirements for transparency.

III. THE SCOPE OF NORMATIVITY, SOURCES OF NORMATIVITY

In conclusion, let us return to a point to which I alluded earlier. Normativity in a common law system may reach more private judgments than we think, and in particular, more than in a civil law system.

The common law is generally thought to require less of its subjects. It imposes fewer mandatory terms, fewer substantive obligations between strangers and also between intimates. Most notably, there is no duty to rescue, no duty to bargain in good faith, and no duty to leave property to your children or to care for adult family members.

But there is, I want to suggest, another sense in which the very method of common law norm generation by way of adjudication actually subjects private actors to a much wider swath of legal norms than does the civil code in civil law countries. The institution of the common law makes a difference for what counts as law at all. And much more is binding on private actors than in civil law countries, where it is more plausible to say that the law just requires compliance with norms anointed by the legislature. If there is a background norm that entitles judges to make law, the boundaries of law itself are more porous and actually stretch out further just by virtue of the fact that judges do a lot more talking and thinking aloud than do legislatures.

I cannot claim to have shown that this is so. It might turn out that the best way to understand legal reasoning is just that it is helpful but not binding at all. That all the justificatory talk gives rise to no content independent reasons for private action. I would disagree with this characterisation but see it as at least as plausible as a view that law is not binding on private actors at all and merely generates prudential or moral reasons that we can account for without claiming any special species of legal normativity. However, for those who accept that law is a normative system, my suggestion is this: the boundaries of normativity depend on institutional considerations and, in a common law system, it is pervasive. In fact, it might permeate our judgements about most interactions with other people. In this respect, common law's substantive forbearance, its desire to leave as much space for private judgement and agency, might be partially offset. And the very idea of legal normativity is burdened by the burdens on private judgement implied by this idea.

7

Can We Escape Normativism in Law?

MICHAEL POTACS

I. INTRODUCTION

THE TERM 'NORMATIVISM', it seems, was first used by Carl Schmitt in order to define Legal Positivism as the object of his critique. For Schmitt, it is characteristic for the 'pure normativist method' that it 'isolates and absolutizes the norm or rule'.[1] In contrast, Schmitt prefers what he calls 'concrete-order-thinking', for which '"order" is juristically not primarily "rule" or a summation of rules, but conversely, a rule is only a component and a medium of order'.[2] The 'concrete-order-thinking' of Carl Schmitt does, of course, not seem to have many followers in contemporary legal theory or legal doctrine.

Nonetheless, new theoretical approaches have evolved which consider themselves as opposed to Normativism[3] or the 'abstract normative understanding of rules'[4] of Legal Positivism. This includes the System Theory on which Thomas Vesting's recently published book 'Legal Theory' is based. The System Theory understands the legal system not so much as a system of norms but rather as a 'social system, as a permanently running communication system'.[5] Differing from Legal Positivism for the System Theory 'the operation of the legal system is not an "application" of an already given order'.[6] According to *Vesting*, the System Theory proceeds on the assumption of an ostensible 'widely shared' view that 'order is the result of praxis, and not its presupposition'.[7]

---

[1] C Schmitt, *On the Three Types of Juristic Thought*, trans J Bendersky (Westport, London, Praeger Publishers, 2004) 49.

[2] Ibid, 48.

[3] T Vesting, *Rechtstheorie* (Munich, Verlag C.H. Beck, 2007) 20 ff.

[4] T Vesting, *Legal Theory*, trans A Shoichet (Munich, Oxford, Baden-Baden, Verlag C.H. Beck, Hart Publishing, Nomos Verlagsgesellschaft, 2018) 23.

[5] Vesting (n 4) 4.

[6] Ibid.

[7] Ibid.

In the following, I will first address the question if and to what extent this criticism of a Legal Positivism with 'normativist' characteristics is justified. In a second step, I will try to answer the question of which understanding is required by democratic constitutions based on the rule of law: an understanding of 'law' as a normative guideline for the use in practice which is in line with Normativism or, conversely, an understanding of 'law' as 'result of practice' in the sense of the System Theory. As all legal orders are normative orders, I will finally try to give an answer to the question: can we escape Normativism in law?

II. CONCEPT

In order to do so, it is necessary to outline the basic idea of Normativism as criticised by Carl Schmitt and the System Theory. It is a form of Legal Positivism that does not address a justification but rather provides a description of norms of positive law. Normativism, thus understood, certainly has to accept that norms can ultimately only be derived from other (higher-ranking) norms and not from facts.[8] However, this 'dualism of is and ought' in the concept of normativist Legal Positivism is only relevant for the *description* of validity relations within a positive legal order. The validity of norms within a legal order cannot be derived from facts, but results from the authorisation of other norms in this legal order. From a normativist point of view, all norms of a legal order must ultimately find their validity in the constitution of this legal order (or in the opinion of Hans Kelsen in the acceptance of a basic norm[9]).

Nevertheless, Normativism does, thereby, by no means construct 'an insurmountable barrier between the world of facts, to which actual (human) behaviour also belongs, and the normativity or validity of legal norms',[10] as alleged by the System Theory. Normativism's object of reflection are legal provisions. The purpose of these provisions is to regulate social life. Therefore, it is needless to say that Normativism starts from the premise that legal norms aim to have an influence on social reality. Accordingly, the meaning of legal norms can never be understood as detached from their objectives.[11] In this sense, Normativism understands legal norms as the legislator's 'act of will'.[12]

In this respect, the System Theory objects that thereby 'law in the modern (liberal) society would be a random "steering mass" of political institutions, authorized to posit law in the context of constitutional "proportionality"'.[13]

---

[8] H Kelsen, *Pure Theory of Law*, trans M Knight (Berkeley, University California Press, 1967) 5 f.

[9] Kelsen (n 8) 8 f. Sceptical against the necessity of the assumption of a 'basic norm' to describe positive law, M Potacs, 'Objektive Rechtswissenschaft ohne Grundnorm' (2005) 36 *Rechtstheorie* 5.

[10] Vesting (n 4) 23.

[11] M Potacs, *Rechtstheorie*, 2nd edn (Vienna, Facultas Verlag, 2019) 187 ff.

[12] Kelsen (n 8) 5. In the words of Vesting (n 4) 24, 'acts of *volition*' (emphasis in original).

[13] Vesting (n 4) 100.

However, this objection fails to recognise the intention of Normativism described by Hans Kelsen with the following words: 'The theory attempts to answer the question what and how the law is, not how it ought to be. It is a science of law (jurisprudence), not legal politics.'[14] Or more precisely: Normativism is interested in the characteristics of *legality* and not in the *legitimacy* of positive law. Social facts as well as moral considerations are only relevant to the extent that they provide support for the detection of the content of legal provisions.

III. EXPRESSION

The interest of Normativism is therefore focused on the adequate method to describe norms of positive law. In this regard, it is of particular importance that legislators make use of the natural language in order to convey their instructions. This was, of course, also not ignored by Hans Kelsen who refers to a 'linguistic expression of the norm'.[15] However, it is also not entirely unjustified if, according to the critique of System Theory, Kelsen's 'strict normativism' addresses acts of will that are to be interpreted as norms without sufficient consideration of a 'social sets of rules and practice-proven conventions' such as 'colloquial customs'.[16] The relevance of the social context for the interpretation of legal provisions may indeed be underestimated by Hans Kelsen's Pure Theory of Law.

It has to be noted that the rules of natural or general language usage do not only consist of semantics which means the ordinary sense of words expressed in literal interpretation. A merely semantic interpretation is neither sufficient in everyday communication nor for the analysis of legal texts, since the semantic meaning is often vague and unclear and statements sometimes have a wider or narrower meaning than what semantic suggests. These aspects are taken into account by pragmatics, which concerns additional rules of communication such as, most notably, the context of a statement in its different forms.[17] This is also reflected in the traditional 'methods of legal interpretation' which include not only semantic rules of interpretation of the wording (literal interpretation), but also pragmatic criteria such as the systematic, teleological and historic interpretation or analogy. This also makes sense, since legislators use general language to convey their orders and thus want to have them understood according to the rules of general language usage.

On that basis, legal provisions can thus be understood as 'speech acts'[18] which express the 'linguistic will' of a legislator according to the rules of general

---

[14] Kelsen (n 8) 1.

[15] Kelsen (n 8) 350.

[16] Vesting (n 4) 23 f.

[17] See A Marmor, *The Language of Law* (Oxford, Oxford University Press, 2014) 22 ff; Potacs (n 11) 145 ff.

[18] Marmor (n 17) 11 ff; Potacs (n 11) 51.

language usage (comprising semantics and pragmatics). The consideration of 'colloquial customs'[19] does, however, in this understanding not lead to an abandonment of Normativism, as assumed by the System Theory. On the contrary, the consideration of 'colloquial customs' takes the objective of Normativism into account, which is to develop an adequate method to describe positive law. Such a method has to regard 'colloquial customs' which include pragmatics as manifested also in the traditional methods of legal interpretation.

However, for the System Theory, the reference to traditional methods of interpretation cannot in principle lead to a satisfying result as the System Theory considers the interpretation based on legal methodology (which was developed from the general language usage) as insufficient. In the view of the System Theory, *'each* legal interpretation' is confronted with a 'normative indeterminacy'.[20] Therefore, legal practice should attach greater significance to the 'mystery of the decision', that according to Vesting 'consists merely in that the moment of decision itself remains obscure, unassailable, absent'.[21]

Against this view of the 'indeterminacy of each legal interpretation' it can be objected that legal methodology is based on the rules of everyday communication that mostly works well. It can, therefore, hardly be assumed (and it would contradict legal experience) that *each* legal interpretation is characterised by 'indeterminacy'.[22] However, it is true that semantics and pragmatics can both express the content of a 'speech act' in everyday communication as well as in the interpretation of legal texts with a different persuasive power. It is for this reason that ultimately only a 'flexible system of interpretation criteria'[23] is capable to adequately reconstruct the will of the legislator. The result is that the meaning of a legal provision can in many cases (so called 'easy cases'[24]) be identified without any difficulties. In *some* cases (so called 'hard cases'[25]), however, semantic and pragmatic criteria have to be weighted and balanced against each other in order to identify the *attributable will*[26] of the legislator. It cannot be denied that in these cases a legal solution requires a judgement and is, hence, not without a 'decisionist rest'.[27] Nonetheless, also in these cases it is possible to limit the 'decisionist rest' by balancing the weight of semantic and pragmatic

---

[19] Potacs (n 11) 51 f.

[20] Vesting (n 4) 129 (emphasis added).

[21] Vesting (n 4) 129 f.

[22] See in more detail against this view K Greenawalt, *Law and Objectivity* (New York, Oxford, Oxford University Press, 1995) 11 ff.

[23] Potacs (n 11) 148.

[24] See F Schauer, 'Easy Cases' (1985) 58 *Southern Californian Law Review* 399.

[25] See L Fuller, 'Positivism and Fidelity to Law – A Reply to Professor Hart' (1958) 71 *Harvard Law Review* 661 f; R Dworkin, *Taking Rights Seriously* (Cambridge, Harvard University Press, 1977) 81 ff.

[26] Potacs (n 11) 52. See also A Marmor, *Interpretation and Legal Theory*, 2nd edn (Oxford, Oregon, 2005) 23 f, who speaks of 'attributing intentions'.

[27] AJ Merkl, *Allgemeines Verwaltungsrecht* (Vienna, Berlin, Verlag Julius Springer, 1927) 142, calls this 'decisionistic rest' the 'autonomous determinant' of a legal provision.

criteria in order to determine the 'attributable will' and to make the judgment comprehensible. Therefore, it is hard to see why the phenomenon of 'decisionist rest' should provoke the abandonment of Normativism in favour of a largely elusive doctrine of the 'mystery of the decision'.

IV. OBJECTIVITY

In choosing between Normativism and System Theory, more fundamental considerations have to be an issue instead. Normativism assumes that legal provisions are in principle to be understood in accordance with their *original meaning*. This is due to the fact that in the use of natural language 'speech acts' are principally interpreted according to the circumstances at the time of their expression. In fact, in every day communication the content of an utterance is the attributed meaning of the author which of course depends on the circumstances when this 'speech act' was set. As legislators use natural language to convey their orders it can be assumed that they want their provisions to be understood in the same way. That does, of course, not exclude that sometimes a dynamic interpretation that takes the current meaning into account is also possible and legitimate in a normativist view. However, it is a precondition that such a dynamic interpretation is in accordance with the will attributed to the legislator who can express this by employing terms which imply a dynamic meaning such as 'state of the art', 'state of scientific knowledge' or (as we will see later[28]) by providing 'principles' which have a 'dimension of weight'. In these cases, a dynamic interpretation can be considered in line with the 'attributed will' of the legislator as the key aspect of Normativism.

In this sense, legal provisions have an objective meaning as the attributed will of the legislator that can in general be identified and described. From a normativist perspective, the decisionist rest in the interpretation of some legal provisions does not change this. The acknowledgement of such a decisionist rest just means that the objective sense of legal provisions is in some cases vague or ambiguous. For Normativism, it is the task of legal science to identify this objective meaning of legal provisions including their decisionistic rest. Insofar, it is not totally inaccurate when Carl Schmitt states that 'normativist thinking can appeal to being impersonal and objective',[29] which he, of course, observes critically.

But also the System Theory opposes this 'model of application and subsumption'[30] of Normativism including its 'static ideas of regularity'.[31] Although from the point of view of the System Theory, 'rules and employment

---

[28] See ch VII.
[29] Schmitt (n 1) 49.
[30] Vesting (n 4) 110.
[31] Vesting (n 4) 36.

of rules' do not coincide, they are 'linked to each other in a kind of network and are carried by their earlier and later practice'.[32] Hence, the relationship between norms and application of norms is, in the understanding of the System Theory, 'circular' by which 'right and law are continuously updated anew through interpretation'.[33] The System Theory tries to take account of this understanding through a 'postmodern' methodology, which focuses on the 'mystery of the decision' (the so-called 'decision paradox'[34]), as already outlined above. The mystery of the decision characterises, in the eyes of the System Theory, each legal interpretation. In the opinion of the System Theory, the solution to this decision paradox is to be found in the 'common knowledge' that is 'produced and reproduced through continual practice in communication, in the use of language and media'.[35] It is crucial that for the System Theory this knowledge is not, as in Normativism, 'anchored in a historical continuity that is superordinate to the decision'.[36] In view of the System Theory, it is rather a 'dynamic common knowledge that is continuously changing' which should, however, avoid 'all vertical authority'[37] and must be 'continuously generated anew in a changing society'.[38]

V. CONTRAST

Normativism and System Theory can thus be concisely contrasted in this way – according to the concept of Normativism, legal provisions are 'speech acts' which express the will of the historical legislator. This meaning of legal provisions is objectively determined and can, in principle, be identified and described. It is the task of legal science to reconstruct this act of will through interpretation as an 'attributed will' and to apply it to specific circumstances. In contrast, the System Theory assumes that there is no objectively determined meaning of legal provisions ('mystery of decision'). Instead, the content of legal provisions is the product of a circular relationship between norms and application of norms and is continuously updated as a result of this relationship. Therefore, what is of crucial importance for the identification of this content is not the 'attributed will' of the legislators, but the 'common knowledge' which is in principle dynamic and subject to constant change.

An assessment of these different approaches is to be preceded by the fact that neither Normativism nor System Theory can be subject to proof in a strict

---

[32] Vesting (n 4) 37.
[33] Vesting (n 4) 131 f.
[34] Vesting (n 4) 131.
[35] Vesting (n 4) 134.
[36] Ibid.
[37] Ibid.
[38] Vesting (n 4) 136.

empirical sense. They constitute two different models of legal theory which are based on *different assumptions*: the assumption of an objective meaning of legal provisions as an 'attributed will' on the one hand (Normativism) and the assumption of a meaning of legal provisions as a dynamically changing 'common knowledge' (System Theory) on the other hand. This does, of course, not mean that a decision between these models cannot be reasonable. It depends particularly also on the specific legal system if and to what extent the respective models seem to be adequate. On that basis, I would like to address the question of which of these two models is more likely to meet the demands of a democratic constitutional state under the rule of law.

VI. DEMOCRACY AND RULE OF LAW

It is characteristic for democratic systems that government action should be bound by the will of the democratically legitimised legislator. Consequently, changes in the law and adjustments to evolving social and political circumstances should in democratic systems primarily be made by the parliamentary legislator and not by courts or administrative authorities. Of course, it depends on the particular legal order if and to what extent also courts are authorised to create law in addition to the statutes issued by the Parliament. In this respect, the power of the courts in Common Law-systems might be quite significant even though also in these systems the importance of statutes is growing.[39] In any case, in democracies the law enacted by the democratically legitimised legislator should prevail in the end.

It is highly questionable if the approach of the System Theory with its 'postmodern' methodology satisfies these requirements of democratic legislation most appropriately. This is because in this approach, the interpretation of the law in accordance with a continuously changing 'common knowledge' and hence also an adjustment of legal provisions to new circumstances is not brought about by the legislator, but to a significant extent created 'dynamically' by the jurisprudence. Such an approach runs the risk that less the will of the democratic legislator but more the view of the opinion leaders, those in possession of the 'common knowledge', prevails. In contrast, Normativism meets the demands of a democratic system to a greater extent because it places special emphasis on the attachment to the will of the democratically legitimised legislator. This is because Normativism aims at identifying the (attributed) will of the legislator and, thus, leaves the adjustments to changing social and political circumstances basically (except the law requires a dynamic interpretation) to the legislator and not to administrative authorities or courts. Insofar, Normativism

---

[39] F Schauer, *Thinking Like a Lawyer. A New Introduction to Legal Reasoning* (Cambridge, London, Harvard University Press, 2009) 105.

ensures that it is the democratic law that governs[40] and not a more or less nebulous and permanently changing 'common knowledge'.

This assessment is further reinforced by the obligation to publish laws in democratic systems under the rule of law. The basis of interpretation in such systems has thus to be the legal text which is, in principle, written in natural language and, hence, also to be interpreted according to the rules of natural language to which the traditional legal methods of interpretation correspond. Therefore, legal provisions are, as already mentioned, 'speech acts' which express the will of the author also in general language usage and, thus, are to be understood according to their original meaning. It is important to stress this again, because it is hardly usual in the use of natural languages to identify 'speech acts' in accordance with 'common knowledge' in principal dynamically and thereby largely independent from their historical context. As democratic legislators express their commands in natural language it seems unreasonable to assume that they want to have them understood as detached from their original meaning basically in accordance with a dynamic 'common knowledge'.

After all, the principle of a *rational justification* of decisions which is an important feature of the rule of law speaks preferably for Normativism and against the System Theory. This is because according to the System Theory 'common knowledge' is indeed essential for the interpretation of legal provisions, but the System Theory does not provide a theory of 'strength' of arguments. It can notably not be decided on that basis if common knowledge in terms of the content of a particular provision proves to be untenable and, thus, needs to be abandoned or not. In fact, however, we cannot rule out that on any particular point of law the whole community of legal officials or legal scientists who believe in such a 'common knowledge' can collectively be in error.[41] In contrast, Normativism is able to provide a criterion for the persuasiveness of legal arguments by reference to the 'will of the legislator'. In the view of Normativism, this will of the legislator is expressed 'objectively' by semantic and pragmatic criteria in the legal provisions and, thus, also exists independently from the respective current common knowledge about these legal provisions. As a result, new (for example historical or teleological) insights about this objective meaning can question the present common knowledge about the respective provision. The 'attributed will' (based on semantics and pragmatics) of the legislator is in Normativism the decisive criterion by which the 'strength' of arguments can be assessed in the 'flexible system of interpretation criteria'.

As Normativism has such a criterion, it proves to be *more rational* than the System Theory which cannot provide such an equal guideline. In a political community under the rule of law in which the transparency of decisions

---

[40] See T Smith, *Judicial Review in an Objective Legal System* (New York, Cambridge University Press, 2015) 219.

[41] M H Kramer, *Objectivity and the Rule of Law* (New York, Cambridge University Press, 2007), 9.

plays a decisive role, this is not to be underestimated. Therefore, compared to the System Theory, Normativism does not only better suit the requirements of democratic orders but it can also be better integrated into the concept of the rule of law as it satisfies its demand of rational reasoning to a larger extent than System Theory.

VII. PRINCIPLES

Against this result the objection might be raised that it does not take the distinction between rules and principles into account which was pointed out particularly by Ronald Dworkin. While rules 'are applicable in an all-or-nothing fashion',[42] principles are characterised by a 'dimension of weight'.[43] Fundamental rights can be understood as typical examples of such principles.[44] Based on the distinction between rules and principles, it might on the one hand be admitted that the model of Normativism could at most be suitable for rules in democratic states under the rule of law. On the other hand, however, it might also be argued that for the explanation of principles the System Theory seems to be more suitable. That is because the consideration of the present values and standards when weighing the justification seems to be an important feature of principles as the example of fundamental rights interpretation impressively demonstrates.[45] Therefore, the line of argument might be that principles fit much better into the model of System Theory and its understanding of legal provisions as a dynamically changing common knowledge.

In response to this objection, it should be recalled[46] that the phenomenon of principles in law is not at all in contradiction to the model of Normativism. If legislators enact law as principles, they empower the administrative bodies and courts to apply these provisions by balancing different aspects. From a normative perspective, the objective meaning of the principle is this 'dimension of weight' that leaves at least some scope for application. It is basically compatible with this objective meaning if within this scope contemporary standards are also considered by legal authorities. In the light of a normativist approach, principles insofar express a 'living originalism'.[47] Of course, it depends on the

---

[42] Dworkin (n 25) 24.

[43] R Dworkin, 'The Model of Rules' (1967) 35 *University of Chicago Law Review* 35.

[44] See already Dworkin (n 25) 27 and especially R Alexy, *Theorie der Grundrechte* (Frankfurt am Main, Suhrkamp, 1986) 122 ff.

[45] See, ie, the reference to the 'present day conditions' in the case law of the ECHR, eg, *Tyrer v UK* App no 5856/72 (ECHR, 25 April 1978), para 31; *Bayatyan v Armenia* App no 23459/03 (ECHR, 7 July 2011), para 102. See to the foundations of this case law N Bratza, 'Living Instrument or Dead Letter – The Future of the European Convention on Human Rights' (2014) 14 *European Rights Law Review* 116.

[46] See ch IV.

[47] See J M Balkin, *Living Originalism* (Cambridge, London, The Belknap Press of Harvard University Press, 2011) 44 ff.

particular principle if and to what extent a dynamic common knowledge has to be taken into account. It is also possible that principles not only allow but even oblige to consider changing circumstances.

But the regulation of all these aspects should in democratic states primarily be undertaken by the democratically legitimised (constitutional) legislators and not by the administrative bodies or courts referring to a common knowledge. Therefore, also with respect to principles, it seems to be more compatible with the idea of democracy to see the attributed will in the first place as the goal of interpretation and not a continuously changing common knowledge. Furthermore, also in relation to principles, the search of the attributed will makes interpretation at least to some extent more rational than the mere reference to an elusive common knowledge as it offers an additional aspect for justification. All in all, the objection with regard to principles does not convincingly question the result that the model of Normativism fits better into democratic systems under the rule of law than the model of System Theory.

VIII. CONCLUSION

As a result of my considerations, the following can be concluded: Normativism can neither be 'proven' nor 'disproven'. Just as other approaches it is a model designed to enable an appropriate handling of the law. Normativism is based on specific assumptions such as the will of the legislator and an objective meaning of legal provisions which correspond to the requirements of democratic states with a rule of law. The answer to the question 'Can we escape Normativism in law?' should therefore be: Yes, we can, but we should refrain from doing so in a constitutional democracy under the rule of law.

8

Real Constitutional Law: A Revised Madisonian Perspective

ALEXANDER SOMEK*

I. THE RECEIVED CONTRAST

O F MAJOR CONCERN to modern constitutionalism is the question of what it takes to sustain the authority of the constitution as law. In their requisite attempts to answer this question, both the common and the civil law tradition have gravitated towards the judiciary and either embraced generalised judicial review or accorded special status to constitutional tribunals. While merely on the patient leaves of academic controversy the jury is still out on the merits of judicial review[1] it is by now taken for granted in many jurisdictions. Attempts to tinker with constitutional courts are regularly met with great anxiety and utter revulsion.[2] These existing habits may explain why the question is scarcely asked whether it is wise or even possible to entrust this guardianship of constitutional law to merely *one* institution within a political system, even if that institution is a court. The alternative that is by now all but forgotten is to view the protection of the law of the constitution always and already handed over to the real constitution and to regard this as a good thing, too.

A 'real' constitution is the opposite of its 'formal' counterpart. Of course, it is not entirely clear what we understand by a 'formal' constitution beyond and aside from an authoritative constitutional text; but the matter is even less clear when it comes to the real constitution. The candidates eligible to receive

* Earlier versions of this chapter were presented at the Humboldt University in Berlin in 2018 and at the Hebrew University in Jerusalem in 2019. I would like to thank the participants in the discussion for their thoughtful comments.

[1] J Waldron, 'The Core of the Case Against Judicial Review' (2006) 115 *Yale Law Journal* 1347–1406.
[2] See various entries on Poland and Hungary on https://verfassungsblog.de.

this appellation range, ontologically speaking, from the parsimonious to the opulent.[3] The ordinarily sparse semantics uses the term to mark the contrast between legal norms and the manner in which institutions and actors employ these in order to get things done. Richer vocabularies of the real constitution appeal to broader historical and social contexts.

The following remarks embrace and defend the parsimonious approach. They do so, however, in a somewhat 'dialectical' fashion. The defence grows into reclaiming the relevance of a richer understanding of the real constitution that has been eclipsed in the course of the ascendancy of modern constitutional law. This richer understanding is more specific than notions of the 'real constitution' that invoke social conditions of unity or substantive objectives.

The path leading to this conclusion begins with viewing the real constitution not at all as 'external' to its counterpart. It will be argued that the real constitution is intrinsic to the formal constitution. The former is, indeed, the latter's very own mode of being what it is by growing beyond itself.

II. USING CONSTITUTIONAL LAW

A straightforward and rather thin understanding of the real constitution views constitutional *norms as means* used by socially powerful agents to pursue political objectives. It does not matter whether these agents exercise official law-making functions or whether they are recognised as public bodies. The instrumental nexus with either guaranteed liberties or the exercise of public authority makes their existence and acts relevant to the real constitution.

A good example for what counts as an element of the real constitution is the social partners – representatives of labour and capital – that may have enormous impact on the design of government policies and legislation. Even though the relevant collective bodies may not be recognised in this capacity by the constitution, their role in the formation of public policy is decisive for the functioning and success of the political system. From this perspective, the real constitution comprises relations of real power and influence within a space established by formal constitutional norms. The normative force of law becomes thus supplemented with the inevitable relevance of those who are socially too powerful to be ignored. Only by paying attention to how their influence and social power is funneled into parliamentary law-making can one perceive clearly who is calling the shots in a constitutional system. The norms of the constitution would never reveal such influence, not least because they are not intended to 'describe' political realities. Rather, it takes political science to perceive this.

---

[3] For the latter see, under the name of the 'material' constitution, M Goldoni & MA Wilkinson, 'The Material Constitution' (2016) 20 LSE Law, Society and Economy Working Papers, https://papers.ssrn.com/sol3/papers.cfm?abstract_id=2875774.

III. PRUDENT CONVENTIONS

Another, slightly different example for the real constitution in such a parsimonious sense are *constitutional conventions* that emerge in the shadow of formal norms. For example, the President of the Austrian Republic is supposed to commission the leader of the party that has emerged as the strongest from the most recent national election with the task of putting together a government. This is a constitutional convention. Departing from it would not amount to a breach of constitutional law. It would, however, definitely raise eyebrows concerning the stability of the republic, for it would be considered entirely improper. The convention reflects a formal allocation of power that makes the government dependent on the support of the majority in Parliament. If it lacked such support, it would be subject to recall by a vote of no confidence. In the midst of the formal constitution grows a convention that facilitates good state practice against the backdrop of a potential of disruption that the constitution permits.[4]

Of course, neither the status of such a convention nor the standing of social partners, such as the trade unions and associations of businesses, are expressions of formal constitutional law. Taking heed of both is a matter of prudence and, using old-fashioned parlance, of statecraft.

IV. ENTER MADISON

And, yet, there is more to the real constitution than a set of prudent practices and influential institutional players. The real constitution is what allows the formal constitution to exercise its force.

Most prominently, we encounter this idea, even if only implicitly, in *Federalist* No. 51, where Madison offers, famously, his solution to the problem of sustaining the authority of the constitution *as law*.[5] As is well known, there are a number of institutional alternatives that Madison dismisses one at

---

[4] Arguably, the emergence of this convention is an 'invisible hand' effect. It is of human making, but not of human design. See E Ullmann-Margalit, *Normal Rationality: Decisions and Social Order* (ed. A. Margalit & C Sunstein, Oxford, Oxford University Press, 2017) at 130: 'The basic picture underlying invisible-hand explanations, then, is that of a bird's eye view that encompasses numerous individuals, each busily doing his or her own narrow private bit, such that an overall design, unsought as well as unforeseen by them, is seen to emerge. The point, of course, is that the emergence of the overall design is not left mysteriously unaccounted for, nor, specifically, is it attributed to accident or chance: it is the detailed stages of the invisible hand process which are meant to supply the mechanism that aggregates the dispersed individual actions into the patterned outcome.' Ullmann-Margalit later (139–140) distinguishes this 'aggregative' account with its 'evolutionary' counterparts, which she does not regard as mutually exclusive (140).

[5] See A Hamilton, J Madison & J Jay, *The Federalist* (ed C Sunstein, Cambridge, Mass, Harvard University Press, 2009) 339–345. For an introduction, see J Ferejohn, 'Madison's Separation of Powers' in S Kernell (ed), *James Madison: The Theory and Practice of Republican Government* (Stanford, Stanford University Press, 2003) 126–155.

a time: frequent appeals to the people, regular constitutional conventions or the Pennsylvanian Council of Censors.[6] None of these appear apt, for none can guarantee what Madison wishes to achieve.

What he intends to find is essentially twofold.[7] First, the provisions of the constitution are to amount in practice to more than mere 'parchment barriers'. The constitution is made up of mere words. How can they, even if they are not devoid of content, constrain human conduct in a field in which passion and ambition are not unlikely to wreak havoc?[8] Second, an answer must be found to the question whether the organ of the constitution that is supposed to exercise this real constraint vis-à-vis others is either immune to interest group capture or invariably, using more old-fashioned language, disposed to fall prey to factional interests. Madison believes the second alternative to be correct. This explains why he finds all the proposals that he discusses to be wanting, for they refer the resolution of the constitutional question to *one* special body even though it cannot be ruled out that this body is likely to be seized with passion or partisan zeal. Not even referring all constitutional questions to the people at large would do the trick. If the interval separating the incidence in question and vote of the people were short, the passionate atmosphere of partisan struggle would be carried over into the resolution of the constitutional question; if the interval were long, the people would no longer care.[9]

Madison believes that members of bodies such as the Council of Censors[10] are not disposed to listen to the cool voice of reason and thus to direct their attention to what the constitution says. The only solution he finds convincing consists of fully integrating the preservation of legality into the quotidian operation of the constitution.

This is the core intuition underlying the system of 'checks and balances'. It rests on the quite ingenious *holistic* idea. No special institution, not even, for example, a constitutional court, is a reliable candidate for sustaining legality. Rather, the only force that can maintain the law of the constitution is the system of acting and counteracting forces that is unleashed by the constitution itself.

These forces are very human.[11] The chief and relatively simple idea of sustaining the authority of the constitution through a system that separates

---

[6] See RF Williams, 'The Influences on Pennsylvania's 1776 Constitution of American Constitutionalism During the Founding Period' (1988) 112 *Pennsylvania Magazine of History and Biography* 25–48.

[7] See *Federalist*, (n 5) at 325, 338.

[8] In other words, this is not the field of 'Brandomian scorekeepers' where people aspire to keep track faithfully of their deontic inferential commitments. Rather, it is the field in which people regularly manipulate those commitments. See RB Brandom, *Making it Explicit: Reasoning, Representing and Discursive Commitment* (Cambridge, Mass, Harvard University Press, 1994) at 157, 180.

[9] See *Federalist*, (n 5) at 336.

[10] See Section 47 of the Pennsylvania Constitution of 1776, available at www.phmc.state.pa.us/portal/communities/documents/1776-1865/pennsylvania-constitution-1776.html.

[11] Even though the debate over whether Madison just faithfully adopted Hume's ideas concerning faction or departed from them is not terribly interesting it should be noted that Madison shifted the emphasis from keeping faction at bay to their multiplication as a result of which the forces are

powers is to link the legal authority of offices with the individual ambition of office-holders.[12] The eagerness to throw one's weight around is supposed to be the force driving the assertion of the powers associated with the office itself. The well-known strategy is to have ambition counteract ambition. Linking the interest of the person with the interest of the place is the chief means of upholding the authority of the constitution.

V. MATCHING DE FACTO AND DE JURE

Of course, the idea sounds drearily mechanistic. Worse, still, upon closer inspection, it even turns out to be rather mystical.[13] It is not terribly convincing on its face, for it fails to take into account that members of multimember bodies may encounter serious obstacles in mustering the support of others when it comes to asserting the power and prestige of their institution. It may also be the case that many members have very little interest in boosting its standing. Hard-core conservatives, for example, may not really have the supremacy of the legislature via-à-vis the executive branch at heart. Moreover, there is no rational choice explanation for why people holding temporary appointments should have an interest in expanding or asserting the standing of their institution. What would it be that they would thereby personally gain? The greatest mystery, however, inherent in the idea appears to be that there is no guarantee that the equilibrium of forces that emerges, if at all, de facto from the competitive struggle matches exactly with what had been anticipated de jure by the constitution qua proper allocation of powers. What Madison does not and cannot explain is why the patterns of constitutional practice that emerge at coordination points[14] between and among self-interested agents[15] would coincide with constitutional norms that are independent of such interactions. Why would, for example, the allocation of legislative powers within a federal system coalesce at a point that is equal

---

supposed magically to cancel each other out. See MG Spencer, 'Hume and Madison on Faction' (2002) 59 *William and Mary Quarterly* 869–896 at 883, 886.

[12] See *Federalist*, (n 5) at 341.

[13] On the following, see EA Posner & Adrian Vermeule, *The Executive Unbound: After the Madisonian Republic* (Oxford, Oxford University Press, 2010) at 18, 24.

[14] From the perspective of rational choice theory, such a point is an arrangement, institution or convention from which no individual has an incentive to defect. See T Christiano, 'Is Normative Rational Choice Theory Self-Defeating?' (2004) 115 *Ethics* 122–141 at 127. It is easy to imagine how the interpretation of powers conferred by the constitution can indeed be based upon coordination points. They are reached when the organs involved mutually understand that any attempt to push the envelop further in their favour might invariably result in chaos or destruction. At this point, they lose any incentive to do so, unless they want to change the system.

[15] The patterns themselves would be amenable to an invisible hand explanation. As Ullmann-Margalit, (n 4) at 127, so aptly explains, such an explanation replaces the judgment according to which a pattern appears to be of human design with an account that demonstrates how the pattern *could have* been or *has* been brought about by the separate actions of many individuals who mind their own business and do not intend to produce the ultimate outcome.

to what the constitution legally requires?[16] Have we not seen enough examples of constitutions in which the allocation of powers developed in a matter that had not been anticipated by the founders?[17]

VI. REASON OVER PASSION

Several questions arise here.

The *first* concerns the relation of reason and passion. Madison clearly contrasts one with the other and associates the partisan energies of factions with the latter. He also leaves no doubt which one ought to rule over the other:[18]

> But it is the reason, alone, of the public, that ought to control and regulate the government. The passions ought to be controlled and regulated by the government.

No matter how much this terminology may be due to the influence of Scottish enlightenment philosophy on Madison's thinking,[19] the whole contrast is perfectly consistent with how ancient political philosophy would have looked at the major task of a constitution. Any successful constitution has to make sure that the reasonable part of the human souls governs another that, even though amenable to reason, is in itself driven by desires and emotions. From an ancient perspective, hence, one would expect a well-ordered constitutional system to establish the control of passion by reason. In the context of politics, reason is more than an ethereal quality of thinking (or a matter of 'deontic scorekeeping'). Rather, it is embodied in a group, notably in an aristocracy.[20] One would have concluded, from that angle, that in order for reason to rule over passion an aristocratic body must have decisive influence on the interpretation of law.[21]

This is not, however, the idea underlying modern separation of powers.[22] The idea appears to be, rather, that any power stays within its proper sphere if

---

[16] Vermeule has a slightly different take on the issue. He regards, correctly, Madison's optimistic view of the separation of powers as an instance of an 'invisible hand argument' (see above nn 4 and 15). He points out that Madison's view of the separation of powers – should he have been concerned about aggregate social welfare – cannot rely on prices and fails to explain why an invisible hand effect comes about. See A Vermeule, *The System of the Constitution* (New York, Oxford University Press, 2011) 17–18, 39.

[17] The American Constitution and the importance that accrued to the office of the President is a case in point. See B Ackerman, *The Failure of the Founding Fathers: Jefferson, Marshall, and the Rise of Presidential Democracy* (Cambridge: Mass, Harvard University Press, 2005).

[18] See *Federalist*, (n 5) at 335.

[19] See Spencer, (n 11) for the relevant influence of David Hume and Adam Smith.

[20] See *Federalist*, (n 5) at 414–420 (on the Senate and its quasi-aristocratic function).

[21] Even *Federalist* 78, in which Hamilton defended judicial review of legislation, abstained from making this argument. See *Federalist*, (n 5) at 508–520. The virtues of the judiciary are, however, already in this essay the 'passive virtues' (neither 'force nor will') that allegedly make the judiciary the least dangerous branch.

[22] It was quite clear to Madison that a constitutional system cannot be built on the expectation that one public-spirited class will dominate the political process in virtue of its commendable character. See R Strahan, 'Personal Motives, Constitutional Forms, and the Public Good: Madison on Political Leadership' In J Madison (ed) *The Theory and Practice of Republican Government*, (n 5), 63–91 at 73.

the right amount of ambition – not too much, not too little – from another power keeps the ambitious office-holder in check (for example, a president threatening to pardon the criminal defendants that the judiciary wishes to convict). In other words, passion is supposed to constrain passion. Reason is the desired result.[23] It is however, unclear, which mix of passions is necessary or sufficient to give rise to a reasonable result.

From an ancient perspective, this is nothing short of miraculous. While the double negation of passion is supposed to bring about reason, it remains inexplicable how this would work. It seems, however, as though the core idea is the same that underlies the creation of 'the extended republic of the United States'.[24] The multiplicity of contending forces and the insecurity whether any coalition of opponents may not be capable of at least *temporarily* ascending over others gives rise to uncertainty with regard to the position of each. While nobody can be assured to be immune to attacks and oppression, the potential oppressors cannot be confident about being spared future defeat by the oppressed. This resembles the situation of a Rawlsian veil of ignorance,[25] at any rate, as viewed by rational choice theorists.[26] If the parties involved are sufficiently risk averse then they will agree to pursue a strategy of fair play in which no one will suffer insufferable defeat.[27] They will play by the rules that they can accept ex ante.[28] Perhaps this matches with how Hume assumed the 'artificial virtue' of justice to arise as part of a strategy to pursue mutually one's long-term interest.[29]

Such solutions are notoriously plagued with the difficulty that there will always be opportunities for defection.

VII. DEMIGODS

But perhaps checks and balances are based upon a slightly different idea. Possibly, limits on powers are of human design and merely appear to be an unplanned aggregate by-product of action. It may well have been intended by the framers of a constitution to make the organs interact in a manner that brings about

---

[23] There is a 'naturalism' presupposed by this argument in the sense that what is desirable from the perspective of practical reason is supposedly brought about by causes that are not amenable to practical reason. For a discussion of such naturalism in the context of Kant's philosophy of history, see C Horn, *Nichtideale Normativität: Ein neuer Blick auf Kants politische Philosophie* (Berlin, Suhrkamp, 2014) 240, 256–270.

[24] See *Federalist*, (n 5) at 344.

[25] See J Rawls, *A Theory of Justice* (Cambridge, Mass, Harvard University Press, 1971) 136–142.

[26] For the difference, see J Rawls, *Justice as Fairness: A Restatement* (ed E Kelly, Cambridge: Mass, Harvard University Press, 2001) at 106–107.

[27] See E Ullmann-Margalit, *The Emergence of Norms* (Oxford, Oxford University Press, 1977) 25, 41.

[28] Part of the self-interested reason may be that they want to appear trustworthy. See Christiano, (n 14) at 136–137.

[29] For a reconstruction, see B Barry, *Theories of Justice* (Berkeley, University of California Press, 1989), 148–149.

these limits even though it is by no means part of the intention of the organs to do so.[30] Conceivably, the interaction of passions can be calibrated by some ingenious constitution-maker – a sibling, as it were, of Rousseau's *legislateur* – in such a manner that the emerging balance matches exactly what the constitution requires as law. Outward pressure would make each branch of government stay within its proper channel. This idea presupposes, of course, that the legal requirements of the constitution can be grasped, in principle, independently of the interaction of constituted powers. This explains why a *second* question must arise, namely, whether for reasons of the inevitable corrupting effect of passions on constituted bodies no particular office or institution within a constitutional system can ever be entrusted with the exclusive task to say what the constitution says from a legal point of view and whether, conversely, divining true constitutional meaning untarnished by the perspectivism of an office or personal ambition is possible only by stepping outside of the system.

By definition, the only ones unaffected by the maelstrom of political strife that engulfs all branches are the demi-divine founders. They stand outside of the system and have a fair chance at designing a system that in its actual operation will inadvertently give rise to the desired result. What is susceptible to being designed from the outside on the basis of pure practical reason can be attained on the inside *only* by giving free rein to passionate conflicts. Such conflicts produce constitutional limits as their side effect. The framers are in a position to anticipate the invisible hand mechanism and use it to enforce the norms of the constitution.

It is obvious, though, that the belief in such cunning constitutional mechanics commits one also to believing in the exceptional wisdom of the founders. If the founders failed at designing a system of checks and balances that in the final result converged with the original constitutional meaning, there would be no reason to trust such a system to begin with. Belief in the founder's wisdom is the *conditio sine qua non* of allegiance to the constitutional system. It must be the *transcendental faith* of those participating in the political process.

VIII. A TACIT INTRASYSTEMIC PREFERENCE

The *third* question implicitly challenges this view. It objects that the very idea of a disembodied and disinterested perspective on the constitution is already tacitly complicit with the *judicial* exposition of law. The purportedly external

---

[30] Invisible hand mechanisms can be part of a deliberately chosen institutional design. See Ullmann-Margalit, (n 4) at 141. This would then be a case of the planned emergence of a spontaneously formed order. Arguably, it would also be a very special case. Planners may simply plan to have *some* spontaneous order. In this case, however, they would intend to have agents unwittingly bring about a *particularly patterned* spontaneous order.

perspective on the constitution is merely a generalisation of one particular institutional outlook that embraces what Hart memorably called the 'internal point of view'.[31] It presupposes that the constitution has a meaning that is fixed from the outset and is therefore capable of guiding judicial expositions of law, unless this law is not sufficiently clear.

The objection suggests that viewing the framers ascribe to the constitution a stable meaning that is to be realised as a side effect of passionate struggles betrays an intra-systemic bias in favour of the judiciary. It indicates what the judiciary would have the framers intend in order to boost the authority of judicial expositions of law. The premise that there is stable meaning to begin with is already biased in favour of the judicial perspective on constitutional law. From the perspective of Federalist No. 51, this premise is false and unfair. It implies partisanship with one specific branch of government. Hence, Federalist No. 78, which defends the role of the 'least dangerous' branch[32] of the constitution qua purveyor of authoritative constitutional meaning, appears to be in tension with Federalist No. 51, which does not rest its hope on the judiciary, even though an emphasis is laid in Federalist No. 78 on the comparatively harmless nature of the judiciary, an emphasis that reflects the spirit of No. 51.

If the third question has to be answered in the affirmative and it has to be admitted that positing stable constitutional meaning is a partial perspective on securing the legality of the constitution then the *fourth* and perhaps final question needs to be asked whether sustaining the authority of the constitution by means of the separation of powers does not have to let go of the idea that there must be something like a meaning of the constitution outside of the mechanics of the separation of powers. Plainly and simply, the score of each game of passion verses passion would determine the meaning of the constitution in the sense of constraining or facilitating action.[33] It would thus be basically up to game theory to explain how such meaning and its authority are generated.[34] Any normative order that arises as a result of settlement would be entirely unplanned. The irony ought to be noted. The instrument that represents, as the first American constitutions had it, the 'plan of government' would work in practice in a way that is inaccessible to human design.[35]

Actually, this is the direction into which the revision of the Madisonian conception has to move. It has to *drop* the belief in the existence of an original normative meaning. But it will be seen that this is not tantamount to debunking all normative commitments.

[31] See HLA Hart, *The Concept of Law* 2nd edn (ed. PB Bulloch & J Raz, Oxford, Clarendon Press, 1994) 89–91.
[32] See *Federalist*, (n 5) at 509.
[33] The final score would mark the relevant 'coordination points'. See above (n 14).
[34] See the classical contribution by Ullmann-Margalit, (n 27).
[35] This is consistent with a major claim of public choice theory, namely that political institutions are not of human design. See Christiano, (n 14) at 124–125, 135.

IX. THE EXTERNAL IS THE INTERNAL

This matter needs to be stated as clearly as possible. The formal constitution establishes offices and institutions and invests them with requisite powers. It is possible to arrive at different constructions of the scope of these powers. The necessary condition for the system to operate is that the office-holders mutually recognise one another in their capacity. In Brandomian terms this means that they consider each other entitled to speak on behalf of their position and to assert how what they *take* to be their powers fits into the overall framework. What is, however, basically up for grabs is whether their relevant assertions will also stick. Of course, the relevant interpretations will usually draw a line between what the power associated with an office *permits* or what it legally facilitates and what would be, even if it were possible, an *imprudent* course of action (see the convention mentioned above according to which the President has to appoint the leader of the strongest party to the position of the Prime Minister). The interpretive claims concerning what is or is not either possible or permissible are in most cases arrived at against a backdrop of a range of options.

From the Madisonian perspective, which is arguably consistent with modern rational choice and game theory, the office holders are by definition eager to arrive at interpretive constructions that promise to maximise the scope of their own powers. The chief executive, for example, may want to support interpretations of her powers to adopt ordinances that are likely to be to the detriment of the powers of the legislature.[36] The legislature, in turn, may contemplate reacting to what it perceives to be an encroachment of its powers by declaring the relevant ordinances null and void. Whether or not the legislature decides to react in this manner depends on several factors, such as, whether there is a chance to have such declarations recognised in administrative offices and courts or whether the subject matter merits creating the risk of uncertainty and upheaval or whether it is prudent to challenge and thereby possibly to weaken the executive branch. Several or all of these factors may influence the decision by the legislature. They are therefore decisive for whether or not what the chief executive takes to be her powers is likely to prevail and to be accepted, at least for the time being, as a plausible construction of constitutional law. Some kind of 'equilibrium' may well be achieved so long as the persons and institutions involved are interested in avoiding system disintegration. Under this condition, each may have sufficient incentive to settle for 'less' power than they might be able to exercise on the basis of frequent appeals to the people, mobilising the street, prolonged government deadlock or violent conflict.

Now, from the perspective of garden-variety legal positivism the factors mentioned above would have to be regarded as 'external'. In and of themselves

---

[36] This is, of course, not at all a fictional example. See B Ackerman, *The Decline and Fall of the American Republic* (Cambridge, Mass, Harvard University Press, 2010) 87–116.

they seem to have nothing to do with the question whether the constructions of powers arrived at by the chief executive are correct, legally speaking. Rather, they seem to concern the altogether different question of whether pursing a counter-strategy of nullification promises to be crowned with success. They seem to be relevant not for legal, but for prudential purposes.

The great lesson to be learned from revising the Madisonian perspective slightly by dropping the belief in predetermined limits is, however, that these factors are indeed *internal* factors. They are internal because the system of checks and balances permits them to be relevant for the purpose of constitutional construction. They cannot be ignored. Even though they seem to concern only the question of additional conditions that have to be met by interpretations in order to be *successful* – an interpretation that is *taken to be* correct by several or all branches – the correctness or incorrectness of a constitutional interpretation *cannot* be determined independently of such additional conditions. Within a context where assertions of powers are pit against one another competing ambitions are the key to determining what the constitution really *means*. They are the constitutionally warranted context of constitutional interpretation.

This is the radicalism of the Madisonian idea.

X. EX FACTO IUS ORITUR

The real constitution is set into motion by a mutually *recognised* formal distribution of the offices and branches of government. The formal constitution then comes to mean what the real constitution permits it to mean.

Indeed, this represents what social system's theorists call a 'virtuous circle'.[37] Alternatively, constitutional law can be characterised as an emergent property or a systemic effect of the existence of the constitution.[38]

If, for example, a government, aided and abetted by a legislative majority, signals its ability and readiness to repack a constitutional court in order to alter its jurisprudence, then changes in the case law undertaken by this court with a view to avert such repacking are the constitutionally warranted result. They are unobjectionable because they reflect how checks and balances work. It would be wrong to say that the old jurisprudence was right and the new is wrong simply because the judiciary yielded to political pressure. The old jurisprudence was just a reflection of a different equilibrium of forces. There is no right or wrong in how the constitution operates as long as it operates.

Constitutionalism has to confront the sobering truth that questions of interpretation are eventually settled de facto. What works and what does not

---

[37] See G Teubner, 'Breaking Frames: Economic Globalisation and the Emergence of *lex mercatoria*' (2002) 5 *European Journal of Social Theory* 199–217.
[38] See Vermeule, (n 16) at 4–5.

work within a constitutional system is not just determined by appeal to the text and fundamental ideas, but also with an eye to what is likely to fly and to be considered palatable to others.

XI. TWO GENUINE NORMATIVE CONSTRAINTS

It may be objected that the revised Madisonianism defended here sells the normativity of the constitution short and deflates it into mere superficial refraction of the interaction of political forces. It no longer captures what Madison must have had in mind when he introduced checks and balances as means of sustaining the authority of the constitution qua law.

This objection can be countered by taking into account that the interactive process of constitutional interpretation is subject to two genuine normative constraints,[39] one of which has been briefly mentioned above. If there is anything normative about constitutional law, it is inherited from them rather than inherent in one or the other norm of the constitution.

The first normative constraint is about avoiding disintegration.[40] Constitutional interpretation takes place in a context that is politically prone to crisis. Depending on the expectations that parties harbor about what others accept without revulsion it is possible to arrive at mutual understandings. Of course, the most powerful actors are calling the shots.[41] On this level, the construction of the constitution is indeed a matter of political compromise.

The second normative constraint involves the core idea of modern constitutionalism, which consists of submitting the exercise of public authority to the discipline of law. In his otherwise troubling and highly polemical book *Legality and Legitimacy* Carl Schmitt[42] observed entirely correctly that in a liberal constitutional democracy, a major legitimating factor of political action is to observe the constitution as law. The subject of legitimacy is, of course, the people. Hence, modern constitutional law is not just a tangled web of dyads asserting their influence and striking deals in the field of constitutional construction; actually, it is based upon a *triadic relation*. While the organs are keen to assert, either through the use of arguments or by means of threats, their powers and privileges vis-à-vis others, it is decisive from the perspective of the people that

---

[39] In speaking of 'genuine' normative constraints a contrast is made to how game and rational choice theorists believe normativity to 'emerge' in situations that are 'prone' to give rise to norms in order to overcome cooperation or coordination problems. See Ullmann-Margalit, (n 34) at 22. Norms presuppose real commitments; they are not merely invisible hand effects.

[40] The approach defended here shares with 'political constitutionalism' the belief that the democratic process has to be self-sustaining. See R Bellamy, *Political Constitutionalism: A Republican Defence of the Constitutionality of Democracy* (Cambridge, Cambridge University Press, 2007) at 5.

[41] See R Hardin, *Liberalism, Constitutionalism and Democracy* (Oxford, Oxford University Press, 1999) at 3.

[42] See C Schmitt, *Legality and Legitimacy* (trans. J Seitzer, Durham, Duke University Press, 2004).

the constitution is adhered to by public authority since that is the only safeguard against their being 'enslaved' by their rulers.[43] The organs of the constitution point out to one another what the constitution says, but their saying and explaining is determined by their interest to assert and to augment their power. In the relation to the people, however, they have to observe the constitution as though it were a valid law.[44] A compromise needs to be *cast* as an application or observance of a norm. As a result of the triadic relation the organs are linked to one common perspective.

This second constraint does in no manner subordinate jurisdictional deal-making to some method of constitutional interpretation. The most fundamental norm of constitutional law is to avoid disintegration. Compromises are struck in light of this end. It is, however, necessary to present tacitly negotiated results in the language that is about observing constraints.

This is not to say that the interpretive construction of constitutional law is bound to remain mere window dressing. Indeed, it is conceivable to adopt conventions of constitutional interpretation as media to make out uncontroversial middle ground, for example, by appeal to acts of founding in which representatives of the relevant parties participated. The general acceptance of a 'passivist' style of interpretation can actually serve as a medium of conflict avoidance. Hence, the determining influence can run not only downstream from compromise to interpretation, but also in the reverse direction.

XII. STRATEGIC LEGALISM AND OBJECTIVITY IN INTERPRETATION

Constitutional practice begins, however, with a prototype of law, namely, the establishment of organs with powers. Owing to their mutual recognition as players within the system, the system of checks and balances is set into motion. It results in determinations of powers that are cast as interpretations.

Drawing on an idea explored by Adrian Vermeule, it can be said, therefore, that all legalism has to be strategic.[45] Even if one were to believe sincerely in the correctness of one particular method of constitutional construction – in other words, an interpretive approach that does not take competing claims by other

---

[43] See J Madison, 'Memorial and Remonstrance against Religious Assessments' in J Rakove (ed), *Writings* (New York, Vintage Books, 1999) 29–35 at 30–31.

[44] Students of the late Kelsenian theory of norms will recognise the tacit reference to Kelsen's final characterisation of the *Grundnorm* as a true fiction in Vaihinger's sense. See Hans Kelsen, *General Theory of Norms* (trans. M Hartney, Oxford, Oxford University Press, 1991).

[45] See Vermeule, (n 16) at 135. As Vermeule explains (137, 153–4): 'From the standpoint of any given judge, choices by other judges create constraints that implicate the logic of *second-best adjudication*: what is best to do given the constraints arising from others' choices may well differ from what it would be best to do of all other judges adhered to the same theory. [...] [E]ven judges who decide strictly according to law must consider the possibility that the best attainable legal outcomes, by their own lights, will occur if they vote differently than they would if other judges agreed with their views.'

branches into account – one would still have to choose, within the embedded context of checks and balances, the one method that is most likely to attain the result that would follow from the preferred approach. For example, an avowed originalist who joins a bench composed of living constitutionalists may have to articulate what in her view the original meaning requires in a vocabulary that appeals to social morality, evolving understandings or moral background principles.[46]

More generally, the belief that constitutional construction has to arrive at disembedded interpretations – interpretations that do not anticipate and accommodate the potentially disruptive interventions of other players in the constitutional system – is wrong-headed, for it misunderstands the nature of a constitutional system. Within the context of checks and balances one needs to anticipate that the 'coordinate branches' will do everything to assert their power and hence develop interpretive stances and vocabularies that they find appropriate.

From this follows that constitutional construction is necessarily a political process that involves anticipating the reactions of others and the readiness to accommodate their views even at the expense of compromising one's own preferred perspective. This readiness engages deeply held political beliefs. What must count, at the end of the day, is the good faith effort to comply with one's own best understanding of political morality.[47]

XIII. THE CONSTITUTION DETERMINES ITS OWN INTERPRETATION

Upon closer inspection, it turns out that there is no unresolved tension between Federalist No. 51 and Federalist No. 78 (see above, Section VIII) after all. Judicial review and checks and balances are fully compatible with one another. Whether or not constitutional courts enjoy greater or lesser authority depends on how much authority is conceded to them by other branches. When they lose this authority, as it arguably happened in Bavaria in the wake of the crucifix case, they need to reflect on whether constitutional disobedience can be regarded as a one-time occurrence and can consequently be ignored, or has to give rise to adaptations in the case law. Dealing with this question is almost the daily business of the European Court of Justice. The *Taricco II* case is an example in which the Court arrived at a particularly amazing interpretation of supremacy in order to accommodate a challenge by the Italian Constitutional Court.[48]

---

[46] For a similar example see Vermeule, (n 16) at 150–151.

[47] See M Loughlin, *Political Jurisprudence* (Oxford, Oxford University Press, 2017) at 6.

[48] See Case C-42/17, M.A.S. and M.B., Judgement of the Grand Chamber of 5 December 2017, EU:C:2017:936), a challenge that remained unresponded by the ECJ. For a discussion, see C Rauchegger, 'National constitutional rights and the primacy of EU law: *M.A.S*' (2018) 55 *Common Market Law Review* 1521–1548 at 1541–2.

Most interestingly, given that constitutional interpretation takes place in a systemic context, it becomes actually difficult to say whose interpretation ultimately counts. If, for example, the European Court of Justice needs to determine whether an interpretation of European Union law, for example, the Framework Decision on the Arrest Warrant,[49] could potentially offend the constitutional essentials ('identity') of a Member State and arrives at a milder interpretation of European Union law (as it happened in the *Taricco* case)[50] it is no longer clear whose interpretation it is, namely, the European Court's or the Member State's. It is one in reaction to the anticipated reaction of the other. It becomes, thus, the interpretation of the *system* of the constitution.[51] Moreover, it is not possible to say that one court prevails. Just as in a case of a parallelogram of forces the interpretation becomes remarkably *impersonal* and, with an eye to the constitution, *objective*.[52] This is how the real constitution allows the formal constitution to speak. The meaning of the latter is the product of the former even though the former could not exist without the latter. Again, it is a *systemic* relation that one encounters here.

XIV. THE QUESTION OF REASON

The revised Madisonian perspective on sustaining the authority of the constitution is utterly persuasive. It allows us to realise that the belief in disembedded judicial supremacy is partial vis-à-vis the judiciary and totally oblivious to the political realities of constitutional law. The formal constitution facilitates the emergence of the real constitution that lends the former its voice. Putting the matter bluntly, without being supported by political compromises that have to be repeatedly struck between the branches, the formal constitution could not assert its authority. And by giving the matter a more dialectical twist it can be said that the formal constitution needs to be mute in order to speak through the actually operating branches of government.

---

[49] 2002/584/JHA, Council Framework Decision of 13 June 2002 on the European arrest warrant and the surrender procedures between Member States – Statements made by certain Member States on the adoption of the Framework Decision.

[50] This case, I hasten to add, did not concern the European arrest warrant but rather whether observing a statute of limitation is essential to Italian constitutional law because of the principle of the 'legality' of punishments. See F Fabbrini & O Pollicino, *Constitutional Identity in Italy: European Integration As the Fulfillment of the Constitution* (2017). EUI Department of Law Research Paper No 2017/06. Available at SSRN: https://ssrn.com/abstract=2930106 or http://dx.doi.org/10.2139/ssrn.2930106.

[51] See Vermeule, (n 16) at 16, who would possibly call it a 'fallacy of division' if one attributed an interpretation by an organ of the constitution arrived at within a systemic context to this organ rather than to the real constitution as a whole.

[52] It is 'objective' in a dual sense. It is not arrived by the subject speaking but rather by the subject qua element of a systemic context. In addition, it is a social reality and not just a view developed by someone.

As we have seen above (see section VI), the Madisonian approach nevertheless fails to explain how the system of checks and balances can ensure that reason will rule over passion.[53] We have not yet come beyond the point at which nothing but the unexamined faith in the superior wisdom of the anointed framers would warrant the conclusion that the antagonism of passionate assertions of powers effectively sustains the rule of law (and, a fortiori, 'reason').

It has also already been mentioned that from an ancient perspective, which may have had some impact on Madison's thinking, the overall objective of the constitution is to facilitate the rule of reason over passion. How that might be possible is what Madison left unexplained, at any rate, in the context of the separation of powers. Instead he came up with elementary ideas concerning representation in a large or 'extended' republic. As is well known, he believed that it would be impossible within a larger constituency for local factions to dominate the legislative process. The futility of all attempts to pursue a partial agenda would lead representatives to support impartial designs.

We do not need to discuss the soundness of Madison's idea. What matters, for the purpose of our analysis, is that Madison shifts the constitutional focus on reasonableness from the interaction between and among various branches of government to one branch, namely, the legislature. As a result, the reasoning about constitutions undergoes a profound transformation.

XV. ANCIENT AND MODERN CONSTITUTIONALISM

Ancient political thought perceived practical reason to be embodied in a particular group, such as Aristotle's *mesoi*,[54] or to be distributed unevenly across constituencies. Practical reason is something that has to be acquired and internalised into habits of behaviour.[55] Overstating the point a bit, whether or not a polity avails of a good constitution depends on the character of its citizens. If the citizens are virtuous, the whole polity is in good shape.

Modern constitutional law, by contrast, works with a disembodied understanding of practical reason. It is manifest in the quality of the will of the collective. This will is expressed in legislation, not least because its quality

---

[53] Vermeule, (n 16) at 48–49, pursues an easy way out. He views overall social welfare as the equivalent of reasonableness and focuses on the representativeness of the overall system even if it involves interactions between and among some highly imperfectly representative institution. The view of constitutional democracy underlying this perspective is rather narrow. The constitutional system is believed to be a vehicle for preference aggregation and tied to a perspective on political morality that is notoriously insensitive to distributive concerns. What is more, Vermeule loses track of the problem to have reason rule over passion and thus renders the challenge inherent in designing a constitutional system less complex than it is.

[54] See Aristotle, *Politics* 2nd edn (trans. C Lord, Chicago, University of Chicago Press, 2013) 1295b 8–9 (p 114).

[55] See A MacIntyre, *After Virtue: A Study in Moral Theory* 2nd edn (Norte Dame, Notre Dame University Press, 1984) at 155.

depends on the generality of norms.[56] The practical reason underpinning the will of a collective is considered to be the outcome of a process that has to meet conditions of impartiality. Universal suffrage, electoral accountability, adequate systems of representation and the weight of public opinion are supposed to secure these conditions. Thus understood, legislation becomes the main, if not the sole, fountain of practical authority in the political sphere.[57]

Unsurprisingly, the executive branch and the judiciary are demoted to a relatively lower status, namely, to that of loyal and humble servants of the legislature. They do not contribute to the constitutional system by adding some form of reasonableness that is originally their own. The judiciary, in particular, is supposed to serve as the tractable agent (*'la bouche'*) of legislation.[58]

This centralisation of all reason in the legislature is, of course, fully consistent with conceiving of constitutional authority through the lens of sovereignty. *Lex est quod suprema potestas iussit.* The law can be reasonable only as long as the sovereign is reasonable.

XVI. THE INCONSISTENCY

This shift of emphasis from the reason that is embodied in the players composing the system to the reason articulated in legislation may explain why Madison fails to answer the question how the mechanics of passion is able to be generative of reason. This failure is intrinsic to the project of modern constitutional law and definitely not one of its accidental features.

Modern constitutional law attempts to overcome the imaginary of the mixed constitution (to which John Adams was then still clinching)[59] and to replace the relevance of estates (lords, commoners, the Crown) with mere functional specifications of sovereign power. Undeniably, this was a major prerequisite for reconciling the idea of mutual checks, which was an old staple of the theory of the mixed constitution, with popular sovereignty. No longer are the branches of government associated with various groups or players that each avail of their own virtues and vices (or embody aspects of practical reasonableness, such as judgement, determination or love of liberty). No longer is it a hallmark of constitutional statecraft to arrange these players such that the presence of one creates an obstacle for others whenever they are tempted to stray from the path

---

[56] See F Neumann, *Die Herrschaft des Gesetzes: Eine Untersuchung zum Verhältnis von politischer Theorie und Rechtssystem in der Konkurrenzgesellschaft* (trans. A Söllner, Frankfurt aM, Suhrkamp, 1980).

[57] For a similar observation, see C Schmitt, *The Crisis of Parliamentary Democracy* (trans. E Kennedy, Cambridge, Mass, MIT Press, 1985) 42–47.

[58] See Montesquieu, *The Spirit of the Laws* (trans. AM Cohler, BC Miller & HS Stone, Cambridge, Cambridge University Press, 1989) at 160, 163.

[59] See J Adams, *Revolutionary Writings* (ed. CB Thompson, Indianapolis, Liberty Fund, 2000) 287–288.

of virtue. No longer is a constitution an instrument that arranges groups in a manner that averts the corruption of their character and harnesses the beneficial energies of each for the benefit of all. No longer is the cooperation of the separate branches through the combination and aggregation of virtues (courage, wisdom, love of liberty) considered to be conducive to the common good.[60] The modern constitutional law that we encounter in Madison's work breaks away from the ancient foundations that had until then been sustained in the theory of the mixed constitution.

This gives rise, however, to a severe inconsistency concerning the legality that undergirds the constitution as law. Transforming the legislature into the sole well-spring of practical reason in the political sphere involves either of two inferential commitments. One can endorse the view that legal norms are more than mere 'parchment barriers' and hence amenable to faithful application in a constitutional context. This will only be the case if those in charge of applying constitutional constraints engage in good-faith efforts to draw out their true meaning. But Madison believed this view to be politically naïve. Alternatively, one may subscribe to the idea that in virtue of some mysterious invisible-hand mechanism the meaning of the constitution that emerges from the incessant jostle among organs is destined to coincide with its true meaning. This idea presupposes, however, the belief that the founders were demigods possessing immense intellectual abilities (see above section VI). While the first commitment is politically implausible, the second must strike one as outright bizarre.

If the operation of checks and balances works in the manner in which it has been sketched above and if, therefore, the revised Madisonian perspective is plausible, then the interpretation of norms cannot be regarded as a transmission belt conveying the practical reason embodied in legislation to the resolution of singular cases. If the interpretation of the constitution and of statutes is eventually tied to political compromise and sustainable only under this condition, then the practical reason inherent in legislation is *systematically* threatened to become eclipsed by the mechanics of checks and balances.

We are now in a position to appreciate *the loss* that modern constitutionalism has incurred vis-à-vis the theory of the mixed constitution. This theory offered an explanation for how reason can rule over passion and how a constitution can

---

[60] All these ideas are summarised in one of the most wonderful documents of modern constitutional history, namely, in Charles I. Answer to the Nineteen Propositions. The 'Nineteen Propositions' were made by Parliament in 1642 in order to contain an increasingly defiant king. They included matters such as approval of the appointment of ministers and parliamentary involvement in the conduct of foreign affairs. Had the king accepted this proposal and not cleverly given his famous reply, England would have been transformed into a parliamentary monarchy. See the text of the Answer to the Nineteen Propositions in JP Kenyon, *The Stuart Constitution 1608–1688* 2nd edn (Cambridge, Cambridge University Press, 1986) at 223–225. Viscount Falkland and Sir John Colepeper prepared the king's answer to the Nineteen Propositions. See A Tomkins, *Our Republican Constitution* (Oxford, Hart Publishing, 2005) at 91.

be conducive to the common good by having each player counteract others or by forcing several into relations of cooperation. While the potential vices supposedly cancel each other out, reason is in the position to predominate in virtue of the combination of actually embodied virtues – or, put differently, in virtue of the real constitution.

More disturbingly, perhaps, vesting all reasonableness in the legislature makes liberal democracy vulnerable to all kinds of attacks that try to expose the working of the deliberating body as a mere sham.[61] The debunking of legislative wisdom is then often trailed with viewing wisdom or political ability vested in a different branch of government, notably, the executive branch.[62]

Taking up a core idea of Vermeule's systemic approach to constitutionalism it can be said that our faith in modern constitutional democracy is guilty of a 'fallacy of composition'.[63] It suggests that only if the institution that makes, owing to its design and operation, its members disposed to arrive at reasonable results plays a leading role and dominates subordinate institutions then the constitutional system as a whole can be reasonable, too. The system can only be as good as its constituent elements. But this is a mistake, for the supervening systemic properties can be different from the constituent parts.[64] Modern constitutional law, in contrast to its ancient predecessor, fails to take into account that the interaction of imperfect institutions and groups that are not public spirited can lead to the supervenient reasonableness of the overall system.

XVII. A MACHIAVELLIAN REVIVAL

The real constitution in the parsimonious sense explains how constraints emerge from having constitutional law determined by the forces that the constitution allows to unfold. This is consistent with the Madisonian approach. But this approach needs to be complemented with a critical perspective on the reasonableness of constitutional arrangements. Without such a perspective one would have little or no reason to rest one's faith in the mechanics of the separation of powers.

In order to develop such a perspective, we need to return to the point at which Madison left off when he perceived all reasonableness to be concentrated in the legislative branch. This means that an exploration of the real constitution in a richer sense needs to take up central themes of ancient constitutional

---

[61] See, most famously and infamously, C Schmitt, *The Crisis of Parliamentary Democracy* (trans. E Kennedy, Cambridge, Mass, MIT Press, 1985).

[62] For a more recent instalment, see A Vermeule, *Law's Abnegation* (Cambridge, Mass, Harvard University Press, 2016).

[63] See Vermeule, (n 16) at 9, 16, 26.

[64] See Vermeule, (n 16) at 14.

thinking. Two themes come to mind, not least because they have figured most prominently in the ancient tradition. The first theme is to view the constitution as an arrangement that protects communities against the corrosive impact of time.[65] A good constitution prevents disintegration that results from civic strife. The second theme concerns the participation of different groups with different ambitions and temperaments.

The concluding observations focus on this second theme. It concerns types of people – groups or individuals – that participate in the political process, broadly understood, and what they contribute, if they do, to joint action that is supposed to be conducive to the common good. In the ideal case, the habits of the groups and the character of its members are embodiments of practical reason. This explains why, from the ancient perspective, reason is not enshrined in texts and commands. The interpretation of utterances is therefore also not considered to be the main business of constitutional analysis.

Modern constitutional law altered the picture profoundly. The people supposedly are the wellspring of all authority. The people are one because the sovereign is one. Owing to the presupposed unity of the people it becomes an anathema for constitutional law to take it for granted that the people are split into two different social classes, namely, the rich, who are few, and the poor, who are many. Moreover, modern constitutional law ignores, consistently and persistently, that each group is characterised by different *umori*, as Machiavelli would have put it. These different moods or temperaments are the desire to dominate and to exploit others, on the one hand, and the desire to be left alone and to live an unruffled ordinary life, on the other.[66]

Quite remarkably, we have recently seen a revival of the second element of ancient constitutional thinking in the context of a critical analysis of the European Union. Wolfgang Streeck points out that in Europe's postwar situation capitalism and democracy have simultaneously mutually supported and undermined each other. Democracy needs capitalism for the reason that social wealth is the fruit of private profit maximisation. Capitalism needs democracy in order to make private wealth accumulation socially acceptable. The concept designating the reconciling element is that wealth would 'trickle down' from the top to the bottom. At the same time, democracy is opposed to capitalism. The inequalities of wealth that capitalism gives rise to and its hierarchical organisation of production would not find the support of majorities if these were able to control production and distribution effectively. The reason that such effective control is out of reach is, again, owing to the fact that capital is opposed to democracy, for capital owners are quick in evading constraints by moving to

---

[65] See, generally, JGA Pocock in his *The Machiavellian Moment: Florentine Political Thought and the Atlantic Republican Tradition* (Princeton, Princeton University Press, 1975) 31–47.

[66] See N Machiavelli, *The Prince* (trans. HC Mansfield, Chicago, University of Chicago Press, 1985) ch 9, p 39.

other places or to react to political interference with divestment.[67] Streeck sums his observations up as follows:[68]

> [W]hile an economic equilibrium is necessary for a democratic society to reap the collective benefits of private capital accumulation, it is put at risk by the very same policies that are needed to make private capital accumulation socially acceptable; and while a political equilibrium is needed to generate consent also with capitalism, it is threatened by the policies that are required for economic equilibrium.

It is not by accident, then, that democratic societies are caught in a circle of crises in which the resolution of a political crisis triggers economic crisis and the other way round. Increasing the tax revenue with the aim of funding social programs diminishes investor confidence in the amount of expected returns; boosting economic performance by making labour markets less 'rigid' is likely to give rise to resistance by trade unions.

The uneasy relationship between capitalism and democracy can be linked to two different constituencies to which policies are addressed. Streeck refers to them, roughly speaking, as citizens and creditors.[69] What he appears to have in mind when speaking of 'creditors' are not merely those owning government bonds or other debt instruments, but everyone having a stake in a consolidated budget and a 'lean state' that does not spend too much on public programmes. A consolidated budget – a not excessively growing public debt – is a major factor for creating confidence that the state is capable of servicing this debt and not creating more money by mere fiat. The measures taken in order to attain consolidation targets usually do not involve the raising of revenues, for exam-ple by increasing the rate of the income tax, but the cutting of expenditures. For the consolidation state it is the supreme law to rank, at least outwardly, its obligations to the debtors above all other obligations. According to Streeck, the people of the state (*Staatsvolk*) – ie, those depending on the state's intervention into the economy – systematically lose out against the people of the market (*Marktvolk*):[70]

> [...] [V]oters range below creditors, the results of elections are less important than those of bond auctions, public opinion matters less than interest rates and citizen loyalties less than investor confidence, and debt service crowds out public services.

In this way, the rights and obligations of citizenship become subordinated to commercial market obligations. The traditional relation between the state and civil society is turned on its head. Market signals – credit ratings – advance to the level of guideposts of public policy.[71] The interest on the part of the few in profitable returns on investments trumps the pursuit of social justice.

---

[67] See RM Unger, *False Necessity: Anti-Necessitarian Social Theory in the Service of Radical Democracy* (Cambridge, Cambridge University Press, 1988) 44–49.
[68] W Streeck, *How Will Capitalism End?* (London, Verso, 2016) 192.
[69] See ibid, 124.
[70] See ibid, at 124.
[71] See J Vogl, *Der Souveränitätseffekt* (Berlin, diaphanes, 2015).

Each of the two colliding regimes comes with different embodiments of reasonableness: the rational profit-maximising investor, on the one hand, and the loyal and sympathetic citizen, on the other. It is as though one encountered the Machiavellian *humori* in different guises:[72] the ambitious wealthy that kick others around for their own benefit and the many who want to live safe and moderately comfortable lives.

In the European Union it is quite clear that the market people are represented, in particular, in the context of monetary union and free movement of capital. It is in this context that the intense scrutiny with which supranational institutions supervise the creation and structure of the national budget tends to put the national political process in the position of receivership. These institutions are in a better position than democratically responsible governments to impose on 'unreliable' electorates a 'market-conforming fiscal policy'.[73] The task of macro-managing the economy becomes thereby decoupled from popular democracy. Streeck perceives quite clearly that this real constitution influences heavily how the powers of supranational bodies (the Council, the ECB) are interpreted by Courts and how state practice adopts quickly to changed circumstances, for example by appointing reliable technocrats to Prime Ministers. The 'troika' has intervened massively into domestic politics (in particular in the case of Greece) and has thereby not at all been supportive of any redistributive ambitions of national governments. Governments are no longer able to behave like states that are capable of overriding markets and act more like firms that respond to market signals. State citizens find it increasingly difficult to find an outlet for protest. Not by accident, they are then inclined to join 'irresponsible' populist movements.

The citizens of the market are not restricted to creditors, narrowly understood. They are composed of all of those who stand to gain from more austere government policies, which means less public and more private provision, the privatisation of state activity and the substitution of individual effort for collective solidarity.[74] This means that entrepreneurs, managers, well-educated professionals or people working in all kinds of 'bullshit jobs'[75] stand to gain from this development while the rest are likely to lose. The only arena that is responsive to concerns of the rest is the national polity, for it is there that ordinary people are given a voice.

Alterations in the real constitution give rise to shifts in the formal constitution. This concerns the margin of appreciation, broadly understood, in particular with regard to Article 7 of the European Union Treaty and the precautionary soft law procedures for strengthening the rule of law. In the face of the power of

---

[72] See already A Somek, *The Cosmopolitan Constitution* (Oxford, Oxford University Press, 2014).
[73] See Streeck, (n 68) at 130.
[74] See ibid at 134.
[75] See D Graeber, *Bullshit Jobs: A Theory* (London, Penguin Books, 2018).

populist movements, there is next to nothing that has been accomplished with these.[76] In the context of the internal market it remains to be seen whether and how the obstacle approach will be scaled back in order to avoid in the future such offensive results[77] as *Viking* and *Laval*.[78] The most recent case law on citizenship has indeed seen a retreat from the emphasis on the rights of citizenship that were at the center of the *Ruiz Zambrano* revolution.[79] There is movement in the real constitution of Europe, and the final movers are the constituencies: the market people and the state people.

XVIII. CONCLUSION

Madison took from the separation of powers the core idea that reason and normative force arise from an antagonism of forces. But he abandoned the broader perspective on the real constitution. He took the gold from the ancient constitutional tradition in order to forge the magical ring of modern constitutional law. What was thereby eclipsed was the perspective on the broader context of class conflict from within which any viable constitution needs to be built. With the rise of populist opposition to the institutions of liberal internationalism, such as the European Union, its relevance has finally returned to us with a vengeance.

[76] See C Möllers & L Schneider, *Demokratiesicherung in der Europäischen Union* (Tübingen, Mohr, 2018).

[77] See, eg, F Rödl, 'Transnationale Lohnkonkurrenz: Ein neuer Eckpfeiler der 'sozialen' Union?' in A Fischer-Lescano et al. (eds), *Europäische Gesellschaftsverfassung: Zur Konstitutionalisierung sozialer Demokratie in Europa* (Baden-Baden, Nomos, 2009) 145–160.

[78] Case C-438/05 *International Transport Workers' Federation, Finnish Seamen's Union v Viking Line ABP* [2007] ECR I-10779; Case C-341/05 Laval, un Partneri Ltd, of 18 December 2007.

[79] Case C-34/09, *Gerardo Ruiz Zambrano v Office national de l'emploi* (ONEm).

9

The Concept of Law Revisited:
An Essay in Descriptive Psychology

ANNE VAN AAKEN*

I. INTRODUCTION

'WHAT IS LAW'[1] and what distinguishes law from other social practices? Is morality a necessary feature of law? How does law influence behaviour? These old questions may seem obsolete but are still much debated. I propose to explore behavioural economic/psychological[2] insights to answer these questions but confine myself here solely to experimental public good games which are representative for the question under which conditions social cooperation and order may arise. Having a legal order is of course itself an example of successful social cooperation.[3] Since the most prominent means of social ordering is law, those insights might be helpful also for legal theory. Such an inquiry may open up a fascinating range of new possibilities about how law might matter to its subjects and it is capable of affecting behaviour in ways that have previously

* Universität Hamburg, Alexander von Humboldt Professor for Law and Economics, Legal Theory, Public International Law and European Law, email: anne.van.aaken@uni-hamburg.de. I gratefully acknowledge the support of the Alexander von Humboldt Foundation. I am grateful for the many helpful comments at the faculty lunch seminar at Columbia Law School in November 2014 as well as the comments at the Vienna Lectures in 2018.

[1] HLA Hart, *The Concept of Law*, 3rd edn (Oxford, Oxford University Press, 2012) 1 deems this the most persistent question of legal theory.

[2] I use psychology and behavioural economics interchangeably. The experiments conducted over about 30 years have been undertaken by psychologists as well as economists; both seek to understand how people really behave. The experimental methodology allows us to observe peoples' social preferences and cognition under controlled circumstances.

[3] S Gächter, 'Human Pro-Social Motivation and the Maintenance of Social Order' in E Zamir and D Teichman (eds), *Handbook on Behavioural Economics and the Law* (Oxford, Oxford University Press 2014) 2.

eluded legal scholars. The use of experimental insights is in its infancy in jurisprudence[4] but in spite of that, experimental insights are increasingly used in philosophy on the one hand[5] and in the study of law on the other.[6]

Theories about law often contain *implicit* assumptions or only common sense psychology about how people behave and why. But they are disconnected from social science and behavioural insights.[7] Except for natural law theories which are not as concerned with empirics, public morality and social efficacy are also empirical notions relevant to theories of law. In spite of this, empirics of human behaviour and their perception of morality and justice, traditionally being a domain of inter alia psychology,[8] are mostly not explicitly spelled out in legal theory. The disconnect between positive and normative legal theory has often been deplored and attributed to two recurring conceptual problems: first, the gap between fact and value and second the gap between internal and external perspectives on law.[9] This is diagnosed equally for municipal law[10] as for international law.[11] This chapter is not concerned with the substance of the law as such, but focuses solely on the legal theory, thus it takes an external perspective on the law.[12]

---

[4] But see, eg, R Donelson and I Hannikainen, 'Fuller and the Folk: The Inner Morality of Law Revisited', forthcoming in T Lombrozo, J Knobe, & S Nichols (eds), *Oxford Studies in Experimental Philosophy*, Vol 3 (Oxford, Oxford University Press); M Kneer and E Machery, 'No luck for moral luck' (2019) 182 *Cognition* 331.

[5] J Knobe and N Schaun, *Experimental Philosophy* (Oxford, Oxford University Press 2008).

[6] E Zamir and D Teichman, *Behavioral Law and Economics* (Oxford, Oxford University Press 2018).

[7] cf. LA Kornhauser, 'Governance Structures, Legal Systems, and the Concept of Law' (2004) 79 *Chicago-Kent Law Review* 355: 'No one in the current debate advocates a social-scientific concept of law that best promotes our systematic understanding of the emergence and maintenance of social structures.' Kornhauser uses rational choice to understand institutions and the concept of law but does not use behavioural insights.

[8] Indeed, the understanding of human behaviour is – next to psychology – a common undertaking of neuroscience, see PW Glimcher et al (eds), *Neuroeconomics. Decision Making and the Brain* (San Diego, Elsevier, 2009), anthropology, see JP Henrich et al (eds), *Foundations of human sociality. Economic experiments and ethnographic evidence from fifteen small-scale societies* (Oxford, Oxford University Press, 2004), behavioural economics, see H Gintis et al (eds), *Moral sentiments and material interests. The foundations of cooperation in economic life* (Cambridge, Mass., MIT Press, 2005), evolutionary theory, see S Bowles and H Gintis, *A cooperative species: Human reciprocity and its evolution* (Princeton, Princeton University Press, 2011) and last but not least social psychology, see P van Lange et al, *Social dilemmas. The psychology of human cooperation* (Oxford, Oxford University Press, 2014).

[9] cf. Kornhauser (n 7), 'Governance Structures, Legal Systems, and the Concept of Law' 381.

[10] A Vermeule, 'Connecting Positive and Normative Legal Theory' (2008) 10 *University of Pennsylvania Journal of Constitutional Law* 387 and A van Aaken, 'Towards a Psychological Concept of Law' in S Kirste and M Anderheiden (eds), *Interdisziplinarität der Rechtswissenschaften* (Berlin, Duncker&Humblot, 2015).

[11] A Buchanan and D Golove, 'Philosophy of International Law' in JL Coleman, SJ Shapiro and KE Himma (eds), *Oxford Handbook of Jurisprudence and Philosophy of Law* (Oxford, Oxford University Press, 2002) 869: 'little explicit connection between positive and normative theorizing.'

[12] There are many dimensions to legal theory: 1) normative dimension of law (moral theory of legal doctrine and institutions), 2) analytic dimension (what makes a norm a part of law, what is law?), and the epistemology of law (what are the ways of knowing legal facts of law?). See ibid, 871.

HLA Hart deemed his concept of law 'an essay in descriptive *sociology*', meant to further the understanding of law, coercion, and morality as different but related social phenomena.[13] To the best of my knowledge, hitherto, an essay in descriptive *psychology* in order to understand law, coercion and morality is missing: this is a first attempt to explore elements of a psychological concept of law. Arguments around the concept of law can serve as an essential starting point for trying to reinterpret legal theory and the field of law in psychological terms.[14] Having a realistic picture about human behaviour should also be the basis for any legal theory.[15] This chapter is just a starting point, outlining along which lines of reasoning this could go and it is oversimplifying and selective due to space restrictions at several instances. I therefore discuss the issues on a rather abstract level but hope nevertheless to illuminate central questions in legal theory via psychological insights.

First, I shortly outline my view on the relationship between legal theory and social science (Section II). Then I describe behavioural foundations used – implicitly – in the analysis and theories of law (Section III). Third, I will explore the behavioural assumptions underlying different theories of law, exploring how psychological insights may help to reconstruct those theories (Section IV). The last part concludes (Section V).

II. LEGAL THEORY AND SOCIAL SCIENCE

One may have different understandings of the role or purpose of legal theory in the first place, for example, whether theory should generate empirical predictions that are falsifiable through empirical observation or whether legal theory should generate normative principles guiding the legal order. I would defend both points of view but insist on a solid empirical basis when pursuing normative endeavours. This does not commit a naturalistic fallacy – it informs the normative and analytical debate. Except for natural law theories which are not too concerned with empirics, public morality and social efficacy as used, for example, in legal positivism are in principle empirical notions. More generally speaking, legal theory has been for too long heavily disconnected from social science.[16] Hart did not follow up on his promise in that he used tested

---

[13] Hart (n 1), *The Concept of Law*, 'Preface' vi.

[14] For a similar attempt for national law from a sociological perspective, see R Cotterrell, *Law Community. Legal Theory in Sociological Perspective* (Oxford, Clarendon Press, 1997) 23 onwards; for international law, see M Hirsch, 'The Sociology of International Law: Invitation to Study International Rules in Their Social Context' (2005) 55 *University of Toronto Law Journal* 891.

[15] BZ Tamanaha, 'Socio-Legal Positivism and a General Jurisprudence' (2001) 21 *Oxford Journal of Legal Studies* 1.

[16] This of course does not apply to legal sociological approaches to law which have a very long tradition, eg, M v Rümelin, *Rechtsgefühl und Rechtsbewusstsein* (Tübingen, Mohr 1925) or M Rehbinder and H Schelsky, *Zur Effektivität des Rechts* (Bielefeld, Bertelsmann Universitätsverlag 1972).

sociological (or other social science) insights.[17] This disconnect between positive and normative legal theory has often been deplored and attributed to two recurring conceptual problems: first, the gap between fact and value and second the gap between internal and external perspectives on law.[18] But implicitly, legal theories do use behavioural assumptions. In my view, having a realistic picture about human and/or state behaviour should also be the basis for any legal theory; it does not exclude normative or analytical reasoning. This does not necessarily entail a rationalist approach which, as one may argue, is used by Austinian theories, but also by legal positivists. But it does entail a social science approach with hypotheses being able to be tested in principle (although not all may be tested). Behavioural economics/psychology is stronger in that respect than rational choice in that it tests also the behavioural assumptions of rational choice (or other approaches to legal theory) and thus lays the empirical groundwork for other theories about the smallest unit of analysis – the individual actor. Thus, rationalist approaches are no *conditio sine qua non* for an empirically grounded legal theory, the rationalist but also the behaviouralist approach follow the epistemology of critical rationalism as advanced by Karl Popper holding that scientific theories and any other claims to knowledge can and should be rationally criticised, and (if they have empirical content) can and should be subjected to tests which may falsify them.[19] This epistemological approach should, I submit, also underpin legal theory.

III. BEHAVIOURAL FOUNDATIONS OF LEGAL THEORY

Theories and assumptions about human and state behaviour abound. It is impossible to deal with all of them. I would like to concentrate on rational choice theory and on psychology as it is also used in behavioural economics and only on public good games since those experiments explore social cooperation and law is one phenomenon of social cooperation. Other deviations from rational choice will be mentioned only when influencing the games, such as framing. Whereas rational choice theory is an *assumption* of how people behave[20] and normative decision theory tells them how they should behave, psychology or behavioural economics analyses how people really behave. Experiments are used to observe peoples' social preferences and cognition under controlled conditions. They can be conducted in the field or in laboratory settings, whether of individual or

---

[17] cf. Tamanaha (n 15), 'Socio-Legal Positivism and a General Jurisprudence'.

[18] cf. Kornhauser (n 7), 'Governance Structures, Legal Systems, and the Concept of Law' 381.

[19] KR Popper, *Logik der Forschung*, 3. Aufl. (Siebeck/Mohr 1969) (german original, The Logic of Scientific Discovery as translated).

[20] Seminal on the role of assumptions in economics M Friedman, 'The Methodology of Positive Economics' in M Friedman (ed), *Essays in Positive Economics* (Chicago, Chicago University Press, 1953).

group (that is inter-personal) behaviour. The experimental approach is a promising research method because it best secures internal validity.[21] But it opens up the problem of external validity of the experiments, that is the degree to which it is warranted to generalise results to other contexts.[22] External validity of lab experiments remains challengeable for all social science using them; legal theory is no exception.

A. Rationalist Assumptions in Legal Theory

Many contemporary theories of law and how it works (or not) use the rational choice assumption implicitly but do not spell out their behavioural assumptions.[23] Most clearly this becomes in Austinian command theory which relies on external sanctioning only; external sanctioning is an expression of the underlying presumption that people react to external incentives in a cost-benefit analysis. HLA Hart argues against this top-down, 'pyramidal view of law as order of a sovereign backed by sanctions.'[24] Hart deals with the problem of the functions of law, stressing the 'specific character of law as a means of social control'[25] since '[w]hat is important is that the insistence on importance or seriousness of social pressure behind the rules is the primary factor determining whether they are thought of as giving rise to obligations'.[26] Although his theory is much more complex, it is based upon an implicit premise that people act rationally towards obligations, although one may argue that his internal point of view incorporates what would now be called the 'expressive function of law',[27] namely to guide conduct via information.[28] No game-theoretical language is used though.[29]

---

[21] In scientific research, internal validity is the extent to which a causal conclusion based on a study is warranted, which is determined by the degree to which a study minimises systematic error. It contrasts with external validity, SR Thye, 'Logical and Philosophical Foundations of Experimental Research in the Social Science' in M Webster and J Sell (eds), *Laboratory Experiments in the Social Science* (San Diego, Elsevier, 2007).

[22] For a detailed discussion, see C Engel, 'Behavioural Law and Economics: Empirical Methods' in E Zamir and D Teichman (eds), *The Oxford Handbook of Behavioural Economics and the Law* (Oxford, Oxford University Press, 2014); C Engel, 'The Proper Scope of Behavioural Law and Economics' (2018) Preprint Max Planck Institute for Research on Collective Goods, 2018/02.

[23] The index of the Oxford Handbook of Jurisprudence and the Philosophy of Law does contain one mentioning of 'rationalism' or 'rational choice' but also no other one on behavioural assumptions.

[24] L Green, 'Introduction' in HLA Hart (ed), *The Concept of Law* (Oxford, Oxford University Press, 2012) xxvii.

[25] Hart (n 1), *The Concept of Law* 39.

[26] Hart (n 1), *The Concept of Law* 87.

[27] R McAdams, *The Expressive Powers of Law: Theories and Limits* (Harvard, Harvard University Press, 2015).

[28] Hart (n 1), *The Concept of Law* 88–90.

[29] Game theory models strategic interaction between actors. See for an introduction, DG Baird, RH Gertner and RC Picker, *Game Theory and the Law* (Cambridge (MA), Harvard University Press, 1994).

Past attempts to explain social order in economics and political science, typically relied on the assumption of self-regarding and rational agents[30] using game theory. John Rawls, for example, in his 'Theory of Justice'[31] very clearly uses rational choice assumptions, coupled with the assumption that people are risk averse (thus the Minimax principle).[32] Usually a main distinction is drawn about the underlying problem structure of the game: coordination games and cooperation games. Law also creates social order via its coordinating functions which makes obeying the law also in people's self-interest, eg traffic laws for driving right or left or an air traffic control language. Law can create a focal point. Hart recognises this when he explores mere convergent behaviour and the existence of a social rule.[33] Once the standard is set, no further problems of compliance are to be expected; the law is self-enforcing and expectations converge. I will not discuss pure coordination games, although they might be worth exploring concerning the rule of recognition of Hart,[34] but focus on cooperation games, including mixed motive games, since they pose the biggest problem for social cooperation.

Social order can be conceptualised as a public good game, a cooperation game.[35] Social order is of collective interest but individuals have an incentive to disregard the law if this promises to be more advantageous than abiding by the law. Public goods are non-rivalrous and non-excludable. They are usually modelled as a prisoners' dilemma game where (in a one shot game), the Nash Equilibrium is non-cooperation. It is individually rational not to cooperate although the group would be better off if all cooperated (inter alia, the free-riding behaviour is attributed to that social dilemma). In bilateral relationships, credible commitments (eg an enforceable contract) and the shadow of the future (in repeated games), may sustain cooperation. This is much harder in larger groups – social scientists are much more pessimistic

[30] Starting with T Hobbes, *Leviathan* (London, Andrew Crooke, 1651), available at: https://socialsciences.mcmaster.ca/econ/ugcm/3ll3/hobbes/Leviathan.pdf.

[31] J Rawls, *A Theory of Justice* (Cambridge (MA), Harvard University Press, 1971).

[32] This decision principle is derived from normative decision theory, which is based on rational choice theory.

[33] Hart (n 1), *The Concept of Law* 9; see also Green (24), 'Introduction' xxiii.

[34] See GJ Postema, 'Coordination and Convention at the Foundations of Law' (1982) 11 *Journal of Legal Studies* 165 and Kornhauser (n 7), 'Governance Structures, Legal Systems, and the Concept of Law'.

[35] Each of these subjects in the group is given an initial endowment of money (or tokens). They can then choose to contribute some of their endowment to the public good. The contribution to the public good is multiplied by some factor k, where k is greater than one but less than n. This enlarged pot is then shared out equally between all the group members. Contributions to the public good thus benefits each group member by k=n, which is known as the 'marginal per capita return'. An individual who contributes one unit to the public good thus benefits the group as a whole, since k is greater than one, but loses out herself, since k=n is less than one. The best outcome for the group as a whole is that each individual should contribute her full endowment to the public good. However, each individual has an incentive to free-ride on everyone else's contributions. Standard economic theory predicts that nothing is contributed to the public good. This prediction is known as the 'strong free-rider hypothesis'.

about the cooperative outcome:[36] 'stable cooperation is possible in the two-person prisoner's dilemma but is hard to achieve in large groups because no effective punishment targeted at non-compliant group members exists.'[37] This has similarly been argued by Hart distinguishing thus primitive legal orders from modern legal order.[38] One important insight of many experiments using the public goods game is that cooperation is inherently unstable and tends to unravel to the worst outcome, predicted by self-interest. Does this mean that legal theories assuming only self-interested motivation and change of behaviour *only* through external sanctioning, like Austin's imperative theory, are correct? The answer is a qualified 'no': the 'strong free-rider hypothesis' has been proven to be wrong. But what are the important elements upholding social order?

B. Behavioural Economics

The last 30 years of research in behavioural and experimental economics have challenged the view described above. Experiments on social preferences use game theory including the ultimatum game,[39] the dictator game,[40] and trust games[41]

---

[36] For details, see R Cornes and T Sandler, *The Theory of Externalities, Public Goods, and Club Goods* (Cambridge, Cambridge University Press, 1986) and for global public goods, see S Barrett, *Why Cooperate? The Incentive to Supply Public Goods* (Oxford, Oxford University Press, 2007). For Behavioural Game Theory, see CF Camerer, *Behavioural Game Theory. Experiments in Strategic Interaction* (Princeton, Princeton University Press, 2003).

[37] Gächter (n 3), 'Human Pro-Social Motivation and the Maintenance of Social Order' 3.

[38] Thus, in small groups and tribes 'primitive legal orders' in the sense of HLA Hart might be sufficient to generate cooperation. But in large groups, such as nation-states, a sophisticated, credible legal system might be necessary in order to hold up cooperation. Cf, Hart (n 1), *The Concept of Law* 91–93.

[39] The experiments started with the so-called Ultimatum Game. See W Güth, R Schmittberger and B Schwarze, 'An Experimental Analysis of Ultimatium Bargaining' (1982) 3 *Journal of Economic Behaviour and Organization* 367. The proposer makes an offer of how to share a given amount (usually money) and the recipient can accept or reject the offer. In case of acceptance, the offered division is implemented; in case the recipient rejects, both get nothing. If the recipient is motivated solely by monetary payoffs, he or she will accept every offer. Therefore, the proposer will only offer the smallest money unit: this is expected by the *homo oeconomicus* hypothesis but not found in the experiments. This is attributed to fairness considerations which are, when left unfulfilled, punished even if costly to the punisher.

[40] The 'dictator' determines how to split an endowment (such as a cash prize) between himself and the second player. The second player simply receives the remainder of the endowment left by the dictator. Most people all over the world share the endowment, although there is no sanction for not doing so. This contradicts the rational choice assumption. For a meta-analysis, see C Engel, 'Dictator Games: A Meta Study' (2011) 14 *Experimental Economics* 583. For details, see E Fehr and KM Schmidt, 'The Economics of Fairness, Reciprocity and Altruism – Experimental Evidence and New Theories' in S Kolm and JM Ythier (eds), *Handbook of the Economics of Giving, Altruism and Reciprocity Vol I* (San Diego, Elsevier, 2006).

[41] The trust game is similar to the dictator game, but with an added first step. First, one participant decides how much of an endowment to give to the second participant, and this amount is typically multiplied by the researchers. Then the second participant (now acting as a dictator) decides how much of this increased endowment to allocate to the first participant.

which have been extensively played in different forms. Plenty of experimental research has shown that individuals are also motivated by other-regarding/altruistic and social preferences:[42] 'the principle of rationality, unless accompanied by extensive empirical research to identify the correct auxiliary assumptions, has little power to make valid predictions about political phenomena'[43] – or for that matter – the phenomenon of law. Ultimatum game experiments, eg, have shown that people are generally willing to sacrifice monetary rewards for reasons of fairness when offered (too) low allocations, thus behaving inconsistently with simple models of self-interest as used in rationalist models. Since I am interested here in the law as a means of constructing social order, I will concentrate on those experiments which have been conducted on the role of reciprocity, sanctions, fairness and morality, neglecting other heuristics and biases.[44]

Experimental economists make a distinction (just as legal theorists) between the motivation (the reasons for action) and the behaviour itself. Whereas some people indeed follow the assumption of rational-choice of maximising their own, self-regarding behaviour, others will behave selfishly under some conditions, but are not motivated by selfishness: 'People can be non-selfishly motivated and end up behaving selfishly, but the converse also exists: selfish people behaving pro-socially.'[45] Punishment (ie sanctioning) plays an important role in this but need not in all circumstances: social order can be sustained, to some extent, by internalised norms of proper conduct even in the absence of any formal enforcement (internal reasons for action). Here, morality can play an important role as well.

Gächter discusses three pillars of social cooperation[46] which neatly match with arguments in different legal theories. The first pillar is internalised norms of cooperation, sustained by emotions such as guilt and shame; moral norms may be underlying those (see i. below). The second pillar is the behaviour of other people. Most people are 'conditional cooperators' willing to cooperate if

---

[42] This started with the so-called Ultimatum Game. See Güth, Schmittberger and Schwarze (n 39), 'An Experimental Analysis of Ultimatium Bargaining', for a meta-analysis, see Engel (n 40), 'Dictator Games: A Meta Study'. Other games include the Dictator Game, the Power to Take Game, the Third Party Punishment Game, the Gift Exchange Game and the Trust Game. For details on the experiments, see Fehr and Schmidt (n 40), 'The Economics of Fairness, Reciprocity and Altruism – Experimental Evidence and New Theories'.

[43] HA Simon, 'Human Nature in Politics: The Dialogue of Psychology with Political Science' (1985) 79 *American Political Science Review* 293, comparing in that paper two theories of human rationality that have found application in political science: procedural, bounded rationality from contemporary cognitive psychology, and global, substantive rationality from economics. The word 'satisficing' is a conjunction of the words satisfy and suffice and means a strategy or cognitive heuristics that entails searching through the available alternatives until an acceptability threshold is met (instead of using the best available alternative by optimising). See also HA Simon, 'A Behavioural Model of Rational Choice' (1955) 69 *Quarterly Journal of Economics* 99.

[44] Extensively on other heuristics and biases relevant for law (and probably legal theory) such as framing and endowment effects, Zamir and Teichman (n 6), *Behavioral Law and Economics* and Aaken (n 10), 'Towards a Psychological Concept of Law'.

[45] Gächter (n 3), 'Human Pro-Social Motivation and the Maintenance of Social Order' 4.

[46] For an extensive discussion of those pillars, simultaneously giving an overview on the experiments so far conducted, see ibid.

others do so as well. This motivation can sustain cooperation if enough people cooperate but can jeopardise social order if too many others follow selfish inclinations – it hints at reciprocity as a strong driver of behaviour (see ii. below). The third pillar are sanctions meted out to anyone who does not cooperate; ideally punishment can work as a mere threat without being executed much; this punishment can be peer-punishment (as in primitive legal orders[47] or parts of international law) or third-party punishment as in 'modern legal orders' (iii. below).

i. Moral Judgements

Let's turn to the role of moral judgements. One important determinant of people's pro-social behaviour is most likely internalised norms of what people consider the morally right thing to do. '[T]he real question is no longer whether many people have other-regarding preferences, but under which conditions these preferences have important economic and social effects.'[48] For example, people donate anonymously to charities, they vote for reasons of civic duty although their vote is unlikely to be decisive, in most countries people pay their taxes despite low detection probabilities for evasion, and people also care for the environment out of moral convictions.[49] Those preferences are especially important for explaining collective action central to law. Also, anger and guilt are prototypical morally-linked emotions and are expected to be especially relevant in a context of social cooperation.[50] Gächter reports on a study using techniques from moral psychology that elicited people's moral judgements of free riding on a public good to understand to what extent free riding is perceived to be a *moral* problem. They found that people think that it is morally blameworthy and more so the more others contributed;[51] it triggers anger by the cooperating individual. At the same time, free riding triggers feelings of guilt by the free rider – a feeling most people do not like, so called-guilt aversion.[52] Those emotions are interesting for legal theory, since they trigger two different potential enforcement mechanisms of norms – external and internal punishment. Potential free riders might expect punishment from the angry cooperative

---

[47] As Hart (n 1), *The Concept of Law* 91 et seq. calls them.

[48] Fehr and Schmidt (n 40), 'The Economics of Fairness, Reciprocity and Altruism – Experimental Evidence and New Theories' 617.

[49] With further references, see Gächter (n 3), 'Human Pro-Social Motivation and the Maintenance of Social Order' 13.

[50] Ibid 14.

[51] Ibid.

[52] J Haidt, 'The Moral Emotions' in RJ Davidson, KR Sherer and HH Goldsmith (eds), *Handbook of Affective Sciences* (Oxford, Oxford University Press, 2003) and G Charness and M Dufwenberg, 'Promises and Partnership' (2006) 74 *Econometrica* 1579 as well as M Dufwenberg, S Gächter and H Hennig-Schmidt, 'The framing of games and the psychology of play' (2011) 73 Games and Economic Behaviour 459, 462, defining guilt aversion as the 'dislike of giving others what they expect'.

members and thus act cooperatively on the basis of an extrinsic self-regarding incentive to avoid punishment by contributing. Guilt, in contrast, is a negative emotion that can serve as 'internal punishment' and therefore provide an intrinsic reason for action.[53] Cooperation can thus be supported to the extent that people think cooperating is morally the right thing to do and feel guilty if breaking the social contract.

Traditional game theory does neither capture moral sentiments nor the relevance of beliefs about intentions of others, since it assumes that outcomes (and not beliefs) determine payoffs,[54] but ever more experiments show how important the perceived (good) intentions of other actors are for interaction.[55] Here, trust (or reputation) about the intention can play a role.[56]

Behavioural game theory attempts to capture those insights without giving up the strategic interaction basis.[57] If actors are perceived as moral and legitimate, cooperation is fostered; if actors are deemed unfair, cooperation is undermined. This has been well-documented in experiments.[58] Law itself distinguishes between different causes of non-compliance in many instances and accounts for intentions.

ii. Reciprocity

Second, reciprocity has been recognised by social scientists[59] as being one of the main basic principles that constitute societies. It can help explain the maintenance and development of social norms – and probably legal norms.[60] In its most extensive definition, which is usually used in this literature, it consists of being favourable to others because others are favourable to you (it is thus rational-choice based). Behavioural economics takes a more differentiated look at the reciprocity principle. It identifies three possible rationales:[61] (1) self-sustaining sequences of mutual favours which can be solely self-interested: 'cooperative' or

---

[53] See Gächter (n 3), 'Human Pro-Social Motivation and the Maintenance of Social Order' 14.

[54] But see latest developments: R Bénabou and J Tirole, 'Mindful Economics: The Production, Consumption, and Value of Beliefs' (2016) 30 Journal of Economic Perspectives 141.

[55] A Falk, E Fehr and U Fischbacher, 'Testing theories of fairness – Intentions matter' (2008) 62 Games and Economic Behaviour.

[56] Furthermore, preferences may also depend on the type of opponent, so-called type-based reciprocity. *Cf.* D Levine, 'Modeling Altruism and Spitefulness in Experiments' (1998) 1 Review of Economic Dynamics 593; Fehr and Schmidt (n 40), 'The Economics of Fairness, Reciprocity and Altruism – Experimental Evidence and New Theories'.

[57] It rather expands classical game theory by adding emotions, mistakes, limited foresight and leaning. Cf. Camerer (n 36), *Behavioural Game Theory. Experiments in Strategic Interaction* 3.

[58] Falk, Fehr and Fischbacher (n 55), 'Testing theories of fairness – Intentions matter' (providing further references concerning the experiments).

[59] S Kolm, 'Reciprocity: Its Scope, Rationales, and Consequences' in S Kolm and JM Ythier (eds), *Handbook of the Economics of Giving, Altruism and Reciprocity Vol I* (San Diego, Elsevier, 2006) 371.

[60] V Boehme-Neßler, 'Reziprozität und Recht' (2008) 39 *Rechtstheorie* 521.

[61] Kolm (n 59), 'Reciprocity: Its Scope, Rationales, and Consequences'.

'retaliatory' behaviour in repeated interactions is motivated by future benefits (explicable by rational choice, weak reciprocity); (2) balance (which assumes acts of comparison and matching), often related to equality and fairness concerns (reciprocity *strictu sensu*); (3) liking, because being favoured induces liking which induces favouring (a sort of Facebook effect), or because liking can directly result from being liked. Reciprocal behaviour in one-shot interactions is often called 'strong reciprocity' (since rational choice theory would assume defection) in contrast to 'weak reciprocity' that is motivated by long-term self-interest in repeated interactions.[62] Legal and political philosophy have for a long time relied on weak reciprocity following the rational choice approach. But we might then overlook other reasons for sustaining law.

A reciprocal individual responds to actions he or she perceives to be kind in a kind manner, and to actions he or she perceives to be hostile in a hostile manner.[63] Whereas an altruist is willing to sacrifice his or her own resources in order to improve the well-being of others, a spiteful or envious person is also willing to do this in order to punish others.[64] Many people are strong negative reciprocators with punitive sentiments for wrongdoing.[65] Most individuals are conditionally altruistic or spiteful: they are conditional cooperators.[66] This has been well proven in the so-called ultimate game,[67] where it was shown that most people reject an offer; thus supporting the *homo reciprocans* prediction over the *homo oeconomicus* one.[68]

Those findings have been first studied in bilateral relationships but the same holds in multilateral or group environments. A large number of studies show that most people contribute to a public good in the beginning but contributions

---

[62] See, eg, H Gintis, 'Strong Reciprocity and Human Sociality' (2000) 206 *Journal of Theoretical Biology* 169.

[63] A Falk and U Fischbacher, 'A Theory of Reciprocity' (2006) 54 *Games and Economic Behaviour* 293.

[64] For a discussion of the motives to punish, see A Falk, E Fehr and U Fischbacher, 'Driving Forces behind Informal Sanctions' (2005) 73 *Econometrica* 2017.

[65] Surveyed in S Gächter and B Herrmann, 'Reciprocity, culture, and human cooperation: Previous insights and a new cross-cultural experiment' (2009) 364 *Philosophical Transactions of the Royal Society B – Biological Sciences* 791.

[66] First, there are some unconditional cooperators, who contribute all or almost all of their endowment, regardless of the circumstances. Second, there is some proportion of conditional cooperators, who cooperate as long as others are doing so. Third, there are free-riders, who make small or no contributions from the beginning; it is these free-riders that drives the decay of cooperation in contributions over time.

[67] The proposer makes an offer of how to share a given amount (usually money) and the recipient can accept or reject the offer. In case of acceptance, the offered division is implemented; in case the recipient rejects, both get nothing. If the recipient is motivated solely by monetary payoffs, he or she will accept every offer. Therefore, the proposer will only offer the smallest money unit: this is expected by the *homo oeconomicus* hypothesis.

[68] See G Charness and P Kuhn, 'Lab labor: What can labor economists learn from the lab?' in O Ashenfelter and D Card (eds), *Handbook of Labor Economics* (North Holland, Elsevier, 2011) an overview of experiments supporting for strong positive reciprocity; the ultimatum game gives strong evidence about strong negative reciprocity.

decrease over time in experiments that allow for repetition of the base game.[69] In constellations where subjects make their contribution decisions simultaneously, ie they cannot respond to what they have observed others to do, they have to rely on the beliefs they hold about other group members' contributions and some experiments control for that.[70] The results are consistent with strong positive reciprocity: on average, reported beliefs and own contributions are highly significantly positively correlated. Although this holds for the majority, some people contribute nothing despite the fact they believe others will contribute a lot.[71]

What are possible psychological mechanisms that produce strong negative and positive reciprocity? In the experiments, three important mechanisms were identified:[72] first, a known conditional form of altruism is the so-called inequity aversion[73] which describes a situation in which, in addition to the actor's material self-interest, her utility increases if the allocation of material payoffs becomes more equitable. 'Equitable' is of course an indeterminate notion and usually depends on the reference point; this is mostly the status quo. But it neatly connects to some notions of distributive justice. Other mechanisms are, secondly, social efficiency seeking (ie contributing to the public good) and thirdly, a desire to reward or punish intentions behind actions. In short, concerns for the well-being of others (for fairness and reciprocity) need to be taken into account if behaviour in social interactions is to be understood.[74]

iii. Sanctions

But can cooperation survive without sanctions? The sobering answer of many repeatedly played in numerous public good experiments around the world is that cooperation almost invariably breaks down in repeated interactions. As Gächter holds: 'Thus, the conclusion is inevitable and seems to vindicate Hobbes: in and

---

[69] B Herrmann, C Thöni and S Gächter, 'Antisocial Punishment Across Societies' (2008) 319 *Science* 1362 and Dufwenberg, Gächter and Hennig-Schmidt (n 52), 'The framing of games and the psychology of play'. In all subject pools, people contribute substantial amounts initially but over time contributions dwindle to low levels almost everywhere. See for a rigorous analysis U Fischbacher and S Gächter, 'Social preferences, beliefs, and the dynamics of free riding in public good experiments' (2010) 100 *American Economic Review* 541 and for a survey A Chaudhuri, 'Sustaining cooperation in laboratory public goods experiments: A selective survey of the literature' (2011) 14 *Experimental Economics* 47.

[70] Thus, some experiments ask the participants what they estimate the other group members will contribute (eg, Dufwenberg, Gächter and Hennig-Schmidt (n 52), 'The framing of games and the psychology of play').

[71] Gächter (n 3), 'Human Pro-Social Motivation and the Maintenance of Social Order' 10.

[72] Ibid 13 and Falk, Fehr and Fischbacher (n 64), 'Driving Forces behind Informal Sanctions'.

[73] GE Bolton and A Ockenfels, 'A Theory of Equity, Reciprocity and Competition' (2000) 100 *American Economic Review* 166; Fehr and Schmidt (n 40), 'The Economics of Fairness, Reciprocity and Altruism – Experimental Evidence and New Theories'; G Charness and M Rabin, 'Understanding Social Preferences with Simple Tests' (2002) 117 *Quarterly Journal of Economics* 817.

[74] Fehr and Schmidt (n 40), 'The Economics of Fairness, Reciprocity and Altruism – Experimental Evidence and New Theories'.

of itself, that is, without external enforcement, social order is fragile and the time horizon as such is of no avail.'[75] Cooperation is thus inherently fragile, and needs some support through other mechanisms to be sustainable.[76] This is a strong hint at the necessity of sanctioning devices – such as law – but not necessarily centralised ones.

Sanctioning institutions are the 'undisputed winner in a competition with a sanction-free institution'[77] when institutions can be endogenously chosen. In experiments, it could be shown that although people have an initial aversion against sanctioning, the entire population migrates successively to the sanctioning institution and strongly cooperates, whereas the sanction-free society becomes fully depopulated. Sanctioning institutions can thus be explained even from an evolutionary perspective.[78] And their importance has been intuitively grasped by legal theorists.

But not all sanctions are alike. Whereas social norms and international law are often sanctioned in a decentralised way, municipal law is commonly sanctioned by central institutions. Also, the latter have been mimicked in experiments. In a *third-party* punishment game,[79] the potential punisher is not an affected party, but an independent third party (this feature thus resembles municipal law enforcement in reality). Since the third party is not affected by the decisions of the involved players, third-party punishment is a reflection of normative considerations. The results show that third parties are much more likely to punish a defector if the other player cooperated than if both defected; this reflects the findings above on moral judgements. Additionally, centralised punishment *by one group member only* has been studied and found quite effective.[80]

---

[75] Gächter (n 3), 'Human Pro-Social Motivation and the Maintenance of Social Order' 19.

[76] Ibid 23. But see for crowding out effects also DP Balliet, LB Mulder and P van Lange, 'Reward, punishment, and cooperation: A meta-analysis' (2011) 137 *Psychological Bulletin* 594.

[77] Ö Gürerk, B Irlenbusch and B Rockenbach, 'The Competitive Advantage of Sanctioning Institutions' (2006) 312 *Science* 108.

[78] E Fehr and U Fischbacher, 'Social norms and human cooperation' (2004) 8 *Trends in Cognitive Sciences* 185, 189: 'The human capacity to establish and enforce social norms is perhaps the decisive reason for the uniqueness of human cooperation in the animal world. The evidence indicates that other animals largely lack the cognitive and emotional capacities that are necessary for social norms.' (fns omitted). E Fehr and S Gächter, 'Cooperation and Punishment in Public Goods Experiments' (2000) 90 *American Economic Review* 980 developed an experimental design to study punishment and cooperation in a sequence of ten one-shot (random group members – 'Strangers') and fixed group ('Partners'; same group members) public good game – settings that correspond to different real-life interactions. Strangers cooperate much less than Partners.

[79] Fehr and Fischbacher (n 78), 'Social norms and human cooperation'. They deem social norms prior to legal norms (185): 'Cooperation in human societies is mainly based on social norms, including in modern societies, where a considerable amount of cooperation is due to the legal enforcement of rules. Legal enforcement mechanisms cannot function unless they are based on a broad consensus about the normative legitimacy of the rules – in other words, unless the rules are backed by social norms.'

[80] R O'Gorman, J Henrich and M van Vugt, 'Constraining free riding in public goods games: Designated solitary punishers can sustain human cooperation' (2009) 276 *Proceedings of the Royal Society B-Biological Sciences* 323. This experiment shows that allowing a single individual to punish increases cooperation to the same level as allowing each group member to punish and results in greater group profits.

The mere threat of punishment can be effective to uphold cooperation.[81] This is also what would be expected by rational choice theory: for a norm being effective in guiding behaviour, the *expected* sanction is decisive. This is also how law enforcement works in many instances. Thus, punishment can exert its power as a mere threat effect, yet the threat has to be there. If punishment is impossible, cooperation breaks down.

Furthermore, the perceived fairness of sanctioning is important. If sanctions are perceived to reveal selfish or greedy intentions, they destroy altruistic cooperation almost completely, whereas sanctions perceived as fair leave altruism intact. Fair sanctions are especially those which sanction defectors in public-good games. In common pool resource (CPR) experiments,[82] it was also shown that the possibility to communicate and to sanction alleviates the inefficient excess appropriation of the resource (contrary to the prediction of rational choice theory). Thus, if sanctions are perceived as being unfair or just satisfying self-regarding motives, cooperation breaks down. Modern lawful societies channel punitive sentiments into laws and a formal, institutionalised and centralised sanctioning systems with fair procedures.

Furthermore, there are games which use exclusion and the formation of club goods as a sanctioning device. This kind of punishment has been used in more primitive legal orders but it still has some resonance in modern legal orders.[83] This sort of punishment is cheaper than punishment where the punisher needs to take his own endowment to punish. Those sanctioning devices have a long history: 'ostrakismos' is considered to have been one important pillar in the Athenian democracy: citizens could vote whether to banish individuals (usually for 10 years, afterwards the ostracised individual could rejoin the society (redemption, ie reversed exclusion).[84] The efficacy of those mechanisms has been tested in experiments. The results are quite clear: cooperation is massively enhanced with those mechanisms. One experiment showed that adding exclusion of a group to a game can be very effective at increasing contributions.[85]

---

[81] C Engel, 'Social preferences can make imperfect sanctions work: Evidence from a public good experiment' (2014) 108 *Journal of Economic Behaviour and Organization* 343.

[82] For the classical rational choice prediction concerning CPR, see R Selten, 'The Chain Store Paradox' (1978) 9 *Theor Decis* 127. See also A Falk, E Fehr and U Fischbacher, 'Appropriating the Commons – A Theoretical Explanation' in T Dietz et al (eds), *The Drama of the Commons* (Washington, National Academy Press, 2002) (finding that there is less appropriation in CPR and more contibution to public goods if the institutional set-up allows for (informal) sanctions and communication). Eg, see E Ostrom, 'A Behavioural Approach to the Rational Choice Theory of Collective Action' (1998) 92 *American Political Science Review* 1.

[83] OA Hathaway and S Shapiro, 'Outcasting: Enforcement in Domestic and International Law' 2011) 212 *Yale Law Journal* 252.

[84] G Charness and CL Yang, 'Public Goods Provision with Voting for Exclusion, Exit, and Mergers: An Experiment' (2010) Working Paper, available at: www.researchgatenet/publication/228687877_Public_Goods_Provision_with_Voting_for_Exclusion_Exit_and_Mergers_An_Experiment 21.

[85] M Cinyabuguma, T Page and L Putterman, 'Cooperation under the Threat of Expulsion in a Public Goods Experiment' (2005) 89 *Journal of Public Economics* 1421 (finding that contributions rose to nearly 100% of endowments with significantly higher efficiency compared with a no-expulsion baseline. Expulsions were strictly of the lowest contributors, and there was an exceptionally strong fall-off in contributions in the last period, when the expulsion threat was unavailable).

It is critical that free-riders are not able to exploit cooperators on a long-term basis. Conditional cooperators who succeed in avoiding free-riders will make large contributions in an endogenous formed group-formation. Furthermore, a non-myopic free-rider may well cooperate strategically, as it rapidly becomes apparent that contributing nothing will very likely lead to being excluded. The driving force appears to be the economies of scale of the larger group combined with the awareness that bad behaviour will result in screening in the form of not being able to join a group or being expelled from one. Finally, the possibility of redemption (reversible exclusion) leads a substantially higher degree of social efficiency, that is contributions to the public good.[86]

iv. Any Other Distinctive Feature of Law?

An old question in legal theory has been the distinction between social norms and law (both have sanctions). In addition to the direct deterrent effects of sanctions emphasised by the rational choice approach and Austin's imperative theory, legal scholars have suggested various indirect ways how lawmaking may affect behaviour under the heading of 'expressive law'.[87] Does the 'labelling' law bear upon its moral rightness, goodness, or legitimacy – and may this alone influence behaviour?[88] Law is then different from social norms because of their source – its legitimacy and what that signals. Law per se is a reason for action in the sense of Raz' second order reason.[89] However, the relevance of norm-mediated effects of lawmaking and/or adjudication ('expressive law') has been contested.[90] The disagreement among legal scholars is at least in part due to a lack of conclusive empirical evidence on whether and why a law backed by sanctions induces people to obey the law. Two types of experiments are of interest in the legal context: first, experiments testing framing and second, experiments testing the pedigree of the norm.

---

[86] Charness and Yang (n 84), 'Public Goods Provision with Voting for Exclusion, Exit, and Mergers: An Experiment'.

[87] RH McAdams, 'An Attitudinal Theory of Expressive Law' (2000) 79 *Oregon Law Review* 339; RD Cooter, 'Expressive Law and Economics' (1998) 27 *Journal of Legal Studies* 585; RH McAdams, 'A Focal Point Theory of Expressive Law' (2000) 86 *Virginia Law Review* 1649; CR Sunstein, 'On the Expressive Function of Law' (1996) 144 *University of Pennsylvania Law Review* 2021; E Anderson and RH Pildes, 'Expressive Theories of Law: A General Restatement' (2000) 148 *University of Pennsylvania Law Review* 1503.

[88] Note that the assumed causal effect goes from labelling to behaviour whereas in legal positivism the prerequisite element of law is social efficacy (ie the norm must influence behaviour in order to be called law). Most probably, it is an interaction effect.

[89] J Raz, *Practical Reason and Norms* (Oxford, Oxford University Press, 1999) distinguishes between first- and second-order reasons. First-order reasons are simply reasons to perform this or that act. Second-order reasons, in contrast, are reasons to act for a reason, in which case they are 'positive' second-order reasons, – or they are reasons not to act for a reason, in which case they are 'negative second order reasons' ('exclusionary reasons'). According to legal scholars, people may obey law because of norm-activation.

[90] MD Adler, 'Expressive Theories of Law: A Skeptical Overview' (2000) 148 *University of Pennsylvania Law Review* 1363.

Framing effects play a role in the behaviour in public good games. A framing effect is assumed to be present 'when different ways of describing the same choice problem change the choices that people make, even though the underlying information and choice options remain essentially the same.'[91] In the psychological literature, framing effects are seen as a violation of the axiom of rational choice known as 'descriptive invariance'.[92] Many experiments explore those effects now.[93] An early experiment could show that behaviour is more cooperative when the situation is framed as an international negotiation than when it is framed as a business transaction.[94] Other experiments show that when social identity is created, cooperation is higher when the contribution is for the 'in-group'.[95] This connects to the 'exclusion as punishment device' discussed above. It was shown that frames can influence beliefs and beliefs in turn influence motivation and thereby behaviour.[96] Law can thus act as a frame in two ways: it can enhance beliefs of what others do (legitimate expectations) and it can express a view on what is 'the right thing to do'.

Tyran and Feld experimentally investigated the effects of no, mild and severe legal sanctions in the provision of public goods. They also compare exogenously imposed law and endogenously chosen law and thus the pedigree of the norm. If law is endogenously chosen, people vote in a referendum on whether or not to enact law. If law is exogenously imposed, it is enacted by the experimenter. The results show that severe sanctions almost perfectly deter free-riding – in accordance with the external incentive view. However, people also obey law backed by mild sanctions if it is accepted in a referendum, but not if it is exogenously imposed. Legal scholars may argue that a democratic source generates more legitimacy and this might well be so. But one may also argue that democratically generated laws are like mutual promises: Tyran and Feld show that voting in a referendum for mild law induces expectations of cooperation, and that people tend to obey the law if they expect many others to do so. Their explanation is that voting for mild law is interpreted as a signal for cooperation, and induces

[91] R Cookson, 'Framing Effects in Public Goods Experiments' (2000) 3 *Experimental Economics* 55 and T Ellingsen et al, 'Social framing effects: Preferences or beliefs?' (2012) 76 *Games and Economic Behaviour* 117, 118 for different theories about framing. See also Dufwenberg, Gächter and Hennig-Schmidt (n 52), 'The framing of games and the psychology of play', arguing that psychological-game theoretic models can accommodate framing effects in games, without reference to bounded rationality or cognitive biases. Rather, framing effects can be understood as a two-part process where (i) frames move beliefs, and (ii) beliefs shape motivation and choice. Guilt aversion and reciprocity theory furnish specific statements about (ii), for which they have found empirical support.

[92] Cookson (n 91), 'Framing Effects in Public Goods Experiments' 55 and A Tversky and D Kahneman, 'The Framing of Decisions and the Psychology of Choice' (1981) 211 *Science* 453.

[93] Ellingsen et al (n 91), 'Social framing effects: Preferences or beliefs?'.

[94] RJ Eiser and KK Bhavnani, 'The effect of situational meaning on the behaviour of subjects in the Prisoner's Dilemma Game' (1974) 4 *European Journal of Social Psychology* 93.

[95] Chakravarty and Fonseca, 'Discrimination via Exclusion: An Experiment on Group Identity and Club Goods' (2017) 19 *Journal of Public Economic Theory* 244–263.

[96] Dufwenberg, Gächter and Hennig-Schmidt (n 52), 'The framing of games and the psychology of play'.

expectations of cooperation. These expectations, in turn, are shown to increase cooperation. As a consequence, subjects tend to obey the law if they expect most others to do so.[97] The explanation they suggest thus has two elements: commitment and conditional cooperation.

Engel and Kurschilgen argue that two important empirical questions lie at the heart of the debate: 'Do normative expectations have any autonomous effect on people's behaviour? If so, does this effect rest on the fact that the underlying norm is perceived to be law?'[98] Engel investigates how participants react in the subsequent period to the experiences they have had in the previous period.[99] If they had contributed less than the average and if they react by increasing their contributions, he argues that this can be interpreted as an adjustment to the perceived expectation of others to make a higher contribution. If many do not play by what this player believes to be the rule, she may react by herself ceasing to abide by it[100] – or vice versa. There is thus a convergence of expectations. Legitimacy of the expectations is measured as perceived legitimacy by investigating how behaviour develops if participants are given a chance to express disapproval through costly punishment, decentralised punishment being interpreted 'as a (very embryonic) institutional intervention,'[101] since the punisher sends a signal of her discontent with the behaviour of another participant. Although there might be consequentialist as well as deontic reasons for punishment, if punishment in the last round is sensitive to the deviation from the contribution level in the penultimate round, then punishment demonstrates first, that punishment cannot be exclusively instrumental and second, that punishers regard negative deviations from the norm as unfair, leading to the conclusion that they interpret the contribution level as a *normative* expectation.[102] Engel and Kurschilgen have conducted a more targeted experiment with two treatments. In the first treatment ('Norm'), participants develop normative expectations. In the second treatment ('Law'), expectations are embedded into a legal frame about the creation of customary law. Both treatments are shown to have a substantial positive effect on cooperation, but there is no significant difference between 'Norm' and 'Law.' This changes as soon as they make it possible for participants to sanction each other, at a cost. They conclude that in that case 'the legal frame makes a crucial difference for cooperation as law and sanctions clearly seem to complement each other.'[103] Those findings contradict rational choice approaches in so

---

[97] J-R Tyran and LP Feld, 'Achieving Compliance when Legal Sanctions are Non-deterrent' (2006) 108 Scandinavian Journal of Economics, 135.

[98] C Engel and M Kurschilgen, 'The Coevolution of Behaviour and Normative Expectations: An Experiment' (2013) 15 *American Law and Economics Review* 578.

[99] C Engel, 'The Emergence of a New Rule of Customary Law: An Experimental Contribution' (2011) 7 *Review of Law and Economics* 767.

[100] Ibid, 776.

[101] Ibid, 777.

[102] Ibid, 778.

[103] Engel and Kurschilgen (n 98), 'The Coevolution of Behaviour and Normative Expectations: An Experiment' 2.

far as they rely on forces of acculturation, fairness components and expressive law. But still sanctioning seems to be a decisive element of law.

As mentioned above, the average person is a conditional cooperator who will make a positive initial contribution to the public good and then take the average contribution of the other group members as the new benchmark. Thus, a lot depends on the expectations of what others will do. Law can create exactly those expectations and prevent the breakdown of cooperation. If a norm is promulgated as law, especially in democracies, it signals legitimacy, stability and a majority opinion – thereby also inducing fear of isolation or ostracism.[104]

IV. LEGAL THEORIES AND THEIR IMPLICIT BEHAVIOURAL ASSUMPTIONS

There has been a widening disconnect between theories following Hart and the engagement with social science and their advances in behavioural insights. Psychological insights and the experiments have the potential to bring those together and reintroduce (social) morality and the normative function of law into the system. A caveat is in order: although the amount of experiments testing legal theories is rising,[105] the experiments are far from refined enough for the moment to discuss detailed intricacies of legal theory. Thus, the following thoughts are necessarily (too) blunt and speculative. As alluded to in the introduction, much of the discussions about the theories of law has centred around three issues: social efficacy, authoritativeness, and material correctness (or morality). I will discuss in this order in order to explore what psychology tell us about those problems.

Let's turn to social efficacy. The experiments tell us which conditions are needed to uphold social cooperation. One is surely sanctions, but that is not the whole story. People cooperate conditionally and if too many people do not cooperate, cooperation breaks down completely. A prominent example are states where corruption is rife. If only some people do not cooperate[106] that does not matter for the whole of society. And more so, if 'defectors' are punished fairly. Thus, a legal system needs trust, communication,[107] sanctioning

---

[104] A phenomenon well established in social psychology, see, eg, E Noelle-Neumann, 'The Spiral of Silence. A Theory of Public Opinion' (1974) 24 *Journal of Communication* 43, DA Scheufele, 'Spiral of Silence Theory' in W Donsbach and MW Traugott (eds), *The Sage Handbook of Public Opinion Research* (Thousand Oaks, Sage Publications, 2008).

[105] See, eg, Donelson and Hannikainen (n 4), 'Fuller and the Folk: The Inner Morality of Law Revisited'.

[106] Which is always the case, see early T Geiger, *Vorstudien zu einer Soziologie des Rechts*, 4. Aufl. ((zuerst 1947) Duncker&Humblot, 1987).

[107] Psychological game theory in interesting in this respect since it shows the impact of communication on trust and cooperation. It may influence motivation and behaviour by influencing beliefs about beliefs. Promises may enhance trustworthy behaviour due to guilt aversion and people striving to live up to others' expectations, see G Charness and M Dufwenberg, 'Promises and Partnership' (2006) 74 *Economectrica* 1578.

of non-cooperators (although there are many ways of sanctioning) and a fair procedure for sanctioning. For the early positivists like Austin, positive law has three main features: it is a type of command, it is laid down by a political sovereign ('law set by political superiors to political inferiors')[108] and it has to be backed up by sanctions. This theory is easily compatible with a rational choice theory of external incentives and is mirrored in legal realism and some variants of law and economics: Austin still has his followers, especially in the Law and Economics movement. Whereas they can illuminate the importance of external sanctions, they miss out central elements for constructing a rule of law, like the expressive and informational function of law as found in Hart's Concept of Law (at least rudimentarily).[109]

What about authoritativeness and the pedigree of the norm? Austinians miss out the importance of the pedigree of the norm, especially its legitimacy for rule following. Can experiments also inform about the role of legitimacy and pedigree of the norm? Austin, writing at the beginning of the nineteenth century, did not make a distinction about the authoritarian or democratic authority of the law-maker and thus the pedigree of the norms; he relied on strong sanctions.[110] He thus does not capture the difference shown in the experiments on the social efficacy of the law: endogenously chosen law shows more social efficacy than exogenous law. This experimental insight has long played a role in legal theory. The experiments suggest that therefore the pedigree of the norms matter much more for compliance and the social efficacy of the law. Democratic systems or those with a perceived legitimate authority can be expected to need less grave sanctions to achieve the same degree of rule-following of the populace.

Do the experiments also inform us about the distinction between primary and secondary rules in Hart's concept of law? Primary rules are rules which require people to engage in or abstain from certain actions whereas secondary rules are rules about rules. Experiments of behavioural economics on public goods are more informative on 'primary rules' than on 'secondary rules', since they rather simulate 'primitive' legal orders. Hart assumed that primary rules only may work in a small and homogenous community but under different conditions of bigger groups the defective characteristics would show: uncertainty, static rule system, no authoritative dispute settlement, no uniform enforcement.[111] This may be true; there are not many experiments on the institutionalisation of the system as required by Hart, since most of the experiments (but not all) have a decentralised peer-punishment design and hitherto fail to capture the development of secondary rules.

---

[108] J Austin, *Lectures on Jurisprudence or the Philosophy of Positive Law* in J Austin and R. Campbell (eds), (Frederick D. Linn Company (reprint by Kessinger Publishing Rare Reprints), 1874) 3.

[109] Hart (n 1), *The Concept of Law* 35: 'We can, in a sense, substract the sanction and still have an intelligible standard of behavior which it was desigend to maintain'.

[110] Ibid, 116 (Lecture VI, para 189). 'Every positive law ... is set by a monarch or a sovereign number, to a person or persons in a state of subjection to its author ...'.

[111] Hart (n 1), *The Concept of Law* 91–93.

Can experiments nevertheless inform us about the rule of recognition? What counts as law depends ultimately upon prevailing social practices.[112] A rule must be effectively accepted as common public standard; the reasons 'why officials use the rule is because they conceive of it as representing a shared social practice upon which expectations are built.'[113] Hart requires a unified and shared acceptance of the rule of recognition[114] by public officials; its existence being a 'matter of fact'.[115] Experiments tell us that even under decentralised conditions expectations converge – people adapt their behaviour to the behaviour of the other players. The existence of a convention, in turn, is made possible by a convergence of behaviour and attitude. Furthermore, those expectations can develop a normative force and develop into normative expectation. Indeed, the convergence of expectations into a convention seems to even provoke the notion of law and justify punishment and sanctions: as normative expectations converge, they are backed up by non-instrumental sanctions. Conventions can thus develop even in a decentralised system with repeated play. As Green held in his introduction to Hart's Concept of Law: 'All that matters is that people converge on a standard and use it as a guide to conduct in that way treat it as normative'.[116] Those conventions can bridge the gap between social fact thesis and law as a second order reason for action: a convention is both, a social fact and a framework of reasons for action. This can be based on insights from coordination games[117] as well as from cooperation games, as expressive law theories tell us. The rule of recognition needs repeated play (of officials) and finding common frames may be important.

The separability thesis has been of utmost importance in the discussions about legal theory. While the thesis implies that there are no necessary moral criteria of legal validity, it leaves open the question whether there are possible moral criteria of validity. Inclusive legal positivists (also known as soft positivists) posit that there can be such criteria for legal validity including or incorporating moral principles. Exclusive legal positivists (also known as hard positivists) deny there can be moral criteria of validity. Exclusive positivists claim the existence and content of law can always be determined by reference to social sources alone.[118] But for what it is worth, this discussion was not only confined to analytical analysis but it included questions of

---

[112] See for a thoughtful discussion, BZ Tamanaha (n 15), 'Socio-Legal Positivism and a General Jurisprudence' 8, 9.

[113] K Greenawalt, 'The Rule of Recognition and the Constitution' (1987) 85 *Michigan Law Review* 621, 627.

[114] The Rule of Recognition is a test accepted by officials to determine which normative standards are part of the legal corpus, see Hart (n 1), *The Concept of Law* 100–123.

[115] Hart (n 1), *The Concept of Law* 107.

[116] Green (n 24), 'Introduction' xxi.

[117] Postema (n 34), 'Coordination and Convention at the Foundations of Law'.

[118] KE Himma, 'Inclusive Legal Positivism' in JL Coleman and S Shapiro (eds), *The Oxford Handbook of Jurisprudence and Philosophy of Law* (Oxford, Oxford University Press, 2002).

empirical morality.[119] The latter can be understood as social morality and is then a question of empirics – experiments are uniquely qualified as a method to filter out moral reasons for acting. They are also illuminating under what conditions sanctioning occurs, and they are being developed to include communication. What the experiments show is the importance of moral sentiments in the construction of social order. Guilt and shame play a role, just as fairness considerations (although this can be framed). They also hint to internal (guilt) and external reasons for action (sanctions). Thus, inclusive legal positivism gets closer to reality.

V. OUTLOOK

Disputes about the correct theory of law will not go away. But the discussion can be informed about the insights we have from social science, including psychology about how people behave, when they cooperate and create social order; law being one of the most important manifestations of social order. The experimental research is relatively young and mimics rather primitive and not developed legal orders. Furthermore, it is still too rough for many open questions in legal theory. The role of norms, moral judgements and emotions such as guilt are the least well understood determinants of cooperation in social science. Conversely, reciprocity, although being such an important driver of behaviour, has been neglected in theories of law, although it is deeply engrained in substantive law and can be considered as one element of justice. Furthermore, epistemologically, some questions of legal theory are just not answerable by social science. But some aspects of legal theory are grounded in social science insights and bridging those insights into legal theory seems a promising venture – where a lot is still to be done. This has been a first outline.

---

[119] HLA Hart, 'Positivism and the Separation of Law and Morals' (1958) 71 *Harvard Law Review* 593.

10

The Foundations of Legal Empirical Studies of European Union Law: A Starter Kit

URŠKA ŠADL AND JAKOB v H HOLTERMANN*

I. INTRODUCTION: THE METHODOLOGY OF EUROPEAN UNION LAW AND THE LEGAL EMPIRICAL TIDE

> European Community law represents, more evidently perhaps than most other subjects an intricate web of politics, economics and law. It virtually calls out to be understood by means of a political economy of law or an interdisciplinary, contextual or critical approach.
>
> F. Snyder, *New Directions*[1]

This contribution addresses a disconnect between a seemingly non-positivist (contextual) outlook of European Union lawyers, which Snyder famously and highly successfully encouraged, and the failure to operationalise that outlook in an interdisciplinary and contextual methodology. In other words, European Union law currently lacks an arsenal of methods, which its contextual outlook would warrant or even require. On the one hand, this might be interpreted as inertia, or a general distrust in the new and fashionable, especially when it involves extravagant software and visualisation. On the other hand, it could reflect a more profound distaste of scholars of European Union law for empirical research, a type of genuine intellectual attachment to the logical interpretation as the only method suited for the study of legal norms. Whatever it is, it is perpetually weaved into an almost 100-year-old debate about the value

*We thank Lucia Lopez Zurita for excellent research assistance and Christoph Bezemek for comments and encouragement. We are grateful to the participants of the Lecture Series on topics in Legal Philosophy in Vienna, who gave us an absolutely wonderful and unforgettable hard time defending our claims.

[1] F Snyder, 'New Directions in European Community Law' (1987) 14 *Journal of Law and Society* 167.

of sociological insights for the content of rights and duties of individuals that is so familiar to literally all scholars of all legal disciplines.[2] The arguments seem totally exhausted, their proponents not at all[3] and so *the most challenging intellectual adventure of modern legal thought*[4] continues. It might be *the* moment to reimagine the debate.

This is precisely the aim of the chapter, which investigates the possibility of studying European Union law empirically without renouncing its normative character. The question is central to the debate. Moreover, the answer is consequential for the studies and the students of European Union law in light of the challenge expressed by Somek in *The emancipation of legal dissonance:* legal knowledge in its current form (as the knowledge about legal norms) hardly seems to make any difference at all.[5] As is usual with the author, the diagnosis is fatal. It is methodological, cutting through the core of both (and only) existing normative responses to the jurisprudence of the Court of Justice (the Court), the attitude of celebration and censure. The former (celebration), explaining and justifying the judgments with the teleology of integration (integration is *the* good cause),[6] has been exposed as mere rationalisation bordering on delusion. It is no longer based on a credible or sensible account of judicial reasoning. The latter (censure), its normative opposite, which criticises the Court for overstepping the boundaries of legal interpretation (activism, policy making, legislating), is an act of regression: naïve where it believes that 'method matters.' In fact, Somek concludes, 'nobody listens, least of all courts. [...]. Both normative positions

---

[2] H Kelsen, *General Theory of Norms* (Clarendon Press; Oxford University Press 1990); HLA Hart, 'Positivism and the Separation of Law and Morals' (1958) 71 *Harvard Law Review* 593; LL Fuller, 'Positivism and Fidelity to Law: A Reply to Professor Hart' (1958) 71 *Harvard Law Review* 630; M Weber, *Critique of Stammler* (New York, Free Press, 1977). A succinct summary in R Cotterrell, 'Why Must Legal Ideas Be Interpreted Sociologically?' (1998) 25 *Journal of Law and Society* 171.

[3] Lively debates, eg, J Klabbers, 'Whatever Happened to Gramsci? Some Reflections on New Legal Realism' (2015) 28 *Leiden Journal of International Law* 469; JVH Holtermann and MR Madsen, 'High Stakes and Persistent Challenges – A Rejoinder to Klabbers and Augsberg' (2015) 28 *Leiden Journal of International Law* 487; M Koskenniemi, 'Law, Teleology and International Relations: An Essay in Counterdisciplinarity' (2012) 26 *International Relations* 3; J d'Aspremont, *Formalism and the Sources of International Law: A Theory of the Ascertainment of Legal Rules* (Oxford, Oxford University Press 2011).

[4] G Teubner, 'How the Law Thinks: Toward a Constructivist Epistemology of Law' (1989) 23 *Law & Society Review* 727, 747.

[5] Legal scholars increasingly replaced by economists in the debates re financial crisis in Europe etc. See also Smits on the decline of legal doctrine overall in JM Smits, 'What Is Legal Doctrine?' in R van Gestel, H-W Micklitz and EL Rubin (eds), *Rethinking legal scholarship: a transatlantic dialogue* (Cambridge, Cambridge University Press 2017).

[6] For an example, see the analysis of the case law by Lenaerts and the reply by Weiler: K Lenaerts, 'The Court's Outer and Inner Selves: Exploring the External and Internal Legitimacy of the European Court of Justice' in M Adams, HC Ferdin and JA de Waele and J Meeusen (eds), *Judging Europe's judges: the legitimacy of the case law of the European Court of Justice* (Oxford, Hart Publishing 2013); JHH Weiler, 'Epilogue: Judging the Judges – Apology and Critique' in M Adams, H Clemens FJ Alexander de Waele and J Meeusen (eds), *Judging Europe's judges: the legitimacy of the case law of the European Court of Justice* (Oxford, Hart Publishing 2013).

have lost their appeal: they disappear in tandem. Which raises the question: 'what remains of legal knowledge in Europe?'[7] (And, relatedly: what is left of the European legal science / the science of European Union law?)

This chapter suggests that we should counter the eclipse of European normative methodology by transforming the legal science of European Union law into an empirical discipline. It might not sound a priori convincing. The mere word 'empirical' is most often associated with observation, experience, and related to facts, rather than with theory or logic, the hallmarks of 'modern law.'[8] The suggestion, however, does not simply propose to study European Union law as a set of hard facts by observing human behaviour, but engages with a more foundational question. It implies a specific conceptualisation of 'the empirical' in the sense in which Weber defined the term: as a study of statements about legal validity advanced by legal actors. The definition is based on Weber's distinction between axiological (juridical) and empirical validity.[9] Ross, departing from this distinction, futher demonstrated why statements about legal validity are not normative statements (expressing the norms about how one ought to behave). They are, on the contrary, descriptive statements, which refer to social facts and the beliefs of judges (officials) and which can be empirically verified as true or false.[10] Holtermann and Madsen outlined the methodology of empirical legal research as a single analysis, which explores the construction of legal expressions of validity together with an assessment of historical social structures that give force to those expressions.[11] In terms of methods this implies a contextual reading of judgments and a set of quantitative and qualitative methods, like focused interviews with legal agents.[12]

Before embarking on a long and winding analytical journey, then, let's consider the obvious. In fact, anyone who has learned and / or lived the integration through law narrative and studied jurisprudence (Kelsen and Radbruch) in law school knows that empirical research will spark ideological friction and face a series of practical challenges when claiming equal standing with classical legal research. Law schools do not teach methods and discourage the broadening

---

[7] A Somek, 'The Emancipation of Legal Dissonance' (2009) 09–02 U. Iowa Legal Studies Research Paper.

[8] M Weber, *Economy and Society: An Outline of Interpretive Sociology* (Berkeley, University of California Press 2013) ch VIII; K Tuori, *Critical Legal Positivism* (London, Routledge 2016).

[9] Weber (n 2).

[10] A Ross, *On Law and Justice (with an Introduction by Jakob v. H. Holtermann)* (J vH Holtermann ed, U Bindreiter tr, Oxford, Oxford University Press 2019) 27; A Ross, *On Law and Justice* (Berkeley, University of California Press 1974) 19–20.

[11] Holtermann and Madsen, 'High Stakes and Persistent Challenges – A Rejoinder to Klabbers and Augsberg' (n 3); J vH Holtermann and MR Madsen, 'European New Legal Realism and International Law: How to Make International Law Intelligible' (2015) 28 *Leiden Journal of International Law* 211.

[12] E Korkea-Aho and P Leino, 'Interviewing Lawyers: A Critical Self-Reflection on Expert Interviews as a Method of EU Legal Research' (2019) [12] *European Journal of Legal Studies* 17; P Leino-Sandberg, *The Politics of Legal Expertise in EU Policymaking* (forthcoming). See also J Komárek's project IMAGINE at https://jura.ku.dk/icourts/research/imagine/.

of the traditional legal curriculum, interpreted as unnecessary burdening. If Somek's diagnosis begins to ring the disciplinary alarm bells, the suggestion to turn to legal empirical studies for a remedy could only make them ring louder.

The old claim that social science should be 'on tap rather than on top' sounds familiar (correct, actually) in the field of European Union law and can be directly translated into the debate about the empirical legal science.[13] In the past two decades, European Legal studies have increasingly opened to empirical approaches while keeping a safe distance. On the one hand, law in context has largely replaced a detached search for the 'correct' meaning of legal propositions. The European Union legal scholarship has been flirting with interdisciplinary approaches and even the empirical legal studies (ELS) movement. European law journals are rife with non-doctrinal investigations: tools of network analysis, semi-structured interviews, and machine learning are integrated into the legal research of European Union law and institutions.[14] On the other hand, the most read, the most discussed, and the most cited contributions remain purely doctrinal.[15] European Union law is taught from textbooks, written in the best legal treatise tradition. Defended doctoral dissertations state without hesitation or remorse that they rely on the 'traditional legal method.' Published articles and monographs do not contain a section on the methodology employed.[16]

This testifies to the fact that the empirical turn did not enrich European Union law with new research tools. In addition, 'empirical' seemed to acquire an unfortunate definition: it typically stands for large numbers, data analysis, statistical software, and hypothesis testing.[17] In the broadest of all definitions it includes qualitative methods, most often interviews and different types of text / content analysis.[18] European Union law lacks a vocabulary to describe those methods and a set of meaningful (from the legal point of view) criteria to evaluate them.

Almost paradoxically, interdisciplinarity, the broadening of the horizons, the 'context' and the so-called 'empirical outlook' restored hermeneutics in Europe. The emergence of empirical studies of European Union law confirmed the established (deep-rooted) belief into logical interpretation of legal meaning, the trademark of modern formalism (positivism), as a core and a (per se)

---

[13] Cf for a general claim see Cotterrell (n 2).

[14] J Frankenreiter and MA Livermore, 'Computational Methods in Legal Analysis'.

[15] A good example in the most read articles of 2018 in the ELR (www.sweetandmaxwell.co.uk/Catalogue/ProductDetails.aspx?productid=30791372&recordid=427): four deal with the *Keck* doctrine, two with the legal effect of directives and two are case commentaries of relevant cases.

[16] Observation by von Bogdandy. See A von Bogdandy, 'The Past and Promise of Doctrinal Constructivism: A Strategy for Responding to the Challenges Facing Constitutional Scholarship in Europe' (2009) 7 *International Journal of Constitutional Law* 364, 387.

[17] See an interesting debate between Lindholm and Derlén and Frankenreiter in The German Law Journal. M Derlén and J Lindholm, 'Peek-A-Boo, It's a Case Law System! Comparing the European Court of Justice and the United States Supreme Court from a Network Perspective' (2017) 18 *German Law Journal* 647; J Frankenreiter, 'Network Analysis and the Use of Precedent in the Case Law of the CJEU – A Reply to Derlén and Lindholm' (2017) 18 *German Law Journal* 687.

[18] Corpus linguistics and computational linguistics (machine learning, STM).

preferable method of analysis. Despite the unforgiving criticism by historians, sociologists of law, and a handful of legal scholars, who exposed its ideology, subjectivity and bias, it looks enriched, open, even attractive. A safe bet. The situation is puzzling not least from the comparative perspective. In the US legal realism and critical legal studies movement (CRIT) had the exact opposite effect.[19]

The suggestion of a methodological volte-face is however not as illusional as it would appear. It relies on deep European theoretical roots in legal sociology (Weber, Ehrlich) and Scandinavian realism (Ross), which offer stable ground for the development of a non-normative approach to the analysis of valid law. It also banks on the European Union law's opening to the 'law in context' outlook, which presents a unique necessary first step:[20] a new generation of scholars is practicing legal empirical studies, albeit often unsystematically and without decorative jargon. Furthermore, the suggestion is inspired by an overall practical disposition of even the 'traditionally minded' European legal scholars, their problem-oriented approach, and a passion for actuality, which indicate a deep concern and a commitment to economic, political and social reality, rather than a tendency to a detached conceptual navel-gazing.

Finally, the suggestion is becoming increasingly relevant with the ascent of ELS and its entrenchment in Europe. The development is refreshing and long overdue. That said, it would be quite unfortunate to embrace the epistemologically thin version of ELS as a basis for the new European legal science[21] instead of making a wholehearted attempt to build on the rich philosophical tradition.

The argument unfolds in three steps. The first step presents the problem of legal methodology as a distinct problem for the scholars of European Union law, and more acute. The second step deals with the objections to the European empirical enterprise, especially in the form in which it resurfaced as a delayed twin of the Empirical Legal Studies. The third and final step argues for a sound epistemology of empirical research which would contain the possible negative effects of an unpremeditated jump into the sea of unpredictable methods and novel research tools. By turning empirical, European Union law, in other words, could turn its past methodological weakness into a future epistemological strength.

The chapter is divided in four sections. The following (second) section is divided in two sub-sections. The first traces the historical role of the law in the

[19] See V Nourse and G Shaffer, 'Varieties of New Legal Realism: Can a New World Order Prompt a New Legal Theory?' (2009) 95 *Cornell Law Review*. See also the critique in L Epstein and G King, 'The Rules of Inference' (2002) 69 *University of Chicago Law Review*.

[20] For an argument that empirical legal research enjoys more prestige in EU law than in national legal research see G de Búrca, 'Rethinking Law in Neofunctionalist Theory' (2005) 12 *Journal of European Public Policy* 310; Korkea-Aho and Leino (n 12).

[21] American legal realism as deliberately a-theoretical (a movement): realists did not take the philosophy seriously. See generally B Leiter, *Naturalizing Jurisprudence: Essays on American Legal Realism and Naturalism in Legal Philosophy* (Oxford, Oxford University Press, 2007). Hence ELS, which is based on the realist and later CRITS movements, is decisively no-foundation(alism).

building of the internal market, which resulted in little self-reflection and scarce foundational research, and the 'internal' critique of the European legal method. The second sub-section surveys the proposed solutions, that is, various calls for more theorising, more foundational research, a clear break with the integration project, and the revitalisation of doctrinal research as a critical discipline with transparent assumptions.

The third section considers the objections to legal empirical research by juxtaposing the proclaimed goals of the ELS with mainstream thinking about the methodology of European Union law and looks for potential synergies. The argument is set agains the background of the ELS (or the so-called Americanisation of European Union legal scholarship) as the basis for an unnecessarily rigid (and unoriginal) position that empirical legal studies and legal research explore fundamentally different questions from a diametrically opposite perspective with incommensurable goals, and that the empirical legal studies restrict the concept of empirical to quantitative methods. The main conclusion of the section is that these objections do not hold in relation to European Union law. Namely, the empirically oriented practice and the contextual outlook of European legal scholarship are not averse to empirical research but more than the enthusiasm and intellectual openness they lack their own recognisable vocabulary. A pre-requirement for such vocabulary along with a unique empirical methodology are strong epistemological foundations. The fourth section thus delves into these foundations and the debate about legal validity as the basis for empirical investigation. It outlines a framework for the 'new' European legal science.[22] The fifth section concludes.

II. THE METHODOLOGICAL PROBLEM OF EUROPEAN UNION LAW THAT PROBABLY NEEDS FIXING

A. The Background of the Problem

The answer to the question whether the European methodological problem is 'serious' cannot avoid engagement with two uniquely European features: first, the legal method's complete overlap with its object of inquiry aka the integration process (either through, without or beyond law), and second, the patchy theoretical thinking about the nature of the European legal order, as the basis of all European hermeneutics.

Both features render the methodological problem in European Union law more acute than in the legal systems with none to marginal overlap between

---

[22] In IL and IR this is better known as the new European legal realism as opposed to the 'old' American legal realism or new legal realism proposed by G Shaffer, see G Shaffer, 'The New Legal Realist Approach to International Law' (2015) 28 *Leiden Journal of International Law* 189. For an alternative definition see E Mertz, 'Introduction: New Legal Realism: Law and Social Science in the New Millennium' in E Mertz and others (eds), *The New Legal Realism* (Cambridge, Cambridge University Press, 2016).

legal scholarship and policy building (political process). Unlike national legal systems, the European legal system cannot ground its methodology in the theory of the nation state with its rich conceptual arsenal.

First, regarding the overlap. To restate what is well known and taken for granted: European Union law has created and successfully sustained European integration and institution building; the European Community was envisioned and implemented as a community of law (*die Rechtsgemeinschaft*),[23] to which the (case)law of the Court, and the legal academic, who was naturally placed to interpret, systematise and rationalise it, was central.[24] The European legal science with its method of coherence and the attitude (normative position) of celebration[25] underwrote the success of the paradigm (integration through (case)law narrative) *and* the de facto accomplishment of the internal market. Things have changed for the worse for the project of European integration and the legal science.

The confidence in the force of pure (neutral, apolitical) law as a means to establish and sustain a polity is feeble if there is any left.[26] The narrative of integration through law has been *de*romanticised, bared as a fruitful effort of the Euro lawyers to entrench their role and constitute themselves as the dominant group. The paradigm, it was argued, was not a *post-facto* account of events but elaborated *alongside* the practice it purported to explain and justify; with the judges, their legal secretaries, commissioners and high civil servants, constantly forging theories of the contribution of law to integration shoulder to shoulder with academics and diplomats.[27] Schepel and Wesseling[28] showed that the staff of the Commission, the pro-European academia, the clerks and the judges of

---

[23] For example, as the former German member of the Court phrased it: 'Die Gemeinschaft is Rechtsgemeinschaft [...] und wird nur durch die Autorität des Rechts zusammengehalten'.U Everling, 'Zur Begründung Des Urteile Des Gerichtshofs Der Europäische Gemeinschaften' (1994) 29 *EuR* 127, 143. Or in the words of the first president of the European Commission, W Hallstein: 'Sie is Schöpfung des Rechts, sie ist Rechtsquelle und sie ist Rechtsordnung'; cited in H Koch, 'A Legal Mission: The Emergence of a European "Rationalized" Natural Law' in H Petersen (ed), *Paradoxes of European legal integration* (Aldershot, Ashgate, 2008). Similarly: 'Le droit a été créateur et demeure conservatoire de l'unité de marché'; in Robert Lecourt, *L'Europe Des Juges* (Bruylant 1976).

[24] M Cappelletti and others, *Methods, Tools and Institutions Book 2. Political Organs, Integration Techniques and Judicial Process* (Walter de Gruyter 1986); A Vauchez, '"Integration-through-Law." Contribution to a Socio-History of EU Political Commonsense' (2008) Working Paper http:// cadmus.eui.eu//handle/1814/8307.

[25] Somek (n 7).

[26] See the result of the last Eurobarometer, specially concerning trust in the EU and the overall image of the Union: https://ec.europa.eu/commfrontoffice/publicopinion/index.cfm/survey/getsurveydetail/instruments/standard/surveyky/2253.

[27] A Vauchez, 'The Transnational Politics of Judicialization: Van Gend En Loos and the Making of EU Polity' (2010) 16 *European law journal* 1. It also explains how the integration through law has turned into the integration through case-law theory of integration in the sixties. Vauchez argues that the prominent lawyers like Hallstein and Dehousse were disappointed by the intergovernmental process of lawmaking (and the slow and dubious harmonisation prompted in 1963) and turned their energy and expertise towards the ECJ and its case law, bringing about the *grands arrêts* like Van Gend and Costa v ENEL.

[28] Especially the European Commission. H Schepel and R Wesseling, 'The Legal Community: Judges, Lawyers, Officials and Clerks in the Writing of Europe' (1997) 3 *European Law Journal* 165.

the Court of Justice, and the authors coming from private practice accounted for over 90 per cent of all European law articles in the three oldest, most prestigious and most influential European journals for over 30 years.[29] The same actors from a handful of law schools typically sat on the editorial and advisory boards of a majority of relevant publication outlets.[30] All the while intergovernmental actors exerted almost no quantitative influence on the production of European legal doctrine.[31]

Moreover, on a personal level, there was no clear-cut line between those who theorised integration (the academics) and those who actively participated in it (the judges and the politicians).[32] A typical European Union law figure was 'that of the member of the Court of Justice who writes abundantly in scholarly journals, is an editor of a few of them, and teaches EU law in places such as the College of Europe.'[33]

Finally, legal science has lost the appearance of autonomy. Micklitz and van Gestel tapped into the politics of European legal research. Their study revealed how the Commission effectively (even if unconsciously and with best intentions) stirred European legal research. In practice, this meant a shift 'from fundamental to applied research, from fully independent research to more hybrid forms of contract research where contractors set the agenda, and from sponsoring of research on the basis of trust and confidence towards tendering and competition.'[34]

This sociology of the narrative exposed the normative outlook aka methodology of European Union law as ideological, highly instrumental, and 'for sale.'[35] One would tend to conclude that the analysis of positive law cannot possibly continue to keep the appearance of neutrality, and even less a status of

---

[29] Ibid 172–173. The authors counted the articles that appeared in the period from 1963 (CMLR), 1965 (CDE) and 1966 (EuR) respectively to 1995.

[30] As compared to both international and national authorship. Ibid, 174.

[31] The CMLR, Europarecht and CDE. Ibid, 173–174, 176.

[32] A strong institutional association existed between the academic community and the European institutions, with many commentators crossing the divide between practice, bureaucracy, judiciary and academia, especially with regard to 'the two most 'communautaire' of the institutions – the Commission and the Court of Justice.' As observed by J Shaw, 'European Union Legal Studies in Crisis? Towards a New Dynamic' (1996) 16 *Oxford Journal of Legal Studies* 231.

[33] B De Witte, 'European Union Law: A Unified Academic Discipline?' (2008) 34 Working Paper RSCAS.

[34] Micklitz and Van Gestel detail herd behaviour of European Union law scholars, their mimetic style, participation in making of the internal market, and instrumentalised research projects largely financed by the European Commission. See R Van Gestel and H-Wolfgang Micklitz, 'Revitalizing Doctrinal Legal Research in Europe: What About Methodology?' [2011] Working Paper 11. 'What we have witnessed is a shift from fundamental to applied research, from fully independent research to more hybrid forms of contract research where contractors set the agenda, and from sponsoring of research on the basis of trust and confidence towards tendering and competition. Moreover, research projects were not given to European academia by policymakers in order to learn that their targets could not be reached. The research question was 'how', not 'if'.' See ibid, 12.

[35] Van Gestel and Micklitz (n 34).

European legal science. The loss of authority (medium to long term) is a logical consequence of a biased method, and appears logically inevitable.[36]

Second, the distinctiveness of the problem comes from the fact that European legal scholarship is reactive, event-driven and context-dependent,[37] lacking interest for theory, and even in the more modest middle-range theorising (defined as the explanation or evaluation of internal features of the system in terms of the system).[38] Theoretical concerns, even when they make it into a crowded academic agenda, tend to be shaped by highly specific developments and highlight the peculiarity of the Union's 'legal problems' rather than their continuity with problems which have stimulated theoretical reflection before or elsewhere.[39]

To illustrate, the perhaps dominant account of the European legal system is its sui generis nature. The sui generis thesis, however, is not a product of any deeper thinking about European polity, federal structures and integration but a mimesis of a judicial discourse – a new legal order of international law (with all its implications).[40] The sui generis thesis, to be established, did not require methodological rigor and critical assessment, but case-law journalism; a form of legal writing, which submits problems and methods to the logic of judicial discourse in a way that produces legally cognisable material to be taught and disseminated.[41]

Hence, the methodology of doctrinal studies of European Union law is groundless.[42] It has thus no common fallback position from which it could re-invent itself when criticised. While this might not exactly preclude a common European practice (Kumm might be right here),[43] it can hardly be argued that it

---

[36] For the argument of neutrality as a basis for legal authority see P Bourdieu, 'The Force of Law: Toward a Sociology of the Juridical Field' (1987) 38 *Hastings Law Journal* 814.

[37] N Walker, 'Legal Theory and the European Union: A 25th Anniversary Essay' (2005) 25 *Oxford Journal of Legal Studies* 581, 583.

[38] Ibid, 585.

[39] Ibid.

[40] See Case C-26/62, *Van Gen den Loos*, ECLI:EU:C:1963:1.

[41] P Schlag, 'Spam Jurisprudence, Air Law, and the Rank Anxiety of Nothing Happening (A Report on the State of the Art)' (2009) 97 *Georgetown Law Journal* 803, 823. On dissemination of the sui generis thesis see A Boerger and M Rasmussen, 'Transforming European Law: The Establishment of the Constitutional Discourse from 1950 to 1993' (2014) 10 *European Constitutional Law Review* 199. On the dissemination of other doctrines of European Union law see KJ Alter, 'Judicial Politics in the European Community: European Integration and the Pathbreaking Cassis de Dijon Decision' in KJ Alter, *The European Court's political power: selected essays* (Oxford, Oxford University Press, 2009); R Schutze, '"Re-Reading" Dassonville: Meaning and Understanding in the History of European Law' [2018] SSRN *Electronic Journal* www.ssrn.com/abstract=3150391; A Vauchez, 'The Making of the European Union's Constitutional Foundations: The Brokering Role of Legal Entrepreneurs and Networks' in W Kaiser, B Leucht and M Gehler (eds), *Transnational networks in regional integration: governing Europe, 1945–83* (Basingstoke, Palgrave Macmillan, 2010).

[42] There is no agreed-upon theory of jurisprudence that is shared or likely to be shared in Europe. M Kumm, 'On the Past and Future of European Constitutional Scholarship' (2009) 7 *International Journal of Constitutional Law* 401.

[43] See ibid.

can justify or legitimise this practice or shield it from politics. Or serve as a basis for the science of European Union law.

There is, however, a silver lining on the horizon. European legal scholarship has the potential to gain the intellectual distance to the European integration project. The project is no longer self-explaining and self-legitimising and the law no longer instrumental to achieve and promote integration. If anything, it is deemed largely unfit as a means of European identity-building. The rejection of the European Constitution in 2005, the referendum in Greece in 2015 and the British referendum in 2016 exposed the impotence of law beyond the legal community. In a sense, European legal scholarship has been liberated of the integration shackles and is free to redefine itself.[44]

B. Proposals on the European Union Law's Methodological Table

European legal scholars have been reflecting on the state and the status of their discipline, mostly triggered by external (political, economic) events.[45] Time and again, their commentary explored methodological questions. Although it rarely triggered an in-depth introspection across the scholarly community, a critical mass of scholars consciously maintained a methodological conversation or initiated an independent methodological agenda.[46] This section briefly reproduces such conversations about methods and legal science among legal scholars focusing on their own field, that is, European Union law. Its aim is to give an impression of the variety of proposals for methodological rigor and the renewal of European research agendas that were – even if only sporadically – tabled and debated. While some stayed on the level of sketches and outlines, others represented fully fledged manifestos for a total overhaul of European legal studies. Common to all was the idea of fixing the problems, which legal doctrine and the normative orientation faced, with more critical legal research and enhanced (improved) normativity. In short: resuscitating theory, revitalising doctrine, never abandoning the positivist analysis.[47] All accounts readily accepted the relevance,

---

[44] In that sense see H-W Micklitz, 'A European Advantage in Legal Scholarship?' in R van Gestel, H-W Micklitz and EL Rubin (eds), *Rethinking legal scholarship: a transatlantic dialogue* (Cambridge, Cambridge University Press, 2016).

[45] Cf, Walker (n 37).

[46] Eg, see F Snyder, 'New Directions in European Community Law' (1987) 14 *Journal of Law and Society* 167; Shaw (n 32); J Hunt and J Shaw, 'Fairy Tale of Luxembourg? Reflections on Law and Legal Scholarship in European Integration' in D Phinnemore and A Warleigh-Lack (eds), *Reflections on European Integration: 50 Years of the Treaty of Rome* (Basingstoke, Palgrave Macmillan UK 2009) https://doi.org/10.1057/9780230232839_6; R van Gestel, H-W Micklitz and EL Rubin, 'Introduction' in R van Gestel, H-W Micklitz and EL Rubin (eds), *Rethinking legal scholarship: a transatlantic dialogue* (Cambridge, Cambridge University Press, 2016).

[47] Cf, for diagnosis von Bogdandy with respect to international and constitutional law. See von Bogdandy (n 16) 377–378.

the value, and the 'scientific character' of doctrinal research, albeit not necessarily in its current form.

There was, to be sure, also an opposite tendency, to tone down the methodological problematic of European Union law, for example, by recasting it in terms of academic fashion and fads. Arnull, in that vein, spoke of the Americanisation of European legal scholarship, reassuring the readers that legal doctrine in Europe was in rude health (he was almost right, from the internal perspective), and that empirical research of European Union law and institutions could only prosper (or even exist) as long as it rested on the shoulders of doctrinal giants.[48] Moreover, the complex nature of the European legal system called for mostly doctrinal exposition.[49] Empirical research came on top of this exposition, and could be added on its fringe (that is, exactly where Hart's formalist welcomed the realist[50]).

Several ideas for a renewed European legal scholarship emerged from different corners of Europe. Von Bogdandy argued for a so-called repositioning of European legal scholarship,[51] or 'doctrinal constructivism.' The latter was a more fully evolved and expanded version of the traditional positivist legal method,[52] which historically established and sustained the discipline of public law as an autonomous discipline (the seizing of the crown metaphor). The positivist method (if there is one), one should recall at this point, aims primarily at the structuring of the law via autonomous concepts, which naturally fall under the exclusive competence of legal science. 'The highest scientific goal of the positivist legal method is, in substance, to reconstruct and represent both public and private law as complexes of systematically coordinated concepts. The key scientific competencies thus become abstraction, the development of concepts, and the corresponding arrangement of the legal material.'[53]

The European (constitutional) legal scholarship could thus follow a conceptual approach, in a more sophisticated and open form that would include the analysis of the constitutional context of the law. This is surprising, given von Bogdandy's own characterisation of the 'positivist legal method as a method that denotes a specific understanding of the law, (autonomy-oriented self-understanding by legal scholars, and a corresponding, specific scholarly goal) but hardly gives precise instructions for scholarly study or how to achieve its aims'.[54] It is, in other words, a methodology without research tools.

---

[48] A Arnull, 'The Americanization of EU Law Scholarship' in A Arnull, P Eeckhout and T Tridimas (eds), *Continuity and Change in EU Law: Essays in Honour of Sir Francis Jacobs* (Oxford, Oxford University Press, 2008) 426.

[49] Ibid, 428.

[50] HLA Hart, *The Concept of Law* 3rd edn (Oxford, Oxford University Press, 2012) 154.

[51] von Bogdandy addressed the European Constitutional scholarship. See von Bogdandy (n 16).

[52] While von Bogdandy did not succinctly define the term, his exposition can be read as a call for doctrinal work, not restricted to the analysis of the positive law but aimed at its development as well.

[53] von Bogdandy (n 16) 373.

[54] Ibid, 376.

218 Urška Šadl and Jakob v H Holtermann

Kumm criticised von Bogdandy's historical reconstruction of the positivist legal methodology and especially its power to establish and sustain a whole legal discipline. However, while von Bogdandy's descriptive account was incorrect – according to Kumm the European legal scholarship already integrated formal, empirical, and moral elements of law with little consensus on how they were integrated across and within jurisdictions) – Kumm's proposal was fully in line with von Bogdandy's. A successful reconstructive integrative theory of European legal scholarship would need to account for its three structural features: the idea that the legal scholarship deals with legal norms as opposed to moral norms or non-normative facts; the idea that it takes an internal point of view to establish what the law requires and finally, the fact that any justification and criticism of legal propositions necessarily proceeds from the assumption of a coherent legal system as a regulative ideal.[55] By implication, 'other disciplines' with their own methodology that took the law and institutions as their object of inquiry could only produce novel insights as add-ons to the legal inquiry.[56] Their function was ornamental at best.

The total (as opposed to ornamental) renewal proposals (in the form of new directions) would include Shaw's call for breaking the link between law and integration (between the process and the object of analysis)[57] and Snyder's call for contextual scholarship: the opening of European Union law to its economic, social and political context.[58] Both enterprises involved various degrees and elements of socio-legal analysis, and methodologically, required a construction of legal arguments drawing from positive law and non-legal material. It was (a commendable and truly refreshing) program for a more sophisticated legal analysis.[59] On the flip side, the proposals did not provide concrete guidelines on how to transform the legal analysis into a socio-legal account.

Micklitz and van Gestel put forward the most entrepreneurial and detailed program for a doctrinal overhaul: a doctrinal exposition with a critical distance from its object of inquiry (the process of integration), with transparent assumptions laid bare for the legal community to debate, endorse and dispute. The objective (apolitical) and autonomous mask of legal analysis would have to be traded for a genuine scientific quest for legal knowledge, characterised by persistent questioning of basic premises of integration and the role of law in this process. It would need to ask novel, critical, and original questions. It would have to be freed from 'mimesis,' meaning the role model and research methods

---

[55] Kumm (n 42) 401.

[56] Kumm (n 42).

[57] J Shaw, 'Introduction' in J Shaw and G More (eds), *New legal dynamics of European Union* (Oxford, Clarendon Press, 1995); Hunt and Shaw (n 46); Shaw (n 32).

[58] F Snyder, 'Editorial: Dimensions and Precipitates of EU Constitutional Law' (2002) 8 *European Law Journal* 315; Snyder, 'New Directions in European Community Law' (n 46).

[59] See Snyder, 'Editorial' (n 58); Shaw (n 57).

of the judge as its sole point of reference and look for answers to the question what can be the *added* value.[60]

Methodologically, the program for an overhaul sought to open doctrinal analysis to formal and informal legal sources, taking account of (but distancing itself from) the development of legal practice. However, it would continue to be grounded in the legal method and interested in the question of legality. As authors propose: 'non-legal' research methodologies should not replace the training in doctrinal research but come on top of that training and were to be taught in combination with doctrinal methods.[61] This statement could be interpreted as a call for the integration of non-legal methods through a legal prism (methodological integration through law).

To summarise, the assumption in practically all above expositions is that there is nothing per se objectionable to the established legal method, but rather to the way, in which the method has been applied, and the questions, which it is used to answer. Importantly, because the problem is not the problem of foundations but of techniques and aims, European legal science can retain the status of science: a normative discipline, with its formal rationality, logical interpretation and the search of the correct meaning of legal texts, its arsenal of autonomous concepts and systematisation of legal norms.

The core of the problem is the *scientific* nature of European Union law as an autonomous discipline. On the one hand, European Union law claims autonomy and a sui generis (or international or supranational or a federal-state-in-the-making) form. On the other hand, it is practically oblivious of its sui generis foundations beyond rationalising (celebrating) or censuring the judge-made discourse of a new legal order with direct effect and supremacy. It cultivates (since the 90s) a profound awareness of the social, the political, and the economic, minus clear theoretical premises, methodological rigor or a recognisable set of research tools to pursue it. This, however, is not a death sentence of European legal knowledge in the sense in which Somek would picture it. Quite the contrary, uncertainties can be seen as advantages (in popular parlance of continuous self-improvement, the 'gifts of imperfection'[62]) of a seemingly rootless legal order persistently challenged by national legal systems and international legal regimes with better defined foundations, entrenched ideas about the aims of legal science and caught in a methodological (dogmatic) straightjacket.[63]

---

[60] For the mimetic nature of legal scholarship see P Schlag, 'Normativity and the Politics of Form' (1991) 139 *University of Pennsylvania Law Review* 801.

[61] Van Gestel and Micklitz (n 34).

[62] Cf, B Brown, *The Gifts of Imperfection: Let Go of Who You Think You're Supposed to Be and Embrace Who You Are* 1st edn (Centre City, Hazelden Publishing 2010).

[63] For the argument that comparatively speaking, European Union law is much more willing to engage in interdisciplinary conversations, see Búrca (n 20).

III. THE CONDITIONS OF THE EMPIRICAL SOLUTION
TO THE EUROPEAN METHODOLOGICAL PROBLEM

The previous section presented the European methodological problem as a distinct problem, particular to the structure of the European Union and its legal system. This section shows that at the same time, the European Union lawyers harbour similar reservations toward empirical research, as their international and national law (private or public) counterparts.[64] To this end, it first places the objections of European legal scholars to ELS in the framework of the old new theoretical debate about legal doctrinal verses empirical legal research (subsection A). Then, it looks at the concrete academic studies, using qualitative and quantitative methods to address legal problems, to show that European legal scholars actively and successfully deal with these objections in practice (subsections B and C).

A. The ELS Meets the Old New Intellectual Tussle in Europe

The first subsection focuses on three distinct characteristics of the global empirical turn in legal scholarship, epitomised in the founding of the Society for empirical legal studies (SELS), the official journal of the society (the Journal of Empirical Legal Studies or JELS) and the annual conference (CELS). The old debate has become relevant because ELS came ashore in Europe (with a proverbial delay of at least a decade). The ELS is the newest new thing, which European Union law is currently facing, and which more broadly rekindled the old debate. It presents a tangible yardstick for what empirical legal studies currently stand for and what the European legal scholarship typically renounces. Three distinct points of contention toward empirical legal research frame this debate.

One, legal empirical research and 'classical' (doctrinal) legal research ask fundamentally different questions. The latter is a study of the content of legal rules and their ordering into a coherent system.[65] Methodologically, it requires interpretation, as a way of discovering the correct meaning of the rule, the validity of which is assumed.[66]

However, proponents of empirical approaches to law perceive law as (at its core) an applied social science in the sense of *Rechtspolitik*.[67] Epistemologically

---

[64] See the debate in the LJIL: I Venzke, 'International Law and Its Methodology: Introducing a New Leiden Journal of International Law Series' (2015) 28 *Leiden Journal of International Law* 185; Klabbers (n 3); Holtermann and Madsen, 'High Stakes and Persistent Challenges – A Rejoinder to Klabbers and Augsberg' (n 3). See also Epstein and King (n 19); J Knight, 'Are Empiricists Asking the Right Questions about Judicial Decisionmaking?' (2009) 58 *Duke Law Journal* 1531.

[65] For a historical account see S Vogenauer, 'An Empire of Light? Learning and Lawmaking in the History of German Law' (2005) 64 *Cambridge Law Journal* 481.

[66] Weber, ie, sees logical interpretation as a search for the correct meaning as the main characteristics of the dogmatic approach to (modern) law. See Weber (n 8) 640 and following.

[67] JJ Rachlinski, 'Does Empirical Legal Studies Shed More Heat than Light? The Case of Civil Damage Awards' (2016) 29 *Ratio Juris* 556.

speaking, the central purpose of JELS / CELS has been clear: to add to the repository of knowledge of the legal system based on observation or empirical analysis, including experimental analysis, and make proposals *de lege ferenda*.

Thus, J Rachlinski, one of the founders of the movement in the US, contends:

> The aim of scholars who conduct empirical work is to bring a realistic, scientific understanding of the effects of law on legal actors and legal institutions. Scholars who conduct empirical work attend closely to the purposes behind legal rules and seek to test whether the rules adopted actually advance those purposes.[68]

This understanding, obviously, cannot proceed from the interpretation of meaning of the rules, the validity of which is assumed. On the contrary, as underlined in the first editorial of the *Journal of Empirical Legal Studies*, the journal would encourage, promote, and provide an impetus for the careful collection of empirical data and the dispassionate, rigorous testing of empirical hypotheses with a clear purpose to contribute to policy debates, hinging on empirical assumptions. Thereby, the newly established journal would fill 'a gap in the legal and social science literature that often leaves scholars, lawyers, and policymakers with false or distorted impressions about the legal system.'[69]

The focus to contribute to informed law reform appears close to the CRITS and carries a distinctly American twist. The empirical scholars turn to data not in order to enhance the doctrinal study of law but rather with a view to engaging in social engineering, ie on the assumption that better knowledge of the data holds the promise of optimising law reform. Therein lies the relevance and legitimacy of empirical legal research. Reform is possible only if the impressions of the legal system and its functioning are not false or distorted.[70]

The reformist twist, however, has always been present in European law. The enthusiasm of continental legal science for legal reform in public and private law has been widely documented.[71] European legal scholarship with its high stake in the process of market integration, harmonisation, constitutionalisation etc, is not exceptional in this sense. Historically, 1968 marked a turning point: the reformist and anticipatory scholarship could openly and actively engage in social engineering, not unlike the CRITS. The quest for change guided legal research in European Union law for decades and vice versa. The European Civil Code[72] and the drafting of the Charter are well-known examples from the

---

[68] Ibid, 560. The same perspective on and ambition for empirical work is emphasised eg in the first editorial of the *Journal of Empirical Legal Studies*. T Eisenberg and others, 'Editor's Introduction' (2004) 1 *Journal of Empirical Legal Studies* v, and has since been repeated in the calls for the annual conferences made by the Society for Empirical Legal Studies.

[69] T Eisenberg and others, 'Editor's Introduction' (2004) 1 *Journal of Empirical Legal Studies* v, v.

[70] See Eisenberg and others (n 69).

[71] Vogenauer discussed the 'anticipatory' or preemptive character as a hallmark of German legal scholarship. See Vogenauer (n 65) 658.

[72] H Schepel, 'The European Brotherhood of Lawyers: The Reinvention of Legal Science in the Making of European Private Law' (2007) 32 *Law & Social Inquiry* 183; MR Madsen, 'European Treaty Making: A Structural Analysis of the Genesis and Evolution of the Charter of Fundamental Rights of the European Union' (2010) 60 *Revue française de science politique* 271.

more recent past.[73] Currently, the impact assessments increasingly commissioned by the European Commission dictate and legitimise new legislation. They call for legal knowledge, which is generated from observation rather than via logical construction. There exist the sediments of empirical legal research, and they are necessary (if only, ironically, to assess the impact of the impact assessments).

Second, to the extent that empirical legal scholarship engages with law and legal doctrine, it is predisposed (even if only implicitly) to suppress legal elements. Empirical approaches tend, in effect, to see law as an epiphenomenon reducible to external, non-legal factors. To make matters worse, the doctrinal study of law, which is usually taken to generate knowledge about legal rules, is challenged in the empirical studies as epistemologically unsound. Correspondingly, the beliefs of its practitioners to the opposite is viewed with skepticism and at the most acute derided and treated as a kind of false consciousness.[74] Empirical scholarship is not merely complementary to the doctrinal study of law but actively contradicts the central assumptions of doctrinal scholarship. Instead of aiming to determine valid law it aims to replace this study entirely.

The first conference of SELS in 2006, for instance, featured 'original empirical and experimental legal scholarship by leading scholars worldwide, from a diverse range of fields.'[75] The most recent conference continues to bring together 'scholars from law, economics, political science, psychology, policy analysis, and other fields who are interested in the empirical analysis of law and legal institutions' and 'papers that engage empirical and experimental scholarship on legal issues spanning all areas of empirical legal studies.'[76]

The first European conference of empirical legal studies (CELSE) departed from the same premise as its American counterpart, aka 'increasing pressure as well as growing demand – from research-funding institutions, policy-makers and legal practitioners – for European academic lawyers to investigate the empirical foundations of their theoretical claims and to explain how legal rules emerge from social interactions and shape social outcomes.' It sought to bring together 'academics from law and other fields who embrace the empirical turn and seek to develop empirical accounts of law and legal institutions in Europe.'[77]

Third, ELS tendentially identifies *empirical* analysis with *quantitative* methods, especially with large-N data, thus excluding from the realm of the empirical not only traditional hermeneutic approaches to law but also qualitative social scientific studies. It presupposes an implicit scientism, which conceives of quantitative work as constituting the only truly scientific approach to the legal field, and thus reduces other approaches to pseudo-science.

---

[73] Madsen details the process of the drafting of the Charter in Madsen (n 72).
[74] See Búrca (n 20); Cotterrell (n 2).
[75] https://law.utexas.edu/conferences/cels2006/.
[76] www.lawschool.cornell.edu/CELS2017/index.cfm and 2019 upcoming conference in LA: https://cels2019.cmc.edu.
[77] http://celse2016.acle.nl/.

Admittedly, from the point of view of classical doctrinal law as legal dogmatics, these three features, prominent in much contemporary empirical work, provide prima facie reasons for rejection. They are anything but a cure for any of the challenges facing the study of European Union law.

B. The Newest New Thing is about Interpretation, Too

Let us first consider a concrete example of premature labeling of empirical methodology as quantitative. When legal scholars object to the citation network approach[78] to law as quantitative, they typically react to its use in political-scientific research. Their critique turns to a study applying citation network analysis to the case law of the Court of Justice, mapping case citations to show that European judges are more likely to cite judgments authored by judges appointed by Member State governments with similar preferences regarding European integration.[79] Such study can provide concrete evidence that the political preferences of Member State governments are reflected in the behaviour of European judges.[80] These empirical legal accounts of judicial decision-making, one could imagine, will only irritate legal research agendas[81] by not generating legal knowledge and asking the wrong questions. They will be forgotten like every other newest new thing.

The objections will come from the unawareness about the roots of the approach and a variety of its applications. The history of social network analysis suggests that the network perspective was not conceived with quantitative methodology, statistical modelling, or hypothesis testing in mind. In fact, the pioneering work comes from sociology, anthropology, and social psychology, all largely disciplines that rely on qualitative methods, such as interviews, questionnaires, and participant observation. They do not require quantification. The first mapping of interactions between girls and boys in a classroom was presented by a pioneer of group psychotherapy.[82]

---

[78] See, eg, Y Panagis, U Sadl and F Tarissan, 'Giving Every Case Its (Legal) Due The Contribution of Citation Networks and Text Similarity Techniques to Legal Studies of European Union Law', *30th International Conference on Legal Knowledge and Information Systems (JURIX'17)* (2017); U Sadl and F Tarissan, 'The Network Approach' in C Kilpatrick and J (eds), *New Legal Approaches to Studying the Court of Justice* (Oxford, Oxford University Press, forthcoming).

[79] J Frankenreiter, 'The Politics of Citations at the ECJ-Policy Preferences of E.U. Member State Governments and the Citation Behavior of Judges at the European Court of Justice: The Politics of Citations at the ECJ' (2017) 14 *Journal of Empirical Legal Studies* 813, 839.

[80] O Larsson and D Naurin, 'Judicial Independence and Political Uncertainty: How the Risk of Override Affects the Court of Justice of the EU' (2016) 70 *International Organization* 377.

[81] For a lively debate in international law on the New Legal Realism advocating the empirical study of law see J Klabbers, 'Whatever Happened to Gramsci? Some Reflections on New Legal Realism' (2015) 28 *Leiden Journal of International Law* 469, as well as the articles in the special issue.

[82] The study was conducted by the psychosociologist and psychiatrist Jacob L Moreno. Its presentation was reported in a column on the NYT on April 3, 1933 (www.nytimes.com/1933/04/03/archives/emotions-mapped-by-new-geography-charts-seek-to-portray-the.html). The article contained the first reproduction of a sociogram.

Anthropologists continue to embark on small-scale studies of kinship relations, friendship, and gift giving among people; social psychologists focus on affections. Research history – and present research trajectories – show that investigations of social ties among actors do not have to involve hypothesis testing: the approach can remain exploratory and limited to the ties that can be mapped without computer software. The central objective of the network approach is to map relations and reveal patterns that are not plainly visible. Expressed differently, it is an approach that seeks to detect and *interpret* patterns of ties among units of analysis. In social networks these units are social actors, in academic citation networks they are academic works, and in legal citation networks they are usually the references to legal sources. The findings obtained via network methods must be interpreted legally. Only the aim of causal explanation of these patterns would include hypothesis testing. All interpretations would require a contextual reading of judgments and legal doctrine, as the immediate legal context of such references.

Applications that use elaborate computer software to visualise and examine large networks as well as applications written on a napkin to visualise the relationships among schoolboys and schoolgirls are all interested in social detail. The method follows the research question, and not vice versa.

Within the European Union legal context, the use of citation networks can answer questions of legal importance and relevance. Clearly, the limitations are not trivial and thus the method must be accordingly calibrated to cater to the needs of a legal scholar. To illustrate, the trickiest aspect is related to the reasoning of the Court and its tendency to repeat normative arguments without an explicit reference to a legal source. An algorithm would pass over them obliviously. Hence, a method relying on explicit citations would produce an entirely inaccurate map of the case law, where case importance would not reflect its 'true' legal importance. By contrast, a (learned) legal scholar would immediately recognise such arguments 'for what they are and what they mean.'

One alternative to dealing with the objection is to pair citation analysis with text analysis. Let's say that the most cited paragraphs typically include a concept or a formulation indicating relevance in the process of construction of legal arguments. An approach that would allow one to gauge such aspects would also have to acquire information concerning whether the case is relevant for one or several legal aspects. For instance, if only one paragraph of a case is repeatedly cited, the case is most likely important for resolving one legal issue. If, by contrast, several different paragraphs of one judgment are cited, the case might be important for resolving more than one legal issue. Text similarity techniques will increase the precision of the reference. An instance of a reference to an entire case is when case A is citing case B. A case to case citation network – as employed by studies using the network approach thus far – is typically constructed on the basis of these references. However, newer studies break the case to case citation networks into a network of case paragraphs.[83] For instance,

---

[83] Methodology outlined in detail in Panagis, Sadl and Tarissan (n 78).

we might find that case A, paragraph 10, cites case B, paragraph 5. Hereafter, by looking only at the language of the Court, we can identify the relation between case A, paragraph 10, and case B, paragraph 5, *even if* case A does *not* cite case B explicitly by case name (B) or cites it by name but does not specify the paragraph. Hence the language similarity technique is a technique used to identify 'lost' citations and construct a complete and detailed network that reflects the legal importance of cases accurately. It gives every case its legal due.[84]

Moreover, the technique can be used to identify legally relevant aspects of individual cases. As an illustration,[85] let us consider three (very) famous cases in European Union law: *Dassonville*, *Defrenne*, and *Francovich*.[86] Doctrinally speaking, *Francovich* stands for judicial innovation.[87] It established a principle (all trading rules enacted by Member States which are capable of hindering, directly or indirectly, actually or potentially, intra-Community trade are to be considered as measures having an effect equivalent to quantitative restrictions) that did not originate from a written legal source of European Union law and laid down the conditions under which it could be applied. The reasoning of the Court invoked the legal cornerstones of the European legal order: primacy, direct effect, the duty of cooperation of national courts and the power to create new legal remedies, as well as respect for the principles of effectiveness and equivalence.[88] *Dassonville* is prominent among legal scholars for one legal innovation (the definition of measures having the effect equivalent to quantitative restrictions) in a well-defined area of European Union law (free movement of goods).[89] By contrast, legal scholars typically situate and consider *Defrenne* in several areas of European Union law. For instance, the case is relevant to the debates on the general principle of non-discrimination on grounds of gender (the principle of equal pay for equal work), the limitation of temporal effects of judgments of the Court in exceptional circumstances, and horizontal direct effect of the Treaty as fundamental characteristics of the EU legal order.[90]

---

[84] Ibid.

[85] The example is take from Sadl and Tarissan (n 78).

[86] Cases C-8/74, *Dassonville*, ECLI:EU:C:1974:82; C-149/77, *Defrenne*, ECLI:EU:C:1978:130; C-6/90, *Francovich*, ECLI:EU:C:1991:428.

[87] See, eg, M Poiares Maduro and others, *The Past and Future of EU Law: The Classics of EU Law Revisited on the 50th Anniversary of the Rome Treaty* (Oxford, Hart Publishing, 2010). It is also one of the most commented on cases in the history of the Court. See, ie, Tridimas, who mentions the 'vast bibliography' resulting from the case: T Tridimas, *The General Principles of EU Law* 2nd edn (Oxford, Oxford University Press 2006) 498.

[88] See *Francovich* (n 86) at 11 and following.

[89] MP Maduro, *We the Court: The European Court of Justice and the European Economic Constitution: A Critical Reading of Article 30 of the EC Treaty* (Oxford, Hart Pubishing, 1998); JHH Weiler, 'Epilogue: Towards a Common Law of International Trade' in JHH Weiler (ed), *The EU, the WTO, and the NAFTA: towards a common law of international trade* (Oxford, Oxford University Press, 2000); Schutze (n 41).

[90] PP Craig and G De Búrca, *EU Law: Text, Cases, and Materials* 6th edn (Oxford, Oxford University Press, 2015).

As the figure below demonstrates, the citation patterns clearly reflect differences in legal content between the three cases. The *Dassonville* sub-network consists almost entirely of one star, with incoming citations only to paragraph 5, whereas in *Defrenne* and *Francovich* the citations to several legal aspects produce a number of smaller clusters. The manifold character of *Francovich* is reflected in the high number of different paragraphs that are cited in subsequent cases.

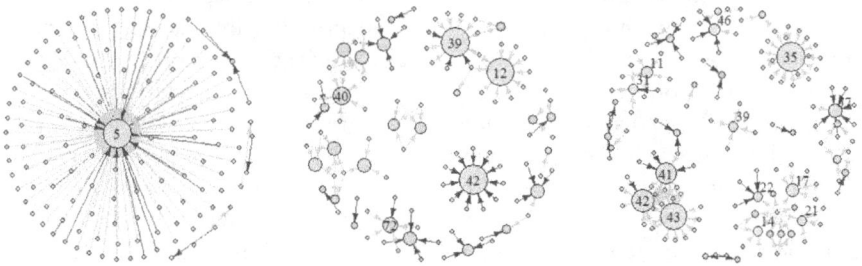

Figure 1 Different profile of cases based on the PARAGRAPH-TO-PARAGRAPH citation network and the extraction of explicit and implicit citations with language similarity techniques. The left image shows the network of citations to different paragraphs of *Dassonville*. the middle image shows the network of citations to different paragraphs of *Defrenne*, while the image on the right shows the network of citations to different paragraphs of *Francovich*

C. The Method and the Vocabulary of Empirical Studies

A new generation of European scholars has tentatively operationalised the general contextual outlook of European Union law by a more systematic and transparent analysis of formal legal sources. Exceptionally, it has made a theoretically informed case for enriching the legal analysis with qualitative methods and non-legal sources. Below are a handful examples, which illustrate this progress.

Scholars of European Union law increasingly seek to ground their legal arguments drawing on empirical methodology. Sometimes, all that is missing is the explicit empirical vocabulary. Zglinski, for instance, shows the rise of deference of the Court to the national authorities by judicial review and proportionality analysis.[91] He uses a sample of judgments of the Court of Justice to substantiate his claim. He patiently describes his research strategy:

> The search covers every complete fifth year of free movement case law from 1974, the year in which the Court first deferred to a Member State institution, 37 until 2013, the last full year available at the time of the research (taken instead of 2014). The sample includes, for the years studied, every judgment turning on the four freedoms

---

[91] J Zglinski, 'The Rise of Deference: The Margin of Appreciation and Decentralized Judicial Review in EU Free Movement Law' (2018) 55 *Common Market Law Review* 1341.

and alleged Member State violations thereof. Preliminary references and infringement actions, the two types of proceedings that can feature deference to national authorities, were considered. This yielded a total of 247 decisions, which amounts to approximately one fifth of all free movement cases ever decided.[92]

This description indicates a type of systematic sampling, and in the course of the analysis, this indeed turns out to be the case. However, because the author omits the commonly identifiable vocabulary of qualitative empirical research, as well as the discussion of the pros and the cons of the adopted research design, the legal reader (let us say, the referee, who disagrees with the argument of rising deference based on her own selective reading of case law) might start suspecting two things. First, that the author must have omitted some 'important' judgments and hence produced an inaccurate account of deference in the free movement law (meaning: the findings based on a sample of 1/5 of all cases cannot be generalised to the free movement of goods case law). Second, she might develop a more general doubt in the legal value added by 'counting' deference. Both would be unfortunate because the understanding of deference and its different forms can only be enriched by a systematic empirical study of its use over time in different historical, economic and social contexts in which the Court must operate.[93]

It would be false to speak of qualitative empirical studies as a recent phenomenon. Micklitz conducted a multitude of interviews for his treatise The Politics of Judicial Cooperation to reconstruct the national and European legal, social and political contexts of the Court's jurisprudence.[94] Micklitz described his methodology as a legal-sociological analysis, which did not only compile empirical data for a case study but with a distinct goal to decode the structure of meaning in the process of argumentation that shaped a case. These ambitious goals could only be achieved with ambitious techniques, combining interpretation of formal legal sources, such as legislation, and informal sources of law, in particular various types of non-binding legal documents, interviews with the participants.[95]

By comparison, a more recent phenomenon in the European Union law is a meta-dialogue in the sense of a critical reflection on the application of qualitative methodology for the purpose of legal empirical research. A good example is

---

[92] Ibid, 1352.

[93] A similar study is A Wallerman's analysis of the principle of national procedural autonomy, where she applies purposive sampling without the sampling vocabulary. See A Wallerman, 'Can Two Walk Together, Except They Be Agreed? Preliminary References and (the Erosion of) National Procedural Autonomy' (2019) 44 *European Law Review* 159.

[94] H-W Micklitz, *The Politics of Judicial Co-Operation in the EU Sunday Trading, Equal Treatment and Good Faith* (Cambridge, Cambridge University Press, 2005).

[95] Another example to understand legal doctrines by relying on non-doctrinal methods is The Making of a European Constitution, where Michele Everson and Julia Eisner used surveys and semi-structured interviews with judges and lawyers in England to examine the role of national lawyers in the acceptance of the supremacy of European Union law. See M Everson and J Eisner, *The Making of a European Constitution: Judges and Law beyond Constitutive Power* (London, Routledge-Cavendish 2007).

Leino's and Korkea-aho's contribution, which focuses on the challenging aspects of interviewing legal experts, and more broadly, on the debate of how to generate legal knowledge from informal sources of law.[96] In particular, they address questions of access, confidentiality, and control of the research process and data, and offer useful practical advice alongside methodological self-reflection. Such contributions are an indispensable tool for further reflection on empirical epistemology.[97]

This brief sketch of the field shows that European legal scholars do not reject knowledge about the law generated on the grounds of empirical methodology nor that empirical research is a new appendix to the exhausted legal field. They accommodate non-normative facts in their normative analysis. As Micklitz and van Gestel submit, the important part of legal curriculum in Europe should be teaching the students how the normative and the empirical interact.[98] We interpret this as an advice to teach the student of European Union law a combination of Weberian legal theory and Scandinavian legal realism. Those, as argued in the next section, offer the necessary conceptual resources in the attempt to develop a promising empirical legal science.

IV. THE DEBATE REIMAGINED

Let us return to the key question: can European Union lawyers pursue empirical research agendas without denouncing law's normative dimension? One cannot but think that if empirical research could anchor its various methods in a sound epistemology, the debate normative verses empirical would finally become intellectually truly rewarding.

Thus far, the analysis shows that first, empirical in Europe means more than an infatuation with the newest new thing in computer science and statistical large N-data. Second, European scholars pursue empirical agendas using their own vocabulary. Finally, European Union law has long operated in the law reform mode albeit unsystematically, from the methodological point of view.

Generally, there are two modes of embracing empirical legal studies, or two ways for European Union lawyers to turn empirical. The first could be described as enhanced toleration.[99] It is toleration+, or more than a peaceful but asymmetric co-existence between empirical studies and doctrinal law, with the latter

---

[96] Korkea-Aho and Leino (n 12).

[97] See also C O'Brien re reflection on her personal participation in the litigated cases used for academic research in C O'Brien, *Unity in Adversity: EU Citizenship, Social Justice and the Cautionary Tale of the UK* (Oxford, Hart Publishing, 2017).

[98] Van Gestel and Micklitz (n 34).

[99] The concept is based on Hotermann's and Madsen's concept of toleration, outlined as part of a general typology of the empirical turn, see J vH Holtermann and MR Madsen, 'Toleration, Synthesis or Replacement? The "Empirical Turn" and Its Consequences for the Science of International Law' (2016) 29 *Leiden Journal of International Law* 1001.

in the driving seat. The premise of a relative supremacy of doctrinal law would have to give way to a more symbiotic relationship, where the knowledge generated by empirical research would be more than an add-on. It would enlighten doctrinal research, via empirical methods and contextual outlook. In the latter sense it would strive for cross disciplinary research, without presenting an epistemological challenge to the foundational premise: the idea of law as a normative discipline, where legal knowledge can validly be generated from the 'internal point of view.'

The second mode is the full empirical turn. The premises of doctrinalism will have to be replaced. This means that legal science would become a science of descriptive ('is' or sein) statements about the normative world. Methodologically, this would mean a complete abandonment of the internal point of view and an adoption of a methodological program that builds on qualitative and quantitative methods designed to identify, analyze, and interpret normative statements. Such a turn appears of course epistemologically more radical and threatening, and methodologically more demanding. On the flip side, it is theoretically more consistent.

The starting point readily available is the conception of legal validity, developed in parallel by Ross and Weber.[100] Ross and Weber distinguish between two types of (legal) validity, the axiological (juridical) and the empirical. The distinction creates an epistemologically sound framework, in which to articulate the premises of the European legal science as an empirical discipline.

Axiological validity is the validity that guides the analysis of doctrinal scholars, whether legal positivists or natural lawyers. From the perspective of axiological validity, the key questions that can be raised about a rule are those that can be answered with the traditional legal method. These are the questions about the pedigree, involving chains of reasoning back towards the fundamentals, and about the conceptual extension, involving application of given canons of legal interpretation. Such activity (method) will establish the juristic truth. At the same time, however, the ambition of establishing axiological validity will *simultaneously* establish itself as a genuinely empirical object of enquiry.

By contrast, empirical validity refers to the world of facts about juristic validity. It is a fact that jurisprudence exists, and it is a fact that there are persons concerned with establishing the juristic validity of legal rules. There are 'intellectual habits' that are governed by this 'jurisprudence,' habits which develop in an empirical-historical fashion. This fact is of tremendous practical significance for the organisation of human affairs. Within this empirical reality there are 'judges' and other 'officials' who can influence human behaviour by employing certain physical and psychological instruments of coercion. They conform to certain maxims, defined as shared ideas about something obligatory

---

[100] Weber (n 2) 128–129; Ross, *On Law and Justice (with an Introduction by Jakob v. H. Holtermann)* (n 10) 13–26; Ross, *On Law and Justice* (n 10) 6–18.

(axiologically valid), which determine their conduct. Correspondingly, to Weber and Ross, to observe of any given legal order or rule that it exists as a maxim is to observe that it has empirical validity. Hence, the discussion of the empirical existence of social life cannot legitimately be based upon the foundation of axiological dogmatics.[101]

Weber mentions briefly how, from the point of view of empirical validity, 'a "legal order" may be analysed as a complex of maxims in the minds of certain men who really exist,'[102] without providing much direction beyond his ideal-types of legal rationalisation. Ross, by contrast, is more concrete, and maintains that the focal point of a study of empirically valid legal doctrine must be what he calls *the judge ideology*:

> To understand and predict judicial behaviour can only be achieved through ideological interpretation, that is, by means of the hypothesis about a certain ideology which animates the judge and motivates his actions.[103]

Legal decision-making 'does not take place in a capricious and arbitrary way [...], but is determined by attitudes and notions – by a common normative ideology which is present and operative in a uniform way within the minds of [...] judges when acting in their vocation as judges.'[104]

The study of these maxims is what counts as an empirical study, regardless of whether the method is qualitative or quantitative. At the same time, it is therefore more than behaviourism.

Ross tries to break down the judge ideology into its constituent parts and to reveal the underlying logic that structures the particular 'complex of maxims in the minds' of judges at any given time. In rough outline, Ross ascribes a central role to the doctrine of *the sources of law*, which he identifies as '*the sum total of the factors exercising influence* on the judge's formulation of the rule on which he bases his decision.'[105] This implies that the shift from axiological to empirical validity does not necessarily imply a complete shift with regard to the legal rules in question. The key question is whether the rules under study are considered valid because of their logical relation to other rules (normative approach) or because they are believed by judges and other officials to be thus logically related (empirical approach). And it is obviously possible for the same rule to be identified as satisfying both these criteria if they are applied in separate investigations.

To repeat, a statement about axiological validity is straightforwardly a normative statement. It directly expresses a normative fact, a maxim (eg that a certain right exists) and as such it belongs, as Kelsen would say, in the realm of

---

[101] See Holtermann and Madsen, 'European New Legal Realism and International Law' (n 11).

[102] Weber (n 2) 130.

[103] Ross, *On Law and Justice (with an Introduction by Jakob v. H. Holtermann)* (n 10) 48–49; Ross, *On Law and Justice* (n 10) 37.

[104] Ross, *On Law and Justice (with an Introduction by Jakob v. H. Holtermann)* (n 10) 89; Ross, *On Law and Justice* (n 10) 75.

[105] Ross, *On Law and Justice (with an Introduction by Jakob v. H. Holtermann)* (n 10) 91; Ross, *On Law and Justice* (n 10) 77.

the ought (Sollen).[106] A statement about empirical validity, even though concerning certain maxims/norms, is a genuinely descriptive assertion, and belongs to the world of is (Sein). European Union law as legal science would concern itself exclusively with the latter.

V. CONCLUSION

This chapter defended the claim that the EU law could reinvent itself as legal science by going empirical, and laid out the foundations (a starter kit). It did so under the assumption that European scholars either already used a variety of empirical methods or were sufficiently open to legal empirical approaches.

The glass is half full. Europe has not walked the American way. There has been more reflection or effort to define the key concept: empirical. CELSE 2018, for instance, accompanied the call for papers with an addendum: 'Empirical analysis is understood to encompass any systematic approach to quantitative or qualitative data analysis, including statistical analysis, machine learning, experiments, text-mining and network analysis techniques.[107] The conferences were a great success, demonstrating that Europe had a 'taste' and the 'market' for empirical legal research.

European legal scholars endorse the knowledge *about* the law as part of their legal discipline, meaning that they integrate (assimilate) contextual, non-normative and to an extent empirical accounts in their normative analysis. They do not shy away from making policy proposals. The problem is not, as might appear at first sight, the reactive and problem oriented approach, but the way (the normative approach) in which they typically address the problem and the tools, which they use to solve it (aka the method). There is, to our mind, no pressing reason for not making contextual legal accounts more rigorous (quite the contrary) via formal education: by introducing empirical and socio-legal scholarship in the legal curriculum. Calls to familiarise students with the mechanisms, through which the normative and the empirical interact, is hardly a call to erode the normative study of law. A combination of Weberian legal theory and Scandinavian legal realism is not a subversive discipline but an arsenal of indispensable conceptual foundations for the legal empirical science.

The glass is half empty. EU law does not base its contextual outlook on clear theoretical premises, methodological rigor, nor research tools. The reflection on theoretical foundations has not been pursued. So far, neither the traditional nor the empirical camp bit the foundational bullet. While the doctrinally oriented European lawyers seem busy with mimesis, the empirically minded lawyers seem completely overcome with trying out the newest computer software or scheduling interviews with judges and stakeholders.

---

[106] Kelsen (n 2).
[107] www.law.kuleuven.be/pub/en/cltej/CELSE.

Moreover, the method of analysis and the traditional approach to legal materials have been rather sticky. One possible explanation is of course the somewhat schizophrenic nature of the discipline: EU law is transformed, adjusted, and domesticated across dozens of legal systems. The enforcement mechanisms are weak.[108] The method might be perceived as the last mark of disciplinary identity and relevance in the multilateral system. The erosion of the method would logically imply further fragmentation of the field. This, we argued, was not necessarily the case.[109] The question is, ultimately (and almost ironically), empirical.

A. An Afterthought

Very often the takeaway of a thorough doctrinal study is rather underwhelming: the author either concludes that the text is ambiguous of that the judge can consider the purpose of this or another rule but not change the text as if she were a legislator. The insight into the content of rights and duties, carefully established in the analysis, vanishes.

At times, doctrinal scholars address broad questions of policy. Should we reform the Court? (Oh, but we did, based on numbers and little analysis.[110]) Is the chamber system appropriate to achieve the ideal of a coherent legal system and the uniform application of European Union law? And the perhaps oldest debate regarding the Court and the quality of its reasoning: should we allow open dissents?[111] These hinge on the interpretation of enacted rules (Treaties, Statutes, Rules of Procedure) and the guiding values and principles of the European legal order. Anecdotal evidence and armchair sociology are used to underpin various (even opposite) normative positions. European legal scholarship can do better.

---

[108] Eg, The impotence of law against the rule of law crisis: C Closa, *Reinforcing EU Monitoring of the Rule of Law: Normative Arguments, Institutional Proposals and the Procedural Limitations* (2016) http://cadmus.eui.eu//handle/1814/43687; L Pech and KL Scheppele, 'Illiberalism Within: Rule of Law Backsliding in the EU' (2017) 19 *Cambridge Yearbook of European Legal Studies* 3; GGbor Halmai, 'The Possibility and Desirability of Economic Sanction: Rule of Law Conditionality Requirements Against Illiberal EU Member States' [2018] SSRN Electronic Journal www.ssrn.com/abstract=3126231.

[109] Cf, A Dyevre, W Wijtvliet and N Lampach, 'The Future of European Legal Scholarship: Empirical Jurisprudence' (2019) 26 *Maastricht Journal of European and Comparative Law* 348; G van Dijck, S Sverdlov and G Buck, 'Empirical Legal Research in Europe: Prevalence, Obstacles, and Interventions' (2018) 11 *Erasmus Law Review* 105.

[110] Critically on the reform see A Alemanno and L Pech, 'Thinking Justice Outside the Docket: A Critical Assessment of the Reform of the EU's Court System' (2017) 54 *Common Market Law Review* 129; A Alemanno and O Stefan, 'Openness at the Court of Justice of the European Union: Toppling a Taboo' (2014) 51 *Common MarketLlaw Review* 97.

[111] JHH Weiler, 'Epilogue: The Judiciary Après Nice' in G De Búrca and JHH Weiler (eds), *The European Court of Justice* (Academy of European Law, European University Institute; Oxford, Oxford University Press, 2001); A Arnull, *The European Union and Its Court of Justice* 2nd edn (Oxford, Oxford University Press, 2006); M de SO L'E Lasser, *Judicial Deliberations: A Comparative Analysis of Judicial Transparency and Legitimacy* (Oxford, Oxford University Press, 2004).

11

Preserving us from Regulatory Power? Legal Normativity and the Possibility of Agency

SYLVIE DELACROIX*

I. INTRODUCTION

EW CONCEPTS CAN be said to divide the jurisprudence community quite as much as the concept of normativity. While this divide is largely the result of different disciplinary backgrounds (with contrasting explanatory ambitions), it is often associated with the Anglo-Saxon and Continental traditions' propensity to talking past each other. Not that there have not been valiant efforts on both sides. In the 1950's, Hart declared that he and Kelsen shared a 'common goal': explaining the normative dimension of law.[1] In itself, that declaration is nothing short of remarkable. It is hard to think of a single other example where the respective flagbearers of Continental and Anglo-Saxon jurisprudence so explicitly declare that they 'share a common goal'. Yet this goal was common in name only. What Kelsen and Hart respectively had in mind was very different. Whereas Kelsen meant to explain what conditions the possibility of law's binding force, Hart is sometimes taken to have given a grand expression to something actually pretty mundane.

From a minimalist perspective,[2] all Hart would have been trying to explain is law's capacity to *guide* our conduct. Interpreted like this, the task of explaining

---

* S.Delacroix@bham.ac.uk Professor in Law and Ethics, University of Birmingham.

[1] 'I share with him [Kelsen] the conviction that a central task of legal philosophy is to explain the normative force of propositions of law [...] None the less [...] my main effort in these two essays is to show that references to both psychological and social facts, which Kelsen's theory in its excessive purity would exclude, are in fact quite indispensable' HLA Hart, *Essays in jurisprudence and philosophy* (London, Clarendon Press, 1983) 18.

[2] You might doubt that anybody would ever adopt such a minimalist interpretation of the term 'normative', and the nature of Hart's explanatory ambition, were it not for the fact that

the normative dimension of law is really no different from the task of explaining how *recipes* can guide our behaviour. Under such a minimalist definition, an awful lot of things will be normative, including trivial 'oughts' such as adverts or recipes, while some hard to follow or obscure laws won't be. As an alternative (surveyed in section II), one may move a little notch higher, and state, with Hildebrandt, that something is normative if it 'induces or enforces, inhibits or rules out certain types of behavior'.[3] As Hildebrandt notes, under this wide definition a Berlin key will be just as 'normative' as law, adverts or games. Section III highlights this definition's problematic omission of any reference to normative agency,[4] which prevents it from distinguishing regulatory power from normativity. Just like it is central to the articulation of the dynamic relationship between autonomy and authority, agency is central to our understanding of law as a normative practice. Yet in legal theory agent-centred narratives that take us from human beings with needs, desires etc to a society with a variety of norms are few and far between.

When legal theorists do inquire into what makes legal normativity possible in the first place, the narratives they develop tend to assume deliberative agency all the way through. Aside from leaving us with a poorer understanding of legal normativity (section IV), this assumption also makes us blind to the extent to which it is not just our deliberative selves, but also our habitual selves that need protecting from undue influence if our capacity for normative agency is to be adequately preserved. Section V unpacks the role played by law's institutional structure in preserving us from a rigidification of the patterns of behaviour underlying our habitual practices. Such rigidification can be the result of our getting 'hooked' by technologies that are designed to durably influence our behaviour while bypassing our deliberative selves. It can also stem from some state-sponsored endeavour to maximise compliance while minimising the need for enforcement. An extreme example of the latter – the 'Wall-E scenario'– and the extent to which the standards that are complied with in such a scenario may cease to be adequately referred to as 'legal norms', will be discussed in section III.

John Gardner himself once took such a minimalist stand (unpublished correspondence) – until he changed his mind, in 'Nearly natural law' J Gardner, 'Nearly Natural Law' (2007) 52 *American Journal of Jurisprudence* 1.

[3] M Hildebrandt, 'Legal and Technological normativity: more (and less) than twin sisters' (2008) 12 *Techne*.

[4] In her more recent 'The force of law and technology', Hildebrandt notes that this 'generic' understanding of norms 'does not imply human agency (it does not address "action") but it does imply some kind of agency (it does address "behaviour")': M Hildebrandt, 'The force of law and the force of technology' in M McGuire and T Holt (eds), *The Routledge handbook for technology, crime and justice* (London, Routledge, 2017). It is important to emphasise at this early stage that this agency need not be deliberative: section IV highlights the important, and largely unacknowledged role of habitual agency in the process of giving rise or norms.

II. UPSTREAM VERSUS DOWNSTREAM PERSPECTIVES
ON 'NORMATIVITY'

While for Kelsen the task of explaining the normative dimension of law entailed a search for the ground of legal normativity, Hart's non-foundationalist stance[5] stems at least in part from the deflationary effects of JL Austin's method. The latter aimed to elucidate even the most complex concepts by reference to the 'things people do with words'. Along this line, Hart's analysis of legal statements as statements from an internal point of view refers to the attitude of part of the population in order to account for the normative dimension of those statements. In this respect, Hart is keen to emphasise the need for a 'hermeneutic' method. The latter 'involves portraying rule-governed behaviour as it appears to its participants, who see it as conforming or failing to conform to certain shared standards'.[6]

To explain the 'crucial' difference between 'merely convergent habitual behaviour' and behaviour that is guided by norms, Hart emphasises the 'internal aspect of rules'. The latter entails that at least some people 'must look upon the behaviour in question [to which the rule refers] as a general standard to be followed by the group as a whole'.[7] Yet Hart's aiming to capture the normative status of law by describing how certain people treat it as normative –hence adopting a 'critical reflective attitude' towards legal rules – does not commit him to explaining what it is about law, or about the context of interaction in which it is embedded, that would give rise to the adoption of such an attitude.[8]

---

[5] The contrast between Hart's and Kelsen's respective accounts of legal normativity is outlined in detail in S Delacroix, 'Hart's and Kelsen's conceptions of normativity contrasted' (2004) 17 *Ratio Iuris* 501.

[6] HLA Hart, *Essays in Jurisprudence and Philosophy* (Oxford, Oxford University Press, 1983) 13.

[7] HLA Hart, *The concept of law* 2nd edn (London, Clarendon Press, 1994) 56.

[8] Hart's specification in the Postscript that the Rule of Recognition should be understood as a conventional rule – 'But the theory remains as a faithful account of conventional social rules which include, besides ordinary social customs (which may or may not be recognised as having legal force), certain important legal rules including the rule of recognition' ibid, 256 – may be regarded as the beginning of such an explanation, which Stephen Perry nevertheless deems to be 'incomplete', 'because he does not say why general conformity could be part of a reason for accepting a rule' (SR Perry, 'Hart's methodological positivism' in Jules Coleman (ed), *Hart's Postscript, essays on the Postscript to the Concept of Law* (Oxford, Oxford University Press, 2001) 341). It is interesting to note here that the lack of interest Hart showed for the question of the emergence of the Rule of Recognition can be analysed along the same lines as Kelsen's determination to preserve the autonomy of the normative sphere. It results from the wish to exclude from the scope of legal theory any potentially compromising consideration (because it might refer to some ideological content). A deep-seated wariness towards any ideological or political content, which leads to the relegation of any moral or ideological conviction to the sphere of private autonomy (the latter lies beyond the reach of legal theory), pervades Kelsen's work, and may be described as one of the key features of the liberal spirit which, a few years later, openly influenced Hart's work. this trend will constitute one of the main targets of Carl Schmitt's doctrine, which describes liberalism as 'the negation of politics'.

By contrast, Kelsen's theory does seek to understand what conditions the possibility of legal normativity, only Kelsen's methodological dualism does not allow him to ground the ought dimension of law in factual propositions. Kelsen thus has to resort to a transcendental argument, relying on the Basic Norm as the last (and presupposed) reason of validity for all the norms of the system. Allowing one to interpret the subjective meaning of the initial acts of will as their objective meaning – ie as normative – the Basic Norm is what allows the passage from is to ought, or rather what takes the place of such a passage.

The perils inherent in overlooking the significant difference of outlook that separates Hart and Kelsen's respective accounts of normativity find their clearest expression in Raz's flawed interpretation of Kelsen.[9] I have outlined the nature of these flaws elsewhere.[10] For our present purposes, what matters is to understand the contrast between the explanatory ambitions that characterise Hart's and Kelsen's respective accounts, as these divergent explanatory ambitions help shed light on very different contemporary uses of the term 'normativity'. As an example, Korsgaard's inquiry into the 'sources' of normativity[11] stands in sharp contrast to Hildebrandt's endeavour to develop 'a generic concept of normativity'. The latter's ambition to account for 'the impact of both technologies and law on human interaction'[12] fits within a wider umbrella of theories whose focus is on the downstream manifestations of normativity. Hildebrandt's emphasis on the independence of such a 'generic' concept of normativity from 'the intention of whoever designed either a law or a technology'[13] partly reflects the perceived inadequacy of overly voluntarist accounts of normativity. It is also representative of a wider, sociological school that was influenced by Wiener's 'cybernetics'. Concerned with the emergent, constraining properties of a variety of systems, such an approach can be directed to the study of the social forces that structure human behaviour, whether these forces are the result of deliberate human intervention or not.

From such a perspective, the salient difference between legal normativity and the 'normativity' of socio-technical infrastructures consists in the ability of the latter to 'self-enforce' to various degrees. As a famous – and fairly simple – example of such self-enforcement, Latour's discussion of the Berlin key[14] is

---

[9] Joseph Raz suggests quite a different way of accounting for Hart's and Kelsen's contrasted understandings of the concept of normativity, based on a distinction between what he calls a 'justified' and a 'social' conception of normativity. According to the justified conception of normativity, 'legal standards of behaviour are norms only if and in so far as they are justified'. On the other – social – view, 'standards of behaviour can be considered as norms regardless of their merit. They are social norms in so far as they are socially upheld as binding standards and in so far as the society involved exerts pressure on people to whom the standards apply to conform to them'. J Raz, *The authority of law* (Oxford, Oxford University Press, 1979) 134.

[10] Those flaws are analysed in detail in Delacroix.

[11] CM Korsgaard, *The sources of normativity* (Cambridge, Cambridge University Press, 1996).

[12] Hildebrandt (n 3), 'Legal and Technological normativity: more (and less) than twin sisters'.

[13] Ibid.

[14] B Latour, *La clef de Berlin et autres leçons d'un amateur de sciences* (La Découverte 1993).

helpful. 'In this case the designer of the key has inscribed a program of action [after entering the house, the door can only be closed by turning the key and thus locking the door] into the hardware, delegating the task of insisting on locking or not locking the door to the key'.[15] In contrast, Hildebrandt rightly notes that 'though legal rules can constitute what it means to count as a road user or even a car driver, they cannot constitute the driving of a car in the sense that in the case of non-compliance one cannot drive'.[16]

While this socio-cybernetic perspective brings important insights, not least because it corrects the perduring, wrong-headed assumption that normativity presupposes intentional agency (more on this below), it has its own limitations too. Because of its downstream focus – it emphasises the constraining impact of a variety of social forces – it misses the significance of another important difference between legal normativity and the regulatory power (problematically referred to as 'normativity') of socio-technical infrastructures.

III. HOW LAW AS A NORMATIVE PRACTICE PRESUPPOSES A MINIMAL DEGREE OF AGENCY

Whereas the regulatory power of socio-technical infrastructures is established once and for all, the normativity of law is not. It is dependent upon a minimal degree of continuing engagement on our part. Imagine a 'Wall-E'-like scenario, where a community of highly machine-dependent, video-games addicted individuals comply with 'legal' requirements in a permanent zombie-like fashion. In that case all we would be faced with is a pattern of behaviour that has been successfully shaped by a technological infrastructure. The aim of the latter is to make sure those behaviour patterns comply with a set of requirements that are only called 'legal' because they were once legal norms. While such norms' necessary infringement upon the sphere of personal autonomy was once the object of debate and contestation, the general state of utter dependence upon machines has led to atrophied 'normative muscles'. Without an ability to mobilise the latter, the very capacity to question the way things are, to articulate aspirations which might in turn call for some modified normative framework, is gone. There is no normativity to speak of: only highly conditioned patterns of behaviour expertly and efficiently administered.

From a socio-cybernetic perspective, by contrast, the only relevant difference with legal systems as we (still) know them is the fact that, in such a 'Wall-E scenario', the 'governmental authority apparatus'[17] which law typically depends upon for its enforcement has become redundant. The latter perspective overlooks

---

[15] Hildebrandt (n 3), 'Legal and Technological normativity: more (and less) than twin sisters'.
[16] Ibid.
[17] Ibid.

the fact that law's authority is not just an 'apparatus'. For all its limitations, Raz's 'service conception of authority' remains the sharpest crystallisation of the dynamic relationship between autonomy and authority, and the extent to which this dynamic structures our[18] understanding of law. I have described this dynamic – and the limitations inherent in Raz's account of it – in detail elsewhere.[19] The following starts with a brief reminder, to explain both the conceptual and normative stakes inherent in preserving a distinction between regulatory power (which need not claim any authority) and normativity.

Raz's prime question is: what does it take for law to have authority over us? Given 'the intrinsic desirability of people conducting their own life by their own lights',[20] how can our abiding by law's precepts just because they are 'legal' be desirable as well? Roughly put, Raz's answer works like this: if, when considering all the various requirements that apply to her, the individual concludes that abiding by the law actually enables her to best balance all these demands, thus putting her on the path of 'right reason',[21] then law's authority may be deemed beneficial, rather than detrimental to her autonomy. Freeing the individual from the task of balancing a complex set of reasons (a task for which the individual often – but not always – lacks information or expertise), law is supposed to 'mediate' between its subjects and the reasons that apply to them.[22] It is in that sense that Raz sometimes refers to his account of authority as a 'service conception': for a legal system to do its job, it must successfully simplify our practical reasoning, at least most of the time. Yet the problem is: if, in order to assess the legitimacy of law's claim to authority, the individual has to keep peeking back at the underlying reasons in order to assess whether law still has a sufficiently high 'normal justification score',[23] it is not clear when that 'legitimacy assessment' should stop.

This unresolved (and perhaps unresolvable) tension between autonomy and authority is crucial to understanding what is missing in the 'cybernetic' understanding of law's 'normativity' described above. Just like it is central to the articulation of the dynamic relationship between autonomy and authority,

---

[18] The 'our' reflects an understanding of law that is structured around a commitment to the rule of law and democracy.
[19] See S Delacroix, *Legal norms and normativity: an essay in genealogy* (Oxford, Hart Publishing, 2006), ch 5.
[20] J Raz, *The morality of freedom* (Oxford, Clarendon Press, 1986) 57.
[21] This concept of 'right reason' unfortunately allows Raz to circumvent the need to spell out his understanding of the status of the moral values that are meant to guide the individual's deliberation. I have argued elsewhere that Raz's arguments, particularly in J Raz, *The Practice of Value* (Oxford, Clarendon Press, 2003) ibid seem to presuppose a pretty robust kind of metaphysical realism.
[22] Raz (n 20), *The morality of freedom* 58.
[23] In order to avoid the impracticality (and the possibility of mistakes) inherent in having to reassess the authority of a particular rule or set of rules in every different situation, the individual may rely on an aggregation strategy, granting the law a certain 'credit' based on its overall performance in enabling her to comply with the demands of 'right reason'. J Raz, *Practical Reason and Norms* (rev. ed, with postscript edn, Princeton, Princeton University Press, 1990) 194.

agency is central to our understanding of law as a normative practice. This is the case at least since legal theorists took stock of the implications of the 'revolution' which Korsgaard brilliantly describes in her preface to *The Sources of Normativity*.[24] This 'revolution' took place when, in the process of transition from the Ancient to the Modern world,

> [T]he problem of value has become the reverse of what it was before [...] If the real and the good are no longer one, value must find its way into the world, somehow. Form must be imposed on the world of matter. This is the work of art, the work of obligation [...] it was Kant who completed the revolution, when he said that reason – which is form- isn't in the world, but is something that we impose upon it. The ethics of autonomy is the only one consistent with the metaphysics of the modern world.[25]

Montaigne was the first philosopher to consider the implications of the above revolution for our understanding of law's normativity. Having rejected as vain any search for natural laws,[26] Montaigne is confronted with the challenge of explaining how law, with its purported authority, can emerge from the 'tiny spring' unveiled by his sceptical critique: the contingency of power and the arbitrariness of human activities. 'Laws are often made by fools [...] but always by men, *vain authorities* who can resolve nothing'.[27] Beyond the foolishness of lawmakers, what Montaigne fears cannot be 'resolved'[28] stems from their being 'always between birth and death',[29] thus subject to finiteness, which does not agree easily with the purported permanence of their task as lawmakers. If men (and women) are the exclusive authors, without any other guarantor, of their own laws, they can undo what they have done. Or to put it in Montaigne's language: if lawmakers are unable to bind their will to anything but 'unstable weak opinions', is there any hope of ever relating the purported 'grandeur' of the law – it being meant to bind us – to those seemingly hopeless, contingent beginnings?

Now, Montaigne was not only the first, modern exponent of this question, he also inaugurated a way of circumventing it. To spare his 'lay' contemporaries

[24] Korsgaard.

[25] Ibid.

[26] 'What kind of Good can it be, which was honoured yesterday but not today and which becomes a crime when you cross a river! What kind of truth can be limited by a range of mountains, becoming a lie for the world on the other side! Philosophers can hardly be serious when they try to introduce certainty into Law by asserting that there are so-called Natural Laws, perpetual and immutable, whose essential characteristic consists in their being imprinted upon the human race. There are said to be three such laws; or four; some say less, some say more: a sign that the mark they bear is as dubious as all the rest.'

[27] M de Montaigne, *The complete essays* (London, Penguin Classics, 1991) III 13.

[28] For a detailed analysis, see Delacroix (n 19), *Legal norms and normativity: an essay in genealogy.*

[29] 'We have no communication with Being; as human nature is wholly situated, forever, between birth and death, it shows itself only as a dark shadowy appearance, an unstable weak opinion.' (de Montaigne, II 12, p 680).

the perilous discovery of law's precarious origins,[30] Montaigne posits a 'Law of Pure Obedience', enjoining one to obey the law 'because it is the law' without asking any further question: 'Now laws remain respected not because they are just but because they are laws. That is the mystical basis of their authority'.[31] The parallels between Montaigne's circumvention strategy and Kelsen's transcendental argument (which for its part posits a 'Basic Norm') are striking.[32] For different reasons, neither Montaigne nor Kelsen were in a position to develop a narrative that takes us from human beings with needs, desires and aspirations to a society with a variety of norms. The next section emphasises the extent to which such a narrative is necessarily dependent upon one's understanding of agency, in contrast to those narratives explaining the emergence – and persistence – of various forms of regulatory power (from anodyne Berlin keys to automated systems of behaviour optimisation).

IV. WHY AN AGENT-CENTERED NARRATIVE NEED NOT COLLAPSE INTO SOME CRUDE VOLUNTARISM

As none of us have the resources necessary to living our lives entirely by our own lights, according to self-posited norms, we cannot but defer to a wide range of externally posited norms. Some of these norms are issued by entities whom we deem to have authority over us. Now, it may be naive to assume that we are all reflective enough to regularly check that those authorities keep enabling us to live the lives we aspire to – or lives that conform with 'the demands of Right Reason', as Raz would put it (such regular checks would be necessary to comply with Raz's 'Normal Justification Thesis'[33]). Yet what matters is that we can at least query the grounds of those various authorities. Answers to these queries will seek to present convincing reasons. Query the grounds of regulatory power, by contrast, and all you will get are brute facts: sometimes these facts clearly proceed from intentional action (as in the Berlin key), sometimes they do not, or less clearly so (think of the durable, constraining power of wifi-routers, or social-media platforms[34]).

To establish whether something is an instance of regulatory power, all you have to do is establish whether it has succeeded in *durably* affecting or

---

[30] 'Laws gain their authority from actual possession and custom: it is perilous to go back to their origins; laws, like our rivers, get greater and nobler as they roll along: follow them back upstream to their sources and all you find is a tiny spring, hardly recognizable': ibid.

[31] Ibid.

[32] These parallels are outlined in Delacroix (n 19), *Legal norms and normativity: an essay in genealogy*.

[33] Raz (n 23), *Practical Reason and Norms*.

[34] The ethical issues inherent in the fact that the regulatory power of social media platforms is made possible by covert manipulation are discussed in detail in S Delacroix, 'Beware of "Algorithmic Regulation"' (February 1, 2019) Available at SSRN: https://ssrn.com/abstract=3327191 or http://dx.doi.org/10.2139/ssrn.3327191.

constraining our behaviour.[35] To establish whether a purported normative claim really is normative,[36] by contrast, necessarily involves some justificatory effort. When a norm is posited by an authority, this justificatory effort might be indirect – whether an authority is recognised as such through agreement (boy-scout leaders) or whether we grant them that status for pragmatic (coordination-problem solving), religious (spiritual leaders) or moral reasons. In such cases, their being granted authority is meant to enable us to enjoy the benefits of simplified practical reasoning, for a while, at least.[37] Provided they are deemed legitimate, those authorities' normative claims are meant to be taken at face value.

In contrast, when a friend argues I should be better dressed, or give half of my income to charity, I am not meant to take those normative claims at face value. I might, if I am lazy, or psychologically conditioned to never question my friend (in which case she may not be much of a friend). Since she is my friend, I will be pondering the reasons – which need not be moral – underlying these normative claims.

If I come across an ad enjoining me to wear a pink hat, however, I am likely to dismiss it as one of the very many trivial 'grammatical ought' statements I come across on a daily basis. But suppose I pay attention to this ad, and that evening I am proudly wearing the pink hat in question. Is this ad 'normative'? Since it 'can be used for guidance', and it can be said, as Hildebrandt puts it, to 'induce a certain type of behaviour' (the better designed the ad, the better it will push the right emotional buttons), those who adopt a downstream, minimalist understanding – see the approaches described in section II – would have to answer positively, and count this advert as normative. Those who wish to resist that conclusion will have to look upstream. Just how far they are prepared to look upstream will vary.

One may, like Montaigne, seek to halt enquiries into the sources of normativity at a point that is safely removed from its precarious, contingent origins. I have outlined elsewhere[38] the striking parallels between the circumventing strategies that inform Montaigne's and Kelsen's respectively resorting to a 'Law of Pure Obedience' and a 'Basic Norm'. Adopting this kind of strategy

---

[35] The 'durably' is important. When I hold a gun at you, I certainly have the power to constrain your behaviour, but to do so durably I would have to be prepared to keep holding the gun in this way, hence guns generally tend to be pretty poor tools when it comes to establishing regulatory power. Technologies like Berlin keys – or social media platforms – fare much better, in this respect, and often end up yielding considerable regulatory power, sometimes unintentionally so. But that doesn't mean that these technologies are normative, at least not in the way I, and I think mainstream moral and legal philosophy, understands the term 'normative.'

[36] 'The problems of philosophy always or at least very often take the form of trying to understand why some purported normative claim really is normative' CM Korsgaard, 'Internalism and the sources of normativity: an interview with Christine M. Korsgaard' in H Pauer-Studer (ed), *Constructions of Practical Reason: Interviews on moral and political philosophy* (Stanford, Stanford University Press, 2003).

[37] Though Raz would add: not for too long, as we are meant to check that each authority still has a sufficiently high 'normal justification score.'

[38] Delacroix (n 19), *Legal norms and normativity: an essay in genealogy.*

would entail that, in the absence of a 'presupposed' norm that would warrant an interpretation of the 'subjective meaning' of the pink hat advert as its 'objective meaning' – ie as normative – that advert does count as normative.

The alternative to such circumventing strategies is to develop some agent-centered narrative. The relevant narrative could take us from a person whose 'emotional buttons' have been pushed in such a way that she finds herself compelled to buy a pink hat that afternoon, for no particular reason other than some impulsive desire to do so. Or this narrative could evolve from a person seeking some means of demarcating herself, to the same person now uphold-ing the need to wear a pink hat in public at all times (it might be to to mark one's political allegiance). In such a scenario, one may argue that this person has made the wearing of pink hats a norm for herself (and others). The 'gram-matical ought' contained in the ad has played a causal role in a complex process involving background norms and expectations that make the wearing of pink hats appear to be a suitable norm to uphold. We will come back to this pink hat scenario in section V.

For now, it's important to underline that the latter scenario will be highly unusual. The context of social interaction that contributes to the gradual emergence of social – and eventually legal – norms will involve complex inter-subjective practices. The latter will typically emerge from patterns of behaviour that may well be wholly habitual,[39] in contrast to the overly voluntarist under-tones characterising the 'upholding a pink hat wearing norm' story described above. Highlighting the unusual character of the latter story is important: theo-retical endeavours to develop a narrative that takes us from human beings with needs, desires etc to a society with a variety of norms have too often collapsed under the assumption that such narratives were doomed to result in some empty form of voluntarism. Kelsen comes close to acknowledging this assumption when he explains why his Pure theory should not be misunderstood as 'a doctrine of recognition':

> [T]he doctrine of the Basic Norm is not a doctrine of recognition as is sometimes erroneously understood. According to the doctrine of recognition positive law is valid only if it is recognised by the individuals subject to it [...] The theory of recog-nition, consciously or unconsciously, presupposes the ideal of individual liberty as self-determination, that is, the norm that the individual ought to do only what he wants to do.[40]

It is somewhat baffling to see just how influential this crude voluntarism has been – or more precisely, the assumption that one must necessarily either come to terms with such a voluntarism's sceptical implications or embrace heavier metaphysical presuppositions.[41] Hart alludes to this dilemma in his review of

---

[39] For more details see section V.

[40] H Kelsen, *Pure theory of law* (University of California Press, 1967) s 34, ibid.

[41] Whether they take the form of a 'noumenal self' or some 'true' values that are meant to be wholly independent of our contingent nature as human beings.

Bernard Williams' *Ethics and the Limits of Philosophy*,[42] where he acknowledges some longing for some external, rational foundation for ethics while at the same time expressing the fear that, were we to look for the grounds of the moral 'I must' in 'what is most deeply inside us', it would not prove 'enough' to sustain a sense of moral necessity.[43] I think it is largely because of this dilemma that Hart cautiously avoids having to tie his understanding of legal normativity to any 'upstream' narrative of the kind described above.[44] In this respect Hart's 'lack of interest' in the practices giving rise to law as a normative phenomenon is not that dissimilar to Kelsen's neo-Kantian arguments (or Montaigne's recourse to a 'Law of Pure Obedience'):[45] all end up safeguarding law's normativity from the contingency of law-making practices.

The resulting separation of law's normativity from the social practices conditioning its possibility is an enduring feature of contemporary jurisprudence. It is also unfortunate. My genealogy of legal normativity[46] was an attempt to remedy this situation, but it under-estimated the importance of one key question: the dual role played by habit and habituation within the background of social practices giving rise to law – and enabling the fact that it binds us.

V. THE UNACKNOWLEDGED ROLE OF NON-DELIBERATIVE AGENCY IN THE PROCESSES GIVING RISE TO NORMS

Considerable work has been devoted to delineating the ways in which 'practices' (conventional or otherwise[47]) may give rise to legal norms. A lot less attention has been paid to the patterns of repeated behaviour – ie habits – that feed such practices. Some legal theorists will tell you there's a good reason for such scant developments. As Shapiro puts it: 'habits are not the right sort of things that can

[42] B Williams, *Ethics and the Limits of Philosophy* (Cambridge, Mass, Havard University Press, 1985).

[43] 'Why should anyone be disturbed if Williams is right in his claim that there is no independent rational foundation for ethical thought ... In fact fears of two different kinds have been excited by such skeptical thought. The first is that if it becomes widespread we shall have nothing – or not enough – to say to the immoralist ... The second kind of fear is more realistic ... once it [a general acceptance of the view that there is no objective foundation for ethical thought] is accepted it will be no longer possible to interpret ethical experience, as many do, as a demand coming from outside. The sense of necessity (the moral "I must") in which the recognition of moral obligation often terminates, will have to be seen as coming not from outside, but from what is most deeply inside us ... The fear is that this will not be enough ...' HLA Hart, 'Who can tell right from wrong?' (1986) 33 *The New York review of books*, Section 4. As Amanda Perreau-Saussine puts it: 'Hart seems to have striven to keep jurisprudential thought open to a moral truth that he feared might not exist.' A Perreau-Saussine, 'An outsider on the inside: Hart's limits on jurisprudence' (2006) 56 *Toronto Law Journal* 371, 388.

[44] I develop this point at length in S Delacroix, 'Meta-ethical agnosticism in legal theory: mapping a way out' (2010) 1 *Jurisprudence* 225.

[45] For a detailed account see Delacroix (n 5), 'Hart's and Kelsen's conceptions of normativity contrasted'.

[46] Delacroix (n 19), *Legal norms and normativity: an essay in genealogy*.

[47] A Marmor, 'Legal conventionalism' in J Coleman (ed), *Hart's Postscript, essays on the Postscript to the Concept of Law* (Oxford, Oxford University Press, 2001) GJ Postema, 'Coordination

impose obligations'.[48] Shapiro unambiguously dismisses the conceptual relevance of habits to our understanding of law because 'habits are not normative activities'. Given 'the normative nature of legal activity', to allow some conceptual link between law and habits would fall foul of 'Hume's challenge', which supposedly forbids any 'derivation of an ought from an is'.[49]

Aside from the fact that it is unclear whether Hume is correctly understood to rule out such a 'derivation' (Putnam convincingly argues otherwise[50]), to take 'Hume's challenge' this seriously is consistent with a meta-ethical stance that has dominated twentieth-century jurisprudence (including Kelsen's robust methodological dualism). I outline the assumptions informing the latter stance – as well as its contrast with a 'non-reductive' naturalism – elsewhere.[51] For our purposes, what matters is to expose the underlying assumption according to which an effort to account for law's normative force goes hand in hand with a demonstration of the way in which law differs from 'mere' habits. The latter are not only confined to sphere of 'is's' (and hence the province of sociology). They are only deemed of interest to the moral or legal philosopher if and to the extent that they constitute a threat to personal autonomy. On a naturalist understanding of ethical agency, by contrast, habits not only condition but enable normative choices. To show the extent to which the 'ethical sensitivity' that informs such choices is heavily influenced by the environment we inhabit, recent empirical studies have for instance studied not just automated responses to environmental triggers – such as smell – but also the role played by factors like early care experience[52] in developing what DeSouza calls our 'ethical know-how'.[53]

---

and convention at the foundations of law' (1982) 11 *Journal of Legal Studies* 165; GJ Postema, 'Norms, reasons and law' 51 *Current Legal Problems* 149; ME Bratman, 'Shared cooperative activity' (1992) 101 *The Philosophical Review* 327 Marmor.

[48] 'Fortunately, plans are the right sort of things [...] Plans have this normative power in virtue of their capacity to organize the behavior of participants' SJ Shapiro, 'Law, Plans, and Practical Reason' (2002) 8 *Legal Theory* 387, 438 ibid. The roots of the long standing intellectualist tradition that still dominates much of contemporary jurisprudence are outlined in S Delacroix, 'Law and Habits' (2017) 37 *Oxford Journal of Legal Studies* 660.

[49] SJ Shapiro, *Legality* (Harvard, Harvard University Press, 2011) 2615 (loc.) ibid.

[50] 'The logical positivist fact/ value dichotomy was defended on the basis of a narrowly scientistic picture of what a 'fact' might be, just as the Humean ancestor of that distinction was defended upon the basis of a narrow empiricist psychology of 'ideas and impressions'. The realisation that so much of our descriptive language is a living counterexample to *both* (classical empiricist and logical positivist) pictures of the realm of 'fact' ought to shake the confidence of anyone who supposes that there is a notion of *fact* that contrasts neatly and absolutely with the notion of 'value' supposedly invoked in talk of the nature of all 'value judgments' (H Putnam, *The collapse of the fact/value dichotomy and other essays* (Harvard, Harvard University Press 2002) 26 ibid).

[51] Delacroix (n 48), 'Law and Habits'.

[52] D Narvaez and D Lapsley, 'Becoming a Moral Person – Moral Development and Moral Character Education as a Result of Social Interactions' in M Christen and others (eds), *Empirically Informed Ethics: Morality between Facts and Norms* (Cham, Springer, 2014).

[53] 'On the ethical level, human beings do just this: they collectively enact and re-enact the ethical fabric of their world each and every day through their actions and interactions. And they do so only on the basis of having first been immersed in that world themselves and having acquired ethical second natures as a result.' (N DeSouza, 'Pre-Reflective Ethical Know-How' (2013) 16 *Ethical Theory and Moral Practice* 279, 291).

Now, because the focus of these studies is to describe the way in which our environment shapes our ethical sensitivity,[54] we know a lot less about the factors that prompt us to question widely accepted norms when they are wanting.[55]

To understand our capacity to stand at odds with the usual, a Kantian framework would point at our shared capacity for practical reason, taking us from the phenomenal to the noumenal by virtue of the capacity for autonomous agency we all share. Yet because the goals and principles informing practical reason are themselves 'filtered through socially conditioned interpretations and perceptions',[56] practical reason cannot be trusted to wake us to the reality of a perverted ethical environment. To understand what underlies our capacity to trigger normative change, one must cast a wider net, considering appeals to our emotional intelligence to be just as important as our more cerebral capacities. This will entail stories of the kind Williams had in mind when he called for philosophy to be conceived as a 'humanistic discipline'.[57] The latter call proceeds from a commitment to avoid the pitfalls of a scientific naturalism, ie a naturalism that lets the current results of our natural sciences define what belongs to nature and what does not.

In contrast to such a 'scientific naturalist' stance, there cannot be any discontinuity between the ethical and the natural in a habit-centred account of normative agency. And that's not because the ethical is 'merely' natural but rather because, as Hans Fink nicely puts it: 'Nature is never *mere* nature. That which is *more* than *mere* is nature, too'.[58] Habits (along with the historical, the aesthetical, the man-made) are among those things that are 'more than mere' nature. To understand the process whereby we come to develop evaluative stands towards these 'more than mere nature' aspects of our lives, all we need, Blackburn reminds us, is to make room for 'creatures with needs to meet'.[59]

---

[54] Or what McDowell calls our 'second nature': '[h]uman beings are intelligibly initiated into this stretch of the space of reasons by ethical upbringing, which instils the appropriate shape into their lives. The resulting habits of thought and action are second nature' J McDowell, *Mind and World* (Harvard, Harvard University Press, 1996) 84.

[55] Besser-Jones for instance reminds us that this environmental conditioning does not preclude normative hopes or ambitions to change the way in which we relate to our environment: 'As long as it remains possible for people to diverge from these ways of behaving, such descriptive accounts should not be mistaken for accounts of how we should make moral judgments and of what should motivate us. Rather, they should be treated as a starting point for normative considerations: given that this is how we tend to judge and act, what changes can we make to improve from this basis?' L Besser-Jones, 'The Role of Practical Reason in an Empirically Informed Moral Theory' (2012) 15 *Ethical Theory and Moral Practice* 203, 211.

[56] H Pauer-Studer and JD Velleman, 'Distortions of Normativity' (2011) 14 *Ethical Theory and Moral Practice* 329, 340.

[57] B Williams, 'Philosophy as a humanistic discipline' (2000) 75 *Philosophy* 477.

[58] H Fink, 'Three Sorts of Naturalism' (2006) 14 *European Journal of Philosophy* 202, 217.

[59] '[B]y the time we have these "is's" up and running we have all that our normative natures require.' So there is 'no unmoved mover: no intervention of the divine spark, or gifts from unexplained quarters': S Blackburn, 'Normativity a la mode' (2001) 5 *Journal of Ethics: An International Philosophical Review* 139. As to why this does not necessarily expose Blackburn to the infamous 'bald and shallow metaphysics' of empiricist naturalism, as McDowell once contended, see Delacroix (n 44), 'Meta-ethical agnosticism in legal theory: mapping a way out'.

These (human) creatures will train themselves to meet these needs against a background of prior practices. In the process of learning to live together, and developing tools such as tables,[60] we will develop standards that lead us to value flatness in a table[61] (and criticise tables that are not flat).[62]

Now, where does this get us in relation to the pink hat example I mentioned earlier? Unlike table building, the process that might lead me to eventually deem hat wearing to be a normative requirement, not just for myself, but for society around me, may take its roots in non-deliberative agency. Let's say the advert pushed exactly the right emotional buttons and I find myself compelled to acquire such a pink hat. This pink hat has become my pride and joy. I also happen to be involved in a woman's rights movement. A lot of my peers in that movement start to wear the same pink hat, partly because of the advert, partly to look like their peers. Years later, everybody has forgotten about that ad, but all members of this movement wear a pink hat, which they have come to deem essential, to the point that it is disrespectful to be seen in public without such a hat. At this stage you might say we have a conventional, social norm, which arose out of a mix of habitual, repeated patterns of behaviour and some minute, intentional but non-deliberative action. The members of this movement might come to acquire political power, and eventually make it a legal requirement to wear such hats in public spaces.

This is but one story among many possible 'upstream' scenarios. The diagram below illustrates what the 'upstream' of legal normativity might look like – if indeed one is at all interested in this upstream aspect – once we stop presupposing deliberative agency all the way through.

Figure 1

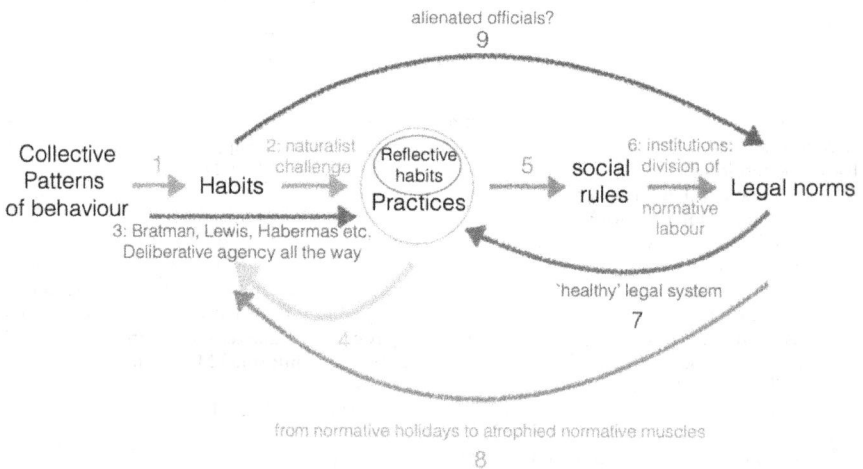

[60] Here Blackburn refers to Wittgenstein's carpenter example to illustrate the extent to which there is nothing so mysterious about the way in which we come to develop normative standards.
[61] That some tools can be designed in such a way as to make any form of normative engagement on our part seem redundant (or impossible) will be addressed in the conclusion.
[62] Just like we will come to develop an understanding of what makes for a good friend, and criticise those relationships that fall short.

This diagram is borrowed from my 'Law and Habit'[63] article, where it is fully unpacked. The following is meant as a quick summary outlining the continuum that stretches from collective patterns of behaviour all the way to legal norms, via habits and/or practices. Practices (whether they are characterised as 'reflective habits' or not) stem from collective patterns of behaviour, and they presuppose a reflective awareness of the needs or purposes served by those patterns of behaviour, with a concomitant ability to change those patterns in light of those needs or purposes. Those practices that are not reflective habits distinguish themselves from the latter by their genesis, which presupposes some deliberative agency[64] all the way through.

Of particular importance is the fact that, in a 'healthy' legal system, there will be a continuous feedback loop (see '7') that goes from legal norms to practices and back again. Symbolising the possibility of continuously challenging the existing legal framework in the name of emergent aspirations, this feedback loop can be compromised by factors both internal and external to a legal system's particular institutional structure. To illustrate the former, internal factors: a legal system that seeks to minimise the extent to which it is exposed to public challenges or protests (and hence maximise seamless compliance) is likely to foster what I have described elsewhere as 'rigidified habits'. Because the latter are not capable of giving rise to practices,[65] the 'feedback loop' will soon be broken.

Aside from these internal, structural factors, the possibility of continuously calling into question the norms structuring our way of living together can also be compromised 'from the outside', so to speak. Here the distinction between 'normativity' and 'regulatory power' that was introduced in section II becomes particularly important. Figure 2 (below) seeks to illustrate the regulatory power of social-media platforms.[66] The absence of feedback loop – except for some attempted legal interventions – stems from the fact that regulatory power does not presuppose any kind of normative engagement on our part (as outlined in section III), hence its potentially corrosive effect on autonomy.

---

[63] Delacroix (n 48), 'Law and Habits'.

[64] 'We exercise deliberative agency when we deliberate or reflect on what we ought to do, attempting to evaluate our reasons for action in the light of our values, convictions, and beliefs about the world. This kind of agency has rightly impressed philosophers largely, we suspect, because deliberative agency seems to be uniquely human – but in fact only a small proportion of our actions involve much in the way of deliberation or reflection.' (N Levy and T Bayne, 'Doing without deliberation: automatism, automaticity, and moral accountability' (2004) 16 *International Review of Psychiatry* 209).

[65] This is explained in detail in Delacroix (n 48), 'Law and Habits'.

[66] S Delacroix, 'Beware of "Algorithmic Regulation"' 1 February 2019 https://ssrn.com/abstract=3327191.

Figure 2

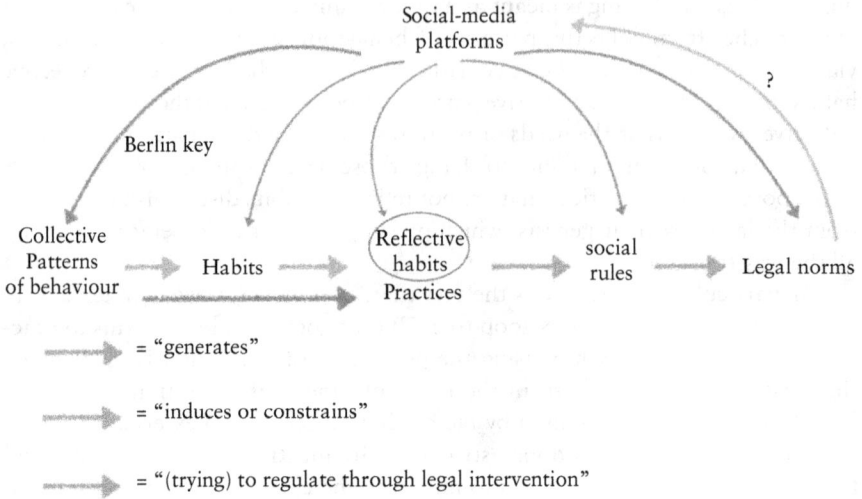

The emphasis on (and valuing of) autonomy that is characteristic of liberal democracies can be described as an endeavour to 'stem the tide' of regulatory power. This endeavour aims to preserve as much space as possible for the constructive exercise of autonomy – understood as the ability to articulate norms for oneself and one's community (ie 'normative agency') *from within* a background of prior normative attachments and expectations. Today the growing reach and influence of digital technologies means the tide of 'raw' regulatory power is rising faster than ever. It is also more insidious. Hence it's never been more important to carefully distinguish regulatory power from normativity: unlike the former, the latter is dependent upon (and engages with) our continued ability to exercise our normative agency. Such agency stems from the uniquely human capacity to see how one's way of living (individually and/or together) could be better, and to project that vision into the future by committing to norms and standards of various kinds. Far from necessarily compromising the latter ability (as is often assumed by overly intellectualist accounts of agency), habits typically enable – and often improve – our capacity for normative agency, provided the automaticity that underlies such habits has not been artificially rigidified. Such rigidification can be the result of technological interventions designed to get us 'hooked'. Or it can stem from an institutional structure that is designed to seamlessly maximise compliance and minimise dissent (as an extreme example, see the 'Wall-E' scenario discussed in section III).

VI. CONCLUSION

This chapter highlights the extent to which it is misleading to speak of something being 'normative' if it does not ever call for (or give rise to) any form of 'normative engagement' on our part. As an artefact that makes us lock a door from the inside, whether we engage it or not (or like it or not), a Berlin key is a good example of something that should not be referred to as normative. If we find that the resulting habit of locking ourselves in has unexpected, negative consequences on community life, our only option is to get rid of Berlin keys and replace the locks. That it is possible to do so is important: the durable, constraining power of the various machines humankind has become irreversibly 'hooked' upon in the 'Wall-E' scenario described in section III is infinitely more sinister.

In such a scenario, the machine-enabled, all-encompassing optimisation of our environment is designed to pre-empt any form of normative questioning. Because of the fine-tuned, personalised optimisation of each person's environment, no one ever experiences the kind of 'dissonance'[67] that would prompt one to consider a different way of living from that which is expertly facilitated by machines. The resulting lack of normative exercise leaves this 'Wall-E' population with irreversibly atrophied normative muscles. Now, these machines may well follow to the letter what used to be legal norms. Yet because the latter are shielded from any form of questioning or normative engagement on the part of the expertly managed, 'Wall-E' population, it has become misleading to refer to such regulatory standards as 'normative'.

Thankfully we may still be some way from the above, Wall-E scenario. Yet it's never been more important to draw clear conceptual lines that distinguish normativity from regulatory power. To explain why the latter should not be used interchangeably, attention needs to be paid to the different types of agency which underlie the context of social interaction giving rise to law as a normative practice. Hart's scant concern[68] for this 'upstream' side of normativity has only partly been remedied by accounts such as the conventionalist or 'SCA' models put forward by Lewis, Bratman etc.[69] The latter, 'hypercommital'[70] models indeed perpetuate the dominant (and intellectualist) assumption according to which the social practices giving rise to law must presuppose some deliberative agency all the way through (or route '3' in Figure 1).

Not only are these types of social practices unlikely to account for the vast majority of the social processes that give rise to law. The exclusive focus on this narrow, deliberative type – rightly denounced by the 'socio-cybernetic' understanding outlined in section II – has also hindered our chances of understanding

---

[67] The danger inherent in our growing appetite for profile-based optimisation are described in greater detail in S Delacroix and M Veale, 'Smart Technologies and Our Sense of Self: The Limitations of Counter-Profiling' in M Hildebrandt and K O'Hara (eds), *Life and the Law in the Era of Data-Driven Agency* (Cheltenham, Edward Elgar 2019).

[68] As argued in Delacroix (n 19), *Legal norms and normativity: an essay in genealogy*, ch 3.

[69] Bratman, Michael E 'Shared Cooperative Activity.' *The Philosophical Review* 101(2) (1992) 327–41. DK Lewis, *Convention: a philosophical study* (Harvard, Harvard University Press, 1963).

[70] Matthew Smith questions the extent to which such 'hypercommital' models are apt at conceptualising the bulk of social practices at the root of law's institutional structure: MN Smith, 'The Law as a Social Practice Are Shared Activities at the Foundations of Law?' (2006) 12 *Legal Theory* 265.

the crucial role played by law's institutional structure. The success of the latter in keeping in check various forms of regulatory power is indeed critical to the continued exercise of normative agency – without which the 'feedback loops' described in section V all but disappear. Far from being driven solely by deliberative processes, the vivacity of the social practices at the root of these feedback loops also depends on the type of habits fostered by the environment we interact with (including things like social media platforms *and* legal institutions). When repeated patterns of behaviour are encouraged in a mechanistic fashion, a rigidification of those patterns typically ensues. This rigidification will hinder our ability to both learn from -and strive to improve- our environment:[71] in short, it will compromise our capacity for normative agency.

---

[71] The latter ability indeed requires a type of automaticity that retains a degree of adaptability to goal changes. This is discussed in greater detail in S Delacroix, 'Habitual Sophia? Retaining one's ability to learn from within each lay-professional encounter' https://papers.ssrn.com/abstract=3242026.

Index

www.ingramcontent.com/pod-product-compliance
Lightning Source LLC
Chambersburg PA
CBHW061144220326
41599CB00025B/4351